Leonie Gilmour

When East
Weds West

Edward Marx

BOTCHAN BOOKS

2013

Leonie Gilmour
When East Weds West
By Edward Marx
First Edition

©2013 Botchan Books
www.botchanmedia.com
All rights reserved

ISBN: 978-1939913012 (paperback)

Set in ITC Legacy Sans and ITC Legacy Serif

10 9 8 7 6 5 4 3 2

Contents

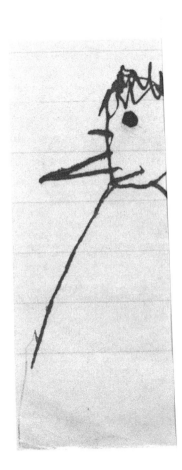

Isamu Noguchi. *Mama*, 1910. Ink on ruled pap

"Fortunately for the world, there are artists of mother-hood as there are artists of painting and sculpture . . . But such mothers are rare." —Léonie Gilmour's kindergarten teacher, Fannie Schwedler Barnes in *Kindergarten Magazine*, November 1897.

Preface

Léonie Gilmour mainly used her typewriter for other people's ideas. Though proud of her occasional publications, she was usually too busy to indulge her literary muse. When she did sit down with an idea, something would often prevent her from reaching the end of it, and if she did finish it, chances were good it would not end up getting published. Toward the end of her life, at the request of her son, Isamu Noguchi, she attempted to begin putting together a sort of autobiography—"the book," as she called it—but found it hard to get started. She had never liked chronicles: "The things worth keeping seem not to be in them. If one could capture the bright winged moment that like a humming bird flits over the garden and is gone, or net the shy anemones that bloom in the deeps of the heart and cannot be brought out into the sun! The real things are so far from speech." Nor was her memory "a well-ordered storehouse from which one can fetch out things at a moment's notice"; rather, it was "like a treacherous sea, where things are so covered with sand they are completely lost. Sometimes, it's true, the tide ebbs, and behold clearly revealed are the long lost days, bright and untarnished. I feel sure they are all there—somewhere—oh very safe. Not arranged chronologically. All quite equal in value and without any time sequence whatever." Her best source of information was a packet of her letters saved by her best friend, Catharine Bunnell. "The letters are quite entertaining," Léonie wrote Isamu in September 1932. "They are supposed to be help on 'the book' which I haven't yet had time even to start." Gilmour's literary talents were particularly suited to letters and brief anecdotal essays, contemplating events in the present or recent past before they became covered in her sands of lost time. They are quirky, droll, quickly executed pieces that reveal the texture of her personality—humorous, whimsical, tenacious, independent, fatalistic—amid the unexpected places she found herself as she followed her unconventional course of life.

Though for the most part content to play a supporting role in the lives of her somewhat famous husband, the poet Yone Noguchi, and her more famous son, the sculptor Isamu Noguchi, the story of this "strong willed, independent woman, with a keen intellect and a deep interest in the arts," as art historian Robert Maeda once described her, has always been too interesting to remain quietly hidden in the background. There is a good deal of heroism in it: the rise from the poverty of New York's Lower East Side to the elite lecture halls of Bryn Mawr and the Sorbonne, the personal battle against racism she undertook when she decided to marry Japanese poet Yone Noguchi, her struggle as a single mother in a foreign country, guiding her son inexorably towards a career as one of the leading sculptors of the twentieth century.

It would be the rare artist whose mother did not play some crucial formative role. Perhaps the artist's mother taught her young son how to paint in watercolors, like Mary Newbold Sargent did, or provided some other artistic stimulant: collecting pre-Columbian artifacts, like Aline Gauguin, or stocked her kitchen with Campbell's Soup and Brillo Pads, like Julia Warhola, who lived with her son, Andy Warhol, during most of his career, and sometimes signed his paintings. The force of a mother's presence on an artist can seem almost unearthly; sitting on a hard chair, severe face seen in profile, Whistler's Mother becomes the iconic figure of American art. Yet, even granting that the artist's mother almost always plays a powerful role, few have so decisively steered a child toward an artistic career as Léonie Gilmour. Isamu was only fourteen months old when Léonie declared she "would like to put him to an Art school somewhere, where he will have eye and hand trained to express his idea"; two decades later, when a well-meaning friend tried to put Isamu through medical school, Léonie raised an "awful row," accusing him of "turning a boy of artistic temperament toward a career for which he was entirely unsuited."

Several books have been written about Whistler's mother, but Léonie's story seemed unlikely to receive much attention outside of biographies of her famous son and husband. Emeritus professor Marleigh Ryan, who studied Gilmour for many years, told me it was "difficult . . . to put her in a context that would do justice to her accomplishments" and that interest seemed "quite limited within academic publications." But "certainly she deserves a strong place in the history of feminism in America."

Then, by chance, Gilmour found an admirer in film director Hisako Matsui. Reading Masayo Duus's biography of Isamu Noguchi, Matsui found inspiration in Gilmour's story of raising a child as a single mother in a foreign country. She herself had come to filmmaking after a trau-

Contents

Isamu Noguchi. *Mama,* 1910. **Ink on ruled paper.** *Isamu Noguchi Foundation.*

"Fortunately for the world, there are artists of mother-hood as there are artists of painting and sculpture ... But such mothers are rare." —Léonie Gilmour's kindergarten teacher, Fannie Schwedler Barnes in *Kindergarten Magazine*, November 1897.

Preface

Léonie Gilmour mainly used her typewriter for other people's ideas. Though proud of her occasional publications, she was usually too busy to indulge her literary muse. When she did sit down with an idea, something would often prevent her from reaching the end of it, and if she did finish it, chances were good it would not end up getting published. Toward the end of her life, at the request of her son, Isamu Noguchi, she attempted to begin putting together a sort of autobiography—"the book," as she called it—but found it hard to get started. She had never liked chronicles: "The things worth keeping seem not to be in them. If one could capture the bright winged moment that like a humming bird flits over the garden and is gone, or net the shy anemones that bloom in the deeps of the heart and cannot be brought out into the sun! The real things are so far from speech." Nor was her memory "a well-ordered storehouse from which one can fetch out things at a moment's notice"; rather, it was "like a treacherous sea, where things are so covered with sand they are completely lost. Sometimes, it's true, the tide ebbs, and behold clearly revealed are the long lost days, bright and untarnished. I feel sure they are all there—somewhere—oh very safe. Not arranged chronologically. All quite equal in value and without any time sequence whatever." Her best source of information was a packet of her letters saved by her best friend, Catharine Bunnell. "The letters are quite entertaining," Léonie wrote Isamu in September 1932. "They are supposed to be help on 'the book' which I haven't yet had time even to start." Gilmour's literary talents were particularly suited to letters and brief anecdotal essays, contemplating events in the present or recent past before they became covered in her sands of lost time. They are quirky, droll, quickly executed pieces that reveal the texture of her personality—humorous, whimsical, tenacious, independent, fatalistic—amid the unexpected places she found herself as she followed her unconventional course of life.

Though for the most part content to play a supporting role in the lives of her somewhat famous husband, the poet Yone Noguchi, and her more famous son, the sculptor Isamu Noguchi, the story of this "strong willed, independent woman, with a keen intellect and a deep interest in the arts," as art historian Robert Maeda once described her, has always been too interesting to remain quietly hidden in the background. There is a good deal of heroism in it: the rise from the poverty of New York's Lower East Side to the elite lecture halls of Bryn Mawr and the Sorbonne, the personal battle against racism she undertook when she decided to marry Japanese poet Yone Noguchi, her struggle as a single mother in a foreign country, guiding her son inexorably towards a career as one of the leading sculptors of the twentieth century.

It would be the rare artist whose mother did not play some crucial formative role. Perhaps the artist's mother taught her young son how to paint in watercolors, like Mary Newbold Sargent did, or provided some other artistic stimulant: collecting pre-Columbian artifacts, like Aline Gauguin, or stocked her kitchen with Campbell's Soup and Brillo Pads, like Julia Warhola, who lived with her son, Andy Warhol, during most of his career, and sometimes signed his paintings. The force of a mother's presence on an artist can seem almost unearthly; sitting on a hard chair, severe face seen in profile, Whistler's Mother becomes the iconic figure of American art. Yet, even granting that the artist's mother almost always plays a powerful role, few have so decisively steered a child toward an artistic career as Léonie Gilmour. Isamu was only fourteen months old when Léonie declared she "would like to put him to an Art school somewhere, where he will have eye and hand trained to express his idea"; two decades later, when a well-meaning friend tried to put Isamu through medical school, Léonie raised an "awful row," accusing him of "turning a boy of artistic temperament toward a career for which he was entirely unsuited."

Several books have been written about Whistler's mother, but Léonie's story seemed unlikely to receive much attention outside of biographies of her famous son and husband. Emeritus professor Marleigh Ryan, who studied Gilmour for many years, told me it was "difficult . . . to put her in a context that would do justice to her accomplishments" and that interest seemed "quite limited within academic publications." But "certainly she deserves a strong place in the history of feminism in America."

Then, by chance, Gilmour found an admirer in film director Hisako Matsui. Reading Masayo Duus's biography of Isamu Noguchi, Matsui found inspiration in Gilmour's story of raising a child as a single mother in a foreign country. She herself had come to filmmaking after a traumatic divorce, and entering the world of film directing in her fifties, found herself an industry outsider. Yet she had persevered and created two respected films. The story of a woman who simply did things her own way, regardless of the consequences, deeply appealed to her. "I was divorced in my early thirties," she explained on an NHK radio interview a few months before the film's premiere. "I think I learned more from that harrowing experience than from my marriage. Life doesn't always go the way one has planned. And bringing up children is very much like doing battle against things that don't seem to turn out properly. But I managed to plod along and it suddenly occurred to me one day that I was a stronger person for it." The project was a labor of love, for which she spent years speaking to audiences throughout Japan, raising money through grassroots support, promulgating the idea of the film to her supporters as "My Leonie," a kind of community project. With the help of public relations strategist Hiromi Saitoh, Matsui assembled a team to promote the project

When I talked with Hisako Matsui in Matsuyama some months into her fundraising effort, she told me she had drawn much of her material from Masayo Duus's recent biography of Isamu Noguchi. She was curious about letters and articles I told her of, but she had already formed her own conception of Léonie, and had little time for further investigations and story revisions. The film would be a work of imagination built on a foundation of fact.

Matsui's endless fundraising speeches paid off when a wealthy technologist (referred to as "Mr. M." in her autobiography) kindly offered to contribute 1.2 billion yen—about ten million dollars. She was now able to sign top talent for her bicultural film. Leading the impressive cast were English actress Emily Mortimer as Léonie and Shido Nakamura in the role of Yone Noguchi. Mortimer, known for her moving portrayal of a single mother in the 2004 film, *Dear Frankie*, had also appeared in Woody Allen's *Match Point* and was soon to appear in Martin Scorcese's *Shutter Island*. Co-star Shido Nakamura, a kabuki-trained actor whose international roles included Clint Eastwood's Iwo Jima saga, *Flags of Our Fathers*, and Gan Xing's *Red Cliff*, would play the role of Yone Noguchi. Matsui, who had worked in casting for many years before becoming a director, was depending on her actors to draw on their own life experiences to breathe life into their characters. Emily Mortimer, like Gilmour, had attended a top university and worked for a time in journalism. (Matsui's original choice for the part, *Sex and the City*'s Cynthia Nixon, had also had life experiences paralleling Gilmour's). Shido Nakamura was thought ideal for the part of Yone Noguchi because the two men shared a history of scandalous extramarital affairs. Behind the camera was acclaimed cinematographer Tetsuo Nagata, best known for his award-winning work on the 2007 biopic of French chanteuse Edith Piaf. Costumes would be designed by veteran designer Aggie Rodgers and Kazuko Kurosawa, with art direction by Giles Masters and Osamu Yamaguchi. A haunting score created for the film by Academy Award winning Polish composer Jan Kaczmarek helped smooth over the unresolved gaps at the heart of the story.

But these gaps were substantial. On the foundation of Duus's biography, Matsui had worked hard to reconstruct Gilmour's world. Duus's biography was the best available on the subject, but its subject was Isamu Noguchi, not his mother. The information about Léonie in the book was limited, and Duus had incorporated a number of prior misinterpretations and outright errors about such basic facts as Léonie's birthdate, the spelling of her name, and whether she had graduated from college, from long chains of erroneous sources usually originating in the confused recollections of Isamu Noguchi, that had, after many repetitions, come to seem reliable. Biographers cannot, of course, research every secondary character to the same depth as the main subject. Moreover, Duus was a writer who preferred bold judgments to timid academic equivocations. "The problem was that Leonie herself was not forceful enough," she tells us, or "Yonejiro tended to lose control when fascinated by someone." Though her confident interpretations were often justified, and made for a livelier story, it was a story that seemed, at times, to be told by the omniscient narrator of a novel. And where Duus's risky interpretations missed their mark, Matsui's film, building scenes out of her misreadings and misinterpretations, would multiply their effects.

Matsui's plan—to use imagination—hers and her actors'—to fill in some of the gaps, worked to some extent, but beyond a certain point, the actors seemed at a loss, finding no choice but to act around the gaps. Emily Mortimer's Leonie is a kind of cipher—having no back story on which she can build her character's motivation, she seems merely going through the motions of her life. Shido Nakamura has an easier job playing Yone as a selfish, philandering artist, but we get few clues as to his motives, and we see little of the charm and talent that attracted Léonie to him.

Of course, we don't always need to know why people do what they do; sometimes we can't know, and sometimes they don't know themselves. We can never expect film, or even biography, to be a faithful mirror of reality. What saves the film, in the end, is the beautiful production design. But here, too, there was a disappointment. Matsui had hoped to use Isamu Noguchi's artworks but found it difficult to obtain permission from the Isamu Noguchi Foundation. Frustrated, she removed most of the artworks from the film. (The Foundation staff, for their part, were mystified as to why Matsui had not followed up on her initial inquiry).

Throughout the production, Matsui kept in close contact with her legions of supporters, inviting them to participate as extras in a number of scenes, giving speeches on the progress of the film, and attending endless dinners. The film was released in Japan in October 2010 and had a respectable run, assisted by the MyLeonie supporters' well-organized promotional efforts. The following year, Matsui began the difficult task of arranging the film's international release. The American producer, Hyde Park Entertainment, accustomed to more mainstream films, expressed concerns over the film's theatrical prospects, and over-two-hour running time. Matsui would have to arrange for a major reedit and find a distributor. The reedit (for which Matsui made some use of an early draft of this book) cut the film to ninety-ninety minutes, reorganizing the narrative into a more straightforward sequence, and placing stronger emphasis on the relationship between Leonie and Yone. The quest for a distributor proved a challenge, for Matsui was an outsider not only to Hollywood, but to the Japanese studio system as well. Fortunately, Matsui had a staunch supporter in star Emily Mortimer. In August 2012 Mortimer's agency brokered a deal with Monterey Media to handle the U.S. release.

The film opened in American theaters on March 22, 2013. Early reviews were somewhat mixed but mostly positive. Rex Reed in the New York *Observer* enthused about the "rich tapestry of cross-cultural revelations" and Mortimer's "exquisite" acting. Frank Scheck in the *Hollywood Reporter* called the film "deeply heartfelt but only intermittently compelling," praising Mortimer's "superb portrayal" and the "stellar support" of Shido Nakamura and Mary Kay Place, and finding the screenplay "frustratingly sketchy and at times overly florid" but "also moving and inspirational." *Variety* reviewer John Anderson thought the story "curious and intriguing" but complained that "Matsui seems more interested in Gilmour as an earnestly envisioned message-delivery system than as a creature of flesh and blood." Still, he thought that Mortimer created "a real character." Rachel Saltz in the *New York Times* and Alan Scherstuhl in the *Village Voice* came down hard on the "plodding" script with its frequently "mortifying narration." "Too bad," Saltz added, "that the film that bears her name ultimately reduces her to the mother of her child."

For American viewers, clearly it was Mortimer who carried the film.

Her performance, forceful and compelling, does not give a final portrait of Léonie Gilmour, but invites viewers to reconstruct the enigmatic woman and the world she inhabited.

This book is, in effect, a true story inspired by a fictional film, a story this time told through Léonie Gilmour's own writings and the words of those who knew her intimately.

The story of the documents that form the basis of this book goes back to the summer of 1969, when Ikuko Atsumi, a graduate student at Tokyo's Aoyama Gakuin studying the forgotten poet, Yone Noguchi, visited Isamu Noguchi in New York at the suggestion of Isamu's brother-in-law, Professor Usaburo Toyama. "He took me to his atelier on Long Island and to my surprise showed me a box of his mother's articles left behind. I could not but feel grateful to this incredible good fortune, because he explained that he had just lately inherited those articles from Miss Florence (his mother's aunt) in California at her death, with whom Leonie Gilmour, Noguchi's first wife and Isamu's mother, had entrusted them before she passed away. Taking out letters and photos one by one, Mr. Noguchi seemed to get his heart touched as he himself was looking at them well for the first time. I had an urge to stay there, if possible, long enough to read all the letters, but since my schedule at Buffalo, Berkeley and Hawaii was fixed, I had to leave there in an hour promising him to return after receiving a grant." Atsumi was able to secure a small grant from the Keio University library, and returned the following summer, persuading Isamu to introduce her to his half-sister, Ailes Spinden. "Mrs. Spinden invited me to her house and showed me a big wooden tea box full of Gilmour's belongings which had been left on the garret for forty years," Ailes having "no courage to confront them." As they took the letters out of the box one by one, Ailes's "long complications toward Japan and her mother fretfully changed into sobbing."

At Isamu and Ailes' request, Atsumi organized the disposition of the letters to two libraries (Keio and Berkeley) and the future Isamu Noguchi Foundation, in the course of preparing her edition of Yone Noguchi's *Collected English Letters*. Some material, however, remained in Atsumi's possession, and was still in her unluckily waterlogged basement some two decades after Atsumi fled the halls of academe in order to pursue a brighter future as president of Intercultural Business Systems. When I visited Atsumi's home in Framingham, near Boston, in August of 2001, we spent the better part of the day cleaning out her basement, and I returned to Kyoto with an unexpected assortment of rare books, manuscripts, and letters. Among these are several of Léonie Gilmour's unpublished manuscripts, which, though few in number, add much to our understanding of who Léonie Gilmour was, and provide a glimpse of the autobiographical project she had begun in the last year of her life at the request of her son. Thanks to the power of Matsui's film, there will finally be a readership for these fascinating documents and the materials preserved by the Isamu Noguchi Foundation and the University of California at Berkeley.

For the most part this book follows Léonie Gilmour's story chronologically, but I have chosen to start with a prologue telling a part of the story Hisako Matsui left out of her movie: the story of Yone's other American love interest, Ethel Armes. Originally, blonde bombshell Nichole Hiltz was cast to play the role of Ethel, which would have made Yone's motivations more comprehensible, but the Ethel scenes, Matsui told me, could not be included due to time constraints.

I have gone to some lengths here to reconstruct aspects of Léonie's early life, with the help of an unpublished autobiographical fragment, "St. Bridget's Child," published here for the first time, and a good deal of investigation into the history of Léonie's primary school, an extraordinary institution whose influence on her and her children has been mostly overlooked; and I have tried to provide a clearer picture of the Bryn Mawr School and Bryn Mawr College, both also extraordinary institutions, that also influenced her course of life.

Léonie did not, in fact, graduate from college, though she completed seven semesters of work with an additional year at the Sorbonne. This was sufficient to get her a job teaching French at a private school in Jersey City, and similar jobs in Japan, but she would probably have had an easier time finding jobs if she had completed her degree. Much of what we know about Léonie comes through her college friend Catharine Bunnell; from Catharine's letters home, we get glimpses of at school; Léonie's own letters to Catharine begin during her years teaching at St. Aloysius' Academy, and continue to the end of her life. Gilmour's relationship with Yone Noguchi is well documented in letters (though at first only Yone's). Through these letters one may also get a better sense of why Léonie was impressed by Noguchi's literary talent and charmed by his personality. Yone Noguchi was an important and interesting writer who introduced haiku and Noh drama to the West, was the first writer of Japanese ancestry to publish an English novel, and developed friendships with many of the leading authors of his day. His use of English was fascinating though imperfect—the British critic Laurence Housman, describing a meeting with Noguchi in 1904, found his pronunciation "so far removed from anything ever heard, that I had the greatest difficulty in understanding him." Noguchi's relations with various editors and publishers were more complex than Matsui's single figure of Frederick Stokes, publisher of *The American Diary of a Japanese Girl*, nor did Gilmour have anything to do with the decision to publish that book anonymously. She did, however, prove a very helpful editor, and occasionally collaborator, on many of Noguchi's projects. She was first and foremost, as Isamu Noguchi once said, "an excellent editor for him." That was, of course, a large part of the problem: their relationship, like many workplace romances, was founded on a workplace camaraderie that slipped—but only temporarily—into passion. In contrast, Noguchi's relationship with Gilmour's rival, Ethel Armes, developed in an atmosphere more conducive to romance. But the workplace relationship had its benefits, allowing Yone and Léonie to develop a casual intimacy that later helped them find practical ways of transcending their often incompatible attitudes, opinions, and cultures.

Another important character missing from Matsui's film is Frank Putnam, a writer and editor Noguchi had met in Chicago, who subsequently relocated to Boston. Putnam was indirectly responsible for Léonie's first meeting with Yone (it was his misguided editing of Noguchi's verse that had driven Noguchi to place an ad in the *New York Herald*) and more directly responsible for reuniting the estranged couple after the birth of their son. Gilmour never met "dear Frank," but it was he who published her first stories in the *National Magazine*, channeling much-needed funds to her in Los Angeles while she debated relocating to Japan, and overcoming her and Yone's objections to reuniting with a steady onslaught of Midwestern family values and common sense. Of course, there was also another factor that, as Matsui's film suggests, pushed Léonie to Japan: the growing racism against the Japanese in California and the passage of discriminatory laws against women who married foreigners. Faced with the choice of losing her respectability or her citizenship, Léonie chose a third option: Japan.

In Japan Léonie had little hope of marital bliss: in the two years she had taken to decide, Yone had begun a relationship with a Japanese woman. (Yone, following his usual habit, seems to have neglected to inform Léonie of this complication for several years). But Japan did give Léonie an opportunity to explore a different way of life. Her thirteen years in Japan were lived in a long string of houses stretching through Tokyo to Chigasaki about thirty miles south. In Los Angeles she had organized the construction of a tent house for her family, turning the experience into a humorous article for Frank Putnam's magazine; in Japan again she found she could turn her domestic arrangements into literary material. Though she never aspired to anything so grand as a novel, she was, at this stage, surely the master of her own story, capable of writing it, when the mood and opportunity arose, with verve and style. One may regret her overly selective subject matter—she rarely wrote, for example, of her professional life and never of her romantic life, though the unexplained appearance of her daughter, Ailes, in 1912 suggests it must have been an interesting one. She does reveal much about domestic life in Japan and about the development of the future artistic legend, Isamu Gilmour. Perhaps in writing of conventional "women's topics" of home and children she hoped to minimize criticism for her unconventional life choices.

Isamu Gilmour returned to the United States in 1918; Léonie and Ailes followed in 1920. It is not always easy to reconstruct these American years, but—at least until the years of the Great Depression—they were probably less pitiful than Duus and Matsui suggest. On her return Léonie established her own import-export business, which gave her a steady if not always reliable income for the remainder of her life, and in most years, she was able to use her business as an opportunity for summer travel to places like Miami Beach and the austerely beautiful Maine coast. At times, especially in the Depression years, it was difficult to make ends meet, but for Léonie poverty—so much a part of her childhood—was merely a challenge to her ingenuity which she never regarded as more than a minor inconvenience. Léonie's sense of achievement, when Isamu arrived at artistic greatness in the late 1920s, was profound. Isamu was only fourteen months old when Léonie wrote Yone, "I would like to put him to an Art school somewhere, where he will have eye and hand trained to express his idea—No matter if he become artist or not." In 1928 Isamu won a coveted Guggenheim fellowship allowing him to travel to France, the country that had first opened her eyes to the world outside of America, and study with one of the greatest living sculptors, Constantin Brancusi. By the early thirties, he was charging hundreds of dollars for portrait commissions and receiving national attention as an important young artist. Ailes, too, had established herself as a dancer in Martha Graham's noted company. Though Léonie would have liked to spend more time with her busy children, she declared herself content in solitude. Returning to New York City in the winter of 1933, she caught a chill that led to her hospitalization at Bellevue hospital, where she died on New Year's eve at the age of sixty.

This book is designed for readers with a variety of interests in its subject, and for that reason favors inclusiveness over selectivity. Readers who might have preferred a briefer account I hope will indulge those who find illumination in small details. Those inclined to take routes through these pages different than the customary one from beginning to end have

Léonie's sanction, for her memory, she told her son, was not "like a well-ordered storehouse" but, rather, "like a treacherous sea"; the "long lost days, bright and untarnished," were "all there—somewhere . . . all quite equal in value and without any time sequence whatever." Those seeking further information will find summaries of sources and suggestions for further reading in the reference section at the end of the book.

Isamu Noguchi, Portrait of Léonie Gilmour, 1932. *Isamu Noguchi Foundation.*

Prologue

On a day in late March, 1905, a letter arrived at the Riedesel house, an old Revolutionary War era house on Brattle Street, a few blocks from the Harvard campus. In the house Dr. William Woodworth and his houseguest, the writer Charles Warren Stoddard, were making their final preparations for a long train journey to the West Coast. For Dr. Woodworth, the forty-year-old director of Harvard's Museum of Comparative Zoology, the trip was merely a short working holiday, but for the melancholy sixty-two-year-old Stoddard, it was a long-deferred return to the Northern California of his youth. The letter, addressed to Stoddard, was from his young journalist friend, Ethel Armes, in Birmingham, Alabama. Ethel had also enclosed two letters from her Los Angeles friend, Elizabeth Converse. The letters told a shocking story about Ethel's fiancée, the Japanese poet Yone Noguchi.

For months, Stoddard had been struggling with Yone's announcement that he intended to marry Ethel. Stoddard's own fondness for the exotic Japanese poet went far beyond the platonic. "How I long to see you; to hold you in my arms again and tell you how dearly I love you and how I shall miss you when you are gone far away," Stoddard had written when Yone told of his marriage plans and departure for Japan. Stoddard was horrified at the thought of Yone being shackled to a woman, even one as charming as Ethel. Yone and Ethel were both Stoddard's "kids," as he called his young intimates; they had first met each other in 1901 at his Washington, D.C. bungalow before Stoddard had been fired from his teaching job at the Catholic University. "If I had my Bungalow and the money to run it, I should implore you to come to me and dwell with me forever more," he lamented. Though Stoddard was fond of Ethel, he believed that "a poet should be free." But his advice merely angered Yone. "Ethel is coming to Japan, and so give some encouragement, will you?" Yone insisted. "I love her—you know. I like to make her happy and beautiful. I promised myself I will do everything for her own sake. And I am doing so. I suppose she will start on the first week of March, and take the 18th steamer which will leave San Francisco." The steamer had departed a week ago but Ethel was still with her family in Birmingham.

Stoddard's brief sense of relief that Yone had been spared the yoke of matrimony was quickly followed by a new horror: Yone, it appeared, had a child in Los Angeles by a woman named Léonie Gilmour. Stoddard

Charles Warren Stoddard.

ought to have recalled the name: he had once accompanied Yone to supper at the apartment Miss Gilmour shared with her Bryn Mawr College
friend, Catharine Bunnell. But to Stoddard those New York days, before
his nervous breakdown, now seemed a horrible dream.

Ethel's letter explained how she had sent her friend Elizabeth Converse to investigate the Los Angeles woman. The results of her investigation were documented in the two enclosed letters. Stoddard opened the
first. "Ethel—" it began, "Have just had Yone Noguchi's baby in my arms
and had a cup of tea with its mother. I will try to stick to facts. It is all
more than I can comprehend." The letters went on to describe a woman
of the most unconventional character, a woman "in appearance Middle-
West as they hang over the back fence" yet "in manner as English as a
queen." Her manner of living was also beyond comprehension: "She and
her mother are keeping this cottage, a most poor one, for two men who
own it and the men take their breakfasts and suppers with them." Converse's awkward, intrusive questions had been met with relaxed, cheerful
answers. "Her attitude has simply swamped me," Converse confessed. "I
knew I could understand your agony and Yone's and expected to find the
third dose of it, but not calm cheerfulness instead." She described "Yo,"
as the baby was temporarily called, "a charming child, a glorious creature of vibrant body and sparkling eyes and sunshine of disposition," and
Léonie's mother, "an old white-haired lady who held the baby while I

Ethel Armes.

drank tea and Léonie ate her supper."

Léonie's winning cheerfulness—"you would like her," Converse insist-ed—had done little to alleviate Ethel's agony. "I am not unhappy at all—Do not think I am feeling more than I do," Ethel feebly insisted. But she admitted she had not been able to write a sane line since it all happened.

Reaching for his bottle of purple ink, Stoddard copied out the con-tents of Converse's letters before returning them to Ethel, thus preserv-ing for posterity the intimate portrait of Léonie Gilmour destined for the flames. "I thought he cared so much," Ethel lamented, "—but—you see—he never loved me once and never cared at all." A few days later, Stoddard and Dr. Woodworth departed for California. "Yes—go see the woman, Dad," Ethel had suggested. Not that it could make any differ-ence anymore: "nothing can—there is the child—his treatment of that woman . . . " Stoddard was not greatly worried for Ethel's sake. "I guess Ethel will come out all right," he wrote Frank Putnam from California. "The bloodless tragedy has probably done them both good."

It was not until the following spring that Stoddard wrote a letter po-litely addressed to "Mrs. Noguchi" from the San Jose sanitarium where he was taking a rest cure after a relapse of his chronic malaria. "I shall be glad to see you and know you and the little one, by and by when I go to Los Angeles. I wonder if I may—may I?" But before Léonie's reply reached him, Stoddard found himself "in the teeth of a temblor," as the great San Francisco earthquake threw everything into chaos.

Yone Noguchi.

On September 12, 1906, five months after the earthquake, a letter from Léonie reached Stoddard, who had relocated to Monterey. "Your letter," he replied, "is so bright, so jolly, so hopeful—and so mis-addressed, I hasten to reply and put you on the right track." Stoddard was well aware that for more than a year, Frank Putnam had been advising Yone on what he euphemistically referred to as "ethics of civilization." As managing editor of *The National Magazine*, Putnam had taken under his wing not just Yone but Yone's whole extended literary family—Ethel, Léonie, and Stoddard. The "good and sensible" Putnam, in whose "great wisdom and direction" Yone trusted, had done more than anyone to reconcile the estranged couple. Under the relentless pressure of Putnam's Midwestern values and common sense, even Stoddard had to put aside his bohemian scruples and admit that the proper course was for Léonie and the baby to join Yone in Japan.

"Nothing could please me more," Stoddard told Léonie, "than to see you and Yone and the wee one all together in Japan. What you write of the Boy makes me love him and covet him. I hope you are keeping one of those kid chronicles in which all the quaint and clever things he says or does are recorded. Are you? If you will, some day you can make a fascinating book of it. This Baby Boy is to be like no other Baby Boy in all the world. Mark my words and heed me!" Léonie knew her child was special. Not yet two years old and still without a proper name, Léonie

Frank Putnam.

had already decided to "put him to an Art school somewhere, where he will have eye and hand trained to express his idea—No matter if he become artist or not." But she scoffed at Stoddard's proposal. Chronicles of "quaint and clever" sayings and doings could never capture the things worth keeping: the "bright winged moment," the "deeps of the heart."

Or so she felt a quarter of a century later, as she reconsidered Stoddard's letter. Baby Boy had become a famous artist as she planned—winner of a Guggenheim fellowship, subject of a *Time* magazine story—and now he, too, was pestering her for chronicles, commanding her to write of their early days in California and Japan, hoping to find some keys to the puzzle of his identity that would torment him throughout his life. And so Léonie sat down at her typewriter and began sorting through her collection of old letters, trying to decipher dates and simply make sense of all that had happened over six decades. Spreading Stoddard's letters beside her typewriter, she began to tell the story of "the kid chronicle that was not written." Stoddard's letter, "written when the boy was a little over a year old," seemed as good a place as any to start, but when she finished typing it, she had second thoughts. On another occasion, she thought she would begin with the story of her own childhood—"St. Bridget's Child" she would call it, thinking of the back alley of the old Greenwich Village church where she lived as a child.

Origins (1873-1896)

June 17, 1873, the day Léonie Gilmour was born in New York City's Lower East Side, was an important day in the history of women's rights in the United States. Upstate, pioneering women's rights activist Susan B. Anthony was brought to the Ontario County courthouse to stand trial. The charge: illegal voting. The previous November, Anthony and her female cohorts had registered to vote, threatening to sue election inspectors if they refused. Anthony insisted that the Fourteenth Amendment of 1868, granting citizenship and voting rights to "all persons born and naturalized in the United States," applied not only to freed male slaves but also to another disenfranchised group: women. The argument, clever enough to frighten local officials, had not impressed their federal superiors, and a few weeks after the election Anthony and the fourteen other women who voted with her, along with the unhappy election inspectors who had registered them, were arrested on charges of violating federal election laws. The arrest drew national attention, which Anthony used to publicize her views: the views of an extremist, for the still-common view was that giving women the vote would destroy the sanctity of the home and threaten the functioning of democracy itself. At the close of the trial, sentenced to pay a $100 fine and prosecution costs, Anthony castigated the court as a fraud, declaring she would never pay. This was the world Léonie Gilmour was born into, a world where women were beginning to loudly demand equality, questioning laws made for the benefit of men, a world beginning to take heed of these demands, but a world of laws and institutions that were painfully slow to change. Some, like Anthony, defied discrimination loudly, while others, like Gilmour, did so more quietly. Though history remembers mainly the protests, the women who broke new ground by quietly finding their way around seemingly insurmountable barriers just as surely deserve our attention, for they, too, helped create the modern world.

When Léonie Gilmour was three months old, another event occurred that would have a more immediate impact on her life: the so-called Panic of 1873, a banking collapse resulting from speculation in American railroad expansion, exacerbated by similar investment failures in Europe. The panic threw the American economy into a severe depression that lasted for five years and lingered until the 1890s. Léonie's father, a poor Irish immigrant, was among the large segment of the population left unemployed by the massive layoffs. Léonie and her sister, Florence, born two years later, were fated to grow up in poverty and chaos.

Isamu Noguchi's stories of his mother's background were sketchy at best, but among her papers there is a story entitled "St. Bridget's Child" in which she writes of her origins. She must have had thoughts of publishing the story, for in it she conceals her true name, saying that her parents named her "Elizabeth." Otherwise, however, the details about her family are essentially correct. The alternative names, "Bridget" or "Brigitta," used here, were names she often used to sign letters to her friend Catharine Bunnell. The name and story derive from St. Brigid's Place, an alley behind St. Brigid's Church in New York's Lower East Side where Léonie grew up.

"Saint Bridget's Church." *The Catholic Churches of New York City, 1878.*

St. Bridget's Child

Unpublished typescript

It is a story of poverty and heroism, those grim fairies who presided at my birth, to whom I owe whatever fibre of strength is in my being. So often have I heard my father and mother speak of these things that it seems as if I remembered them, as if I wept when my mother bent her slender neck in toil for my sake—I yet unborn—as if I still felt the cold kiss of the snow on my cheek, while my father paced under the stars watching my feeble breath of life.

They were such an amazingly foolhardy young couple to marry, my father earning—was it six dollars a week?—my mother a spoiled darling, as innocent of the old time art of housekeeping as of the more modern art of earning money. And when my father fell "out of work" I can well imagine my mother's dismay in telling him of the wonderful dignity of motherhood that was come upon her, a dignity, alas!—too heavy for poor folks to bear. He walked the streets in a frenzied despair, demanding work, work, at any cost, while she made the best pitiful woman-struggle to help that ever it were possible for woman to make. What could she do, oh, what could she do? As a child she had watched the printers setting type for the printing of her father's paper—the *Brooklyn Daily Eagle*, in the days when he and James Gordon Bennett had been partners in that enterprise ("I furnish the money, and you, Smith, the brains" had laughed Mr. Bennett)—and so she knew "upper case" and "lower case" and "font" and "stick" and other words of the printers vocabulary. She boldly went to a printing shop and asked for work. "I can set type," she declared. So she made a grand bluff at typesetting perched on a hard stool before the "case" all the day long until she actually had earned twenty-five dollars. She carried it everywhere in her pocketbook, tightly clinching her hands and ready to cry and laugh at once with fatigue and delight of triumph. Her excitement would be evident to all in the car on which she rode back and forth, and pathetic to those with a heart to understand. One day a man—God knows it must have been a long time since he had thought of his mother—snatched the purse. Oh, how she cried! "Hush, dear, hush!" my father gripped her empty hand. "For heaven's sake, stop! Do you want our child to become a miser?" And so my mother dried her eyes and went to work to earn another twenty-five dollars. It was the bravest thing and I can truthfully say that no touch of the awful taint so feared by my father has manifested itself in my own character, my fingers having spaces between them exactly suited to the spilling of small coins—large ones I haven't tried.

Now it was in St. Bridget's Alley where we lived. There is a St. Bridget's Place, over on the East side, about Tenth Street, close to the East River, and close to a strange white cemetary—tombstones rising everywhere from the barren ground. How hard it is for even a blade of grass to grow in the city atmosphere! When people asked my mother where she was living, "St. Bridget's Place" she would always promptly reply. But there is a St. Bridget's Alley, back of St. Bridget's Place, and there it was truly that we lived, in one room in a rear house. And there it was, under the auspices of the blessed Irish saint, that I first opened my eyes. "Brigitta," my mother laughed and cooed at me. "She shall be named Elizabeth," declared my father. So I have a saint to my honor whichever way you put it, whether I choose to pray to the royal Elizabeth whose lapful of bread for the poor turned into roses to save her truth, or the quaint little Bridget of Ireland whom the fairies stole away. And although when I think of the poor my heart glows with love and pity like the roses of St. Elizabeth, yet I must confess that my mind and my heart are generally too full of the fairies and romance and "Whisht, acushla!" to think long of the poor. Yes, my grim schoolmarm, Dame Poverty, I am grateful to you for all you have done for me—I give you every respect, and humble thanks—yet I love, Oh I love—the velvet-footed romance who steals past me unawares, leaving but a breath, a warmth, a light, the echo of a heavenly laughter, to make me dream in happy indolence, forgetting the Poverty, forgetting the Work, forgetting the Duty, ah, almost forgetting Honor and Pride.

I dare say it was the same fairies that stole away the little St. Bridget who put out stealthy hands about my baby couch. "She will not live," said the terrible doctor. "The only hope would be to take her to the country. "She shall live," replied my father.

The country was far and far away, just as far as the land of sunset clouds to poor folks. But there was Central Park. So every night my father trundled my little carriage to Central Park—yes, after such a long day's work—and spent the nights up there with me, praying in silence, no doubt, and peering often up to the stars for a message of hope. Hope he had not, but fierce will. "She shall live," how often he cried against despair. Yes, he kept up his work of love and heroism—oh my father, why didn't you let the little life free that was to be so useless upon this earth—yes, he kept it up far into the winter, when the snow petals hastened in a breathless silence to throw themselves as a mothering warmth over my sleeping body. "The faster the snow falls, the sounder did you sleep," narrates my father. "It was wonderful to see you sleep. Of course I always took care that you were well-covered." It was my father who, clad in a thin overcoat, stalked up and down in the bitter cold, keeping his heart warm in the thought that his child at least was warm.

So that is how my father saved my life when it was just begun.

And this is the beginning of my story of poverty and heroism.

I will write more about that another day—now there is one calling me away— "Elizabeth, Bridget, Oh, Bridget!"

Entrance to the alley once known as St. Brigid's Place. *Edward Marx.*

St. Brigid (as the name is properly spelled) was an Irish saint (c. 451-525) who came, as a child, under the influence of Saint Patrick, became a nun, and devoted her life to the church. Regarded as a saint in her own lifetime, she became one of Ireland's patron saints. Since New York already had a St. Patrick's Cathedral, the name of St. Brigid, known as a great aid to the poor, was a natural choice for the large church that began construction in 1848 during the great Irish famine which brought so many Irish immigrants to the city. The church, sometimes called "the famine church," was completed in 1856, and still stands in somewhat truncated form facing the east side of Tompkins Square, having narrowly escaped demolition in 2004 thanks to a large gift from an anonymous donor.

Léonie's mother was correct about the name of the alley in which they lived: the high-sounding "St. Bridget's Place" was in fact an alley behind the church, sandwiched between Seventh and Eighth Streets. Although "St. Bridget's Place" is not named on any map I have seen, the name does appear in a list of streets in *New York as it Was and Is* (1876) which identifies its location as "rear 185 Seventh street," an address close to Avenue B. The alley is now mainly used as a playground for the St. Brigid's School. There is still an entrance at 185 Seventh Street, but it seems no longer in use and is covered with graffiti. The nearby "strange white cemetary" was probably the old Catholic cemetery at Eleventh Street between Avenue A and First Avenue. In 1883, the Church, claiming that "the old cemetery has been neglected and has become a scene of desolation," attempted to sell the land and remove the bodies to the suburbs, but angry protests prevented the plan from being carried out until 1907, when the land was finally sold to a real estate developer to build tenements for Jewish immigrants.

Léonie Gilmour's birth certificate states that she was born on June 17, 1873, in the borough of Manhattan, New York. The place of birth is given as 185 Seventh Street, St. Bridget Place. Her mother's name is misspelled as Albiania Gilmour (maiden name Smith). Her father is identified as Andrew Gilmour, a clerk, age 30.

Andrew Gilmour, 1892, by Charles DeForest Fredricks. *Isamu Noguchi Foundation.*

From the birth certificate we may suppose that Léonie's father was born in 1843 or 1844; from an 1887 letter in this volume, we know his middle initial, J., and from Léonie's 1920 passport application, we know that he emigrated from Ireland to the United States in 1868. Isamu Noguchi wrote in his autobiography that Andrew had "fled Ireland." Léonie listed "Coalraine" as her father's birthplace on a 1920 passport application and in 1933 urged Isamu, "Don't forget to go to the north coast of Ireland if you have time, and to visit Coaleraine, the town of my father's home." The entry for the father's birthplace on Léonie's birth certificate is difficult to make out: my best guess would be "Zeloisto," which does not seem to correspond to any identifiable place in northern Ireland or elsewhere. Masayo Duus makes several statements about Andrew Gilmour that I have not been able to corroborate: that he "appears to have left home to escape a complicated family conflict," and that "Albiana was, in practice, a single mother." A clearer picture of the Gilmour's marital troubles can be gleaned from Léonie's friend Catharine Bunnell: "the housekeeping arrangements" (a euphemistic reference to Andrew and Albiana's separate apartments) were the result of Andrew Gilmour's quarrelsome tendencies: he was full of wild anarchist theories and expected everyone to agree with him, while "Mrs. Gilmour smiles at his notions contemptuously and the fat's in the fire immediately." For all his crazy notions, Mr. Gilmour, Catharine thought, "has much the finer nature of the two and she jars on him. Neither has anything to say against the other; they meet amicably, but they simply can't stand each other's constant society. Which being the case, I think they are wise in separating rather than perpetually quarreling." Albiana, who worked at various times as a typesetter, nurse, piano teacher and housekeeper, eventually moved to California without Andrew. Léonie never spoke ill of her father, and in her later life, she identified almost exclusively with her father's Irish ancestry. In "St. Bridget's Child," she takes pains to present her father as a man who preserved her fragile life with his tender care. Though the story implies that he was often "out of work," his occupation is listed on Léonie's school records as "clerk," Duus notes. In 1909, Léonie considered bringing her father to Japan where he and Isamu "would be amusement and occupation for each other" digging and growing vegetables together; though he never came, she occasionally sent money through her sister. Léonie's 1920 passport application gives a last glimpse of Andrew Gilmour at age seventy-six, retired and living in Detroit.

But let us return to "St. Bridget's Child." Léonie wrote that she supposed her life threatened by "the same fairies that stole away the little St. Bridget." But it was a different Bridget who was kidnapped by fairies in the old ballad. As the ballad, "The Fairies" (written by Anglo-Irish poet William Allingham in the 1850s, and later included in Yeats's 1888 anthology, *Fairy and Folk Tales of the Irish Peasantry*) explained,

> They stole little Bridget
>   For seven years long;
> When she came down again
>   Her friends were all gone.
> They took her lightly back,
>   Between the night and morrow,
> They thought that she was fast asleep,
>   But she was dead with sorrow.
> They have kept her ever since
>   Deep within the lake,
> On a bed of flag-leaves,
>   Watching till she wake.

Contrary to Léonie's suggestion, this fairy-protected sleeping Bridget of Irish legend has little connection with the Catholic saint after whom St. Brigid's Church was named; it is sometimes suggested that the legend derives from a once popular Celtic fire-goddess who "lost her friends" with the coming of Christianity.

The park where Léonie remembered her father taking her could hardly have been Central Park. Such a distant trek uptown through the lawless horse-driven traffic of New York's mostly unpaved streets would hardly have been conducive to health. It would, of course, have been Tompkins Square Park just across the street—a fact Léonie probably suppressed to emphasize her father's sacrifices and because Tompkins Square was "infamous for being hot, dusty, and low . . . 'the resort for poor people.' Nobody has a good word for it." The bad reputation was not entirely deserved, as Albert Webster tried to point out in 1873; the square was not really, as well-heeled West-siders supposed, a place where "the sun biteth like the serpent, and all manner of foulness riseth up from out the earth." Though a poor cousin to Central Park, it had many advantages: "Even Central Park, with all its glory of size and embellishment, does not permit to its visitors an indulgence in those peculiar delights of ease and mirth that are the gifts of the humbler spot." These "peculiar delights" included "careless bareheadedness," (hats were *de rigeur* at the uptown park), the abandonment of shirt-sleeves, and chorus-singing. From half-past six in the morning the thousands of sitters and walkers thronged the gates. Most were German immigrants, for the square was near the great German quarter, also known as "Little Germany" or "Dutchtown" (a corruption of "Deutschtown"). They had brought with them a great enthusiasm for physical culture—German "gymnastics" and a love of the outdoors. These activities were somewhat transformed in the square, with boys throwing base-balls, as well as wrestling and racing.

POOR PEOPLE'S PARKS.—TOMPKINS SQUARE.

Tompkins Square Park. *Hearth and Home,* **September 1873.**

Communal political activism was another German legacy brought to the square, which became the site of one of the nastiest labor protests of the period, the Tompkins Square Riot of January 13, 1874 in which the police dispersed a massive unemployment demonstration. When the police began swinging their batons, most protesters fled in panic, except a local German Workingman's Association, which stood firm until the mounted police arrived.

Andrew Gilmour was clearly not the only one to "fall out of work" in the wake of the Panic, which brought on a global collapse and the Long Depression that lasted until the end of the decade. Banks and insurance companies failed, real estate values plummeted. The protesters at the Tompkins Square Riot were angry because a quarter of the city's work-force had lost their jobs.

Léonie's rendition of her mother's story is also a bit fuzzy, though it is possible to reconstruct the facts from her slightly garbled account of her newspaperman grandfather, Aaron Smith. Aaron Smith did indeed co-found a Brooklyn newspaper: not the *Brooklyn Eagle* but the *Brooklyn Daily Times*, or more accurately the *Williamsburgh Daily Times* as it was known at its founding in 1848—the name was changed when Williamsburgh, once a separate township, was incorporated into Brooklyn in 1855. Aaron Smith did cofound the paper with a man named Bennett: not James Gordon Bennett, the wealthy and flamboyant publisher of the *New York Herald*, as Léonie thought, but the less illustrious George C. Bennett, a twenty-two-year-old English immigrant. George Bennett had been working at the *Williamsburgh Morning Post*, but after quarreling with his associates there, decided to set up a rival paper, taking advantage of a local political rivalry. Bennett and Smith had a third partner, Dr. Egbert Guernsey, "a local physician with literary gifts" who initially edited the paper on "a little hand press." But Dr. Guernsey tired of this job after only a few months. It might have been at this point that Aaron Smith, identified in a history of east Brooklyn as "a shoemaker by trade," was called upon by George Bennett to "furnish the brains" of the operation. Evidently, the pair made a success of it, for in 1850 they were able to move to a three story brick building on Grand Street.

On January 1, 1855, Williamsburgh gave up its dream of being an independent city, and dropping its "h," became Williamsburg, Brooklyn. That summer, the first anonymous edition of what is today Brooklyn's most famous book of poetry, *Leaves of Grass*, appeared, and Aaron Smith's paper, renamed *The Brooklyn Daily Times*, played a key role in its reception. The early response to the book was quiet and mixed. The *New York Daily Tribune* on July 23 found the poems "certainly original" but complained about the "reckless and indecent" language and the "pensive insolence" of the anonymous poet pictured in the frontispiece. A similar, brief review appeared in *Life Illustrated* a few days later, followed, through the whole month of August and into September, by dead silence. Finally, on September 29, *The Brooklyn Times* featured a glowing article entitled "Walt Whitman, a Brooklyn Boy," revealing the poet's identity and lavishing praise as well as stirring up a bit of controversy upon "the man whom our Brooklynites know so well." The review led to "an outpouring of praise and condemnation showered on Whitman." Whitman couldn't have planned it better himself—because as a matter of fact he had planned it himself: the *Brooklyn Times* review was his own work, as scholars later discovered. Bennett and Smith were probably aware of Whitman's subterfuge, but said nothing, and a year and a half later, Whitman, now famous, began contributing editorials to the paper.

The members of the Smith family appear as residents of the Village of

Williamsburgh in the 1850 census. We learn that Aaron Smith was born in Massachusetts, that his wife, born in New Hampshire, was named Hannah, and that they were both the same age: 35 years old when the census was taken (August 13) which would place their birthdates in 1814 or 1815. Albiana, listed as 9 years old (fixing her date of birth as 1840 or 1841) was at this point the eldest of three children, with a brother Jerome, age 5, and a sister Ida, 3. About Hannah Smith, Léonie's maternal grandmother, there are interesting stories but few hard facts. Isamu recalled hearing she was the daughter of a French fur trader and his Cherokee wife; his grandmother, Albiana, he recalled, looked "like an Indian." Albiana would have been about eight when her father began his involvement with the *Times*, and a teenager when Whitman became a regular contributor to the paper.

We have no indication as to how Albiana and Andrew met. Perhaps one might make a story out of an 1870 census record for an "Andrew Gilmore," age 26, living with the family of Russian sea captain Axel Bockelman in Brooklyn, working as a "store clerk." If this was indeed our Andrew Gilmour, we might imagine Albiana as a customer who visited the shop where Andrew worked. Disapproval of the marriage from Albiana's family might explain why Andrew and Albiana were obliged to leave Brooklyn for the relative squalor of an alley behind St. Brigid's Church.

Isamu knew that Andrew "was an unbeliever, as was Mother." The reasons for Andrew Gilmour's religious skepticism are unclear; perhaps he had tired of factional disputes in his home town of Coleraine; perhaps he had come under the sway of the newly fashionable evolutionary theory. He was not alone; religious skepticism was on the rise. New York was full of progressive organizations offering new ideas for the age of telegraphs and steamships.

In 1877 one such organization, the Society for Ethical Culture, began offering free weekly lectures. Its goal was to develop a system free of religious dogma. The leader and chief lecturer was a young German-Jewish Semitics professor at Cornell named Felix Adler, son of a prominent rabbi. Andrew Gilmour might have heard about Adler's Society from their German neighbors. Whether Andrew was attracted by Adler's lectures is uncertain; what certainly interested the Gilmours was the news that the Society had opened a Free Kindergarten, the first in the city. The kindergarten was located far uptown, on West 44th Street, but was run according to high ideals; moreover, it was said to be a "soup school" where students were provided with free food and other necessities, even medical care.

The Free Kindergarten opened in January 1878 when Léonie was approaching her fifth birthday. Sending Léonie to kindergarten meant Albiana had only two-year-old Florence to worry about. The free food and occasional clothing provided by the school meant that Léonie would not have to go hungry and without proper clothes when family finances were dire. The school was even prepared to cover Léonie's transportation expenses.

Toward the end of 1879, the Society announced plans to extend the kindergarten into a full-fledged Workingman's School, entirely tuition-free, and the Gilmours were ready to sign up 6½-year-old Léonie for that as well. The decision was to prove one of the most fateful of Léonie's life, for it rescued her from the probable fate of a daughter of a poor, semi-employed Irish immigrant and working mother—attending the uninspiring public schools if she was lucky, or, more likely, leaving school at an early age to work as a seamstress, factory worker, or domestic servant. The Workingman's School put her on a very different course, giving her a new set of goals and objectives. The impact of the school was so profound that without an understanding of its special purpose and educational philosophy, it is impossible to understand Léonie's life and career, and the lives and careers of her children.

The Workingman's School

Felix Adler, age 27 when the Free Kindergarten opened, had come to the United States from Alsey, Germany (a town twenty miles south of Mainz) at the age of six, when his father, prominent rabbi Samuel Adler, was called to New York's Temple Emanu-El, one of the leading Reform Synagogues in the United States. The Reform Judaism movement, which sought to modernize the Jewish religion by bringing it into accord with modern science and post-enlightenment rationalism, had proved very successful in America, where schismatic disputes were not so bitter as in Germany and Orthodox and Conservative Jewish factions were not as deeply entrenched. Felix trained for the rabbinate and was expected to succeed his father, but with the financial support of the congregation, he also attended Columbia College and was sent to Germany for graduate work at the universities of Berlin and Heidelberg, where he became interested in the ethical philosophy of Kant. He returned to New York with a doctorate in Semitic studies in 1873 and a head full of plans to carry the modernization of Judaism still farther. He is said to have told a friend that, "when he returned to New York, he would 'make things hum' in the religious world."

On October 11, 1873, Felix Adler had made his long-anticipated first sermon at his father's temple, Temple Emanu-El (then located at 43rd Street and Fifth Avenue). Entitled "The Future of Judaism," it was humming with new ideas. Judaism, he told the congregation, was in essence a religion of ethics, "not of creed but of deed," and it was Judaism's ultimate destiny "to embrace in one great moral state the whole family of man." To do so, however, Judaism had to throw off its outgrown superstitions and repackage itself as a time-tested ethical system. The message appealed to many in the congregation who were looking for a more modern approach to their ancient religion. Others felt he went too far. The aging Samuel Adler had already brought in an assistant rabbi from Manchester, and it was he who pointed out that Felix had not once referred to the deity in the course of his sermon. Even the most secularized Reformists were loath to dispense with the idea of God, and after some debate on the matter it was decided that Felix Adler's first sermon at Emanu-El would be his last.

Felix Adler. *New York Society for Ethical Culture.*

The trustees of the congregation still had great hopes for the young man and organized an endowment to place him at Cornell College as an instructor in Semitic languages. But at Cornell, again, Adler managed to offend religious sensibilities, and the college declined to renew the contract for a second year. Adler, however, refused to accept defeat. Encouraged by a visit to Ralph Waldo Emerson, he returned to New York City. His supporters among the Emanu-El trustees were willing to fund a series of lectures, which Adler began in May 1876.

Adler was an impressive lecturer, full of youthful energy and idealism, and his lectures proved successful. Initially, support came largely from the Emanu-El community. When the Society for Ethical Culture was formally inaugurated in February 1877, fifteen men were chosen to serve as trustees; all but one came from German Jewish families. The fledgling society's first president and most generous financial supporter was Joseph Seligman, a prominent Jewish financier who had survived the Panic of 1873. Seligman's was the classic rags-to-riches story: emigrated from Germany at eighteen, he had worked his way from peddler of household goods to one of the nation's most powerful and wealthy men: so powerful, in fact, that he had been offered the post of Secretary of the Treasury by notoriously anti-Semitic President Ulysses S. Grant in 1869, and had turned it down. Other founding trustees included Marcus Goldman, whose business buying and selling "commercial paper"—unsecured promissory notes—was doing very well; he would soon bring his son-in-law Samuel Sachs into the business, thus creating one of the great investment banking houses of the twentieth and twenty-first centuries. (Goldman's son, Julius, married Felix Adler's sister, Sarah). There were two prominent lawyers (Edward Lauterbach and Samuel Speyer), a couple of tobacco traders, and several clothing merchants. In spite of its German-Jewish makeup, the Ethical Culture Society was decidedly not a Jewish organization, and took pains to make non-religiosity an official principle. Its stated aim was "to assert the supreme importance of the ethical factor in all relations of life, personal, social, national, and international, apart from any theological or metaphysical considerations." Meetings were "to consist of a lecture mainly, and, as a pleasing and grateful auxiliary, of music to elevate the heart and give rest to the feelings." Nevertheless, because of its German-Jewish perspective the Society tended to devise projects that addressed concerns of the Jewish community.

Although America was ostensibly a land of religious freedom, anti-Semitism was a very real and visible factor in American life. This was made abundantly clear a few weeks after the founding of the Society when Joseph Seligman arrived with his family at the Grand Union Hotel in Saratoga, New York, their summer vacation spot for the past ten years, and was informed by the manager that Judge Henry Hilton, the owner, had "given instructions that no Israelites shall be permitted in future to stop at this hotel." The manager politely explained to Seligman that Hilton believed the large Jewish clientele the previous year had driven away Christian customers who "did not like their company" and "resolved to run the Union on a different principle this season." Seligman wrote an angry letter to Hilton and returned to New York City, where Edward Lauterbach chaired "an informal meeting of Mr. Seligman's friends and acquaintances . . . to consider what action was desirable under the circumstances." Seligman's letter to Hilton sarcastically pointed out that if Hilton, who was also in the retail clothing business, "did not consider Jews worthy to enter his hotel it would be wise for him to send a circular to all Jews not to make purchases at his Broadway stores." Lauterbach read the letter to the group and concurred with Seligman that "it is time we awaken to defend ourselves." It was resolved "to call a mass meeting of the Jewish residents of this City at an early day." The meeting was written up in the *New York Times*, with Judge Hilton giving a long rebuttal in which he attempted to argue that Seligman was merely a "'Jew' in the trade sense of the word" who "years ago . . . absolutely threw overboard the Hebrew Bible and Moses, and . . . now belongs to the Adler set of liberals; and this being the case, he but plays the mountebank if he attempts to arouse the prejudices of the Orthodox Hebrew Church." "It is the fault . . . of this class of 'Jews' themselves," Hilton argued, "that they are discriminated against." With such comments, and Hilton's publicized comment that "notwithstanding Moses and all his descendents," he could do as he liked on his own property, Seligman had little trouble promoting a boycott of Hilton's businesses that ultimately drove the hotelier into bankruptcy. Ironically, however, the protest failed to halt policies of Jewish exclusion at upstate resorts, and even promoted them by publicizing Hilton's claim that the "notorious characteristics of the Seligman 'Jew' had almost ruined the Long Branch hotels into which they have been admitted" and that "hotel men all over the country were awakening to it, so much so that a man of this type will soon find no admittance at all to such hotels."

Joseph Seligman.

The Ethical Culture Society under Adler worked to develop idealistic answers to the problem of anti-Semitism—incorporating elements of Judaism into a universal ethical system that would also borrow on equal terms from other religious systems—and it also sought to develop practical solutions: the Free Kindergarten and its sister project, which offered free nursing care to the poor. One of the most pressing problems facing New York's Jewish community was the growing influx of Jewish immigrants arriving at the port each day. The immigrants were full of energy, and some were educated, but most lacked appropriate job training and language skills, and ended up crowded into tenements or on the streets. The new arrivals were seen by the earlier generations of Jewish immigrants as contributing to negative perceptions of Jews. Of particular concern was the problem of the immigrant Jewish children, who were often at risk of turning into neglected street ruffians while their parents desperately sought means of survival in poorly-paid sweatshops.

At the time of its incorporation on February 21, 1877, the Society declared its plan for "the establishment of a school or schools wherein a course of moral instruction shall be supplied for the young." Over the course of the year, Adler and his associates worked out the details and on January 2, 1878, the Free Kindergarten of the Society for Ethical Culture opened its doors to eight "small persons," six boys and two girls.

It may well be true that all one really needs to know is learned in kindergarten: "Share everything. Play fair. Don't hit people. Put things back where you found them," etc. But the ideas on which Kindergarten is based were not as simple or obvious as Robert Fulghum's best-selling book might lead one to believe. Kindergartens did not spring up naturally out of the ground; they were the product of a long history of research, experimentation, debate, and social activism. The name "kindergarten" was first used in 1840 by German educator Friedrich Froebel to describe his "play and activity institute" for children. As the concept was developed over the following half-century by Froebel and his followers, kindergartens gradually gained popularity in the United States and other countries, mainly, at first, in German immigrant communities. Initially, kindergartening was viewed as a voluntary social contribution that women of leisure could make for the benefit of children of similar social backgrounds. In America, however, "kindergarten crusaders" began to argue for wider adoption of the system and questioned the elitism of its early proponents. In St. Louis, kindergartens were incorporated into the public school system as early as 1873. Kindergarten exhibits at the Philadelphia Centennial Exposition in 1876 helped promote the concept. In most of the country, however, kindergartens were thought too much of a luxury to be incorporated in school systems burdened with more serious problems. Moreover, many in the kindergartening movement resisted institutionalization, fearing kindergartens would lose their sense of idealistic purpose. In the end it was the practical advantages of kindergarten that overcame these resistances, for kindergartens could provide child care for the increasing numbers of women working outside the home, and could also compensate for domestic deficiencies seen as the root of various social problems. "It was one of the purposes of the Society to send the teachers into the homes of the children," recalled Florentine Scholle, one of the Free Kindergarten's early teachers, "and we were so successful in gaining the confidence of our pupils that the parents looked forward to our visits and, in many instances, we were able to be of real service in what is now called Americanization work."

Adler was fired up with idealistic plans for social reform and brimming with thoughts on religious history and ethics, but he was not greatly interested in the practical problems of child management. Histories of the Ethical Culture Society usually describe the Free Kindergarten as his project, but Adler himself gave much of the credit to others in his own account of the founding in the *Ethical School Record* of 1916, and he was not just being modest, as some of his colleagues claimed. Nevertheless, he took an active role in seeking out students for the school, canvassing the so-called gas house district with Alfred Wolff distributing leaflets. "Soup schools" that gave students free soup lunches were already popular among Italian immigrants, but the Free Kindergarten was the first to target such a young age group. Some parents evidently suspected it to be a kidnapping scheme.

The Free Kindergarten started in the National Assembly Rooms on West 44th Street, between 8th and 9th Avenues, a venue used as a dance hall at night. There was one teacher, Fanny E. Schwedler, a trained kindergartner who became something of an authority in the field; it was she who, in an address to the New York State Teachers' Association in 1897 made the wise comment about "artists of motherhood" quoted at the beginning of this book. (Her occasional columns in such journals as *Kindergarten Magazine* are full of practical wisdom: "Too much can not be said concerning the use of the word 'don't,'" she writes in one comment. "The world is dealing with negatives; instead of teaching how to do right we are continually harping on how not to do wrong; when taught the right way the wrong has no temptation for us.") For the first two years the Kindergarten was merely a kindergarten. As the word spread the number of students soon increased to 80. In October 1879, the Kindergarten was moved to rooms in an apartment building at 1521 Broadway, on the corner of 45th Street.

The Free Kindergarten. *New York Society for Ethical Culture.*

As the Kindergarten became popular, the Society began discussing the possibility of expanding it into a full-fledged school for children of the poorer classes. What allowed the possibility to become a reality was the announcement of an anonymous $10,000 gift in October 1879 from one of the society's trustees. Not surprisingly, the donor was soon revealed to be the Society's wealthy president, Joseph Seligman. Seligman was suffering from heart disease and had made the gift shortly before traveling south for the winter on the advice of his physician; he died of heart failure in New Orleans on April 25, 1880.

With financial problems out of the way, the prospect of a full-fledged school raised many questions. Adler viewed the New York "common schools" as a sort of cross between a factory and a prison. He had many ideas on the ethical aspects of educational reform, and some solid practical assistance from Alfred R. Wolff, an engineer, who served as the school's secretary, and planned and superintended the manual training course. But neither had much practical experience with pedagogy. As the trustees had doubts about American pedagogical training, it was decided to import a specialist from Germany: Gabriel Bamberger, a former rabbinical student, like Adler, who had chosen to pursue a career in education. Bamberger was Adler's senior by about ten years, and was directing a government preparatory school and business college in Hesse when he received the invitation, but found the offer sufficiently compelling to pack his family off to New York. Bamberger left a strong imprint on the school and its methodology during the decade he spent as its principal and it is he, no doubt, not Adler, who appears at the center of Léonie's 1887 graduation picture.

The Workingman's School, which opened in February 1880, was, as the name implied, "primarily intended for the children of working people." "Instruction is gratuitous, only children whose parents are too poor to pay a tuition fee being admitted." The policy of refusing admittance to anyone able to pay tuition was continued, with a few exceptions, until 1890. Nevertheless, the school aimed at offering an education far superior to that of the state-funded public schools. Relocated to the Ethical Culture Society's newly acquired building at 109 West 54th Street, the school contained "125 children, gathered from the poorest families, who are kindly clothed—so far as is needed—fed, and taught, and generally cared for every day." Even medical care was provided: Florence Scholle recalled that "it was in our kindergarten that the practice of medical examination of the pupils was first initiated."

The Workingman's School was admittedly experimental, a testing ground for the ideas of Adler, Schwedler, Bamberger, Wolff, and the other teachers. Adler served as the school's spokesman and sought to harmonize the ideas that came out of the discussions of the Society, the day to day work of the school staff, and the concerns of the Trustees. In some ways these ideas were radically progressive, in others, they represented a compromise between newer, progressive educational ideals and traditional notions of working-class education. Social class had always been a factor in American education, and the wealthy supporters of charity schools for working-class children—as well as the children's working class parents—hoped these schools would produce competent and contented workers, not idealistic Kantian philosophers. Public schools, which were also aimed at the lower and middle classes, focused on teaching basic skills of reading, writing, and arithmetic, and attempted to include some rudimentary job training. Adler's approach was different. He felt American democracy, idealistic in character, called for something more than mere job training. "It is the business of the school to cultivate every individual pupil as an individual; to develop, not some particular faculty, but, so far as possible, every one of his faculties; to liberate all the powers of the mind and heart latent within him; so to educate him that he may become, not a breadwinner, but a man." At the same time, he wholeheartedly embraced the idea of manual training. "The educational objects aimed at are to cultivate the eye and the hand, to develop skill, to call out the active side of the pupil's nature." Adler wanted his school to bridge the gap between manual training and intellectual idealism, indeed, to turn manual training into a kind of idealism.

THE MODELING-ROOM.

The Workingman's School. *Century Magazine,* **1889.**

The enthusiastic sense of democratic idealism with which Adler and his associates approached manual training was something peculiar to European Jewish immigrants, as Rabbi Joseph Leiser, explained in a tribute to Bamberger. "Industrialism, during the last four centuries, had sunken the lowest among the Jews. Proscribed from the gilds, and forbidden to engage in the manufacture of articles of use, the Jew was compelled to resort to the direst means of supporting himself. Driven from farm, field, and factory, he was enclosed within his Ghetto walls, where he gradually unlearned the use of handicrafts." The Workingman's School was specifically designed to reintegrate skills Jews had lost over centuries of exclusion from guild-controlled professions in Europe. For this reason, immigrant Jews regarded even the exploitative drudgery of garment district sweatshops as a valuable democratic privilege.

"Hand culture, apart from its value per se, is a means towards a more effective brain culture," Adler explained in "The Democratic Ideal of Education." Through shop lessons, pupils were to "learn the properties of things by making the things, by toiling over them." Modeling in clay, drawing and designing were used to "cultivate the taste." "The results obtained in this department by children twelve years old, and even younger," Adler reported, "are surprising." The artistic capacity of the American people was like "the deposits of the precious metals underneath our hills, which remained so long undiscovered but yielded an astonishing return the moment they were systematically mined."

Adler's emphasis on hand culture was refreshing, and his enthusiasm infectious, but his methods did, at times, seem a bit extreme. "The method everywhere is to excite the pupils to self-activity," he wrote. "Hence our anxiety in the science department to make the laboratory method available for elementary instruction. Hence our eagerness to put tools into the hands of the little workmen six years old. Hence in the teaching of history, geography, etc., our determination to exclude as far as possible the use of text-books, to deprive teacher and pupils alike of those props of indolence, to make them construct their text-books as they go along." Later Léonie zealously followed Adler's method in raising her own children. Nothing Isamu did, whether buying books or making them himself, could induce his mother to teach him to read—it might spoil his eyes, she said. Isamu's fondest childhood recollection was of his mother reading to him. But she would not allow him to slip into the dreamy indolence of poetry, the world of his father's books: he must remain active. "It is the mission of the school," Adler wrote, "to convert potential into kinetic mental energy; to build up faculty and ever and only faculty; to be, in the Socratic phrase, 'the midwife' of the soul in its process of self-manifestation." The school "does not attempt to load the memory of its pupils with facts, it is not solicitous about the amount of positive knowledge which they may carry away with them; it is satisfied to train them in such a way that they may be able later on to attain the ends of knowledge and virtue, to whatever degree their nature permits, through their own exertions. The school is a gymnasium of the faculties." This was the environment of the Workingmen's School, where Léonie Gilmour developed her unconventional views, and it was the environment she created for Isamu—in some ways more effectively than Adler could have managed in a Manhattan schoolhouse. Isamu became the model Adlerian student, shaping clay, metal, and stone into the self-manifestations of his soul. Adler's methods encouraged the student's discovery of his or her own individuality. "The gravest charge which can be brought against the prevalent methods," Adler had said, is "that they take too little account of the specific differences by which human beings are distinguished from one another, and endeavor to fashion all alike upon a preconceived and arbitrary pattern." The educator, he thought, should be "not a master but an interpreter of nature, to guide it in the way it would go."

The school's first graduation ceremony in 1887 attracted attention in the press, no doubt in part because mayor Abram Hewitt was scheduled

to speak. But Hewitt canceled and a visiting English industrialist and for-
mer parliamentarian, William Mather, gave an address instead. Andrew
Rickoff, the school's new "director" also gave a speech. Rickoff, noted
for having reformed Cleveland's public schools, would take over Gabriel
Bamberger's job in 1890 when Bamberger left to take a job supervising a
Jewish manual training school in Chicago.

Léonie (far left) with her graduating class. *New York Society for Ethical Culture.*

Eight Years of Study

First Commencement of the Workingman's School

New York Times, June 12, 1887

The Commencement exercises of the Workingman's School were held
last evening at the school building, 109 West Fifty-fourth-street. Prof.
Felix Adler presented diplomas to Leonie Gilmore [*sic*], Agnes Schuster,
Lydia North, Laura Bamberger, Lizzie Friebolin, Robert Menzer, Abram
Cohen, Charles Whitney, and Adolph Groh, who compose the first class
that has graduated from the Workingman's School. The work of the

pupils was on exhibition last evening in several rooms of the building.

In opening the graduating exercises Prof. Adler explained that the school is the first institution in which an attempt has been made to connect manual training systematically with the ordinary branches of a public school curriculum. The school has been in operation for eight years, which is the length of time necessary to the education of a pupil under the system in operation.

Several of the graduates read essays, the majority of which were on historical subjects, and were well composed. Mr. Mather, ex-member of Parliament for Manchester, delivered an address in which he spoke in the highest terms of the good work which the school was performing and incidentally praised in enthusiastic language the beauty of American women. Mayor Hewitt was to have delivered an address, but was unable to attend. Andrew J. Rickoff, one of the Directors of the school, also delivered an address.

As Léonie approached graduation she was faced with the difficult decision of her future plans. The boys in her class were mostly destined to fulfill their teachers' expectations by entering fields connected with the manual arts. Adolph Groh attended night school and became an interior decorator. Robert Meinzer became an ornamental plasterer. Giles Whiting, the most successful of the first graduates, attended CCNY and Columbia and became president of a Persian rug manufacturing company before he was thirty. But what of the girls? Felix Adler's views on women were somewhat ambivalent. Like most Americans of the period, Adler saw motherhood and housekeeping as women's primary social roles. "At the same time," he argued in his 1877 book *Creed and Deed*, "we should not close our eyes to patent facts, facts such as these . . . that well nigh two millions of women in this country are engaged in working for their livelihood. Is it not cruel mockery to say to these women that their business is in the household? If the condition of things is such that they must seek outside labor; if we permit them to toil by hundreds of thousands in the fields and factories, on what plea of right or reason can we deny them admission to the higher grades of service? Is it not simple justice to admit them to all the professions, and to allow them the same advantages in colleges and professional schools as are enjoyed by men?" Adler had no fear of the supposedly dangerous effects of education on women. The effect of competition would quickly discourage them from unsuitable pursuits, he said, and, far from seeing higher education as a detriment to marriage, he argued that "higher education can alone make marriage what it ought to be." Léonie's female classmates were not destined to challenge the status quo, however. Lydia North and Agnes Schuster would end up as housewives; Lizzie Friebolin would attend an evening high school while training for kindergarten work, and eventually married a veterinarian; Laura Bamberger moved to Chicago when her father took an offer to direct the Jewish Manual Training School there, but died the following summer in an unfortunate boating accident on the Ohio River.

And Léonie Gilmour seemed likely to finish out her education in the dreaded public school system. The new school year was already under way when an alternative course presented itself. There was an opening at the Bryn Mawr School, a new elite private school in Baltimore, which also offered a scholarship. Felix Adler had proposed Léonie as a candidate and it seemed to require little more than her father's approval.

The Bryn Mawr School was designed to be a feeder school for the new Bryn Mawr College in Pennsylvania, a few miles outside of Philadelphia: both schools had opened their doors in the fall of 1885. The driving force behind both schools was a group of five Baltimore women informally known as "the committee." The leader of the committee was Martha Carey Thomas, who preferred to be known as M. Carey Thomas or, better yet, Carey Thomas. Thomas, like Felix Adler, had gone to Germany for her doctorate, not by choice but by necessity, as doctoral study for women was all but impossible in the United States. With determination, strong family connections, and help from her four like-minded friends, she pushed her way into the planning of a new women's college being developed from a Quaker physician's bequest, convincing the trustees to scrap their plans for a conventional sort of ladies' college and build instead one that would offer women the most rigorous academic program in the country. The lack of suitable applicants for such an institution necessitated the creation of an affiliated preparatory school, the Bryn Mawr School, to be run by Thomas's wealthy heiress friend, Mary Garrett. The plan was undoubtedly an impressive one, but many parents and educationists thought such a demanding curriculum unsuitable for girls, and for some years, the two institutions had difficulty fulfilling their enrollment quotas.

Carey Thomas's conversation with Felix Adler about the prospects for taking one of the Workingman's School graduates to the Bryn Mawr School must have been a delicate one, since Thomas, it would later emerge, was not in favor of admitting Jewish students. For the right applicant, however, the Bryn Mawr School (or rather Mary Garrett) was prepared to offer a full scholarship, including room and board. Moreover, if the applicant could stay the course, the two top graduates of the

Bryn Mawr School each year were promised a four-year college scholarship. It was an astonishing opportunity for a poor student with the determination to succeed. Adler and Thomas discussed the matter and settled on Léonie Gilmour as the appropriate choice. On October 15, Adler wrote to the Bryn Mawr School's secretary:

Felix Adler to Eleanor Andrews, October 15, 1887

Miss Eleanor A. Andrews;—

Having received word from Miss M. Carey Thomas that there is one more vacancy in your school and that Leonie Gilmour, a graduate of our Working-Man's School, will on proper application be received by you, I herewith present the young girl for admission and beg to introduce to you, Mr. Andrew J. Gilmour, her father, who is ready to make the necessary arrangements on her behalf.

Yours respectfully,

Felix Adler

Within days, Léonie was en route to Baltimore, embarking on an entirely new course of life.

Eutaw Place, looking toward Eutaw Street, the neighborhood of the first Bryn Mawr School. *Library of Congress.*

The Bryn Mawr School, 1887-1891

The goal of the Bryn Mawr School was to prepare women to enter college and, to enforce it, graduation was made contingent on passing Bryn Mawr College's grueling entrance examination. Foreign languages, history, science, and English were the main subjects of study. Aside from drawing and elocution, the coursework made no concessions to the frivolous feminine accomplishments usually taught in girls' schools.

From September 1885, when it first opened its doors, until 1890, the School occupied an austere three-story building at 715 North Eutaw Street, between the fashionable neighborhood of Seton Hill and the elite Mount Vernon district where most of the committee members' family mansions were situated.

The dominant force at the Bryn Mawr School was Mary Garrett, the school's president and main benefactor. Garrett's father, "Railroad King" John W. Garrett, late president of the Baltimore and Ohio Railroad, had left a huge fortune at his daughter's disposal. Though Mary Garrett had not attended college herself, she was highly cultured; it had been she, in fact, who opened Carey Thomas's eyes to the worlds of drama and literature neglected by her strict Quaker upbringing. Nor was Garrett's involvement with the school merely financial; she took a very active role in its management.

Léonie's benefactor, Mary Garrett, president of the Bryn Mawr School. *Bryn Mawr College Archives.*

The students were nearly all from white, wealthy, Christian families. In 1886, the year before Léonie's arrival, Mary Garrett had angered Carey Thomas by admitting a Jewish student, Sadie Szold, daughter of a local Jewish newspaper editor. Although Garrett held her ground and continued to occasionally admit Jewish students, objections from Thomas and committee member Mamie Gwynn kept the numbers low. The school's anti-Semitism became a public scandal in 1890 when the school's headmistress carelessly told a reporter posing as a rabbi that his daughter could not be admitted because the school's quota of Jewish students had already been filled. Thomas, forced to reply to the accusations, denied the policy, blamed the headmistress, and pointed out that two of the school's best students were "Jewesses." But the truth about the school's anti-Semitic policies—deplorable, though hardly exceptional—was evident enough. Class prejudices were also evidently strong at the school. For Léonie, whose classmates at the Workingman's School had been mostly poor and mostly Jewish, the transition to a world of privileged Baltimore girls must have been a shock.

The Bryn Mawr School on Cathedral Street. *Bryn Mawr College Archives.*

In 1890, the Bryn Mawr School moved to its own newly-designed building on Cathedral Street, a six-storey edifice with Tiffany glass lamps adorning the entrance, replicas of classical statuary lining the hallways, and an indoor swimming pool and gymnasium in the basement. By this time, however, Léonie had little time for swimming and gymnastics, for her examinations were coming up. Unless she could pass the Bryn Mawr College entrance exam, said to be harder than Harvard's, she could not graduate. Students needed proficiency in three of four languages—ancient Greek, Latin, and either French or German—they would be expected to master the fourth at Bryn Mawr College. Latin and Greek were each subdivided into three sections: grammar and composition, prose authors, and poetry. There were examinations in algebra, geometry, and science. There was a daunting reading list for the English exam, where one could expect to encounter essay questions like the following: "How far, in your opinion, does the interest of *Comus* lie in the story and in the delineation of character, and how far in the beauty of description and of language? Give full reasons for your opinion." Only the history exam gave any indication of leniency: students could choose ancient, English, or American. Somehow, Léonie survived the gauntlet.

The hope of obtaining one of the two scholarships, funded by Mary Garrett, must have been a powerful incentive. The Bryn Mawr School catalog promised that "the two pupils of each year who have completed the entire course most satisfactorily, will be entitled to four years' residence, free of expense, at any college at that time approved by the School." Considering the relatively small class size and high attrition and failure rates, Léonie had a good shot at one if she could only make it through.

Léonie's graduation picture. *Bryn Mawr School archives.*

"According to our list of graduates," archivist Elizabeth Di Cataldo informed me, "she was the first to be awarded what later became known as the Bryn Mawr Scholarship, which provided full four year tuition 'to any college at that time approved by the School', but was really intended for and was later limited to Bryn Mawr College. This was funded by Mary Elizabeth Garrett, financial supporter of BMS, BMC, and the Johns Hopkins Medical School. Leonie is listed as the only graduate in a *Baltimore Sun* article of 13 June 1891, but there was one other girl who may have also graduated from that class. We did not have formal diplomas or ceremonies until 1894 and Leonie is listed in another *Sun* article (June 9, 1894) as one of the previous graduates who would receive one. From the school's founding in 1885 to 1891 only six or possibly seven girls successfully passed both the curriculum and the entrance exams for Bryn Mawr College, which was a requirement for graduation through the mid 1920s."

Bryn Mawr College, 1891-1896

In September of 1891, Léonie Gilmour entered Bryn Mawr College, then commencing its seventh year of operation, as a hopeful member of the class of 1895. Isamu Noguchi recalled: "My mother was a devoted Bryn Mawr alumna, keeping in touch with her classmates. (She later took me to meet President Clara Thomas.) She majored in chemistry, but had become more interested in literature, and had translated George Sand when she met my father." Technically, his mother was not an alumna; despite completing seven semesters at the college and a year at the Sorbonne, she was always listed in college directories among the "Former undergraduates that have not received their Degrees," although she had plenty of company since about forty percent of students also failed to graduate. And it was not literature she majored in after giving up chemistry, but political science and history. Léonie would never have confused the name of the college president: Carey, not Clara, Thomas.

The portrait of Carey Thomas by John Singer Sargent, commissioned by the college in 1898, shows a forty-one-year-old woman of powerful intellect and considerable beauty, her body concealed in a black academic gown that blends into the darker background. The painter has endowed his subject with an ambiguous expression that could be mild amusement or slight disgust, sympathy or disdain; she gazes with a penetrating attention disconcerting to an ordinary viewer, and perhaps terrifying to a student about to take her German exams. One hand clutches the left knee a little too firmly, the other apparently brushes something into the background (perhaps the pleas of the failing student). Although the portrait had not yet been painted when Léonie arrived at the college in 1891, students soon acquired their own image of Miss Thomas, for it was very much her college, and she ran it with firm hands.

**M. Carey Thomas
portrait by John
Singer Sargent.** *Bryn
Mawr College.*

In spite of its strong Baltimore connections, Bryn Mawr College was a very different place from the Bryn Mawr School. The environment of the converted farmland campus was decidedly rural. It was still a work in progress when it opened in the fall of 1885. Taylor Hall, named after college benefactor Joseph W. Taylor, a large granite building with a clock tower, was the sole academic building, combining classrooms and faculty offices. Merion Hall, a student residence, accommodated up to fifty students. And there was a simple red brick gymnasium. Houses for faculty accounted for the few remaining buildings. The two main buildings, Taylor and Merion, were built in an austere Victorian Gothic style. A second residence, Radnor Hall, the first of six buildings designed by Cope and Stewardson in a half-Quaker, half-Oxbridge style known as "collegiate Gothic" or "Jacobean Gothic," opened in 1887, followed by a third, Denbigh Hall, in 1891, each a bit more English than the last, until the ostentatious Pembroke Hall, in 1894, boasted a castle-like tower complete with four crenellated battlements. Academic buildings progressed more slowly; during Léonie's stay the only addition was Dalton Hall, a spartan science building constructed after a tiresome fundraising effort, the trustees viewing a separate science building as an unnecessary luxury.

Bryn Mawr entrance, approaching Taylor Hall. *The Lantern,* **1892.**

Pembroke Hall. *Bryn Mawr College Archives.*

At the end of the nineteenth century, American universities had two approaches to curriculum: the prescribed course of study, employed at most universities, and the elective system, instituted at Harvard in 1869. With the concept of a "major" still unknown, colleges struggled to find a balance between the two extremes. Bryn Mawr's "group system," modeled on the one at Johns Hopkins, was one attempt to have it both ways. "All alike must devote one third of one year's work to studying some science, another third of a year's work to another science, or to a course in political economy, history, law or mathematics, another third to the history of philosophy, another third to the fourth language omitted at entrance, and another third for two years to the study of English literature and of the correct writing and the correct pronunciation of the English language. In the two years that remain to her of the four years' course she may study exclusively any two allied subjects, though she may also diversify her work in certain prescribed ways." These "two allied subjects" constituted the student's group, which determined the sequence of required courses and electives. There were only five possible groups: "1. Any language with any language. 2. Any science with any science. 3. Mathematics with Greek and Latin. 4. Mathematics with Physics. 5. History, with Political Science." Léonie was initially drawn to Chemistry, but gave it up, she later told Marie Stopes, because "it was no mental discipline," a comment that must have surprised Dr. Stopes, who was herself a botanist. Instead, Léonie settled on History and Political Science.

Dr. Elmer Kohler presides over a chemistry class. *The Lantern,* **1893.**

The college placed a great deal of emphasis on language. A full sixth of the entire undergraduate course was devoted to English literature and English expression. The student, Helen Thomas explains, "must study not only the construction of sentences and paragraphs and the meaning of words, she must also learn the proper enunciation of vowels and consonants and the proper accentuation of syllables in so far as they can be taught in a short time. Her attention is called to the provincialisms and inaccuracies of her individual pronunciation, and exercises are given to help her to correct her faults." Such exercises could be ruthless. "When mimicked by her teacher, her way of vocalising a given sentence leaves her no possibility of self-delusion. She may make jokes about the matter, and often in fact does, she may practise trilling her R's, for instance, so persistently and so loudly as to be a nuisance to all her neighbours, until a skit in the college paper celebrates her wilful zeal to her great delight, but she can never again be wholly careless of her speech." The linguistic habits of the Bryn Mawr graduate therefore tended toward the fastidious linguistic precision of a Marianne Moore (class of 1909) or a Katherine Hepburn (class of 1928). You'd probably have to have been at Bryn Mawr to appreciate why Léonie Gilmour always delighted in using down-home provincialisms like "we-uns" and "I s'pose."

But English was not the real challenge. "The greatest trial of the average Bryn Mawr student in her whole college course is perhaps her French and German senior oral examination," Helen Thomas explained. In this ordeal, "the seniors are brought up one by one to translate a few passages in each language at sight. In a little quiet room, awfully quiet, sit around a long table a member of the French or German department and another member of the faculty with the president of the college presiding." That the president was now a woman, Carey Thomas, was no consolation; that she was, in fact, the elder sister of Helen Thomas, who wrote these words, no help. President Thomas scoffed at professors who did not fail a few students each term, just for form's sake. Sitting in the hot seat opposite Miss Thomas, the student "feels keenly the ignominy of stumbling through sentences that are perfectly intelligible to the three grave, attentive persons about her." So "from the time she is a freshman the wise student does a little reading in French and German in preparation for this inevitable moment, and she sometimes even manages to use it as an excuse for persuading her family to spend a summer in France or Germany with her, which, if not quite necessary, is distinctly pleasant."

Of course, Léonie Gilmour could not hope for such a family vacation, but the dream of a year overseas must have been powerful. There was no chance the college would fund such a trip; the one "European

Fellowship" offered each year going to some brilliant graduate like Edith Hamilton, the distinguished classicist who would go on to succeed Mary Garrett as head of the Bryn Mawr School. But there was a way: according to the terms of her scholarship, Léonie was "entitled to four years' residence, free of expense, at any college at that time approved by the School." She would have to pay the steamer fare herself, and the loss of a year meant she would almost certainly run out of funds before graduation. But that was a problem that could be solved later. Léonie did the math, and the answer was Paris.

In the fall of 1893 she was on a ship to France, to spend an academic year at the Sorbonne. It must have been a daunting prospect, attending a foreign university, in a foreign language, where women, though greatly outnumbered, were expected to compete on the same terms as men. She had to manage it with as little expenditure as possible, in spite of the constant temptations of the resplendent City of Light. We do not know how, for Léonie rarely discussed her time in France; perhaps she was too busy studying to see much of the city. For Léonie, it seems, the Latin Quarter really was a place to study Latin. No doubt in order to conserve her funds, Léonie did not stay the summer in Europe: in early July she took passage from Boulogne on the S.S. Werkendam, a Dutch-operated Belfast-built steamer, returning to New York on July 10th.

The most important change at the college during her absence had been the controversial appointment of Carey Thomas to the presidency after James Rhoads became too ill to continue. The debate had begun in February of 1893 and carried on through the summer and fall, with the trustees continuing to insist that a man was needed for the position and Thomas intimating she might resign as dean. Mary Garrett played her financial trump card to break the deadlock, promising a $10,000 gift to the college contingent on Thomas's appointment. In November, the trustees approved the appointment with a seven to five vote, but denied Thomas a position on the Board of Trustees.

With French and Latin out of the way, Léonie now had to concentrate on her major fields of history and political science. Initially, there had been only one professor covering both fields: a twenty-eight-year-old Johns Hopkins history scholar about to receive his doctorate, by the name of Woodrow Wilson. Wilson proved too good a choice, though, for three years later, he was lured away to a more attractive position at Wesleyan, which in turn became a stepping stone to Princeton and a subsequent career in politics. He was replaced by Franklin Henry Giddings, a sociologist influenced by the evolutionary theories of Herbert Spencer; soon after, a specialist in colonial American history, Charles

McLean Andrews, also joined the faculty. Giddings left in 1894 to chair Columbia's sociology department. The college then hired Lindley M. Keasbey, a friend of Woodrow Wilson, who seemed to stick.

Keasbey was a man of the hour, a political theorist of the age of American expansionism. At the time he joined the faculty, he was writing an enthusiastic polemical study arguing for the construction of a Nicaragua canal: a plan he considered superior to the proposed Panama route. Keasbey was not a man of dispassionate inquiry; he argued his points energetically, approaching international politics as great global game America should play confidently aided by historical hindsight and clever strategy. "At the terminus of the easterly trade routes," he wrote in 1896, "Russia and England are at present battling for supremacy in Asia, and France is supporting the Muscovite in the struggle. But in between the European rivals, little Japan is now bravely forcing her way to the front; and thus, despite these long centuries of Western exploitation of the East, an Asiatic power may, after all, have to be reckoned with in the final adjustment of affairs." In spite of his support of American expansionism, Keasbey was later accused of harboring socialist sympathies, and his anti-war activism during the First World War led to his being fired from the University of Texas in 1917, effectively ending his academic career.

History professor Lindley M. Keasbey. *University of Texas at Austin.*

During her second period at the college (1894-96) Léonie formed an unlikely but enduring friendship with a younger classmate Catharine

Tomlinson Bunnell. Twenty years later, Léonie still pictured Catherine (whose name she always insisted on misspelling with an "e") in the blue dress with a little pink about the collar she had worn at eighteen. Catharine came from a family as wealthy as Léonie's was poor. Her maternal uncle was Yale-educated Wall Street lawyer John W. Sterling whose $15 million bequest to his alma mater in 1918 (at the time the second largest gift in the history of American education) paid for the university's main library building, the Sterling Library. But this connection to vast wealth had limited benefits for the Bunnells, who lived mainly on the architectural earnings of Catharine's father, Rufus. Catharine's letters to family members, preserved in the Sterling Library's Manuscripts and Archives department, give a vivid account of her year sharing a dormitory with Léonie at Bryn Mawr, and their later time as roommates in New York.

John Sterling's portrait (right) watches over the Sterling Library reference desk. *Edward Marx.*

Catharine, a Bridgeport High School graduate, sat for the Bryn Mawr entrance exams in June 1894, accompanied by her mother and a friend who gave up and went home after the first day. "The girls who come are regularly coached for these exams," Catharine's mother wrote on June 5. "Every one of them is astonished that Catharine has dared try it at all. We are told that one rarely passes without conditions; four are allowed.

Catharine says if she has too many, she will not try to come here this year, but take some special course of study at home, and enter in '95 with an advance in one department at least." Catharine passed. On September 18 she informed her brother Frank that their mother was soon to put her "last remaining pet lamb" (Catharine's words) on a train to Philadelphia.

"Yes, the least member of the Bunnell tribe did turn out all right, by the skin of her teeth," Catharine told Frank a few days after her arrival. In June, hopeful that she would pass the entrance exam, Catharine had wisely reserved a room in the brand-new Pembroke Hall. A congratulatory telegram from their elder brother, Sterling (a mechanical engineer then based in Minneapolis) "arrived at my room very soon after I did on Monday afternoon, and found me casting one rueful eye at the unswept carpet, the other at the unmade bed. However, these little evils were soon remedied and we couldn't complain very much, even of the fact that no student lamps were ready and we had to go to bed in the dark, when we remembered that this entire hall has been completely built and furnished since the first of April."

Catharine Tomlinson Bunnell. *Stratford Historical Society.*

Catharine Bunnell did not meet Léonie in an art history class as "Catherine Burnell" (played by Christina Hendricks), does in Matsui's film. In fact the college had no art history courses before 1906 when Mt. Holyoke graduate Caroline Ransome was appointed as an associate professor.

"... you'll find it much more pleasant to simply disapprove." *Essen Communications, Ltd.*

Rather, they met in Pembroke Hall, where fate had assigned them to the same dining table along with thirteen other young women. Each had an assigned place, Catharine explained in an October 14 letter to her father. Catharine sat next to the head, hemmed in by four students, a "very conceited Sophomore," a Canadian postgraduate who appalled everyone with her ignorance of U.S. history, another postgraduate who arrived late on the scene, and "the Junior, Miss Gilmore, who sits opposite me and is quite a friend of mine, although very quiet." She found her tablemates "rather dull as a rule, and if they didn't have such a terribly fresh Freshman among them (I am sure that is what they consider me), I am sure that they would almost stagnate."

When Catharine's mother visited the college in in October, Catharine introduced her to Léonie, who had been appointed as a proctor in the dormitory, a position of some responsibility. Catharine hoped to bring her brother Frank, who had recently started teaching in a school across the river in New Jersey, for Thanksgiving and Léonie rather naively encouraged the plan. "I don't know about Frank's Thanksgiving visit, the rules here are so strict," Catharine wrote her mother on October 28. "Léonie told me a few days ago that she had just discovered that no men but our father could be admitted to our studies after dinner, even in the presence of a chaperone, (isn't she a great proctor not to have known the rules when you were down here?) and at other times they cannot be admitted with the college girls without a chaperone."

Frank finally gave up the idea, but Catharine assured her mother that the Thanksgiving holiday had been quite lively. "It did seem rather lonesome Wednesday afternoon when girl after girl departed, until only nine were left in Pembroke East, and I began to wish that I too were going home. But Mary Moody came after me to go shopping for a party she was getting up for Thursday night in the Merion Students' parlor." After attending Quaker Meeting on Thursday morning, Catharine went into Léonie's room and read *Much Ado About Nothing* to her. ("Even reading one play a day," she told Frank a few days later, "we can't begin to keep up with the Dean's lectures.") About four o'clock a box arrived for Léonie from New York, "packed with good things to eat. A small roast turkey, jelly, preserves, pickles, walnuts and wafers were pulled forth and exulted over in turn. As there were too many things for the tea, we decided to give a breakfast party the next morning." Catharine was up at 7:30 to walk to nearby Rosemont for additional provisions and flowers. After tracking down the cream, specially ordered but apparently pilfered by the housekeeper, all went without a hitch: "we treated our guests to hot coffee with real cream, oranges, turkey, Saratoga [potato] chips, bread and butter, pickles, and cranberry sauce. After the girls had gone and the dishes were washed, we made the rounds of the various halls and asked over forty to our tea in the afternoon." About thirty came. "We had the students' parlor fixed up quite prettily with all our sofa-pillows and knick-knacks scattered around. My screen hid the empty fire-place and the silk-afghan made a much admired cover for the big table. Everything went off pleasantly, and we felt that we had done our part to enliven Thanksgiving for those left here." On Saturday Catharine "read some Shakespeare, and went up-stairs to a small tea given by Katherine Dame in her sister's honor. Played whist in the evening in Léonie's room and got badly beaten, owing to the phenomenal luck the other side had, holding at least nine trumps between them every time. After which we played poker and then had tea." She spent the night in Merion Hall with her friend Mary Moody.

As the school year progressed, the teas given by students became more numerous and extravagant, until even Catharine was appalled by the number. "I believe there were six large ones [yesterday]," she informed her brother on March 10. "It was also Katherine Dame's birthday, and she had a whist-party of eight in her room that night. The amount of candy we devoured was truly terrific. Léonie Gilmour and I made candy that afternoon for her; confectioner's sugar was an unknown article to all the grocers in town, as well as to the oyster-shop proprietor, etc., so we had to use the pulverized; but, by putting in plenty of flavoring and using heaps of almonds, dates and figs, we managed to disguise the taste. We discovered, on arriving at Katharine's room, that she had already received three or four boxes of candy that day. We sympathized deeply of course; it is such an affliction to have duplicate presents, and we decidedly lightened every box of it before we left." Yet Katherine Dame's tea was over-shadowed by the one given by Hanna Carpenter in the evening, "with the swellest provisions yet displayed by a Freshman. Ices and most elaborate cake and candy." "I wish the girls would not give quite such elaborate feed," Catharine lamented; "it makes one feel bashful about doing the thing on a smaller scale." She and Mary Moody intended to "return to almost pristine simplicity" the following week "asking only about thirty Freshmen, and furnishing tea, wafers, and home-made candy."

Although teas brought out the differences between the haves and have-nots, class differences were far less visible at the college, with its rural isolation, than they had been in the elite Baltimore neighborhood of the Bryn Mawr School. There was even an atmosphere of enforced egalitarianism. "The individual who attempts to discriminate in the choice of her friends along lines of external worldly importance is at once sent to Coventry as a snob, and life made anything but pleasant for her until she evinces a change of heart." Helen Thomas, as Carey Thomas's younger sister, demonstrated the truth of these egalitarian words knew the truth of these words: a sophomore at the college in 1890 when her sister was accused of anti-Semitism, she later married the older brother of Mary Flexner, one of the first Jewish students, admitted to the college in 1891.

The increasing presence of Jewish students may have raised a few eye-brows at Bryn Mawr, but there were no doubts about the college's first Japanese student, Ume Tsuda. Tsuda, born in 1864, daughter of a prominent Christian agriculturalist, was one of a small group of girls sent to be educated in the United States in 1872. Returning to Japan a decade later, she had worked as a tutor for leading politician Hirobumi Ito, who had recommended her for a teaching position at the elite Peeresses' School. Under the weight of her teaching responsibilities, Tsuda soon came to feel her lack of teaching qualifications, and wrote to sympathetic Quaker friends in America who assisted her in gaining admission as a special scholarship student at Bryn Mawr, where she was enrolled for two and a half years, from 1889 until 1892. Though older than the undergraduates, she was, by all accounts, a model student and a favorite among her classmates.

Matsui's film has Léonie meeting Umeko Tsuda and visiting her room, decorated with Japanese prints. The scene is evidently based on Duus's claim that "for about a year they lived in the same dormitory." But in fact Tsuda was only at the college during Léonie's first four months; in January 1891, she left to spend six months studying teaching methods in upstate New York, after which she returned, soon afterward, to Japan. Léonie later told Stoddard, "I will find one friend in Japan when I go there, that is Miss Tsuda, who went to the same college with me, and in whose school I shall teach when I go over," but the presumed friendship and job never materialized.

Ume Tsuda.

Léonie was more likely to have known the two Japanese students who came to the college after Tsuda left, Masa Dogura and Michi Matsuda. Masa Dogura, the younger of the two, arrived first. Two years older than Léonie, she was said to be a millionaire's daughter. A product of Doshisha Girls' School in Kyoto, Miss Dogura was expected to teach at Doshisha's pioneering nursing school after graduation. Dogura joined Léonie's History and Political Science group and was one year behind Léonie, graduating in 1897. Her planned teaching career did not materialize, however, for shortly after returning to Japan, she married Baron Yasuya Uchida, a rising diplomat who served as ambassador to Peking, Vienna and Washington before being appointed foreign minister. Léonie may also have known Michi Matsuda, another student from Doshisha, who arrived in Léonie's final year; shy and lacking "the attractiveness which personal beauty carries with it" (as Umeko Tsuda frankly noted in her letter of recommendation) Matsuda, who was five years older than Léonie, also joined the History and Political Science group. She went on to a successful career in education, eventually becoming the first female headmistress at Doshisha Women's College in 1922. Though Léonie was probably not close with any of the three Japanese students, their presence at the college gave Léonie a first-hand view of a side of Japanese womanhood very different from the "dear little Jappy, Jap, Jappy" of *The*

Geisha, the hit musical of 1896. These were smart, serious women full of a sense of purpose, and they were at pains to show their Bryn Mawr sisters that Japan was no insignificant, childish country. Their message was reinforced by Japan's decisive victory over China in the 1894-5 Sino-Japanese War.

The arduous ordeals of Bryn Mawr and its isolated location meant that the women tended to form close bonds. But Léonie was quieter and more independent than Catharine. She had always been different from her classmates, in New York, where she was often the only non-Jewish girl, and in Baltimore, where she was the poor scholarship girl from New York who had grown up in a tenement and sewed her own clothes. But she had been taught to value her individuality, and that poverty was not shameful but ennobling. "It sometimes seems as if the angelic aspect of human nature displayed itself by preference in the house of poverty," Felix Adler once wrote. Perhaps the trip to Paris was in part a reassurance that she could have what the other girls had. But it had left her with no real desire to join the pursuit of wealth, luxury or power. The desires she cultivated at college seem to have been more of an aesthetic variety. "Do you know Catherine," she would say, "that you're about the one person of my acquaintance to whom I can quote or read poetry without having them look at me as if I'd gone clear daft."

English lecturer Alfred Hodder.
Bryn Mawr College archives.

Bryn Mawr in the early years was a college with a split personality. It had been intended as a Quaker college, an ideal the trustees continued to maintain. But the heart of the College was Carey Thomas, who had turned away from her strict Quaker upbringing in order to pursue her love of literature and the arts. That Carey Thomas was a lesbian is now generally accepted, and was probably evident to many of Bryn Mawr's faculty and students. During the first decade of the college's existence, Thomas lived with her intimate friend and fellow "committee" member, Mary ("Mamie") Gwinn. Their relationship went back to 1878 when Gwinn, who came from a wealthier and less repressed family, had followed the more diligent Thomas to Europe on her doctoral studies; they had been inseparable ever since. Gwinn had helped Thomas with her Bryn Mawr plans from the beginning; when Thomas was appointed dean, she had brought in Gwinn as a graduate student and instructor, and after bestowing on her a doctorate, installed her in the English department. Gwinn was a popular enough professor, although she was somewhat reclusive and evidently dissatisfied with the enforced austerity of her life at the college.

English professor Mamie Gwinn.
Bryn Mawr College archives.

In February of 1895, Thomas interviewed a candidate named Alfred Hodder for a lectureship in English, a position intended to help Gwinn cope with the growing number of students taking English. Hodder was that rare academic creature, a Harvard-trained philosopher who could write persuasively on almost any topic: over the next decade, he would publish a book on philosophical skepticism, an exposé of sleazy New York politics, and a novel. Those who knew him thought him brilliant, but he is remembered today mainly for spoiling the domestic tranquility of the Thomas-Gwinn household. The romance between the lonesome

Gwinn and the debonair Hodder developed so quickly that by Thanks-giving, Thomas was threatening to fire the Hodder, who evidently had a wife and child, if Gwinn continued to see him, but the threat merely forced the couple into furtive, secret meetings.

A few years later, Gertrude Stein wrote a story entitled *Fernhurst* based on the Thomas-Gwinn-Hodder affair which Stein came to know Johns Hopkins where she was a medical student (the new Hopkins medical school had been opened to women thanks to another clever contingent gift from Mary Garrett). Stein learned part of the story from two Bryn Mawr graduates in her class, the other part from her brother Leo who had attended Harvard with Hodder. That Stein herself was involved in an emotionally tumultuous lesbian love triangle with the two Bryn Mawr women made the story all the more poignant. The story was still continu-ing to unfold. Gwinn and Hodder continued to meet furtively until until Hodder resigned from the college in 1898 and took his wife and child to Europe where he left them. Gwinn's inability to break off the relation-ship led to strain between her and Carey Thomas, and Mary Garrett gradually took over Gwinn's place as Thomas's preferred intimate com-panion. Gwinn continued to live with Thomas until the spring of 1904 when she announced that she was leaving to marry the now divorced Hodder. The final act of the saga took place in 1907 when Hodder's for-mer wife returned from Europe and announced that she and Hodder had never been divorced because they had never been officially married, but that their marriage was still valid according to common-law standards, and Hodder was therefore guilty of bigamy. Hodder was looking to have a hard day in court, with Alice James (wife of his Harvard professor, William James) prepared to testify against him, but Alfred Hodder died shortly before the trial could take place.

In short, if Bryn Mawr, under the watchful eyes of the Quaker trust-ees, was not exactly a hotbed of lesbianism and free love, there was still a good deal of barely-repressed sexual energy simmering beneath the surface. Students may or may not have sensed the drama taking place in the Deanery, where Thomas and Gwinn were locked in battle over Hod-der. In *Fernhurst*, Helen Horowitz writes, Stein, conveying what "students perceived, understood, and misunderstood" about "the Carey-Mamey-Alfred triangle," gives a hostile portrait of Thomas, but portrays Gwinn sympathetically. "Tall, her wavy hair tinged with gray, the brilliant and elusive, innocent and regardless Miss Bruce"—the character modeled on Gwinn—"is above all detached from human contact." "By some quality of her nature," Stein explains, "she never succeeded in really touching any human creature that she knew," but "her desire was to experience the extreme forms of sensuous life and to make even immoral experience her own . . . she was still waiting for the hand that could tear down the walls that enclosed her and let her escape into a world of humans." The women professors also served as models; they were the much-talked-about "new women" of the age, and their love affairs and lifestyles could hardly fail to interest students who might wish to follow in their paths.

When Catharine's mother and brother Frank visited Bryn Mawr during the Thanksgiving holiday in 1895, she introduced them to Dollie Gray, afterwards explaining to Frank that Dollie was her "wife." "She is as cute a girl as you ever saw, always dead broke, always in scrapes, but she manages to pull through and keep jolly at all times," she wrote on December 3. Returning to the subject in a January letter Catharine, explaining that Dollie "wanted to be remembered to her brother-in-law," told Frank the story of their marriage. "She is not my wife in the Yale sense of the term, but we fell into the way of calling each other 'Dollie' and 'Jack' last year, and acting the spooney couple for the benefit of the other girls. We got tired of that this year, and concluded to consider ourselves married. That gives us the use of each other's rooms and possessions without being required for any special case."

The topics of love and sexuality had to be addressed openly—up to a point—at a college committed to the idea that women's education did not simply mean the preparation of women for roles as wives and mothers. Discussions must have returned again and again to questions of women's sexuality and its relationship to society.

Gilmour's one surviving work of literary criticism, "George Meredith—A Study" (see appendix) might well have originated as a paper for an English class taught by Gwinn or Hodder. In it, she specifically addresses Meredith's involvement with problems of women and sexuality. "He is perhaps chiefly intent in solving the problems of women in connection with marriage," a sentence that might have applied to Hodder as well as Meredith. Gilmour was no blind follower of "the numberless new sects that are springing up, the many 'isms' of the day that are raising their rebellious standards against the existing order of things and penetrating with their revolutionary doctrines into all parts of the social structure," which she saw as merely "expressions of the spirit of nonconformity." She was particularly interested in Meredith's novel, *One of Our Conquerors*, where "we have the story of a woman who has taken the 'leap' out of society by leaving her husband to live with another man. The story is told with such sympathy, her life seems so to justify her course, that one does not condemn her. She, however, never seems to get away from the haunting sense of guilt." Meredith's story was unusual in a period dominated by "fallen women" stories, but he did not go far enough for Gilmour's taste. "Her one grand impulse of daring spent, she retreats into the innate timidity that has ever marked her gentle and sensitive nature. How like a woman!" Gilmour's "how like a woman!" seems to echo the views of Gwinn, scoffing at social disapproval and pursuing her tragic relationship with Hodder straight through to the melodramatic finish. But at the end of her essay, Gilmour retreats from this extreme position. "Whether this simple method of cutting the knot, if universally accepted, would be of advantage to the community at large, is an open question. In any case it is to be remembered, as Meredith says elsewhere, that conventions protect the weak, and that women are at present the weaker half of humanity." By the time Gilmour published the essay, in 1905, with a baby in hand and no husband to be seen, the conservative argument for the protections of marriage must have seemed even stronger.

According to the college archivist, Lorett Treese, Léonie Gilmour completed seven semesters of work at the college during the academic years 1891-2, 1892-3, 1894-5, and the first semester of the year 1895-6, and left without receiving a degree from the college, with a note on her transcript indicating that she withdrew for reasons of health. One might suppose "reasons of health" to be a convenient excuse for any of a number of possible impediments, from the financial problems associated with the ending of Léonie's scholarship the previous year to the difficulty of passing the many examinations required for graduation. But Léonie was hospitalized in January 1895, as a letter to Catharine from her mother on the 18th indicates. "Until you wrote of Léonie's illness, I did not know that Bryn Mawr owned a hospital. Is it an institution of the 'University Town' or located among the shanties on the other side of the track?" The hospital was indeed located "among the shanties on the other side of the track," but it was a new building, with an elevator and electric lighting, designed by Philadelphia's premier architect, Frank Furness. The illness that led to Léonie's hospitalization is unclear. But it brought to a close the long educational course that had begun sixteen years earlier in Felix Adler's free kindergarten.

Catharine Bunnell, busy studying for her German condition exam, which a summer spent in Switzerland had not made more appealing, was also having doubts about her academic future. At the end of the year she, too, would give up the daily grind and endless rounds of tea parties to return home to Stratford. She would take a few art classes at Yale, travel, and decide what to do with her life.

New York & New Jersey, 1896-1904

Léonie returned to her family in New York where, after recovering from her illness, she sought work in various fields for which she was qualified: teaching, editing, translation, the occasional office job.

St. Aloysius' Academy

In 1898 she was offered a regular teaching job at St. Aloysius' Academy, a Catholic girls' school in Jersey City. For four years she took the East River Ferry to Jersey City on school days to teach classes in French and Latin. The Academy was conveniently located on Grand Street only two blocks from the river. Across the street was St. Peter's, an Irish Catholic church with an affiliated boys' preparatory school, St. Peter's College. The Jesuit fathers of St. Peter's ran the college while the nuns of the affiliated Convent of the Sisters of Charity ran St. Aloysius's Academy. (The buildings still stand at 107 and 110 Grand Street, though the Academy has become St. Peter's Preparatory School and the church, now the Saints Peter and Paul Orthodox Church, is now Russian Orthodox). If the school's Catholicism was not Léonie's taste, the Irish atmosphere probably was. Her most sympathetic friend among the faculty was Sister Rose de Lima, an instructor two years older than Léonie who later chaired the political science department at the College of St. Elizabeth.

It was also during this period that Léonie undertook a significant translation project, a translation of Victorien Sardou's popular 1860 farce, *Pattes de mouche* (1860). The play was already well known in English through American playwright John Palgrave Simpson's 1861 theatrical adaptation. Gilmour's translation was made for a two-volume anthology of European plays and therefore would be expected to follow the original more faithfully. Gilmour's translation appeared alongside translations by Elizabeth Barrett Browning, Edward Fitzgerald, and William Archer, along with a cohort of Oxford and Cambridge classicists. Though it never really competed with Simpson's popular stage version, Gilmour's version has appeared on stage and was reprinted in several later anthologies.

The St. Aloysius' Academy (now St. Peter's Prep). *Edward Marx.*

In January 1900, with little fanfare, Léonie and Catharine Bunnell set up household together at 448 West 151st Street, in the Washington Heights neighborhood of upper Manhattan. Though far uptown, it was just a few blocks from the last station (155th Street) on the 9th Avenue Elevated Railroad, or "L," which offered quick access downtown. On January 18, Catharine wrote her brother Frank that she and Léonie had been to see French soprano Emma Calvé in *Carmen* at the Metropolitan Opera and to see a show of artist Peter Newell's drawings. They planned to see a matinée each Saturday and were "planning to send cards to our friends and stay home and receive" on Sundays. "We take in about all the good picture exhibits in New York too," she explained; "but most of the time Léonie is working and I stick to the shanty, writing and learning all kinds of housework."

Catharine had met Léonie's father and been treated to a good dose of "Mr. Gilmour's anarchism":

> Léonie came home sick last night and went directly to bed;
> so I looked after her father's supper, and sat in the kitchen
> for a long time afterwards, while he cooked the oatmeal for
> breakfast and told me all sorts of pipe stories concerning

theosophy, Masonry, Vedantic and Hindu philosophy, the pure symbolism of the Bible, and finally his own well matured plan for building an air-ship, launching a few bombs at New York, and abolishing by a word all governments and monetary systems. And each man will work four hours a day and each have absolutely everything he wants. The only flaw in the scheme, as he thought, was his lack of money to build the airship. Just think of a man believing for years that he had an idea in his head which might bring him in millions of dollars if it were not against his principles to sell it. He was so serious throughout and the whole tale was so funny and pathetic that I had hard work looking as though I believed it all.

"It's a strange life down here," Catharine concluded; "I'm getting more theories hammered into my poor little brain between what I'm reading and seeing of actual poverty, and Mr. Ghent's socialism, and Mr. Gilmour's anarchism."

The following week, when Léonie collapsed from eyestrain and over-work at her editorial job, working at the DeVinne Press on East 4th Street, Catharine stepped in as her temporary replacement. It was a con-venient excuse for Catharine to escape her "charmed life" for a taste of the working world, and she was relishing it, as she explained in a letter to her mother:

Catharine Bunnell to her mother, January 23, 1900

My Dear Mother;—

This time of writing rivals yours; it's ten minutes past seven and I'm on my way downtown on the L.

I hardly think late nights were to blame for Léonie's breakdown; we are almost always in bed before ten, sometimes soon after nine. Have to be you know, getting up so early. Generally she works in the proof-room of the DeVinne Press, mornings only, as copy-holder, that is she reads copy while the proofreader corrects the galleys, and acts as fag generally. Last Wednesday she staid all day; it's a free and easy sort of a job down there; they can use much or little of the copy holder's time, depending apparently on how much she wants to give them. In addition to the nine hours' work she forgot her glasses and read without until she fainted away in the course of the afternoon. She would go back to work next morning and repeated the performance.

Then she had to give up and rest; so she showed me what she could about the business, and they've been good enough to put up with me down at the Press. They are a nice set of young women down there, pleasant as can be, and they seem a healthy, happy lot too. I am working all day and shall be there all this week, with only Saturday off for a matinée and earning my six dollars a week, having reduction for the afternoon out, and really, for the first time in my life, having a feeling of self-respect, of really being worth my keep, which would make up for ever so many disagreeable things, let alone the few there are about this job.

I think I have never had any trouble in seeing the heroism in life, it's the alleviating side that I need to see most of. It's maddening often to see sorrow and wrong all about and to bear a charmed life which is never touched by either. The Evanses certainly seem to be at the other end of the scale. No, I shan't sympathize with your idea of our life's taking much heroism. We are not distressingly poor and have as much health as we need.

So in spite of the ticket I can't see you this week. Léonie is under an oculist's care now, and will go to work next week all mended up. Thank Grandmother for her dear note; it would have been a much more effective hint than the ticket had I been able to take it. I have the library books with me, and shall express them on my way home tonight. Charge the dues to me, and take many thanks for them and much love from Catharine.

DeVinne Press Building. *Cornell University Library.*

Catharine Bunnell to her mother, Jan. 31st, 1900

The DeVinne Press, New York.

My dear Mother;—

I'm writing in half minute snatches of time, while "Hully" stops perforce to talk to somebody. "Hully" is a girl whom I knew slightly at Bryn Mawr, when she belonged to the upper ten and came of a family who were worth millions. Since then her father has failed and she has learned proofreading and is happier than ever before in her life. The "Press" people look upon her, as I fancy they do on the other two of us college girls also, as "very nice, but queer." We worked like dogs yesterday over a dry old book on business, which had to be rushed through the Press at a rate distracting to foreman, compositors, and readers. The mixture of bad English and hifalutin language was too much for us as we got tired and late in the afternoon we were laughing ourselves silly over the stuff, to the great disgust of all the other people who had had anything to do with the job. As Miss Walcott said, "There wasn't one of them that knew enough to laugh over anything in this office till I struck it."

There's more to follow of the same stuff today, but we are on the home stretch, and our foreman, Mr. Bigger, positively condescended to get good-natured over the job yesterday afternoon. He's a bully, a coward, a liar, and a mean man generally; but he's been smiling on me ever since I've been here, and I think he'd like to have me stay on. The other people don't know how to smooth his fur the right way. Not for nothing have I lived the best part of twenty-three years in hearing of your blarney.

The point of this letter is, will you send me some spondulicks? My shoes gave out of a suddint like, and I had to have a few other things, so that I shall be living on charity by tomorrow—that will be the first of February, so if you will send me a V. on my allowance, that will tide me over Saturday, when I draws me wages.

The Boer meeting Monday night was a howling success, as you probably gathered from the "Tribune" account. It was the liveliest political meeting I ever attended and you know I have a fondness for them anyway.

The dinner the night before was a much greater pleasure; my French basely deserted me though, and I could hardly speak three consecutive words, but the French people are always polite and complimented my accent highly. They didn't hear much of it to judge by, I assure you. And the rest can wait till I come home. If I write all the little happenings, there'll be nothing left to talk about, and then Auntie would be disgusted.

Excuse dirt please; it's impossible to steer clear of it in this office.

Which much love to all of you,

Catharine

Catharine was still working at the DeVinne Press in March. "Léonie and I are in for company tomorrow," she wrote Frank on March 7. "We invited Helen Saunders to come to lunch; and then, seeing that would keep us pretty well at home, asked Katharine Dame, another Bryn Mawrtyr, who is studying at Pratt, to drop in for tea. She accepted effusively; had we remembered it was her birthday? You may imagine whether we will give ourselves away or not; and we've already made quite elaborate preparations for a lot of nonsensical birthday presents." Catharine also went with a friend to see Léonie's old teacher, Felix Adler, lecture at the Carnegie Lyceum, but came away unimpressed. "I've heard plenty of such would-be broadminded people before expatiate on the glories of their own little rut, and was simply rather bored." Her friend, even less enthusiastic, "waxed madder and madder every instant, and came home a devoted Whiscopalian ready to go to church all through Lent." Léonie was evidently untroubled by Catharine's reaction. "Today Léonie and I have been moseying around downtown, doing some shopping, and visiting the Press, where the whole crowd was very cordial." She was soon to return home to Stratford but had plans to rejoin Léonie in New York in the future.

Several letters from Léonie written in 1900 to Catharine in Stratford are the first of Léonie's letters that seem to have survived. Léonie and Catharine had similar reading tastes and often shared books and magazines; they were reading Elbert Hubbard's whimsical series of pamphlets, *Little Journeys to the Homes of English Authors*, and Léonie particularly enjoyed the last one, on Robert Burns. "All poets are lovers, and all lovers, either actual or potential, are poets," Hubbard explained at the outset. "Potential poets are the people who read poetry; and so without lovers the poet would never have a market for his wares. If you have ceased to be moved by religious emotion; if your spirit is no longer surged by music; and you do not linger over certain lines of poetry, it is because the love instinct in your heart has withered to ashes of roses." Burns had "succeeded in his love-making and succeeded in poetry, but at everything else he was a failure. He failed as a farmer, a father, a friend, in society, as a husband, and in business."

To Catherine Bunnell, May 4, 1900

My dear Catherine,

I'm sending on some of the Roycroft productions to-day and hope you will pardon my dilatoriness. I shall try to do better in future. I thought the Burns one fine. I must acknowledge that Bobby was a ne'er do well, but for a'that and a'that I still have a trace of tenderness left for him tho no respect. I just received a very nice letter from May Wendell. Her handwriting is almost as bad as mine. I like her.

Those narcissus have the most graceful poses of any I've seen. They're on my bookcase in an empty olive jar (forget the olives 'cause I thought the bottle would make a pretty flower glass). Thank you, dear. You do your best to spoil me, don't you?

I don't seem to have any particular news today. Did I tell you that the other branch of my family have moved to 19th Street? Is there any magic in the number? There's another flat to be had in the same house for $24.00 (five rooms & bath). Also a microscopic one of 3 rooms in the same block for $11.00. Have you forgotten our old plans? And what do you mean by annexing yourself to a working girls club to begin in September? Just [thing] you know I shall have started one right here in New York and you'll be in demand to manage *it*. So you'd better hold yourself in readiness. I wonder you don't get the trained nurse to teach you her business while you're about it. You'll be smattered into a perfect paragon if you keep on. But remember there's a market for all talents in the grand metropolis of America, N.Y.

Give my regards to your family. I hope your grandmother is feeling nicely to-day. I'm pretty well, thank you, excepting for a protracted attack of loneliness. I use my eyes from four to five hours daily at least.

Affectionately
Léonie

Léonie at this time seems to have taken an interest in attending church to hear the sermons of William Rainsford, a prominent labor activist who was rector of the nearby St. George's Protestant Episcopal Church, located at East 16th Street east of Third Avenue. But at the same time she was also interested in a local mystical organization (possibly related to the Freemasons) which offered a different view of the workings of the soul.

To Catherine Bunnell, November 20, 1900

331 E. 16th Street, New York.

My dear Catherine,

I wrote a letter to my love and on the way I forgot to post it. Which is to say I did write you a letter last week which is at present reposing on my mantel piece and too stale to offer you. The gist of it was simply to remark that if you want to find out what the dickens I am up to you had better come down and find out.

I had a letter from Alice today holding out the prospect of a glimpse of her around thanksgiving time. Won't that be scrumptious.

I saw May Wendell once this year but she didn't see me. I yelled to her from the window of the elevated car but she was wrapt in uppish thought and wouldn't respond.

Found a card in my box awhile ago labeled "Miss Moody" sans explanations. Where is she at? If you see her tell her how sorry I was to miss her call. Send me her address anyway.

Oh that miserable club of yours! Before I'd let myself get so tied down to the club habit that I couldn't spend an evening with me own fambly! But I'm going to join a club too. A very nice one right around the corner. When you come down you shall go. I'm sure it'll beat the Bridgeport one all hollow. This is an elegant neighborhood and we haven't moved yet. I go to church every Sunday (three times), hear Dr. Rainsford preach right at the corner and the best music in the city, all free gratis for nothing. The mystic circle is also right handy and it is very edifying to go there and find out about the workings of your soul and how it's all one whether you're a sinner or a saint, because in either case you just go and do exactly what you want to do.

Had one call from Mrs. Jule, since I've been here and one from Rose Connelly, my Catholic friend of Washington Heights. So I keep a little in touch with the old neighborhood after all, you see.

Mama expects to go to the hospital about Christmas time to have her eyes operated on and I'm afraid it kind of worries her. I believe there is only the slightest chance of the operation being unsuccessful, however. Still it's a trial to go through with it. Forgive my scrappy scrawl. I'd far rather have a long talk with you.

Lovingly,
Léonie

To Catherine Bunnell, n.d.

My dear Catherine,

Highty, tighty, jiggledly, giggledy jig!

The above is the time to which I danced on my head upon receipt of your note.

So you got a pink waist? I don't want it. It wouldn't jibe with my new hat. O yes, I took the one that I gave to Florence eight years ago back again—you remember it's brown trimmed with some silk that is mostly blue and gold. I added thereto a yard and three quarters of broad scarlet ribbon. Result, an opium dream of a poppy field! Très chic, and quite Frenchy, they say.

I didn't arrive here until Thursday evening, when the janitress promptly put in an appearance to collect the rent. Such a circus! She said the landlord was *furious*. She was really frightened to see him take on so. I believe he swore at us a little. O what a lark! He was sure we had eloped for good—or for bad—especially as my dear pater was likewise in ignorance of our whereabouts.

The janitress made a long and impressive story out of it, and I answered (casting my eyes dreamily about the room): "I wish the landlord would give us a new wallpaper. It's really not aesthetic to have it faded in spots. It pains me."

"Oh, how glad I am to hear you say that word"—the janitress cavorted in her seat. "Now I *know* you don't think of moving."

The butter and egg man paid me a compliment on my improved appearance since going to the country. He especially noticed a sparkle in my e'en that he hadn't seen before.

With best love to my friends in Stratford and will you (please!) ask your aunt for her receipt for Chinese pears? Pears is awful cheap now.

Yours faithfully

Léonie

This is my seventh letter today! Whew!!!

In the following letter, Léonie wrote Catharine about her literary interests. She was enjoying *David Harum*, a popular 1898 novel about an upstate banker, and *Wishmakers' Town*, a volume of whimsical poems by a minor New Hampshire poet-playwright, William Young, that had been reissued in 1898 with an introduction by Thomas Bailey Aldrich. She was thinking out the plot of a problem story, and suggested Catharine might send one of her own stories to Florence, who was now working at *The Criterion*, a New York based monthly magazine of literature and the arts.

To Catherine Bunnell, April 25, [190?]

My dear Catherine,

"There's as much human natur in some folks as in others if not more" and a good deal of it in David Harum. Have you read it? If not you orter. I've steered clear of that book all this time only to fall in love with it the more precipitately at last, just as I did with Trilby. Not that "falling in love" is exactly the term to express my feelings either. But it just goes to the right spot, as a good salt pickle does sometimes. So I've read 275 pages of it without skipping and gotten considerable quiet chucklement thereoutof.

Came across a quaint little poem, or poem-series by William Young, called "Wishmakers Town" that has a primitive sort of charm that quite took my fancy. Something on the style of Schiller's "Die Glocken"—a medley of little snatches just long enough to make you wish for more—Here's some lines that stuck

> Myrtle and eglantine
> For the old love and the new.
> And the columbine with its cap and bells, for folly.
> And daffodils for the hopes of youth
> And the rue for melancholy.

Do you know Catherine, that you're about the one person of my acquaintance to whom I can quote or read poetry without having them look at me as if I'd gone clear daft. And I've come to the conclusion that the average person has nothing but pitying contempt for the whole race of rhymesters and rhyme mongers. I console myself with cynical reflections about the average depth of the human mind, and by pouring out a heartful of most profound pity for "the ear to no great harmony's inclined" etc. etc.

Well, to come down to prose and facts. Let's see—you asked for Mrs. Woodward's address. It is 122 East 27 St. I called on her when I was down there yesterday. Like her better as I know her better, and think she improves in manners, dress, and looks with surprising rapidity. She's really very bright and quick to catch on to things. She patronizes me—He! he! I didn't go to the Barnard tea the other day because of a rampant headache that roared out a warning howl at the last moment. I'm glad you patched up the rag of my character with the Grendel. I've been thinking out the plot of a problem story this afternoon. Gwine to write it down tomorrow if my energies don't evaporate overnight and then perhaps the lady will have some cause to open her eyes and gasp.

That is to say, supposing the story gits written and gits accepted and gits printed and gits read.

How is Alice and when does her school end? Do you think it would amuse her or that she would have time to make me a little visit this summer. It would delight me. Give her my love, please.

Now why did I start on a new page contrary to all precedent. Suppose I must keep my tongue wagging till the end of the other side anyway. I got a new hat. That is, I took an old black straw hat, somewhat dingy, and with a watercolor brush and bottle of ink improved it into a suitable crowning achievement for a lady of literary and artistic tastes. A whole big bunch of cabbage roses stuck on—not automobile, alas! And I'm dying of envy of you. I'm *sure* your bonnet would be more becoming to me and consequently feel as if I'd been done out of something that properly belonged to me.

I'm very glad your hospital is convalescing. I think you must have too high living at your house. Can't you put them on the raw food system? It's still flourishing here and saves cooking & dishes. It is to laugh. Good-bye old girl, I mean me darlint.

Your f.f.st f.f.

Léonie

N.B. Did I tell you Florence is with the "Criterion." Wants you to send them a story through her (for the glory of the connection). How about the Vegetable one?

The teaching job provided steady work, but the salary was not high, and with the expenses of living in Manhattan, and her mother's medical expenses, Léonie was on the lookout for other opportunities, scanning newspaper want ads.

The ads under "Instruction, Colleges, Schools, &c" in the *New York Herald*, on Friday, February 1, contained the following:

Advertisement in the *New York Herald*.

The advertisement appeared to be from some sort of student. She responded, giving her address. No doubt she expected to receive a reply by mail, but the applicant had come to her apartment in person, and finding no one, left the following note.

From Yone Noguchi, February 4, 1901

80 Riverside Drive, New York city

Miss Leonie Gilmour:

Dear Madam:

Permit me! I am a young Japanese who advertised in the Herald and received your letter, I called on your place but not finding even a person.

I don't need any English teacher—yes, I do!—I want one who can correct my English composition. Can you take such a task? I suppose that you are able, with good English and literary ability.

About three pages a week.

How much you charge?

Pray, answer me!

Yours

Yone Noguchi

P.S. Tell me when you can see me, then we will talk about—that's better, I suppose.

New York Herald building at Herald Square. *Library of Congress.*

Gilmour must have been surprised to discover the student was a published author, a Japanese poet two years younger than herself who had published two books in California three years earlier, and was on friendly terms with a number of well-known writers. He had arrived in New York the previous July, having stopped for some weeks in Chicago, where he had written his impressions of the city for the *Evening Post*. But his efforts to establish himself in New York were going slowly. His "California fame as a poet of two or three years back seemed quite nicely forgotten" and he seemed fated "to play a sad young poet whose fate was to die in a garret." He would not have needed to apologize for his poor housekeeping (as he does in Matsui's film), for, like many Japanese immigrants, he had worked extensively as a household servant in California, and was still doing so in New York. "I found a little job in a certain family to wash dishes in the morning and tend the furnace of a winter evening," he later wrote; "here I used all my hours for reading the books which I drew freely from the library near by." The house was a beautiful four-story residence on Riverside Drive, but he was too embarrassed to explain his position to his literary friends. He told Léonie he was revising some poems for publication and wanted her help.

Yone Noguchi in 1901.
Collection of Edward Marx.

Noguchi had earlier rejected the idea of hiring someone to do type-writing on the ground that his poem was "too divine to go to their desk." His enthusiastic new Chicago friend, Frank Putnam offered to help, but seemed to lack the requisite poetical talent. That Putnam was a person of strong opinions and, at the same time, Noguchi's dear friend, made it all the more difficult for the accommodating Japanese poet to reject his suggested changes.

"And I have already got published two volumes of poetry." *Essen Communications, Ltd.*

Two weeks later, Gilmour had performed her first editing and type-writing task for her new client, who was pleased and apologetic.

From Yone Noguchi, February 21, 1901

80 Riverside Drive

Miss Gilmour:

How thankful I am for your task done for me. I feel almost sorry to pay such a little money, but you know, I wish you will believe, that I am a poor student who can not have much money. If my writing were something marketable, you could have some share of its profit—Alas, I am sorry that it is not so!

I console myself saying that my writing is above money. I don't know sure of it!!

I think that "Apollo" ought to be rewritten, because so many an eminent writer at past wrote on it, and fear that some one may take a trouble to compare with mine. I will add some more thought and beauty if possible. And the piece "Glimpse" ought to go to a basket.

I here enclose two more poems which I wish you will put in type.

I wish you will consider well of "The Apparition". It was corrected—O so much was changed by my friend, I am so sorry!—And now I like to have in the original form which I think great deal better.

And another piece which you have read yesterday.

And also.

I wish you will copy O Hana San poem. Am I not asking to you too much? I afraid I do.

Believe me, will you? O what?

And one more thing.

I think that I will come to see you on *next Monday night*. Say, about 8 o'clock. Doesn't it suit you?

Yours,

Yone Noguchi

Noguchi had earlier asked Frank Putnam to correct his poems, but Putnam's poetic enthusiasm exceeded his talent, and Putnam had violated standards of editorial decency by failing to clear his extensive changes with Noguchi before printing "Apparition" in the January *National*. Where Noguchi had written "I raised my eyes and saw / The breezes passing on dewy feet," Putnam added an ill-considered poetical flourish: "I raised my eyes and saw / Naught but the breezes passing on dewy feet."

From Yone Noguchi, [February / March 1901]

Miss Gilmour:

Dear Madam—

Here is the poem I took home, I changed many a place. When I have read over and over, I found so many same words repeated and some line is entirely commonplace. I wish it will be all right.

The man—I mean my friend in Chicago—changed so such, and made it utterly poor, I suppose. That poem appears to me a new poem, I know so much difference from what I wrote in the original piece.

I think now that it has been improved.

Good-bye

Yours

Yone Noguchi

P.S. I think that I will come to you on next Wednesday—about two o'clock. Is that suit you? If not, write to me.

Fortunately, Miss Gilmour proved more tactful. Noguchi sent along more poems.

From Yone Noguchi, March 4, 1901

My dear Gilmour:

I will be glad to see you on next Thursday afternoon (two o'clock!) I wish that all the poems in your hand be all ready. Is it too hard on you?

With my best regard,

Yours

Yone Noguchi

P.S. Also I wish that you will pay much attention on "O Haru"—I mean of its revisions. It has many lines of my own ideal style.

By March, Noguchi had rehabilitated his Japanese girl's diary project, begun with the help of his California friend Blanche Partington, but neglected since the previous spring.

From Yone Noguchi, [April / May 1901]

Léonie:

Here are next three chapters. Say, listen, can't you fix them according to your own idea? I think that you would better make those horribly long paragraph more shorter. *Say, cut them to very short stick.* I think that's better. Of course you cannot do so, some place.

Anyhow I wish you will arrange them to your idea.

And this is broken English, but it got to be literature, you know, therefore I wish that you will take out some unnecessary words, and *condense them nicely.* Try it, please.

I am in mood of writing, but somehow my mind is scattered, so cannot write really clever thing. So I ask you such a task to complete.

This is not poor stuff, but it got to be more careful, but I can't do it.

Please, try best you can. I think that you can fix it remarkably, since I gave you my specimen of broken English.

I wouldn't say anything for what you shall do with it.

This broken English is not refined so well, so you *might change as much as please.*

O please, do it!

After I finish this business, I must do some other work.

Are you busy? Don't you take my interest in this girlish stuff?

Change it entirely. Somewhere it is so poor, I thing [*sic*], make it perfect.

by-bye

Yone

In the summer of 1901, Noguchi left his room on Riverside Drive, and moved to 41 East 19th Street, which he later described to Stoddard as "a Jap boarding [house], full of prank and noise." As the weather warmed up, so apparently did Noguchi's relationship with his new assistant, as the change in address from "Miss Gilmour" to "Leonie," which occurred sometime in May, indicates.

Meanwhile, Noguchi had neglected his correspondence with Stoddard for many months. When he picked it up again, he pointedly avoided any mention of Léonie. "Only books were my comrades. Dark night, friendless daytime," he lamented. But he was happy to tell Stoddard about his new writings: "They are an American diary of certain Japanese girl. Think how charming they must be!" The manuscript had been accepted by *Leslie's Monthly*, and that very day he was going to meet a Japanese artist, Genjiro Yeto, whom the editor had arranged to do the illustrations.

In the following letter, Noguchi told Léonie about a story he was thinking about. His story was apparently for Léonie's edification rather than the collection of short stories he was working on. It was a sort of reverse of Clive Holland's cross-cultural romance novel, *My Japanese Wife: A Japanese Idyl* (1895), which depicted a rather idealized marriage between an Englishman and a Japanese woman. Noguchi's story, which, he told Léonie, should be entitled "My American Wife," would not be so pleasant. His description was curiously prophetic.

From Yone Noguchi, [1901]

41 E 19th St.

Dear Leonie:

I thank you for your suggestion. Your idea seems better than I told you perhaps, but you see that the chief part isn't in the story. The portrayal of Japanese country life will give the book somewhat original appearance.

You know how I hate the plot in a story. Whenever I see any bungling invention in it I am disgusted. See "A Kentucky Cardinal" which have no story whatever!

Anyhow I must improve my idea before I will begin with my composition, of course.

Now here I present you my new variation. How you like?

A young Jap married a young American girl at Yokohama. By the way the story should be entitled "My American Wife". (Don't accuse me with plagiarism—you have heard "My Japanese Wife", haven't you?) He carried her to his country home where his parents were King and Queen. He had to obey to them. They couldn't understand even one word of English with which his beautiful wife could speak. The wife could'nt bring herself to intimacy to her parents-in-law. See! Now she is getting to suffer. She was very unhappy. She dreamed her old love story with an American young chap. She came to understand finally that "Crow should be in comradeship with a crow".

Of course she enjoyed now and then in Japanese country easiness and beautiful scenery, but they couldn't take her blues off.

And so on. I think that this story is so true, to nature. I know so many cases like this.

And finally she couldn't stand even a moment in her Japanese house, and she will run away with a certain missionary. And our Japanese husband will marry again with a girl who was choosen by her husband.

Simply this story tells that Love is not the greatest factor in Japanese life. And that any woman cannot live without any society and intercourse with her own people and all that.

I cannot tell you clearly now, because my hand shakes as your own. And moreover I have no peace of my mind.

This is true and capital story I think.

Yone

Oh, well, plenty time—I'll think more.

Léonie's hand might well have shaken if she could have foreseen her future in Noguchi's lines.

From Yone Noguchi, Wednesday, September 10, 1901

99 W. 8th St., Bayonne

Dear Leonie:

Please don't! Let us laugh! I will come up to see you on Saturday evening. Is the story ready? Change English as much as it ought to be: Will you make it perfect? Please don't feel bad with me! I know of course you don't!

Yours

Yone

From Yone Noguchi, October 2, 1901

Dear Leonie:

I thought I will write you this morning that I will not need money from you. But I did not, as my friend called on me. And I received your letter this evening, with $5. I am so sorry I forced on you with such a matter. I got some money from somewhere else. Maybe I need money some time later, but really I need not at present. So I return it with a thousand thanks. Pray, you finish that article tomorrow, will you? I have something to write up. Today I saw Leslie's Editor who said he had forgotten to pay me for the article I wrote. So some money will come from his also. Then I will pay you for your work you have done for me. Perhaps he, Leslie's Editor, will publish, no, commision me to write up that Thibet expedition I told you. He wished me to see him on next Monday. Something will turn up to be sure.

Yone

P.S. Of course you will send your story to the Red Book, if you wish. Maybe he will accept, maybe not. There's no harm to try. I kept it somewhere in my MS-book. I will get it for you, if you want.

From Yone Noguchi, October 22, 1901

99 W. 8th St., Bayonne, N.J.

Dear Leonie:

Sleepy, sleepy! I slept thirteen hours last night, but that was not enough. I am just sleeping nowadays. Yes, truly, just sleeping! My head actually turned to a wool, unfit to think and write anything in the world. I want change!

For last week I was scamping in the books of English society. I came to conclusion that I will go to London next year (perhaps May or June) and write about "M.G. [Miss Morning Glory] in England."

I don't hear any thing yet from Stokes, but he will take the Diary all right.

I expect to see him within a week, however.

How sleepy I am truly! The paper before me is dancing. I don't know how to write.

I must wake up.

I think I will go to Boston for change, and see some of my friends there.

My old friend at Washington wrote me inviting me to come up. But

I don't like such a sentimental old fool—Yes, Stoddard is an old fool! I like to go to Washington, however, the place is nice and quiet, a genteel town. I think I will go there, if he promise me to act less fantastically. Truly I will go there next month if he would promise me that. He has such a great library—thousand and thousand books.

How sleepy I am!

I am dead in fact—my brain and body all.

Say, I heard again from my home about my mama. She is really serious.

My brothers (three in all) returned to my native country from Tokio to see my mama. One of them wrote me from her sick bed. But he said that the danger had passed.

So long!

Yone

I will see you in a few days. Will you be in Fifth Ave.?

Noguchi had evidently come to think more critically about Stoddard. As he became closer to Léonie, he perhaps sensed her disapproval of his homoerotic relationship with the older writer. Of course, he said nothing to Stoddard, having written two weeks earlier: "Dear Charlie, I like to see you so much! I am lonely."

Yone's increased intimacy with Léonie led to quarrels, such as the one which took place around October 1901, ignited by Noguchi's criticism of one of Léonie's stories, which portrayed a woman's remarriage, to which he had both literary and (somewhat surprisingly) moral objections.

From Yone Noguchi, [November 1901?]

Dear Leonie:

Awfully, awfully, awfully sorry: Did I give you such a pain?

Please say no!

I didn't mean * * well, never mind, I can't take back what I said other night.

Now you will see that a brown Jap cannot be equipped with the very quality to be a gentleman. Here in this country "gentleman" is one who knows how to praise (no matter be truth or —), isn't it?

American gentleman is so charming, full of adjectives fit for your ladyship, but I am not so gallant. *I am only a Jap*, you know, ignorant and "narrow minded". What more you said!

I am really "D—D", I suppose.

You don't be mad with me, will you?

The first thing with me is that I am no critic. I understand all the explanations you gave: truly, truly! But, I wish to say that the natural story (true to nature) isn't very readable story. Your story is so true doubtlessly, but as long as it does not give any strong impression, the story has not much of value, I declaire. I don't say it especially for your story, but in general. Such a story that you wrote is a commonplace occurrence not only in France but anywhere.

Pray, pardon me, I am growing again to "D—D"!

I will not speak again with this subject. Simply I will promise you that I will try my best art to please you next time. Believe me, will you?

Yes, you do!

I am so grateful for your indulging in "Flattering me for long eight months". Truly I am, how I can be otherwise! "What kind sympathetic friend you are" as you said to me! Honestly you are a competent critic, since you have such a patience and art to flatter enduringly.

Now, I understand how kind of woman you are! I am blind of another's beauty and cleverness, except in myself, that is quite true. I admit that I am spoken often so.

You are my friend, are you not? Then you cannot be mad with me, can you?

I was truly severe to you, but I don't mean to undervalue your little story which was written in better English, with certain delicious touch. Just I say what I thought—that is all. You know I am such a damful fellow who never speaks well of another. I know that is wrong. Moreover as long as I keep such heart, I know, I can not be American gentleman, but I can't help it.

Once more of your story.

You defend of the woman who shall marry again—all right. You have a very good sympathetic opinion. But I have another. I firmly believe that any woman or man can't allowed to be so indulging in matrimony. I don't think that people can change husband or wife as if with the socks or underwear. Many weak people often do it, but I despise them. Why? Because if once unsuccessful, the disappoint can't be healed so quickly, except a feeble-minded ignoramus. Matrimony, it seem to me, is an honorable battlefield where if you were successful it would be a great honor. *I don't believe in a small skirmish business,* no body makes a fame or gains any pride in such a little fight. So whenever you enter in matrimony you must prepare yourself that you will return with an honor, or otherwise you will be killed in disappointment which is an honorable defeat, you know. I hate the people who change so often their partner.

I will never put such a character in my story.

You say "Divine womanliness", truly, perhaps. If thus, *woman is turning to a regular "nurse,"* isn't it?

Oh, let these nonsense be dead! *I sincerly fear that you shall praise my story no more in future.* I understand that woman is very revengeful.

Let me shake hands with you, be friend. Can I not? Pray, forgive my wickedness!

Good-bye

I will be a good boy.

Yone Noguchi

Friday

P.S. The report said that my dear Mama is awfully sick. And I fear I shall not see her again.

I am sick also.

In January 1902, Catharine Bunnell took up Léonie's invitation to re-join her in New York. This time Catharine was determined to work to support herself while she tried her luck as a writer, her plan being to write what she referred to portentously as the Great American Novel. Making the ménage even livelier, Catharine's former "wife," Doll Gray, was in the city and happy to serve as Catharine's general factotum. Doll, whose real name was Elizabeth Delano Gray, had graduated with a degree in Chemistry and Biology in 1898, but had yet to find a steady job (she later became a math and science teacher and scientific illustrator).

Catharine Bunnell to Frank Bunnell, January 31, 1902

Dear Kid;—

Thanks for your letter and all the good advice therein contained. The last fits, to come home when I can, I mean to take about the Sunday or possibly the one after that. As for the typewriter part, the best stunt at present in the low state of my finances seems to be to use Léonie's. I am paying her $1.50 a month for its use which helps her out in paying for it by installments and gives me a machine as many hours in the day as I can use one. It's a Wanamaker-Wellington, an easy running affair though I don't like all its arrangements, the shifts for instance. But it has the Universal keyboard which is a good thing to learn. Bessie Gray is dictating to me three or four hours a day and by next week at the latest I hope to get up a respectable speed on it.

So far only a little over thirty pages of the "Great American" are done, but I have written and sent off two short stories to the "black Cat" and "Munsey's." The first is the one upon which we are building our hopes.

It's a woolly tale called "The Opal" and ending "The opal had exploded into a thousand fragments.!" We plan to dado the room in red, buy a guitar and mandolin, and pay unlimited visits to the opera when the returns from it arrive. Meanwhile we quote the fateful sentence, which seems to have had a disastrous effect upon us, for nearly everything we touch explodes. I attempted to saw through a board a few nights ago and upset the gas stove in the process. As we didn't set it up quite right and Dollikins and I were the first ones to use it afterwards and never perceived the trouble, Léonie maintained that it was a wonder the whole flat hadn't done the thousand fragments act. Her own record of breakages yesterday evening, however, was a good one, a clock and a flatiron. O, we're a muscular crowd.

You would love to see our appetites. Mine is at top pitch and regular as clockwork. We live on wholewheat bread, meat, vegetables, cereals, and fruit, with very occasional relishes besides, tea for dinner and cocoa or imitation coffee for breakfast and supper. Isn't that a proper meal for you? Dollikins was sent away from home because she couldn't eat, but we all declare that she could digest a dynamite bomb.

So far however we've seen none such. The anarchists must be wearing their red shirts, since we've seen none waving. Mr. Gilmour takes supper with us on condition of supplying us with milk, and brings us various presents of bread, catsup, etc. He is as full of odd theories as ever, but I've never, since one evening two years ago, heard him mention his plan for reforming society. Next week Doll and I intend to get Mr. Curtis, who is the most harmless of failures, to take us to some of the radical meetings in the city. Also we plan trips to Cooper Union and other haunts of the populace.

Doll is with us for some two months or so and equal to a box of monkeys. We were cheerful enough before she came but now are positively hilarious. We two go trotting around the city; she's never been in it before,—and get beautifully mixed up downtown and have to appeal to squads of friendly policemen to set us right. They regard us with a fatherly air and we remember directions as long as we can and go blundering on serenely.

She makes an ideal private secretary. I never aspired to such a luxury before, and begin to feel like a very successful literary personage. Besides dictating, she offers suggestions for plots, criticises liberally, and proofreads the typewritten manuscript. She is looking for a job, now if only I could afford to offer her a permanent one!

"Mummer" was down Tuesday, but I fear she didn't like our looks over well. Perhaps she feared that I like them too well. There is some truth in that way of looking at it. I sut'nly am thoroughly happy in this place. And yet its no great shucks. The locality is far from fashionable, our furniture is of the simplest and scantiest, and so far we've done all our own work except for having the bed—and table—linen mangled. I wish you could look in on us sometime.

Olive's calendar papers the imitation fireplace, being exactly cut up to fit. I am pining for the book she sent you to make a border above the mop-board. Also we are looking for a set of monk's heads and pipes, to give us a consistently Bohemian atmosphere. But our ship isn't in yet, nor the "Cat" (the Black one) back.

A specimen of your typewriting is always much appreciated. Don't let the length of this scare you and don't cuss because you've got to answer; you haven't.

You would admire to hear Doll dictate to me. A "new paragraph" is "lu," short for "Hallelujah," and since exclamation points have to be made by a queer combination of keys, she expresses them at the "Damn, close quote, dash."

Au reservoir.

Affectionately,

Catharine

Doll says "If I had only sent him my love!"

Wanamaker-Wellington typewriter. *McBride's Magazine,* **1899.**

Towards the end of February, 1902, Yone left New York City for Rochester, where he stayed with an unidentified friend. He was near exhaustion, made worse by an unpleasant meeting with Frederick Stokes, who wanted to postpone publication of the *Diary* for the Christmas market. Noguchi was eagerly awaiting the promised April publication, and thought it "really foolish to wait so long, without any definite idea how many copies should go when it were published in Christmas season." After the meeting he had written again to Stokes, who seemed to acquiesce. But Stokes' lack of enthusiasm was depressing, and Noguchi tried to prepare himself and Léonie for the worst. Though he still thought that "the book will go all the same when it made a fine starting," he also conceded in a postscript that he really didn't see "any bright prospect" for it. "I am not disappointed if it made a failure," he told Léonie. But on account of his exhaustion he had missed their planned Saturday meeting. He owed her money too, as he acknowledged. "Believe me that I am not forgetting about you!," he assured her. But Rochester was a charming town: "every house is covered by two-foot-deep snow."

From Yone Noguchi [February 1902?]

145 Troup St., Rochester

Dear Leonie:

I am sorry to inform that *I am not American citizen.*

Sometime I will, I think. I made up mind concerning about this matter.

"I am called Heathen," somebody said "but as good as any Christian." My reply is that for such a case.

––– o –––

Today I made such a charity.

I saved out one young Jap from the Rochester jail, and sent him to New York giving some coin. I feel very happy, indeed so, and afterward I found out that he was one of my benefactors who gave me some bread and piece of meat when I was tramping round California a few years ago. I did not know him at all, but he told me whole thing.

I could repay, thank God! for his kindness.

He is a young chap, short and keen-eyed, poor fellow! He suffered enough, I think. I wished him godspeed.

Yone

P.S. Getting hot, isn't it?

A few days later, a letter from Stokes assured him that the proofs should begin arriving in about two weeks, so Noguchi settled down to being a "happily lazy fellow."

As spring began to arrive at the end of March, Noguchi wrote to Léonie in better spirits. "What a glorious weather we have here in Rochester! It is a regular Spring day—Oh, so glad! It does make me feel elegant, and more than that, I feel as if I have something great in my future." He was a little concerned about the *Diary*, fearing that Stokes "doesn't make justice to my book," and suggesting that Léonie "might drop in and ask about the proofs," which had still not arrived. "Well, never mind, we will wait till he will send them."

With Yone gone, Léonie had more time for Catharine. The two had set up housekeeping in a cheap apartment on West 15th Street, near Seventh Avenue.

Catharine Bunnell to her mother, March 21, 1902

161 W. 15th St.

My dear Mother;—

I've just come home and found your letter. Hope you haven't been worrying seriously about us. It never occurred to us there was any danger. And not being on the lookout for adventures at that time of night we of course didn't find any.

And I have gotten slept up and am feeling much less tired than on either of the two preceding Fridays and quite in the mood to accompany Mr. Gilmour and Bess to the Radical Club. Next, I haven't so far kept any account because I haven't had any extravagances to curb, and while Bess is here expenses aren't on their normal basis. So I didn't see the use. But I shall start one the first of April. Expenses will be approximately like this, —one week's salary for rent, one for food, one for laundry and scrub woman—gas will come somewhere out of these three amounts and the last quarter for clothes and incidentals. With me gone all day, the longest part of the housework falls on Léonie, so I am to put in forty cents worth of mangling every week,—that will take care of all sheets, towels, and table-linen for the two of us,—and fifty or sixty cents for a woman to scrub the floors. Then I mean to have practically all my laundry done rough dry (at $.30 a dozen) ironing myself the few things that really need ironing, and perhaps tucking a few little things into Léonie's wash for her to do for me.

I think I can live on that schedule; it certainly can be done for less, for Florence Gilmour told me last night that she and her mother had lived for a long time on ten a week and even less—it passes my comprehension though how they did it. They are better off now; I don't know how much Florence is earning, about $14.00 a week I imagine and she said they felt quite rich.

Thanks for the dollar, —but I should hope I could have afforded so much. Doll said she never enjoyed a play so much in her life; and it's been with me all the week and will be for many a day to come. So have the hours with you; I only wish you could come down oftener and that father could really see our shanty. Very many thanks for all my birthday fore and aft.

Supper's ready, so I must run.

Lovingly your

Catharine

On April 19 Noguchi complained to Léonie about her "many weeks of silence." He was planning to "leave here Rochester on 30th or 31st of this month. Then where to go? Perhaps England!!!" In fact, he left somewhat sooner, but his destination was Stoddard's Washington, not England. The attraction of Washington was almost certainly Ethel Armes, not Stoddard himself.

Yone had met Ethel in 1901, the same year he met Léonie. It was at Stoddard's Washington bungalow. Yone knew Stoddard through his California mentor, Joaquin Miller. Back in the 1870s, Stoddard and Miller were part of the group, along with Mark Twain, Bret Harte, Ina Coolbrith, and Ambrose Bierce, that put San Francisco on the literary map. On Miller's advice, Noguchi had written to Stoddard when he was trying to establish his literary credentials in 1897. Stoddard had welcomed Noguchi's overture with overwhelming, even passionate, enthusiasm, and the two men had corresponded warmly until Noguchi was finally able to travel to the East Coast in 1900. Noguchi's feelings toward Stoddard were mixed; at times he felt gratitude, admiration, affection, even love ("We slept in the same bed, Charley and I," Noguchi wrote cheerfully); at other times, he found Stoddard needy, childish, old, and tiresome. Fortunately, Stoddard had another "kid," as he called his young intimates: Kenneth O'Connor, a former street-waif he had more or less adopted. Ethel Armes had first appeared on Stoddard's doorstep as a precocious sixteen-year-old bearing a letter of introduction from a former Hawaiian consul and her visiting card, written in ink, with "The Washington Post" in tremendous letters. Her father, Major George Augustus Armes, was a notorious, scandal-plagued Civil War hero and Indian fighter who spent the greater part of his military career in the capitol, trying to exonerate himself for alleged military offenses he may or may not have committed, while making fortunes brokering real estate on the side. Ethel's mother,

Lucy, was the daughter of the late John Bozman Kerr, a Maryland congressman and sometime diplomat. The second of eight children, Ethel grew up mainly in Washington, D.C., attending private schools, learning to play piano, performing in amateur theatricals, and socializing with the families of Washington's elite. Her father's favorite, Ethel knew how to fight and charm in order to get her way. When she showed up at Stoddard's bungalow for her "first interview with a celebrated man," she was fascinated by Stoddard's quirky ways. His bungalow was filled with odd, exotic artifacts from his far-flung travels and books signed by famous authors. She succeeded in charming the old misogynist with her playful unconventionality and bright intellect.

After that 1893 meeting Ethel's life had been thrown into turmoil when her mother filed for divorce and her father sent her off to a boarding school in Virginia. Upon her graduation she spent a year at George Washington University and then set out to become a reporter, working briefly for the *Chicago Chronicle* and writing special features for other papers from 1899 to 1900 until the *Washington Post* hired her as a staff writer. When she heard from Stoddard about Noguchi, after the Japanese poet's first visit to Washington in 1900, she wrote up an article about this "Dream Child Noguchi." Determined to meet the reclusive Japanese poet, she came to the bungalow one night when Stoddard was out, announcing that she was a reporter for the *Washington Post*. Fearing the Japanese poet, said to be "inaccessible to interviewers," might refuse to see her, she quickly explained that she was also among those who called Stoddard "Dad"; thus, as Noguchi's effective sister, the situation hardly called for formality. When Noguchi came downstairs, he found a young woman playing softly on the piano. "Awfully glad to see you, Yone," she said. He later wrote that he fell in love with her at once. "The snow was covering the land when I saw her home," he wrote in his account of the meeting a few years later. "The indescribable joy I felt is something I cannot forget for the rest of my life."

When Noguchi returned to Stoddard's in the fall of 1901 hoping the "sentimental old fool" would "act less fantastically" he told Léonie it was because Washington was "nice and quiet, a genteel town" and Stoddard had "such a great library—thousand and thousand books," saying nothing of his feelings for Ethel. On that visit, Ethel wrote a long story about "Noguchi the Dreamer," unsigned, for the *Washington Post*, depicting the flirtatious camaraderie of Stoddard, Yone, and an unidentified female "third person" (undoubtedly Ethel) as they lounge around in the bungalow, smoking cigarettes, drinking Madeira wine, eating chocolates, and composing whimsical stories together. Their affection seemed to have deepened. Stoddard warned him that Ethel was merely flirting with him, and he was inclined to agree.

Léonie may have detected something amiss, for they quarreled during Noguchi's brief stopover in New York city. It was affection that made Léonie put up with Yone's annoying demands, affection strong enough to erupt in jealousy, which Léonie expressed through punitive coldness rather than emotional outbursts. After the quarrel he wrote her from Washington:

From Yone Noguchi, April 29, 1902

Oh Leonie:

Did you truly mean that?

O no, you didn't! I know that. Oh, why, goodness, you don't get mad? You know I can do nothing without your help, you know that, don't you? Oh, don't be so childish—Yes, I was wrong at first place—to get anyway so impatiently. I didn't mean that at all. Just, just!—that's all.

Oh, Leonie, come, be nize to me, will you?

Truly I am learning how to swear nowadays, and I am using very rough speech, you know.

I can't think of you otherwise but one of male companion. So I wrote such a letter—of course from my good heart, that God knows.

Oh, please, don't!

Go to typewrite my stuff, pray.

I will be nize as can be next time.

Don't you want to see your letter—I mean what you wrote. I can't be only blamed, I think.

Oh, don't be cruel, please.

Be friend! Leonie, see!

My next good story is almost done now. Truly I tell you that I haven't seen one happy day in Washington. Stoddard is almost ill since first day, you know.

He is speaking from morning till night, "Oh dear me; my Lord!"—such a sort of foolishness. And he went to Hospital two days ago.

And his boy has gone to Devil, drinking all the time, and he hasn't visited Stoddard yet in Hospital. Isn't awful?

So I got to take care of Stoddard, trying to be nice as I can, you know.

How miserably I am situated, you can imagine!

Pity me, not writing such a terrible letter.

Your letter made me upset. Makes me more dreadful!

Yone

At some point in the spring of 1902, Léonie and Catharine left 15th Street for an apartment in Washington Heights a few blocks from their previous one, this time on West 153rd Street, across the street from Trinity Church Cemetery. "Certainly it's a vast improvement on that old 'cold-water flat' on 15th St.," she informed her brother a few months later. Catharine, who had her first literary success placing a poem entitled "Cosmography" in the *Cosmopolitan*, earning her $7, had begun working on her second Great American Novel. Léonie's mother, who lived in a fifth-floor apartment on 19th Street, loaned Catharine her sewing machine and occasionally invited her to dinner. On a Wednesday morning on August Mr. and Mrs. Gilmour came up together with a cousin named Frank, and stayed for lunch. Catharine "had a long talk with Mr. Gilmour, who is always interesting, while the others explored the cemetery." "Sunday morning Léonie started out for a paper and discovered two leaning against our door. Evidently Mr. Gilmour was in the neighborhood and she started out investigating, and found him two blocks up the river, industriously filling a flour sack with earth to carry to Florence. They came home together, and he read the paper, had a nap and lunch here, and altogether made us quite a visit, and praised Léonie's bread, as he should have done. The last batch was simply perfect, made of a mixture of whole wheat and rye flour with rolled oats to flavor it." Catharine's mother had suggested bringing Léonie to Stratford for a visit, but Catharine informed her on August 18 that "Léonie's coming is doubtful. Yone still sends daily manuscripts and bid fair to keep up the good work until school opens. But I may be able to steal her for a couple of days."

Catharine's mother, Catharine M. Bunnell, c. 1898. *Sterling Library, Yale University.*

In September, Léonie did get to Stratford for a brief visit. "Léonie came up with me Thursday night for about a week; talks of going [back] Wednesday but I hope not," Catharine reported to her brother. "We have had rather a quiet time seeing folks who have called, driving, going to Seaside Park with Father Sunday, taking dinner in New Haven today, and coming back by way of Woodmont, where we had a swim if you could call it one, when we weren't off bottom a single minute, I mean not out of shallow water. The water is still fine in the Sound, though it begins to be cold in streaks." Léonie returned to New York alone, leaving Catharine to work on her novel for a few weeks.

To Catherine Bunnell, September 14, 1902

Dearest Catherine

Only the fact of my being rather cerulean in hue of late has prevented my writing. You know one can't be a cheerful cherub *all* the time. I feel like a widder. Made an effort to console myself yesterday by buying stuff for new shirtwaists. Today, bein' as I had a bad cold (the most delicious cough sounding like the bark of a very fierce little dog) I took a stroll through the rain and mud of Broadway and Fifth Avenue, came back with my stockings sopping to the knees, took them off and went bare footie around the house for a couple of hours and topped off by taking a cold bath and doffing a heavy shirt for a thin chemise. Cold is almost gone. Scared off I guess.

I am interested in your selection of reading matter, but say, aren't you afraid of an attack of indigestion?

How goes the G.A.N (This doesn't stand for "gander"—guess again—though they do say every goose has one.)

I have decided not to decide about whether to give you any candid opinion or candid flattery until I see it. After you make a success of yours I suppose I ought to try to follow suit—I likes to live up to my friends—but no! you might suspect me of jealous rivalry—I repress myself. To you be the glory of being the only 'riter of the fambly.

Your note reached its destination in the pocket of a poet—outside pocket, sorry to say—not the heart one. Yone grows in grace though not in height. He is five feet 3 1/2 inches. He sends his best regards.

Tell Alice New York is the best place in the world for throat trouble.

Lovingly
Léonie

Catharine responded with a request to borrow Léonie's typewriter.

Léonie was quite willing to send it. The cold that had been scared off the previous week returned with a vengeance, and Léonie treated it with the remedies of the day: hop tea and catnip tea, mild sedatives thought to be good for the blood and for fever, cascarets (a medicinal candy with a purgative derived from tree bark), red pepper liniment (a home remedy believed to cure fever by inducing sweating), and hot baths.

To Catherine Bunnell, September 19, 1902

Rose la belle,

Your commission was executed. It cost 34 cents. I sent the receipt on to your brother. Hope the typewriter will arrive all right, as the man kept insisting, with a threatening look, that I sent it "at my own risk." Is he thinking of smashing it?

No great news. It is raining. I used all my own shoes and borrowed all yours yesterday (including the red slippers) and changed my stockings six times. Then I resorted to the following:

1 hop tea
1 catnip tea
1 cascaret
1 hot bath
1 rub down with red pepper linament.

2000 applications of handkerchiefs to the tip of me rosy nose. Tore up me nightgown for handkerchiefs. Shall I make the portieres over into nightgowns?

Met another old man yesterday, after tramping miles through Harlem rain in answer to an ad of his. He buttonholed me, and talked and talked. So delighted to find an intelligent listener, you know. His conversation was on many and various topics, including one Sop Hockles, also a book of his about "How to Abolish Poverty." He insisted on my staying to lunch, and as it was one o'clock and I was very tired and wet, it seemed easier to yield than to tear myself away. So we lunched in a large kitchen,—himself, myself, a little girl and a deaf lady. He is a genial old cuss,—but no money in it, so I came away (after inviting him to call, of course). Seems to me this world is chiefly made up of old men.

Glad you [are] having a good time. I'm baking today, for the first time since I came back. Been living on baker's trash, ugh. I really need your manly appetite to help me out in this housekeeping business.

Thank Miss Sterling very much for her recipe. I made a few jars, but concluded there was too much work in it for the result.

I'm due over in Jersey on Monday.

I didn't hear from the Century Co. at all. Funny, isn't it? I wrote a note to them today to know the reason why. I think somebody must have been taken with a severe fit of absentmindedness.

Postman is whistling. Wonder if he'll post this. Ta, ta!

Your loving

Brigitta

Friday

By the end of September, Catharine was back in New York. She was more determined than ever to support herself in the city while continuing her writing. "I want something that will give me a living (fifteen dollars a week in course of time) and not take quite all my hours or much of what little originality I may have," she told her mother on October 2. She had even sent a letter to her rich uncle, John Sterling, who, in a brief spasm of familial curiosity, had written asking for her "theory about living away from home." Catharine complied, hopeful he might write her some letters of introduction, but there was no response. "Funny Uncle doesn't write. 'Spose my letter clean disgusted him?" she wondered to her mother. "I told him frankly that I wanted a home of my own, and to see what I was worth in the world, and to gain a wide experience to make me sometime to write matter worth reading." After three weeks, Catharine wrote her uncle again to ask if he had forgotten, and this time received an immediate reply. "The contents of your note of Sept. 29 had not, as you have inferred, slipped my mind," Sterling wrote. "The letter I have kept in my drawer, unanswered, the only one of the kind that is there, simply because I did not know exactly what to reply. I had no idea that you had really left Stratford, and founded a home of your own. There are two sides to almost every proposition, and one of the sides to yours, I fear you have not looked at as carefully as it would have been wise to do. As I do not wish to appear even to cast any reflection upon the judgment of your father and mother, I forebear to say more upon the subject." It was not clear which side of which proposition Catharine had neglected to consider, but the guess that Uncle was probably "considering her as a backslider and a reprobate," as she speculated in a letter to her brother, was probably not far off the mark. Catharine was unruffled, however. Although Uncle "evidently didn't approve," she wrote her mother, he had "very pleasantly forebore to do more than hint as much." Anyway, Catharine's father (as her uncle had insinuated) was perfectly willing to indulge her plan. "I do not exactly see the real need of it myself," he had written her on October 5, "except that it is a temporary way (it is to be hoped) and an easy and comparatively inexpensive way of coming in contact with more or less people and seeing some of the busy part of the world away from Stratford."

The Washington Heights apartment was certainly inexpensive. "If finances improve of course we may change our location," Catharine told her brother Frank. "But I don't know of any other way in which we could secure anything like as much comfort as we do here for four dollars a week. That covers rent, grub, gas, and some laundry work." Even so, she had to ask a five dollar loan from her mother to make ends meet at the end of October. "Coming up on the L after leaving you I proceeded to reckon up my worldly goods, and found that, after paying my half of a two-months gas bill and laying aside four dollars to put with this week's five for rent, I had $1.39 to live on. Since then Mr. Gilmour brought us a present of crabapples which necessitated buying sugar for jelly, I've telephoned Mary Montgomery, and three trips downtown are looming up before me between now and Sunday night. So that I find myself with forty-two cents to spend for vittles. Worse yet, Léonie missed a day at school and so will absolutely need a loan of fifty-four cents between Monday morning when our landlord calls and Monday night when she brings home her New Jersey money."

In November, Léonie's mother was in the hospital for an eye operation. "Florence Gilmour was up here Monday evening and reported that Mrs. Gilmour's operation was a more complicated one than the doctors had expected," Catharine wrote her mother on the 5th. "They probably will not certainly know the outcome for some time. Meanwhile the hospital people speak encouragingly. Léonie begged off Tuesday morning and called on her mother, reporting that she was in a ward with twenty-five other patients, her eyes, like theirs, poulticed high up till the people looked like bullfrogs." On the 21st, Catharine reported that she had been to see Mrs. Gilmour. "She is getting along famously, and very happy to be home and have the operation over, although there is always the fear of future trouble."

Albiana's convalescence offered Catharine an intimate glimpse into the Gilmours' marital difficulties. "The housekeeping arrangements are not due to her but to Mr. Gilmour who, I think, would quarrel with anybody of whom he saw much. He is 'shtiff wid theouries' and expects everyone to agree with him; Mrs. Gilmour smiles at his notions contemptuously and the fat's in the fire immediately. Then, aside from that fact, he has much the finer nature of the two and she jars on him. Neither has anything to say against the other; they meet amicably, but they simply can't stand each other's constant society. Which being the case, I think they are wise in separating rather than perpetually quarreling."

When Yone did return to New York, it was only for a few weeks. With Yone preparing for his imminent departure to England, Léonie, busy looking after her convalescing mother, failed to notice Yone's frequent visits to Queens to visit his love interest, Ethel Armes. The two were even discussing the possibility of marriage, and were on the verge of telling Stoddard. But when Yone departed in early November, Ethel gave him a playful brush-off. "Ah! sir—you don't suit me. Already you have a successor," she warned. "Who is mine?" she wondered; "The Lady of the Truth?" Perhaps she was thinking of Léonie. "Do you know the sun has quite set on our 'love affair'?," she ended. "You aren't my style, Mr. Noguchi (to run away and leave me!) Oh! but that was a silly thing for you to do! I have to laugh at you now."

Noguchi sent Léonie a postcard on November 24, four days after his arrival in London. Léonie wrote back, sending a letter of introduction to a certain Miss Foster, who Léonie thought might be able to help him find accommodations more suitable than the overpriced Queen's Hotel on Leicester Square. But Noguchi found a West End rooming house on his own, from which he wrote Léonie a longer letter around December 9. "I thank you for your kindness in sending me a note of introduction," he wrote. "I had settled, however, in a little inexpensive room which address I reported in my postal card, a week ago. But I think that I will hunt Miss Forster up as I might want her help some day. London is such a vast city. It takes a day or two to find out where that street is. Isn't it dreadful? It is true!" He was finding London more expensive than expected, and hard to penetrate. "It would be better to give up my hope to bring Miss Morning Glory here in London," he conceded. "She cannot do much actually, you know." He was waiting for an answer from John Lane, the publisher to whom he had submitted his poems. He ended with a plea: "write me some encouraging letter, will you?"

Léonie had trouble complying, for the news from Stokes about the *Diary* sales was discouraging, and prospects for the sequel appeared dim. He was "turning to a pessimist," he told Léonie on January 2nd; if he didn't leave in February, he might starve. But Noguchi's fortunes began to change after he tracked down a Japanese artist friend, Yoshio Markino, whom he had known in California. With Markino's help, he published a hundred and eight copies of a sixteen-page pamphlet of poems, *From the Eastern Sea*, mailing them out to famous writers and critics. The response was immediate and quite favorable. He sent Léonie a copy of the pamphlet on February 2, along with an early review from the *Outlook*. "What do you think about them?" he inquired. "I am sailing pretty well, I fancy, but my pocket—Oh, my pocket! But I assure you that I am far from starvation. It is interesting—what?"

When he wrote again two weeks later he was in much better spirits. Léonie seems to have temporarily relocated to Pine Street (presumably the Pine Street in Jersey City). "I sent my last letter to Pine Street. If you left there, you would write to French-man." She had had a curious adventure of some sort with a Japanese man.

From Yone Noguchi, February 19, 1903

Dear Leonie:

I was delighted—yes, hugely—with your last letter. Who was that damn Jap, I wonder? What a comedy! What a tragedy also! Really I was sorry for you—Oh, no, not for you, I mean for that "My countryman". You truly made me mad calling him "Your countryman". Well, there's no question we have lots of such a funny fellow. Awfully funny fellow, I should say. I will tell you that you must handle such a matter more cleverly than you did this time. You are possible to draw much fun out of it, you know.

Yes, Leonie, London winter has passed, I thank God. No fog, now, really! Fine sunlight is smiling all over the place. I expect some nightingale, then I will try to beat our "Keats" poem. Of course I do not know how serious London is with my poetry, but I think that I can do much better in England with poem than in America— "Your country" (attention!) People—there are only few I fancy—trully care to read poetry, perhaps they do not want to buy, then. My first experiment was successful, I should say. Who could expect much from such a sixteen-page pamphlet? I sold out about fifty copies, you know. That is to say I made twenty five dollars. And that is more—yes, great deal more—than I spent on my pamphlet. I have only three copies left now. I don't think that I will send those three copies to America—Brentano's—and sell them. I thank you for your courtesy (I learned such an expression from Englishman).

Well, what I must go to tell you? To begin with "Letters". You will do what you think right to do with them. I think that they will not do at all. If the magazine doesn't want to take them in, please! keep them in your drawer. Or you may burn them up and keep yourself warm by the fire they will make. I am sure that that is good reward for my two-month'[s] hard labour. I thank God for it, trully. I am trying best I can with the "Diary" and "Letters" in London. Pearson-people were delighted with the "Diary", but they didn't want to publish if they couldn't be certain that the English Diary—supposing I am going to write—were as much clever as the American one. I sent them out some other publisher—Methuen's. Perhaps they will take, because they sent me an encouraging letter already. However, you don't know how things will turn up, till you exchange contract paper, in London. I am almost certain that *my poems have more chance to do better.* My new book will be out within two weeks. It is a tremendously quick work for Englishmen.

Yesterday I went to the British Museum to see Miss Foster. I promised her to be there at 10 at morning, but I was there at 11. Naturally I missed her to my regret. She returned to London only a few weeks ago from somewhere in country. She wrote me that her relative was ill.

I have met with Laurence Housman—the author of "An English Woman's Love-letters", and talked with him upon many a things. He was most agreeable man in London. I have met also with some other fellows whose names were not known to you. Mr. Sydney Colvin was so kind, he used to be intimate with Mr. Stoddard. He said he liked to do something for me when it was necessary. Really I do not know where Mr. Shaw lives. If I can find him out, I am sure I have chance to mention of your name. Just yet, Leonie! I am not so famous that many a people will call on me.

I will send you my new book at the very moment when it is out. I used "From the Eastern Sea." My friend Jap artist made a cover-design which is good. I am living with him you know. So, Sayonara.

Yone

From Yone Noguchi, February 24, 1903

151 Brixton Road, S.W.

Dear Leonie:

Yes, my new book will be out in fortnight at the latest. The proofs were corrected, and the cover was done. Hurrah, book—*London book!*

Oh, no, I shall not destroy your most interesting letter ever I received. I will keep it as long as I live. As to the "Letters"? I wish you will try with some other magazine once more. And if no one didn't want them? And then you will try them for publication as book. Book-publishers I mean. Doubleday Page for instance. Or the publisher of Indianapolis who published "When Knighthood was in Flower"—what name is he? Bowen Merrill? Something—such a name. Perhaps I may have chance to publish them in London, maybe not. Cannot tell yet.

I made many a nice young, lovely, kind friend among literary *genius* (attention!)—W.B. Yeats or Lawrence Binyon, Moore and Bridges. They are so good; they invite me almost every day. They are jolly companions.

Their hair are not long, I tell you.

Good luck and strong health

Yone

English publisher can do anything quick when they want to. That is very rare case. I was fortunate now.

My best wishes to Miss C.

Miss C (Catharine, of course) had recently begun working with Léonie's sister Florence at the Century Company, proofreading new editions of the popular *Century* and *Standard* dictionaries, "salary fifteen a week, hours nine till five with a liberal hour at noon, and all sorts of little advantages," as she informed her mother on January 31. "I read the dictionary and work a paste-pot and a typewriter; it's said there are other stunts to follow." She rarely mentioned Léonie in her letters now, though she was spending a good deal of time with Florence and Mrs. Gilmour. At work, she told her mother on May 22, "Florence and I growl to each other. The Century women-folks laugh at us for being so much together and always having so much to say to each other. It's rather odd that we should have grown to be such chums for she is not a girl who makes intimate friends. She seems to me in many ways like Emily Bronte; in reading Charlotte Bronte's life, the Bronte sisters reminded me strongly of the Gilmours. It was less an individual than a family resemblance, but the younger sisters certainly have much in common."

On March 5, Noguchi reported to Léonie, "my fund for adventure is almost exhausted, so ho, ho, ho, for Ameriky: But it is very uncertain with everything of me. However, some relief may come from somewhere, and then I will stay some months more." He had come a long way from his first impressions of London; now he acknowledged that "here very nice people are living, intelligent and entertaining." "Perhaps again in Autumn," he speculated, "I shall come to London with plenty money—enough to support one year and I will try to establish myself here."

From Yone Noguchi, 12 March 1903

Dear Leonie:

I am coming back to America, and I will take a Boston steamer on 24th of this month. I think I shall stop five or six days in Boston to see my friends there. Then ho, ho, for New York. My book. The book will be out on next Monday. Fine book, you bet! About forty pieces of my Great Poems. My publishers are awfully enthusiastic and I of course. I think it is not necessary to mail it to you, because I am sure I can see you at the beginning of next month.

So, good-bye,

Yone

"This is my famous friend, Charles Stoddard." *Essen Communications, Ltd.*

Noguchi spent a week in Boston with Frank Putnam and his family before returning to New York, where his success was duly celebrated by his literary friends, especially Charles Warren Stoddard, who had been fired from his lectureship at the Catholic University and had come to New York City to consider his options. Stoddard could not long endure the faster pace of New York life, but while he remained in the city, he gave Yone access to his larger literary and social network. Noguchi knew many of these friends already—Bliss Carman, Edwin Markham, Richard Le Gallienne, among others—but Stoddard's flamboyant presence changed the chemistry of the group that greeted the return of the conquering poet. The ever-childlike Stoddard was appropriately staying with Frances Hodgson Burnett, the noted author of *Little Lord Fauntleroy* (1886) and other children's books. Stoddard had friends in the theater world as well. An actor friend, Edmund Russell, was playing *Hamlet*, and offered Stoddard a box of seats for the April 28th performance. "Russell gave us a box for his Hamlet and our party will consist with Mr. Stoddard and Bliss Carman and Percy McKay, who wrote a poetical play for Southern," Noguchi explained in an April 24 letter. "I am afraid that you should feel very uncomfortable if you will join with us. But Leonie, you care to come, I will tell Mr. Stoddard about you. Answer it to me, will you? I wish Russell would give us the free tickets instead of the box. And it is possible to get a ticket for the second matinee, I think." Léonie did not join the party. Yone had told Stoddard little, if anything, about her, and she knew more than she cared to know about "Dad" and his queer ways.

Nevertheless, she was evidently interested to have a look at "Dad," so she and Catharine devised a plan to invite Stoddard and Yone to dinner. It was "one of those little suppers which I and my friend Catherine Bunnell, sometimes gave in our tiny apartment on Washington Heights," Léonie recalled years later. "One of us always played the role of cook, the other was hostess, turn and turn about. That day I was cook, and when, flustered and hot from wrestling in the kitchen (Catherine played that role better than I) I came at last to sit down at the table, Mr. Stoddard seemed to waft away all those kitchen fidgets while he kept us entertained with his suave wit, and vastly amused by the naive self-consciousness with which he enjoyed our appreciation, his fat rosy head hung on one side like a foolish baby's." Léonie did not make much of an impression on Stoddard at the time, for three years later he couldn't remember whether they had met. Léonie supposed he thought her merely "'the cook' of a very simple home-made sort of supper he once took with some of Yone's friends in horrid New York."

Stoddard was, in fact, on the verge of a nervous breakdown. He was eager to join Noguchi and Bliss Carman for dinner, "but we must arrange fully as to the time and place and as to how I am to get there. You know I am lost in this strange city; I am as one grasping in the darkness, and I cannot find my way alone very well." After renting a flat, with the plan to settle down and write, he had become "unnerved by the 'appalling noise, rush, and vulgarity' of Manhattan, and he was afraid to stay in his apartment by himself." In June, he finally collapsed into "nervous prostration," and was taken away by Dr. William Woodworth, keeper of the Museum of Comparative Zoology at Harvard, to his home in Cambridge.

Noguchi had taken an apartment at 315 East 26th Street, close to the East River and Bellevue Hospital. The lively New York spring turned into another depressingly hot summer as American publishers showed little interest in his London success. He therefore hit upon an unusual plan.

From Yone Noguchi, July 5, [1903]

315 East 26th, city

Dear Leonie:

Finally I opened a booth—a Japanese bazar—on Madison Square Roof Garden, and is meeting some favour. I sell things between $5 and 10 every night. It is all right. Many people come to see me and buy things. I have been very busy for last week, so I could'nt write to you. Say, Leonie, do you remember that you did not give me a copy of the "Violet" (a poem of some misty night)? Will you hunt it up, and send it to me? I have some more things to be fined, but my mind is up-set, somehow—but not from my *Business*. I received a very good letter informing me that my book "From the Eastern Sea" is going to be published in Japan. I had a copy to be returned to you, but I am sorry to tell you that I was compelled to send it to my publisher in Japan. I am sure I will have some copies from London pretty soon as I wrote him. Then! S—! Believe me, will you? I am in fog about my publication in this country. D—! What I care! The people in this country don't care much about poetry, anyhow. Well, I will sell China-ware or fan instead of writing poetry.

Won't you come to the Roof Garden? with Miss C. of course. I may send you some tickets for you.

Yone

The Evening World said I was the son of some Marquis Noguchi, mentioning about my booth. What a jolly people! I am glad to become Marquis Jr. once in my life even in a paper.

How are you? All right?

Roof gardens were all the rage in New York, and the one at Madison Square had been transformed for the summer into a Japanese garden. The main attraction of the event, entitled "Japan by Night," was a pseudo-Japanese play entitled *Otoyo*, a "diverting and quaint entertainment" about a Japanese-American intermarriage. Visitors enjoyed the Japanese architecture and paper lanterns while "Japanese waiters, clad in their native costumes, flitted about the Garden, serving tea." The *New York World* reported that Noguchi, "the son of the Marquis Noguchi, a high military official" (Noguchi's father was actually a shopkeeper) and "the author of several books written in English, notably, 'The American Diary of a Japanese Girl'" would be "presiding at a little booth where fans, incense sticks, umbrellas and various other knicknacks will be sold." The slip about Noguchi being the author of the *American Diary* elicited a rebuke from his editor at *Leslie's Monthly*, Ellery Sedgwick: "how often have I told you that you should be under my care to avoid such dangers from reporters and things."

"Yone is busy running a stand in connection with the Japanese roof garden at Madison Square, and says he is doing a hustling business," Catharine reported to her mother on July 10. "We are going down to see him tonight with Florence, taking Kiritchjian for escort." Catharine had brought down her bathing suit from Stratford, and "Léonie luxuriated in it yesterday at the foot of the street."

It was during the summer of 1903 that the relationship between Yone and Léonie reached a point of no return. Ethel Armes had not reappeared, and during the long, hot summer which Yone had spent mostly in New York, Léonie had moved into position as Yone's significant other. Photographs of Noguchi during this period show a handsome and well-dressed youth with chiseled features, a sharply drawn, slightly feminine mouth, a focused intensity replacing the slightly lost expression of earlier years. Léonie, though she would retain her schoolgirlish appearance for another decade, had celebrated her thirtieth birthday in June. Logical and practical, she was not his feminine ideal, but those very qualities made her extremely useful to him. When he left New York at the end of August, some troubling question had been left unresolved.

The second Madison Square Garden.
Library of Congress.

Yone went to Boston, where he spent a few weeks with the Putnam family, making occasional visits to Stoddard, now recovering in Cambridge, and another writer friend, the poet Josephine Peabody. "What is the matter Yone?" Stoddard inquired on September 15. "Why are you so down hearted and so mixed with every body?" He must have intuited that the problem was erotic in nature, for he advised, "I also am down hearted and sometimes very discouraged. Then I say to myself that I shall go into a convent and stay there for the rest of my life forgetting the world."

From Yone Noguchi, September 17, 1903

So kind of you! Really you are. Are you deadly tired of me? Are you really? I should say that it would be the time when I must make a graceful exit. (Oh, if possible!) I am something like a jelly fish which has no head and tail. I don't know what going to do. Just I am contemplating—about what? God knows.

I have read about the terrible weather of New York in your city. Didn't your high building of William street tumble down? If it did, it might have been quite a fun. If you lost your leg, it would sound more romantic—more than an elope with a Hindoo Prince.

(Anyhow, what's the matter with you?)

You are quite blue, aren't you? Come, now, it's awfully foolish to be blue. I don't feel well yet—having a specimen of fever and the terrible cold. I said lots of complaining words in the letter—as it became my habit—but you will find me rather a jolly fellow nowadays—except when I think about my going to Japan. I think it would be quite probable. I am going to see the editor of the Transcript today, (Now, it is only morning yet,) and will talk about the matter.

Mr. Stoddard came back from Nantucket and now is in Cambridge. I am going to see him, and later on I will drop in Miss Peabody's house. Did you ever read her poems, I wonder? Such a sweetness and grace in them! She is quite a poet, and pretty too.

Oh, well, after all, I have nothing to tell you particularly. So wishing you happiness,

Yone

P.S. My best wishes to C . . . please.

Noguchi returned to New York at the end of September. On the 31st, Léonie invited him to the Washington Heights apartment for dinner. "Yone Noguchi was up for dinner last night, and we had quite a party of three," Catharine reported to her brother the following day. "He was full of yarns about Mary MacLane and other Boston celebrities, and we have a date to dine with him and his friend, 'the cook,' before long,—a real genuine Jap cook on a U.S. tugboat." Léonie's father also continued to make frequent visits, bringing quantities of fruit, and Catharine was often to be found in the company of Florence or Albiana, or both. When Catharine found herself without a dress-up suit after receiving an invitation, she brought Florence along as she searched the downtown shops. "Monday night," Catharine reported on October 4, "Florence invited me home with her. 'How much of a home have you got?' said I, for Mrs.

Gilmour and she are just breaking up, Mrs. Gilmour to go up into the country, Florence into rooms on 14th St." The move was Florence's idea: "she wanted to be alone to practice her music, and do as she pleased. She is in a nice house full of artists, men and women, and she will do nothing crazy, and she still supports Mrs. Gilmour, though Léonie now is to help. But I think Florence will yet be sorry. She hasn't Léonie's and my domestic instincts and will probably have a forlorn time with the restaurants." The Monday night dinner was supposed to be Catharine's farewell to Albiana. Catharine agreed to accompany the two to a downtown restaurant, the Maggie Lou, "on condition of its being 'Dutch.'" "I said my tearful farewells at the 'L', promising to write to 'the old lady', and then on top of that she turned up at lunch next day. But she really left Tuesday afternoon, going to some cousins in Massachusetts."

Meanwhile, Catharine's friendship with her housemate Léonie was showing signs of strain. "Léonie says I look like a fat lummox tonight, which may account for the lack of brains in this," Catharine reported. "She had a cold this morning and therefore elected to dine on cabbage, which left the half-pint of cream for my disposal."

Léonie was no doubt spending more time with Yone. In November, on a sheet of paper torn out of his notebook, Yone wrote out the following declaration. There was no ceremony, no announcement; none of Noguchi's friends had the slightest awareness of the progress of events, which took place in conditions of absolute secrecy. If Catharine knew what had happened, she said nothing to her family.

From Yone Noguchi, November 18, 1903

18th November, 1903

I declare that, Leonie Gilmour is my Lawful wife.

Léonie later said Noguchi told her that this "constituted sufficient marriage ceremony," and that afterwards, "for four months, beginning in the autumn and ending in Feb[ruary] or March[, 1904]—they saw each other daily or lived as man and wife, though having separate homes." Outwardly, they conducted their lives exactly as before.

When Léonie arrived in Japan four years later, Noguchi told a reporter he had written Léonie a marriage promise one summer night before going off to Washington, and had begun living with her when he returned in November. The confession seems candid, but Noguchi's memory of dates and events was never very exact. That Noguchi remembered a "summer night" promise, though the written declaration was actually dated November 18, might suggest an earlier verbal promise made before his departure. Noguchi was also mistaken about the destination of the trip, which was to Boston, not Washington.

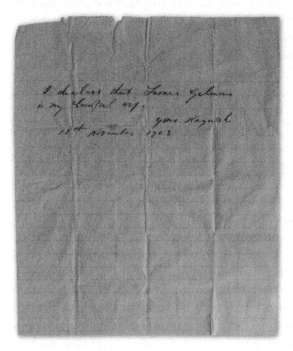

The marriage
declaration.
*Isamu Noguchi
Foundation.*

   Masayo Duus, in her effort to make sense of the declaration, quotes a poem written in the 1920s in which Noguchi writes of giving in to passion and making promises to a young American woman on a winter night walk in Central Park. Hisako Matsui's film transfers Duus's scene to Noguchi's apartment with much the same effect. But the union seems more likely the result of a gradual erosion of resistance on both parts.
   Did the document constitute a legal marriage? In a word, no. For most of the previous century, it might have sufficed. New York state had pioneered the "common-law marriage" in 1809, when the state supreme court, in Fenton vs. Reed, declared that marriage required no formal solemnization, and that a consummated verbal marriage contract by consenting partners was perfectly valid. Léonie's parents were likely among the multitude that had availed themselves of this expedient. Besides evidence of some form of marriage contract, the tests of a common law marriages (besides the eligibility of the partners) were simply cohabitation and reputation, which meant that the partners lived together and were generally reputed to be married. Léonie would have had some dif-

ficulty satisfying both tests, since she told Elizabeth Converse that she and Noguchi had maintained separate homes during the period they were together, and it was hardly the case that they were "reputed" to be married. Nevertheless, with the signed declaration, an evidently half-Japanese baby, and a witness or two, Léonie might have been able to persuade a judge that she was legally married, if common law marriages had still been accepted in New York.

The trouble was that New York's law had changed. In 1901, amid growing concern over abuses of the common law system, the state legislature overwhelmingly passed the Weekes Bill, abolishing new common law marriages in the state beginning in 1902. Couples could still marry "without benefit of clergy," but were required to file a signed and witnessed marriage contract at a local government office. The prohibition proved unpopular and a new law, reinstating common law marriages, went into effect on January 1, 1908. But the reinstatement had no bearing on the six-year period when common law marriage had no legal basis in New York. Noguchi's November 1903 declaration was therefore invalid, regardless of the couple's intentions.

According to what Léonie told Elizabeth Converse in 1905 it was Yone who "drew up" the document, telling Léonie it "constituted sufficient marriage ceremony," an account that presents Léonie as more helpless and naïve than she probably was. Her essay on George Meredith offers some clues to her thinking: "it is to be remembered," she says, following Meredith, "that conventions protect the weak, and that women are at present the weaker half of humanity," and particularly, at the hour of birth, "let it be remembered, woman and child are both utterly dependent upon the caprice of man; and the Mighty Convention of Marriage." "Mighty Convention of Marriage" was Léonie's own phrase.

It is conceivable that Noguchi had heard of common law marriage practice from friends, although Léonie must have had a far better grasp of New York marriage laws, and would certainly have known of the practice. Even if they were aware of the legal problem, they may have supposed, like many couples, that their experimental marriage could be later solemnized, or else dissolved if unsuccessful.

Following the marriage declaration, Noguchi seems to have postponed his plans to return to Japan. In a December 1903 letter to Putnam, Noguchi wrote, "'I shall not go back to Japan some years yet.' This is what I have to announce to you, because I told you about it so often times. There are many a thing in connection to this matter, but it is not necessary to tell you as you have no interest in it doubtlessly." This was Noguchi's way of conveying to Frank the probable consequences of his secret marriage, without actually confessing to it. "There is one thing which is sure—" Noguchi added. "There will be no war in Manchuria. Japan—also Russia are afraid to fight. They think the matter from Business point of view, you know. I think they were quite right."

"Léonie backed out of our theatre party last night," Catharine wrote her mother on January 8, 1904, "so we had a quiet dinner at the Maggie Lou; then as Florence's and my spirits were irrepressible, we two shook 'the old lady,' did a little house hunting." Florence was already regretting her new rental: "she has no heat in her new room but a gas radiator, the gas is frozen, and her landladies won't even lend her the loan of an oil stove while she dresses in the morning. Hence her frantic search for other quarters." Catharine was amused by the evident distance between the Gilmour sisters. "It was funny to hear the two girls praise up the advantages of a flat if only there was someone to share it with. The logical scheme would be for the two to go in together but neither will hear of it." A few weeks earlier, Catharine had given notice to the Century Company that she would soon be returning to Stratford. Her supervisor was sorry to see her go, offering to keep her place open if she wished to return, which she declined, and even suggesting she might continue to work at home. In preparation for her return home, she had been shopping, again with Florence along. A new shirt-waist, a silk petticoat, and some underwear were the result. "I don't want to come home in rags," she explained.

By the end of January Catharine was back in Stratford, having brought to an end her two-year experiment in New York living. But she had done well in her proofreading job and with the help of Léonie and her family, learned to live on her own in the city. Though Catharine enjoyed having a job, and the independence it brought, the work itself was hardly exciting. Her three efforts at writing the Great American Novel had found no takers, nor even her short stories: all she had to show for the countless hours at the typewriter was a short poem in the *Cosmopolitan* and a letter to the editor of the *New York Times* (debating the question of whether a working woman could survive on four dollars a week). She was ready to return to a more stable and privileged family life in Stratford. And Léonie, now with the Washington Heights apartment to herself, was eager to discover whether she and the Japanese poet Yone Noguchi had a future together.

The Russo-Japanese War, which began on February 4 with Japan's attack on the Russian fleet at Port Arthur, changed Noguchi's life dramatically. There was an immediate, positive effect on his literary career; suddenly, every editor was clamoring for articles on every possible subject related to Japan. Noguchi, in the right place at the right time, was in great demand, and began churning out articles by the dozens. He now needed the editorial assistance of Léonie more than ever, but the added strain came at a time when the troubled relationship was nearing its breaking point. The marriage experiment had not proved an immediate success. Noguchi's reawakened plan to return to Japan in order to cover the real war stories was probably not welcomed by Léonie. Yone's disbelief of her intuition that she was pregnant must also have contributed to the strain. "I must have tried his patience by dissolving in tears every time he spoke to me for the last few weeks of our acquaintance," she later told Frank Putnam.

Why did the marriage fail? A 1907 Japanese newspaper account ostensibly based on statements made by Noguchi points to the return of Ethel Armes as a key factor. "But at this time I developed a relationship with another woman who played music, and [G]ilmour and I had a discussion about separating and split up, and going off to the newly-available mistress, I concealed what had happened with [G]ilmour." The sentence in Japanese seems to suggest that the new relationship caused the breakup, although the grammar is sufficiently vague that it might be read as merely saying that the new relationship developed at the same time as the breakup. Moreover, the article itself is not entirely reliable. Noguchi's surviving letters give no clear indication of Ethel's reappearance before the Léonie breakup. The first indication that Ethel has reappeared is a reference in a May 18, 1904 letter to Stoddard. "Did you hear anything about Ethel? I think our connection has been cut off. I did not write her for some long weeks. She was such a dear girl to me, but something made me stop—." Noguchi's complaint on May 18 that he had not heard from Ethel "for some long weeks" gives no clear indication as to when Noguchi began seeing her again. But by the beginning of June, Noguchi was fully immersed in his Ethel romance. "Oh, Dad, Ethel wrote me again—such a pretty letter—" he explained to Stoddard, "and God, I wrote her, I love her, Dad. I cannot help it. She bewiches [*sic*] me so. She may not be worthy. I am not also. (Let us see!)" Stoddard did his best to contain the damage. Ethel, he warned Noguchi, "must toy with you, and tease you, just for the fun of it. She is a very good girl and a very clever one, but I fear she would make a husband very uncomfortable and could not help doing so." Noguchi was not to be persuaded. He was in love with Ethel; she was his new poetic inspiration. "She has more charm than Annabel Lee," he wrote in his Japanese *Homecoming Diary* (*Kicho no ki*). "Her little face, white fingers, abundant hair . . . Nothing about her does not move my heart." He even published a lyrical expression of his sentiments, "To E.A.," in a Japanese journal, *Shin-shosetsu*, in March 1904:

"One touch with thy skin revives memory mine / Of a thousand tales of kiss and life."

Whether or not the reappearance of Ethel was a factor in the break-up, there can be little doubt that Noguchi thought very differently about the two relationships. Léonie had never inspired him to write the sort of romantic nonsense that Ethel did, and this was clearly not a point in Léonie's favor. Ethel offered Noguchi an idealized experience of passionate love he could not find in his relationship with Léonie.

In December, 1902, Ethel had left New York, where she had been staying with her journalist brother Oscar in Flushing, and moved to Birmingham, Alabama to join her mother and younger siblings. Stoddard, who now knew of Yone's interest in marrying Ethel, urged him to forget the idea. "She is not one to think seriously of: she will bring you only unrest and unhappiness," he pleaded. "Write to her, by all means and tell her of your success. But go no farther—if you love me you will heed me! I know what I am saying!" "Love her not, my dearest Yone," he reiterated two weeks later; "she is a flirt and not worthy of the serious passion of a true heart." Yone probably doubted the motivations of Stoddard, who in the same letter begged him: "Now come, place your lips to mine in one long rapturous kiss." But spring came, and then the long hot New York summer, and then fall, and still there had been no contact from Ethel. In the fall, Yone and Léonie had decided to live together as man and wife.

As Yone and Léonie struggled with their secret marriage, Ethel, who had joined her mother and younger siblings a thousand miles south in Birmingham, began writing to him again. Though she had found work writing for the *Birmingham Age-Herald*, she was now evidently inclined to look more favorably on the amorous Japanese poet who promised to take her away to an exotic land. The Russo-Japanese War had begun, and Yone was suddenly in great demand everywhere; he had begun making plans to return to Japan to take advantage of the literary demand. In what must have been an inspired series of letters, he had proposed to Ethel and she had accepted. "Yes, I know she will make me rather uncomfortable perhaps," he wrote Stoddard on July 18. "But Dad, I love her so—don't you know that? I cannot help it. So as you know marriage is nothing but gambling game or horse-race. I will take risk, and bet—if I win—it would be so much better. Oh, Dad, really, truly, I determined to marry her. She confesses also that she loves me more than any other fellow. I think what she says is true. How can I doubt it?"

Love, in the Western sense of the term, was something of a novelty in Japan. Japanese intellectuals spent a good deal of energy debating the meaning of the concept, and even coined new Japanese words like "*renai*" ("passion-love") in an effort to name it. Japanese who traveled to the West, like Noguchi, were eager to investigate the much-talked-about experience firsthand. "Though it is not wise to be madly in love," Noguchi wrote in a November 1905 poetic discourse on the subject, "you gain more that way than when you love intelligently. What do you gain? A history filled with tears!"

Coverage of the Adachi marriage, *San Francisco Call,* **Sept. 9, 1900, p. 19.**

There had been a fair number of marriages between Japanese men and Western women. Attitudes varied regionally and were subject to fluctuations as a result of international politics. In general, racial prejudice, though a powerful force, could be outweighed by considerations of wealth, social class, religion and education. Thus, marriages of white women with Japanese nobles or high officials—like Viscount Shuzo Aoki, Yoshitane Sannomiya, head of the Imperial Household office, and ambassador Shiro Akabane—rarely excited criticism. The marriage of Inazo Nitobe, a Quaker from a samurai family with a doctorate from Johns Hopkins, to coreligionist Mary Elkinton, was also accepted after some initial resistance. The Nitobe alliance took place on the East Coast, how-ever. By the turn of the century most western states had laws on the books prohibiting marriages between whites and Mongolians, a cate-gory which was often believed to include Japanese. Kinnosuke Adachi, a successful journalist from a former samurai family who had done post-graduate work at Vanderbilt and converted to Methodism, was refused a license to marry Los Angeles society belle Thirza Epperson in both Los Angeles and San Diego, before finding a county clerk in San Bernardino willing to do the deed. When the Japanese man was of a lower social class, as was the unhappy case for Gunjiro Aoki, a domestic servant, and Gladys Emery, a clergyman's daughter, in 1909, things could get more than a little ugly.

Coverage of the Aoki marriage, *San Francisco Call,* **March 25, 1909.**

Noguchi, who had no claims to nobility or wealth, was wise to plan his wedding in Japan, and to do so when American attitudes toward

Japan were at their most friendly. He and Ethel might even have married in Alabama, for Alabama's anti-miscegenation law only addressed "marriage between any white person and a negro, or descendant of a negro." (It wouldn't have been wise to try, since Alabamans were not particularly concerned about laws, and lynched an African American almost every month, on one pretext or another). But even before Léonie reentered the picture, his marriage to Ethel had an air of impossibility. Noguchi seems to have sensed impending tragedy when he chose to call Ethel his "Annabel Lee" after the doomed lover of Edgar Allan Poe's poem. On the ship back to Japan in 1904, he wrote of his secret fear that, as in the poem, a cloud might come to chill his beautiful Annabel Lee, and her highborn kinsman take her away to a sepulcher in a kingdom by the sea.

Yone's dreams of Ethel almost certainly contributed to his breakup with Léonie. With the guns of the Japanese navy firing in the distance in February or March the final skirmishing between Yone and Léonie was taking place, according to Léonie's later account to Elizabeth Converse. Léonie had evidently conceived in February, and claimed she "felt it almost as soon as it happened." She told Noguchi, who merely laughed at her "intuition," probably attributing it to the emotional strain of the breakup. "How can you tell?" he asked her; "you have never had such an experience before?" She had no answer for him, and his lack of sympathy helped steel her determination to manage without his help. They had other differences, temperamental and cultural, and even if Noguchi did not actually accuse Léonie of lying, the split was not an amicable one. They seem to have had no further contact during the remainder of Noguchi's stay in New York, although they both continued to live there. Since they were not actually living together, the separation required little apparent effort. Noguchi evidently regarded their brief attempt at cohabitation as a harmless, failed experiment.

Ever the proud independent bohemian, Léonie stubbornly refused to inform Yone about her now certain pregnancy, which had entered its second trimester in May. Meanwhile, the Noguchi who didn't think "people can change husband or wife as if with the socks or underwear" was busy contemplating exactly that.

Stoddard was in a panic. "Now comes a letter from Ethel that fills me with alarm," he wrote Noguchi on July 28. "She tells me that you are to go to her on Tuesday and that you may be married at once. I pray you do nothing rashly! How I wish that you were here that we might talk it all over calmly. My heart is in my throat for thinking of you and worrying over this affair." Noguchi *had* actually written to confess his plan to Dad, but his letters had gone to the wrong address. Now he was a bit hurt by

Stoddard's attitude, and wrote back irritably: "Yes, I was going to leave here on 1st of August. But some people who owes money failed to pay me. And without the money from him it would be impossible for me to return." "And as Ethel wrote you," Noguchi continued flatly, "I decided to marry her. But not so soon, as she said. We once thought so, but it was our second thought that we shall wait awhile, and think it over." He then appealed to Stoddard to take a lighter view of the situation: "Dear Dad, you never took any interest in Ethel, and rather you have had a mean opinion about her. But, Dad, don't say anything displeasing about her! I love her so much—and that settles it, Dad. I will see how things will turn up. Perhaps she may not be perfect, and she is strangely wild. But she has a certain charm which I cannot get over. So I decided to marry her, and see our lot. When I will turn my head toward Japan, I will stop at Birmingham and see her and her family. It seems that her mother has no real objection to our marriage. Pray, say some kind word about Ethel, Dad." "Perhaps I will come up to see you in a few days, since I made two weeks postponement," he added.

Noguchi had also written many of his other friends announcing his departure, though only mentioning his marriage plans to a select few. One was his friend Zona Gale, spending the summer in her hometown of Portage, Wisconsin. "Well Yone—I wish I were there for a while to say many things," she wrote back on July 18. She mildly rebuked him for his secretiveness: "oh, I wish you had told me while you were unhappy, and we could have talked it over. Why didn't you? But now that it is all come right I wish you all the joy in the world."

Stoddard ignored Yone's please and continued his efforts to derail the marriage plan. Though "so disturbed at the turn in affairs" that he could "hardly write a word" on August 1, he nevertheless managed a lengthy letter, beginning by describing how a marriage of two friends he had once encouraged had turned into a "Hell on Earth." "I do not say that yours, if you marry, is likely to be anything of the sort," he wrote, but "I do think that it is a mistake for either of you to marry now and that you will both realize this by and by." He did, however, make some effort to avoid saying anything unkind about Ethel, and added, "no matter what you or she may do it will make no difference in the love I have always borne you and shall ever bear you even unto the very end." He longed to see Noguchi once more, "to hold you in my arms again and tell you how dearly I love you or how I shall miss you when you are gone far away." Noguchi was not pleased and brushed off the emotional appeal. "So you don't like me to marry Ethel," he replied on August 4. "Truly I cannot help it, Dad, since I love her that settles it."

Noguchi later published a journal of the trip as a chapter in his book *Kicho no ki* (Homecoming Chronicle). The journey begins at Penn Station, where unidentified friends see him off. He reflects on his ten years in America and England, concluding "there is not one thing I could be proud of, but I did keep on the straight and narrow doing nothing to be ashamed of in my heart." In Birmingham, Noguchi reunites with Ethel and meets her mother. They dine at the home of Ethel's journalist friend, Anna Walker, where old Mr. Walker tells his Civil War stories. Ethel is the daughter of the Civil War hero Major George Augustus Armes; Noguchi gives a brief, idealized account of this "rare and fearless man," entirely avoiding his long history of scandals and courts-martial that had prevented him from actually serving in the army for most of his career. The general's absence is not noted but Ethel's mother warmly welcomes Noguchi. Noguchi remains in Birmingham another three days, meeting Ethel's two younger brothers and dining at the Armes home. On their last day together, Noguchi and his intended enjoy a picnic lunch and dine at another hotel, then exchange parting gifts. Ethel gives Yone a buckle with a golden eagle, a silver spoon, and a pin shaped like a cloverleaf ("I will always follow you like this cloverleaf, a clinging clover," she says). "When you come to Japan," Yone replies in the same starry-eyed spirit, "I promise you cherry trees in the springtime and chrysanthemum gardens in the autumn, and we'll gaze at the moon in the sky and drink tea together." At 9:30, they part. "Sweetest Ethel!" he declares in his diary, "You may be sure I would not hesitate to sacrifice my life for you."

Before leaving San Francisco for Japan on August 30, 1904, Yone sent a letter to Léonie apprising her of his departure. Now six months pregnant, Léonie was left with few options. A week later, she bought a train ticket to join her mother in Los Angeles.

Los Angeles, 1904-1907

The primitive Pasadena campground to which Albiana welcomes Léonie in Matsui's film is the result of some confusion on the part of Masayo Duus, who wrote that Isamu Noguchi grew up "surrounded by the natural beauty of the Pasadena hills" in a "one-room shanty house Leonie had built for her mother." In fact, Léonie lived during her Los Angeles years in Boyle Heights, the eastern edge of the rapidly expanding metropolis, a neighborhood popular among new arrivals because of its low cost and easy access to the Stephenson Avenue (later Whittier Boulevard) streetcar line. Léonie's first California address was a cottage on First Street at the southwest corner of Evergreen cemetery. Albiana had left New York the previous October to visit cousins in Massachusetts; how she ended up in Boyle Heights remains a mystery. But the two liked the area well enough to buy a parcel of land a mile south at 1144 Marietta Street the following year. Léonie did work in Pasadena for a few months: in a stylish four-storey office building in the heart of Pasadena's bustling business district.

Eight and a half months pregnant, she wrote Catharine Bunnell the following letter soon after her arrival.

To Catherine Bunnell, October 30, 1904

2927 E. First Street, Los Angeles, Cal.

Dear Catherine,

That was a very nice letter you wrote October 5th—I shall keep it always. And I thank you for all your wishes for our happiness, especially for Yone, since that is what I am wishing also. It may be I shall not see him again. I have a fancy as if he were a bird that flew through my room and is vanished. And I console myself—try to—saying that I am more fortunate than other women who must see their lovers grow old, indifferent, perhaps commonplace, whereas mine will be ever young, and ever poet.

Your blanket of softest wool arrived in great good time—in fact I have almost three weeks yet to await the appearance of its claimant.

The time seems long. I have done a great deal of sewing and some reading. I am reading now "Old June Gardens" by Alice Morse Earle, which pleases me. It would delight you surely, since it is full of reminiscences of New England. If I were able to dig up this awfully stiff sticky dobe soil I would plant a few more things in my garden, but have to content myself with watering the things already growing there—mostly roses and green kitchen stuff. I fancy I would like some nasturtiums climbing over the wood shed at the back, and blue iris by the rickety fence to one side, and a bed of thyme close to the door near the drooping peach tree.

Our garden is a sunken affair, which leaves a view of hills, cottages and gardens set against the far away mountains like a picture hung on the wall before you—while to the right the green-veiled mazes of the cemetary look down upon you.

Oh yes, you may be god-mother if you like but of course he-she has to have a Japanese name.

With best love to you and all the girls.

Léonie.

Nurse, unidentified girl, and Albiana bathe the newborn. *Isamu Noguchi Foundation.*

The future sculptor Isamu Noguchi was scarcely a week old when he made his unscheduled first appearance in the news. A reporter from the Los Angeles *Herald* had learned of the birth and talked her way into the room at the Los Angeles County Hospital where Léonie was convalescing after the difficult birth. The baby had been born unconscious, but was in good spirits cradled in a nurse's arms when the photographer snapped the picture. Léonie explained her difficult situation to the reporter and begged her not to write the story: "as we have separated," she explained, "this would not be a very pleasant time to announce a marriage." The reporter was not persuaded. "I won't write about you, but just about the baby," she lied.

It must have seemed an irresistible scoop. The Japanese were the talk of the day. For most of the year, the "little brown men" had been waging war against the great Russian empire on Chinese soil. The fighting was now at its peak: the Japanese had been entrenched around Port Arthur for some weeks, suffering huge casualties as they continued to batter the Russian defenses (which would hold out until the beginning of January). Americans were largely on the side of Japan, the underdog, which seemed to have the moral high ground. A decade earlier, Russia, in a tripartite intervention with France and Germany, had forced Japan to give up her Manchurian gains from the Sino-Japanese War, then took advantage of the opportunity to move into Manchuria by means of a series of deceptive agreements: first negotiating a twenty-five year lease to complete the Trans-Siberian railway, then leasing the strategic Port Arthur, and finally declaring that the terms of the leases would be ignored and Russia would simply occupy the territories. Americans had other reasons to dislike the oppressive Russian empire, where an antiquated, bloated aristocracy ruled a vast population of miserable peasants with the help of Cossacks, violent mercenaries who maintained control by instilling perpetual fear, particularly harassing Jews and other ethnic minorities who emigrated to America in large numbers. Despite Americans' limited interest in faraway places, they could not help but be fascinated by the series of epic battles in which small well-organized Japanese battalions thrashed the numerically superior Russians, who suffered from disorganized leadership and lack of troop motivation.

A few West Coast politicians and labor organizations were beginning to make an issue of Japanese immigration to the United States, but it was still a minor one. Outside a few coastal cities, few Americans had ever seen a Japanese person. These "little brown men," the "Japs"—terms still thought to have an endearing quality, though they could easily slide into derision—were said to be different from the Chinese, targets of more than two decades of immigration and miscegenation laws, though the average American would have been hard pressed to explain how. The Japanese themselves were quite certain of their difference from the Chinese, and tried to argue that they should not be subject to laws targeting "Mongolians," like California's anti-miscegenation law. The competing race theories of the day—a muddle of pseudo-science and half-understood cultural stereotypes—gave no definite account of the ethnic origins of the Japanese, and indeed the question is still debated. According to various authorities of the period, the Japanese might be descended from Malays, Chinese, Koreans, Tartars, or Turanians—but Scythians, Phoenicians, Chaldeans, and Egyptians were also put forth as possible ancestors, and serious consideration was given to the conjecture that the Japanese were in fact descendants of the ten lost tribes of Israel. Wherever the Japanese came from, the war had made Americans temporarily sensitive to their vast ignorance on the subject of Japan, and newspapers and magazines were full of stories about the country and its people.

One of a handful of American urban centers with substantial populations of Japanese immigrants, Los Angeles County was home in 1904 to around 4,000 Japanese who made up about two percent of the local population. California, like most states on the West Coast and in the South, had laws banning interracial marriage, Section 60 of the Civil Code declaring interracial marriages "illegal and void," and Section 69 preventing the issuance of marriage licenses to interracial couples. In 1904, "Mongolians" were only included in the second section, a 1901 amendment adding "Mongolians" to Section 60 having been struck down as unconstitutional in 1902. Thus, California would still sanction Leonie's marriage to a "Mongolian" if lawfully performed out of state. Fortunately for Léonie, the reporter who covered her son's birth did not probe too deeply into the question of whether she was, in fact, lawfully married. This must have been some consolation, though a small one, when she opened the Sunday *Herald* on November 27 and found on page 8 the following article:

LOS ANGELES HERALD: SUNDAY MORNING,

Yone Noguchi's Babe
Pride of Hospital

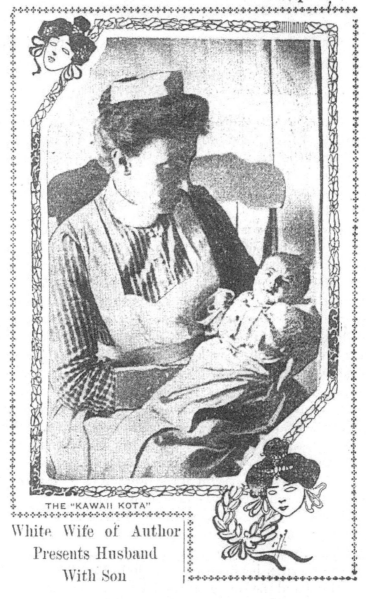

THE "KAWAII KOTA"

White Wife of Author
Presents Husband
With Son

Los Angeles Herald, **November 27, 1904, page 8.**

Yone Noguchi's Babe Pride of Hospital

White Wife of Author Presents Husband With Son

Los Angeles Herald, November 27, 1904.

"Kawaii Kota," meaning dear baby, are the words which Yone Noguchi, the author of "The American Diary of a Japanese Girl," begins his book, and out at the county hospital the story of another little life has begun, and the little son which has been born to the wife of the author and poet, is just such another baby as the one described by him in the first pages of his book.

That the wife of the man who has achieved so much success in the literary world should be lying sick in the hospital, surrounded only by strangers, seems strangely sad, but Noguchi, the father, is far away in Japan and knows nothing of the little son who bears his name, and the American mother in the day of her trial and triumph waits patiently for a time when things will be better for them. The little dark bundle at her side who she declares "Looks exactly like his father," smiles his happy little smile, all unconscious of the conditions under which he was ushered into the world eight days ago.

The young man gives promise of being in every way a fine specimen of the kind that is holding the attention of the whole civilized world. In spite of the fact that baby was born under the flag of Uncle Sam and that his mother is an American woman, of the blue eyed type, he has not a single trace of anything but Japanese and the hair and eyes are as black as his father's ever were. Out at the hospital he is quite the center of attraction and the nurses have endowed him with the name of "Bobbie" for lack of a better one. He is exhibited on all occasions and there is nothing that the son of the illustrious poet can not have for the asking.

The story of the love which brought Laeonie [*sic*] Gilmore [*sic*] and Yone Noguchi together begins five years ago in New York. Miss Gilmore was teaching and the young Japanese was writing and studying in the same place. They met and became friends. She helped him with his work, editing manuscript and reading copy and a year ago became his wife.

Noguchi's work carried him to different parts of the country. He was in San Francisco for some time and was very popular with some of the foremost authors and poets of the day. He has been connected in his literary work with such men as Jack London and Gelett Burgess, and is regarded by all of them as a man with a brilliant future.

He has already achieved a marked degree of success in this country and in London where he has published one of his books of poems. "The American Diary of a Japanese Girl" was one of the most popular of his works. "The Voice of the Valley" and "Seen and Unseen" also received much praise from the critics and the public.

Noguchi left for Japan in August to act as war correspondent for a New York syndicate. His wife came to Los Angeles the same time that he left for Japan, and has been there ever since.

In the meantime the son of an illustrious father lies in his cot in the hospital, and with his mother will wait for the day when peace shall again be restored and Noguchi will return to his adopted home.

The reporter was being unduly optimistic about Yone's return to the United States: it was not likely to happen anytime soon. Léonie remained in the hospital for two weeks, and then returned home, such as it was. She and her mother were now sharing a small cottage with two men, her mother keeping house in lieu of paying rent.

To Catharine Bunnell, January 1, 1905

My dear old Catharine—

Baby has tried on his shoon and he thinks they will fit nicely about the time he gets ready to wear shoes. At present he keeps his feet tucked away in his petticoats. They are very pretty (feet and shoes). Wish I had a decent picture to send. That newspaper picture is rank injustice. He's a sweet pretty boy. Don't know just who he looks like. At first he had a decided resemblance to his daddy, but it's wearing off. He has a funny little Irish-Japanese smile that would do your heart good to see. First he stretches his wee mouth as wide as he can, turns up one corner of it, then shuts one eye and gazes at you with the other. It would do credit to an Irish comedian. First time he did it I thought there was something wrong with one eye, but just as I was beginning to worry, —pop!—shut went the open eye and open went the other, while his lip curled a bit more.

Thank you for the Christmas things. May you live many Xmas's to present me with a nightgown each year—I beheld it with rapture, as I was living on one, as usual. Mama admires her kimono immensely. And I'm so glad the "smallest thing" is twins, so I can give one to my son. With love—from mama also,

Léonie

The Russo-Japanese War continued. In January of 1905, General Nogi took Port Arthur (Lushun), then the fighting moved north to Mukden (Shenyang), where Field Marshall Oyama and General Kuropatkin came together in late February for what was then the largest land battle in recorded history. As the battle commenced, Yone Noguchi sat at a desk in Tokyo writing a difficult letter to Léonie. He had received a telegram from Léonie informing him of the birth of his son and it had thrown all his plans into confusion. He was planning to get married in Japan in a little over a month. He begged Léonie's forgiveness, but wondered if she would consent to it. What would she have him do? What should he do? He wished to God he could love her, but he could not. He knew she was too kind and he was deplorable, but what could they do?

Noguchi in Tokyo, late 1904. *Kicho no ki.*

Léonie replied as he hoped, that she did not wish to stand in his way. For the baby's sake, however, she wanted Noguchi to acknowledge their marriage and his paternity; she could then legally obtain a divorce, and he would be free to marry whomever he liked. She supposed Yone meant to marry a Japanese girl; he had once predicted such an outcome, quoting an old Japanese saying, "Crow should be in comradeship with a crow."

But in fact it was not a Japanese girl Yone intended to marry; it was an American woman named Ethel Armes. Ethel was home with her mother and younger siblings in Montgomery, Alabama, packing her trousseau for the long journey to Yokohama—she was scheduled to sail on March 18—when she received an awkward letter from Yone apprising her of the new and unexpected complication.

Yone told Ethel of the child's birth in Los Angeles and about the newspaper story, but he said he and Léonie were not really married and had lived together for only a week; the newspaper story was a lie. Ethel was at first uncertain whether to take him at his word, and with a journalist's instinctive need to get to the bottom of things, she wrote a Los Angeles friend, Elizabeth Converse, apprising her of the situation and asking her to investigate. She even enclosed a check to cover expenses. On the morning of March 22, 1905, Miss Converse set out on her investigation. She began at the Los Angeles County Hospital, where she examined Léonie's registration and obtained her address. Then she proceeded to the Gilmour home in Boyle Heights, where she interviewed Léonie and examined the baby. By the end of the day she was able to dispatch a hastily written letter:

Elizabeth Converse to Ethel Armes, March 22, 1905

Ethel—

Have just had Yone Noguchi's baby in my arms and had a cup of tea with its mother. I will try to stick to facts. It is all more than I can comprehend.

The child was born Nov 18, '04, at the County Hospital. She entered the Hospital the 17th Nov, and left taking her baby with her Dec 1st. They told me at the Hospital that the baby looked Japanese and that it was beautiful and *Healthy* and bright. And *that* I heard from every source until two hours later I held the child in my arms.

It is Yone's I believe.

Yone's letter, dated Tokyo Feb 20th, was placed in my hands. He asked her forgiveness, her consent to his marriage in Japan; asked about the baby, what she would him to do, that he must do, what she ought to do. He wished to God he could love her, but could not. Appreciated her kindness as kindness and deplored his "temperament."

I met her mother—an old white-haired lady who held the baby while I drank tea and Leonie ate her supper—"If I didn't mind, nursing the baby made her so hungry."

I can't read people—my conceit has fallen out. I will try to tell you of her and you can read her, I can't.

In appearance Middle-West as they hang over the back fence. In manner as English [as] a queen. Simplicity, gentleness; says she was reared in Bryn Mawr (as her Alma Mater); teaches French and does a little writing. She and her mother are keeping this cottage, a most poor one, for two men who own it and the men take their breakfasts and suppers with them. They just moved there a few weeks ago and, she adds, "That is all I have to live on now. When the baby is through nursing I will teach again perhaps."

Says she has friends here that she has made, old college friends of hers at Pasadena. She adores the baby; says "A baby is worth twenty husbands." That she does not want to stand in the way of Yone's happiness; that she wants to shield him; and advises you to wait a while until she can get a *Legal Separation* in order to be sure her baby will be legitimatized.

Her marriage to Yone consists of a document drawn up by him and signed which he told her constituted sufficient marriage ceremony. That was in New York you know. They never lived together; "we were too poor"; but for four months, beginning in the autumn and ending in Feb or March—they saw each other daily or lived as man and wife, though having separate homes; the baby is the outcome of their very last days together.

She intends never to be separated from the child. The baby is a charming child, a glorious creature of vibrant body and sparkling eyes and sunshine of disposition. She said she determined to keep her mind happy so as to make the child happy; she has succeeded.

My first question embraced "Are you going to Japan?"

"Oh no!" very [gently]; "We have separated and will never live together."

Said Yone told her he did not love her as husband should wife—and they parted.

She is peace and happiness and courage and hope. If she were the Mother of Jesus, she could not be more sure of herself or happier.

She says she has a trunk full of his Mss, and this document of matrimony, but wants a legal separation which would prove that the paper is legal; otherwise fears some stain may be cast upon child.

The child's temporary name is Yo, meaning mid-night, she tells me.

She says she would not pity the girl Yone would marry; she believes in him. Oh! I can't understand it. She does not want help, or money, or anything; just her baby. Says calmly she loves Yone dearly; to tell you she does not want to stand in Yone's happiness—but she would like his marriage to her proved legal for the child's sake, though she did not put it in words so crude as that; her rate was a perfect one and perfectly carried out. You would like her. Write me if I have done what you wanted. Elizabeth.

The following day, Elizabeth Converse wrote Ethel again, adding additional information neglected in the rush of her first letter.

Elizabeth Converse to Ethel Armes, March 23, 1905

Dear—

Last night I posted an incoherent letter to you in which I endeavoured to give you the main facts. I enclose herewith your cheque intact—as finding her cost nothing.

On the official slip at the County Hospital her age is given as thirty, occupation, housewife, father, a native of Ireland, mother a native of New York, as she appears as "Noguchi, Ella G." On the blank left for "Married or Single" appears the initial *M*.

A reporter from the *"Herald"* went out to the County Hospital and met her—, it was a woman reporter. Leonie tells me she asked her not to write it up—"as we have separated, this would not be a very pleasant time to announce a marriage"; so the reporter responded "I won't write about you, but just about the baby." They told me it had been written up in the "Herald", at the Hospital, but the remainder I learned from Leonie, who would have shown the clipping to me but I did not have time. I did not let her show me the document of marriage either, although she has it, and I did read his letter written on the 20th Feb. She was so very willing to talk. I had expected frigidity or reticence as that is what I would have handed out to *anyone* and *everyone* who asked me questions under such circumstances.

Her attitude has simply swamped me. I knew I could understand your agony and Yone's and expected to find the third dose of it, but not calm cheerfulness instead. I told her she was the happiest person I had met in a long while. I find no peg on which to hang *regret*, the baby is so health and vibrant with life and joy and its mother equally happy. *She thinks the baby compensates for all else*, so what is there to do? Yone will never be permitted to have the baby, I am sure of that. She expects nothing, and seems to want nothing, *only to make safe to the baby a lawful name*.

Whether the document is legal enough to found a legal separation, I know not. It has *some* legal value in New York, however. She went to a lawyer with it and he said if she was willing to go to court with it, they could hold Yone responsible, but she adds calmly, the less publicity the better for the baby. She does say that Yone knew of her condition. Said she felt it almost as soon as it happened, told Yone and he laughed at her—and said "how can you tell, you have never had such an experience before!" and she insisted that she probably knew something "by intuition," but the Doctor could tell nothing until four months. Yone left New York in August, a week previous to [her] leaving for Los Angeles. She came here direct to her mother, and says he went direct to S.F. because she had a letter from him dated there a week later.

He has written her twice asking her permission to marry in Japan, and she gained the idea that he meant a Japanese girl but thinks now he meant *to marry in Japan* to you when you arrive. She walked two blocks to the car with me and standing there in the dark she spoke about a common-law marriage, requiring some kind of a ceremony—as if she could only have that! That would entail Yone coming to her, I suppose, and I don't see how that could legalize the child. I simply am at sea.

He has known her five years, she says. She has revised all his mss; has a trunk full of them in her possession; and I believe she said she had been in Paris and Berlin but knew him only in New York City.

I will go some time in day time to see her. Will take Norris to see the baby. He will be frantic over it. It is not pudgy and fat like Talcum Powder babies, but like a Japanese doll as to figure, as brown as to skin, and modified as to feature.

She seems to accept as final that he doesn't love her, and can't love her, and there is not the slightest hint of a wail or a whine on account of it. I have indulged in a heap worse antics over a flirtation than she is doing over this. She doesn't look agonized—though she was unconscious 22 hours in giving birth to the baby and *it* was born unconscious. She said the worst part was having to listen to the others sufferings after she got through with hers, as they put about three patients, practically, in the same room in the maternity ward. But any reference to any unpleasantness came as an after-thought—after *I* would *dig* for something of the kind.

She must have been reading Walt Whitman. I don't know much of Whitman, but I felt him when with her. She looks about as [fit and trim], and nice to look upon as Margaret West—and you know now what she looks like in personal appearance—sloppy, and not pretty; wears glasses, neither old nor young, not a bit old maidish nor not a bit "sporty", nor dashing, and not provincial. I never met anyone like her but no doubt you have.

Tell me anything you want me to do further, and talk it out to me if it will help you; but I feel quite helpless in advising you.

The baby will certainly be well cared for and loved. She seems full of common sense—every sentence was a master stroke. I asked her—"As an American girl why did you accept so flimsy a marriage ceremony—just a paper." She did not answer at the time, and later spoke of believing so implicitly in his honour, and still thinks he is a man of honour and sweetness and all the rest.

Elizabeth.

Elizabeth Converse had certainly done more than enough. It hardly mattered whether Léonie might consent to Yone's marriage to Ethel—for Ethel's interest in marrying such a man must have evaporated even before she finished reading the first letter. Yone's case, or rather the case against Yone, was, for a woman bred in the traditions of Southern propriety, simple and devastating. To marry a man who had abandoned a loving wife and baby leaving them to fend for themselves cooking for strangers in a Los Angeles shack was unthinkable. Stoddard saved a fragment of a letter Ethel wrote him soon after she learned of the facts. She was still distraught— "I haven't been able literally to write a sane line since it all happened," she admitted. She approved of Stoddard's idea of going to see Léonie and the baby personally, as he was contemplating a trip down the California coast. Stoddard had only the vaguest recollection of dining with Léonie in New York and had been unaware of her relationship with Yone. But the crux of the matter was, as Ethel saw it, "She says—you know—Yone lived with her the year—all that year he was writing to me & we were engaged—she says he was married to her all that time. I heard from him a few weeks ago & he says he lived with her one week only & that she lies. I do not think she lies. You can give me your impressions at least & find out if that is a lie. But—it makes no difference—nothing can—there is the child—his treatment of that woman—[It is] plain written that he never loved me yet & I do not think ever could love me." She continued, "It is strange—I used to dream he really cared for me & that was why I loved him so—because I thought he cared so much—but—you see—he never loved me once & never cared at all." It was clear that she was shaken by the experience, but she insisted that Stoddard needn't worry. "I am not unhappy at all—Do not think I am feeling more than I do. I feel nothing whatever. I am very well now—though my strength is not back yet. I am however becoming interested in work again—in writing—if—if I could learn to write—That will come maybe some day."

Ethel and Yone's love affair was officially over. A cloud from Los Angeles had destroyed Yone's beautiful dream of Annabel Lee. He had gambled on love, and lost. As for Ethel, recovery proved difficult. "I never saw Ethel happy again," her friend Anna Walker later wrote. "That was a blow that she could not ever recover from." She embraced her adopted city of Birmingham and threw herself into her journalistic work, writing, in 581 pages, *The Story of Coal and Iron in Alabama,* supported by "a pitiful sum" from the Birmingham Chamber of Commerce. The book, published in 1910, helped launch her career as an independent regional historian and she is still fondly remembered as one of Alabama's pioneering women historians, though she eventually gravitated back to the east coast, where she lived until 1945. She never married.

Ethel's reaction was a disappointment to Yone, who wrote to Stoddard on April 25 begging him to come to Japan. "I got a little Japanese house with a bit of garden. Come, Dad, be quick!," he pleaded. In a postscript, he asked, "Did Ethel write you about the Los Angeles woman?" "It is not so black with me as you may fancy," he added. "Don't trouble yourself with that matter, pray. I will settle it myself. And in fact it was all settled—a long time ago." But Stoddard, who was looking forward to some relaxation in California, did not take up Yone's invitation. He told Frank Putnam, "I am likely to locate in some old Mission-Adobe village where I shall be unmolested; then I shall have my books, my siesta, my mass-wine, and no interruptions." Yone would have to bear it out alone. On May 22 Putnam reported to Stoddard, "Yone writes from Tokyo, very sorrowfully, 'I wish Dad were here this minute: he would understand!'" "Poor lad—," Putnam philosophized "—he has his uncomfortable hours to get through, same as Adam and Eve and the rest of us, but it will temper his blade and he'll be the better man for it in the long run, I guess."

By this time, Putnam had appointed himself as Noguchi's moral advisor, using his editorial position at the *National Magazine* as leverage. "Yone writes saying his *Los Angeles woman*—dam'd little rascal, I could break him in two for that phrase—" he wrote Stoddard "—will market his American copy for her benefit and the baby's, hereafter, so I'm to use several of his articles during the next year." "If I had only known what was in his mind when he was with me, I think I should have given less time to poetry and more to ethics of civilization, in my talks and walks with the lad. But he is all right as God made him—and I like him that way."

Putnam had grown up in a small town in Iowa and knew something about the value of parents; his own father had died soon after his birth and he, along with his older brother, had been raised by his mother, Cassie, and a stepfather, Andrew Jackson Cushman, who fathered another eight children with Cassie and never formally adopted the Putnam children. Putnam had come away from the experience with the understanding that childbearing was woman's essential function. In the same letter, he told Stoddard how, on a recent visit to Staten Island, he had turned down Edwin Markham's invitation to meet poet Edith Thomas because he had no interest in female poets. "If there is one creature that never got even the least gain out of our so-called advance up from savagery, it is the female of the genus homo: the savager she is the more I admire her, and the better she fulfills her natural functions, loyally adhering to her one lord and master and bearing to him healthy normal children." Putnam was no doubt exaggerating a bit for the amusement of the woman-scorning Stoddard, but he was not entirely joking.

Noguchi was grateful for Putnam's help and took his advice to heart. "You are so good and sensible. I value you above everybody. I trust in your great wisdom and direction," he wrote Putnam on August 22. "Yes, I firmly believe that Mrs Noguchi is a fine spirit. I am becoming to apprehend it, however late it be. I will try to be good. Rest and trust in my words." Over the following months, Putnam published half a dozen pieces by Yone, as well as Léonie Gilmour's essay on George Meredith and "Founding a Tent-Home in California," continuing all the while to urge them back onto the path of conventional morality by reuniting. Stoddard still thought it "a pity he should have become entangled when he seems never to have really cared for her," but Putnam courted him as well, and soon, even he supported Putnam's reconciliation plan. "I hope that Yone calls in his own out of the open," he wrote Putnam. "They should be with him, as perhaps the Crown Prince will save the throne from toppling."

As the Russo-Japanese War entered its second year Japan seemed the likely victor. In a last-ditch attempt to change the course of the war, the Russian navy sent eleven battleships from its Baltic fleet into the Pacific, intending to slip them through the Korean strait undetected and regroup the fleet at Vladivostok. But at Tsushima island, Admiral Togo's fleet was waiting, and for three days at the end of May, the Imperial Japanese Navy sank or captured virtually every ship in the Russian fleet. Two weeks later, both countries accepted President Theodore Roosevelt's offer to mediate a settlement, and the war came to an end.

Léonie was now working again, "in an office of the Chamber of Commerce Building, where I have desk room and take in what work I can," she told Catharine. The building was located at 212 Schieffelin Street, across the river near what was then the Southern Pacific Railroad depot. She had also made a new Japanese friend, a nineteen-year-old French-speaking student named Matsuo Miyake, who was trying to become a writer, and clearly adored her and her baby. Like Yone, Matsuo was full of idealized notions of literature and art. And he had a seemingly endless supply of postcards depicting the romantic Japan where he hoped she would someday accompany him.

From Matsuo Miyake, June 7, 1905

Mme Noguchi,
Ma chère Madam:—
I can hardly think that sickness comes even to the babe, the earthly angel.
I am sure of that he will be well before I will see you on Saturday evening.
Votre Frère

Matsuo Miyake's June 7, 1905 postcard. *Isamu Noguchi Foundation.*

Miyake was to return to Japan in the fall. Until then, he and Léonie formed an intimate friendship of an indeterminate nature. There was certainly an air of romance to it—forbidden romance. It was not merely the thirteen year age difference and the fact that Leonie was supposed to be married to Yone. The previous March, the California legislature had reenacted an amendment to its anti-miscegenation statute, making marriages between whites and Mongolians "illegal and void."

He told her stories of his hometown, Osaka, and the beautiful city of Kyoto, nearby. Listening to Miyake's stories of Kyoto Léonie began to think the ancient capital might be a viable alternative to Yone's Tokyo.

BUY LOTS IN BOYLE HEIGHTS

WHERE ITS NICE, HIGH AND HEALTHFUL; LARGE LOTS, 50X150, BETWEEN TWO CAR LINES; 5C FARE; ONLY 15 MINUTES FROM SPRING STREET.

From $150 Up
Terms $25 Down

$10 PER MONTH

YOU BETTER GET IN ON THESE LOTS QUICK BEFORE THEY'RE ALL GONE; IT'S THE BEST BUY IN THIS CITY FOR A HOME OR AN INVESTMENT.

The Greater Los Angeles Realty Co.

Phone Main 8515.   433 Huntington bldg. OUR BRANCH OFFICE AT EUCLID AND STEPHENSON AVENUES IS OPEN SUNDAY ALL DAY.   TAKE EUCLID AVENUE CAR GOING NORTH ON BROADWAY OR ON E. FIRST STREET TO EUCLID AND STEPHENSON AVENUES. MAIN OFFICE OPEN SUNDAY TILL 12 NOON.

Real estate advertisements, October 15, 1905. *Los Angeles Herald.*

For the present, however, she and her mother had to make their home in Los Angeles. Sharing a "very poor" cottage with two men was hardly a long-term solution, and now there was talk of her sister, Florence, joining them as well. Since arriving in Los Angeles, Léonie had been intrigued by the idea of becoming one of the city's legions of new homeowners. Makeshift homes were going up everywhere. The land was cheap—lots could be bought on credit for a mere $10 a month—and the mild weather made it possible to make do, at least temporarily, with a mere tent house, which could be had for another $10. Even this seemed more than Léonie and Albiana could manage, and, fearing they might lose everything by defaulting on the payments, they "hesitated, trembling on the brink for a whole year." Finally, with a bit of money coming in from work, and from Yone and Frank Putnam, Léonie took the plunge in the summer of 1905. Tents were going up everywhere. A few blocks away, one hundred and fifty of them were built for the Seventh Day Adventist camp meeting, held in August; two thousand Aventists gathered in the large meeting tent to hear Elder William Ward Simpson and others preach of Christ's imminent second coming.

The plot she had in mind was on a little street called Marietta Street. Perched on a plateau above a deep gully, the backyard would look out over the still undeveloped expanses southeast of the city.

The Marietta Street house on a 1906 transportation map. *Library of Congress.*

A Los Angeles tent house. *Out West,* **1904.**

The following year she wrote up the story of her first house-building adventure for Putnam's *National Magazine.*

Founding a Tent-Home in California

National Magazine, February 1906.

I suppose every easterner who comes to California comes hugging a dream of home. "Back east," he had no home. There, not only the too rich, not only the very poor, even the poor-enough-to-be-comfortable, are so often homeless. Homeless? Largely by their own fault, I grant you. "Home" in one sense is within reach of all. Someone has said that wherever two loving hearts strive to make a bit of a nest for themselves apart from the world, there home is. What if the nest be small? What if every gust voice a threat of ruin? Still it may be home. Yes, even under the blighting eye of the landlord there may be home.

But home without any third party, no land-lord, no "other families" in the house or peering in your back windows; home with the dear sense of ownership encompassing it—why, that's a luxury we come to California to find. "Why pay rent? Why not own your own home?" is a proposition thrust upon the eastern visitor from the moment he steps off the train. Everywhere he looks, the busy real-estate speculator has placarded the quaint device. "Lots for sale! Lots! $10 down and $10 a month," or "$25 down and $10 a month." Well, why not own our home, we said. So after a year of hesitation we struck out for "Home." You see, even in California, poor folks must hesitate before owning their home. There's something at stake. Suppose you are paying rent, and one day comes when you cannot pay. What happens? Why, the worst that can come is to be evicted, and then you go and live in cheaper quarters. But if you are buying your home on the installment plan, and you fail to make one payment—alas, you lose your very home. So we hesitated, trembling on the brink for a whole year. Then a bit of a check came to give us heart. We said, "We will."

Over on the eastern outskirts of the City of Our Lady the Queen of the Angels there lies a high plateau, with a view of San Pedro mountain to the South—yes, there too the twin peaks of Catalina Island lift their heads out of white cloud billows while between roll the miles on miles of mesa land, over which the clean winnowed wind of the mesa sweeps unremittingly. To the north the abrupt rock masses of the Sierra Madre show steely blue and white, or thunderously cloud-gray. On the east the softer forms of the dream-distant San Bernardino range still rim the world. Westward lies the city and the city haze—but we need not look westward. Underfoot the close-cropped pasture land fits the sole and springs to the tread.

Once I had come upon it in a stroll, now I remembered and returned to the spot. The real-estate agent—at every corner you find one peering at you from his hole like the squirrels—hitched up his buggy and got out his best oratory for our benefit. Poor real-estate agents have to work so hard: and dear me, wasn't he amazed! We agreed with everything he said. Undoubtedly the view was superb. We promptly selected our lot, the "sightliest" one for view—while the voice of the real-estate man rolled on, telling of the street one day to be cut through there. We were so pleased to have a deep gully close by that it never occured to us that a street could not possibly ever be cut through there. "I'm afraid ye got badly stuck on that lot," a neighbor afterward condoled with us, "because ye see ye'r sidetracked away off from the street, and your property won't rise in value as if a street could be cut through there" Were we a bit crestfallen to think we had paid for just a view? The view consoled us.

Somebody told us we could buy a tent for $10. We saw one advertised in the paper at that price. "A striped tent in good order, fourteen by sixteen feet," the advertisement ran. Now who would have thought to measure the tent? Or go poking about for rents in the canvas? Not we! The people who sold it us—decent working people they were—needed the money in building their "shack." The "shack" with chicken yard in back and some bright flowers in front is the second step in the evolution of the California "Home." The third step is the neat "bungalow" with levelled lawn and trees of your own planting.

Now the tent needed a floor. A floor will cost you a matter of $5 or $6, one of the wise say-so's informed us. We hunted for a man to lay the floor. "There's a decent oldish sort of a German man will work for a dollar and a half a day and glad to get it," one of our neighbors-to-be told us. Him we sought. Herr Z grunted some guttural objections—he was busy putting up some shacks—well, maybe he could leave for a day for a consideration of $2.50. Agreed. And how much lumber would it take? Herr Z calculated in German and pronounced, "Twelve dollars." It was more than we expected. However, we supposed we were in for it. Would he buy the lumber for us? No, he would not But he would meet me at the lumber yard and help me select the lumber, and then we would know what we were paying for. So I met Mr. Z by appointment at Ganahl's lumber yard. A fine, patriarchal-looking fellow he was, recalling the pictures of Joseph. His bronzed face showed richly against the snowy beard, his brown eyes glowed softly. Afterward I learned to value his gentle and kindly heart. That day he tried my patience. Alas, he had quaffed the cup which puts fetters to the will, wings to the imagination—in short, was drunk. He was enjoying the divine irresponsibility of the heaven-born. He did not feel like work. (Does anyone in California feel like work?) "So much work to do on those shacks. If I stop to do your work those people get angerry mit me," he shrugged deprecatingly. But our tent was bought, our lot bespoke, we wanted to settle at once. "Leave alles to me, dear lady. I find one Seventh Day Adventist, good carpenter, I speak to him tonight. Sure he will lay your floor." In the meantime I bought the lumber: 300 square feet of flooring at $27 a thousand cost $9; eight beams two by four inches and fourteen feet long were $1.50; Four boards one foot wide and one inch thick (as baseboards to raise the tent a little from the floor) cost another $1.50. Add 75 cents for cartage and you have a total of $12.75 for lumber.

And I decided to see Mr. Seventh Day Adventist myself. So that evening, after work, (my days being given over to an "office") I sought out the place. How changed, how dark and pathless the mesa by night: here and there a light twinkled from a rare house. Twice on the way a lighted tent, like a paper lantern set down on the mesa, guided me. A bare-legged boy brushed past me carrying a gunny-sack slung over his shoulder. What was in the sack? Dried chunks of manure, used to keep the hearth-fire aglow in the scarcity of coal. (Coal—a dirty soft kind in irregular lumps—costs 60 cents a sack in California, and wood is 30 cents a sack.) I knocked at the door of the carpenter at last. A woman's voice asked me in. I entered a huge room. A glowing kitchen stove in the middle reached out long, trembling fingers of light to touch the rough beams and rafters, the floor, the walls. A solidly built brick chimney rose from floor to roof. It was the outside shell of an incompleted house, of which the partitions, upper floor, lathing and plastering were still to be done. Before the comfortable fire Priscilla, the Puritan maiden—no, the buxom wife of the Seventh Day Adventist, clad in gray homespun and broad white kerchief sat nursing her knees. Outside the wind blew gustily chill. I was glad to come into the warmth. The good wife gossipped. "Tent? Oh, yes, to be sure, you're the lady of the tent. Well, I'm glad to see you—" "I am afraid you made a mistake," I interrupted. "What, don't you live in the tent across the way? No? Well, there's something very mysterious about that. You know she had that tent built several months ago, and there's never a soul to be seen there—yes, someone saw a man and woman sitting in the doorstep at dusk once. Some folks say they've seen a light in the tent—Well, so it wasn't you after all." I told her I wanted a tent put up. Would her husband do it? Well, maybe, tho' she feared he was too busy. I must wait till he came home. He charged $3.50 a day, working by contract he often made more, much more. Now she prated of her husband. "My husband" was one of the important people of the Adventist community. Had I been to Elder Simpson's meetings? Such an earnest man! A man of property too! Why, he owned—But it was getting late, and I excused myself. Come to think of it, she was sure her husband was too busy to take any more work just now. I took up again my search for a carpenter, was directed from one place to another, always with the same result. Tired and hungry, I stumbled my way back to the road, after losing myself once in the tall dried grasses of the gully. At half-past nine I sat down to supper and the narration of the day's events. For the next three days I hunted carpenters. Finally someone gave me a tip to telephone to Union headquarters. They sent me a man (at $3.50 a day of course) who took nearly two days to plant our fourteen by sixteen-foot tent (charges $5) and incidentally discovered that it measured only twelve by fourteen feet. (Is it true that all Californians are liars? Well, I don't at this moment recall one who has kept his word to me in the matters of time and price. Your real Californian will tell you, however, that these are all Easterners. True enough!) So our tent cost us so far $17.75; no, $18.75, including the expressage.

We were to move Wednesday. But Wednesday it rained, the first time in six months. And Thursday it rained. Friday we took advantage of a lull in the storm to start out. I sat up in front of the express wagon beside a black man. Baby in his carriage was strapped securely on top of the load. The dear little fellow took it to be a pleasure outing. When a few drops of rain splashed his face he crowed with delight. He was laughing and making the sweetest crooning noises all the way. When his carriage rocked like a ship on a rolling sea he clutched my forefinger tightly, and thus fortified feared nothing. The roads were all ruts and miry pools, and the journey was long. When at last our wee bit tent came in sight my heart thumped. Home at last!

Inside was ridiculously small. And there were trunks and boxes, bed and stove and sewing machine, baby's chair and baby's crib and baby's go-cart and God knows what else, to be stowed away in that twelve by fourteen space. But it was a shelter from the rain which sputtered threateningly every minute or so, and it was warmer than outside. Hurrah for home!

Leaving my mother with the baby I started off for work (it was now about two o'clock) and finished out the day downtown. Alas, the rain was soon falling in a steady downpour. Was the tent waterproof? Was it warm? I could tell nothing until I returned at nightfall. The walk over the rough roads was painfully long. I struggled against wind and rain, drenched to the skin. I struggled with sticky "dobe." ("Dobe" a contraction of the Spanish "adobe," a kind of dark loam, hard as brick in dry weather, in wet weather sticky beyond the imagination of anyone who has not encountered it. If you get caught in it, it will pull your rubbers off, even your shoes, before it lets you free. There is only one way to overcome it, which is to tie your feet up in gunny-sacks. Such is the vanity of humankind, however, that the gunny-sacks in evidence on a rainy day are far fewer than necessity demands. The mesa was dark, black with the blackness of a river under storm-clouds. Where was our tent-ship? Was it securely anchored? I saw nothing of it until I was quite close. Faintly the light of it shone through the mist. I steered straight for it over the stubbly field.

Mamma sat in the middle of chaos, holding baby wrapped in a blanket. She had been too frightened by the noises to do anything. The tent groaned and creaked, the ropes that held it anchored were drawn taut and whizzed under the wind. The canvas flapped loudly. The whole floor was wet. The only one dry thing in that room was little Yo (my baby) swathed in blankets in spite of his protesting kicks. I found the coffee pot in the corner half full of rain water. And the coffee was in some box or other. Aha! here it is! Now for hot coffee and hamburger steak, cooked over the little oil stove. "Hamburger steak?" sniffed Mama.

"Certainly! You didn't think I'd come home without fetching something in my pocket? And here are fresh rolls."

"Did the milk come? I told a boy to fetch you some."

"Certainly it came. Baby isn't starved, at any rate."

So we ate our supper off one plate. Of cups, forks and spoons we had found each one.

"What shall we do with this tent? It leaks abominably."

I looked around and found open seams in the canvas, a half-inch space under the baseboard, and other defects. Even the best of tents will become water-soaked in a long, continuous rain. Someone in the office had told me that a "fly" was needed. A fly is a sort of cloth roof, stretched over a center beam a few inches higher than the ridge-pole of the tent and extending over the eaves. This sheds the water, protects and preserves the tent, and makes the place cooler in Summer. Such a one as would protect our tent costs about $6. "That will make the price of our tent come to about $25," said Mamma. "And any day a high wind may come and blow the whole thing away. And we have so many other expenses. Already I have given the agent $25 as first payment on the lot, and you know $9 more went to the water company to have the main water pipe tapped, and we still must buy some piping, a faucet and connections to get the water to the surface—perhaps $3 or $4 more. That makes about $40 for first payment on our lot and for water, and say $24 for the tent, that's $64 already."

"Yes, but think, Mama! After this we will pay out simply the $10 a month we used to pay for rent."

"And seventy-five cents for water-tax," added Mamma.

"And in three years the whole thing will be paid for."

"What trees shall we plant?"

"I want a Norway pine."

"Why not have some fruit trees?"

"A fig tree, of course."

"A couple of orange trees? And the blossoms of the lemon are so fragrant."

"Those are all dwarfish trees. I'd like a glorious spreading maple, or an oak."

"Ah, the maple is for back East, where the Autumn frost can get in his fine work coloring the leaves. We have no Autumn glory here," sighed my mother.

"We'll have a honeysuckle clambering over the back porch."

"We can grow any kind of flowers here all Winter. Strawberries too if we want. We're above the frost line."

"But cold enough tonight.

"The bedding is all wet."

"Well, we must manage to lie on it somehow. I'm deadly tired."

We spread two mattresses on the floor. Mamma's was comparatively dry. Mine thoroughly soaked. I lay down, baby with me, wrapped in all the dry blankets. The icy wet penetrated my nightgown. No use to try to sleep. I sat up. The air was cold too. I lay down. The bed was colder. Things had reached the point of tragedy. I began to laugh. Why? By the same logic that I must cry when my cup of happiness is full. Being a woman I suppose reasons are superfluous. Baby objected to my writhings. He fretted. He would not rest again. He wanted to be held. I sat up with baby in my arms, rocking back and forth in bed, crooning and cuddling and talking to him. Bye, baby! Bye! Hush, my baby dear. Mamma got her little boy! Just listen! Hark! What's that? Why, that's the wind! Patter, patter! Why that's little sea-horses trampling on the roof. Sh! Listen! We're in a funny kind of a ship, we're riding over a big sea.

Whole world is drowned, only not we! Hush, my dove! Mamma's only little white dove! Bye, bye, bye, O! He quieted at last. I laid him down and crept to the door. By this time the tent was full of a strange white light. I thought the morning sun was shining through. I looked out. There the moon was, riding uncertainly through cloud billows. "Clusters of cloud against the moon, the wind for a flower," the Japanese expression of the inexplicable pathos of life recurred to my mind, as I glanced back at baby's dear flower face sleeping in the moonlight. O my own little flower! O could I shield thee from every harsh wind! I covered him warmly, and waited. Neighbors' chickens began to wake. And sweet birds trilled in the tall grass stalks of the gully. Now warm sunshine flooded the tent, from above, from the sides. We needed no window. How glorious the life in a tent! Yo clapped his hands. Happy, happy boy!

I went off singing to work. The mesa held up a face radiant through tears. Every grass blade was shining with the silver drops. Grass? Why, the brown mesa had put on a robe of green overnight. The new grass was half an inch high. Soon it would be four inches. In mid-winter it would be knee deep.

Sunday was our day for setting to rights. We hammered and sawed and swept and dug and sweated. In the afternoon I spied a little figure climbing up the side of the gully.

"So hard to find you—such a long walk I had." A Jap boy stood before me wiping his forehead. "You like ducks? Here are two wild ones; my boss shot them."

Matsuo pulled the feathers off the ducks and we fried one in olive oil with plenty of onion and a dash of curry. We were tired and dirty, but happy as gypsies. We enjoyed our supper. Mamma ate ravenously, having been limited to a vegetarian diet for a couple of days. The duck was delicious.

Yo licked the bones.

The tent house was completed in August; not long afterwards, on August 26, Matsuo Miyake sent his farewell note. "Goodnight, America," he wrote. "Good night, Mrs Noguchi, Ma Soeur."

Yone was now marketing his American articles to help support Léonie and the baby. Only one 1905 letter survives, a short businesslike note about Yone's "Sada Yacco" article for *The Theatre Magazine*, sent on September 1. But there were other letters: in one, Léonie told Yone it was his job to name the baby; in another Yone, now desperate for a good editor, broached the suggestion that Léonie might consider coming to Japan.

In October, Léonie wrote to Catharine Bunnell, who had sent a postcard while on a summer trip to Europe with her family.

To Catherine Bunnell, October 4, 1905

212 Shifflin [*sic*] Street, Room 634,
Chamber of Commerce, Los Angeles

My dear Catherine:— Hello, where are yez? I'm thinking its time ye returned to your own fireside, coming down from the Alpine peaks to a more comfortable region. By the way, a postal came to me from those same dizzy regions directed to "Miss Léonie Gilmour." Kathleen dear, I'm s'posed to be married, tho' I'll admit it don't seem much like it living in this maiden solitude. Now what's your news? I'll tell you mine. First, Baby is growing fast and fair. I named him Yosemité, but his papa has not condescended to set the seal of his august approval thereon. He says: 'I will send some good name soon. I am pondering upon it' And he still continues to allude to his lordship as IT. And he can walk all around the room and has two toofens and can say whole lots of things. He has a lively temper. When he gets mad he jumps up and down so hard I'm afraid he'll injure his feet. He loves his mamma awful much—well, as much as ripe figs, which he doats [*sic*] on.

We heard from Florence that she lives in an eyrie on tenth street—she hinted that she'd like to have a flat with you, but hadn't the courage to suggest it. Mamma said she'd feel so much better if you were there to look after her morals.

I'm writing this in an office of the Chamber of Commerce Building, where I have desk room and take in what work I can. Yone is writing busily, and may possibly be over here before long. I wonder when Mary is coming back? I miss her. End of my sheet. I'll write more next time. This is simply to say "Welcome to America, bird of passage"

Léonie

Léonie had recently seen Mary Moody, a Bryn Mawr friend who had visited Los Angeles with her family.

Office work was not Léonie's forte. Though she could "slide down a column of figures as if it was a greased pole," she could, "alas, . . . slide down seven different times with seven different results." Eager to return to her previous profession of teaching, she sought to revive her connection with St. Aloysius Academy, no doubt in hopes of obtaining a letter of reference. It was a delicate matter to explain her situation, since the merest hint of moral irregularity in her marriage could irrevocably taint her reputation with the nuns. Though she seems to have drawn the line at outright lies, intentionally misleading exaggeration was by no means out of the question. Thus, Yone appears as a devoted husband lured away from his happy home life by the promise of a professorial job in Tokyo. The letter also contains the first suggestion that Léonie was seriously considering going to Japan.

To Sister Rose de Lima, November 5, 1905

Los Angeles

Dear Sister:—

I've been intending to write to you many and many a time, but always put it off for reasons which probably would not seem good to you, so I will not enumerate them. I suppose Sister Ines got the letter I wrote so hastily just before leaving New York, tho' I did not receive any answer. Many things have happened since then, the biggest event being the birth of my little boy, now nearly a year old. He is a lively little Jap, with velvety dark eyes like his father's. Most of my time for the past year has been given up to him, and to looking after the business side of my husband's literary work. Mr. Noguchi is still in Tokyo, where he has been enveigled into giving some lectures on American literature in college there, and now it looks as tho' he may find some difficulty in getting away this winter, as he intended. In that case I shall probably go over to Japan with baby next Spring, and perhaps take up teaching again there in the fall. I am trying to master a few words of Japanese which may stand me in good stead if I do go over there. Teaching has taken on a new interest for me, now that I have my own little boy's mental development to watch over. I should like to begin at the beginning, and teach the very little tots. Yo (that's baby's baby name) is beginning to talk. And he's very fond of singing in his own sweet little voice. He is active and strong, can crawl and climb anywhere, walks holding on to things, and can stand alone when he wants to. He keeps his grandmother and me both busy. And still I found time to do a little writing—I hope to do more in future. If you will look in the December or February number of the National Magazine you may find my name misprinted as Léonie Gilman (I asked the editor to correct it) over my first ventures into the field of literature. However, I don't expect to blossom into fame there. I am glad to leave public life to those better fitted to it. (That might be yourself if you saw fit, Sister Rosa Lima.)

And now I've talked a lot. What have you to say? I should be very glad of a little word from St. Aloysius Academy, and to hear something of my old pupils and friends there. Are you still teaching English literature? I may come to you for points when I take up my work in Japan. And do you still read all the books that come out? For my part, I confess I have hardly read a word. But one thing I did come across, which I commend to you—that is Yeats' Plays for an Irish Theatre—very likely you have seen them already.

Please remember me kindly to the Sisters—best love to little Sister Inez!—and write if you feel like it.

Your friend,
Léonie Gilmour Noguchi
Address me, if you write:
Mrs. Yone Noguchi,
634 Chamber of Commerce,
Los Angeles, Cal.
We live on a street not yet cut through, and which is not on the postman's itinerary.

At the end of November 1905, Yone Noguchi had had a curious visit from a Japanese youth bearing two letters from Léonie. When Matsuo Miyake had returned from his foreign travels to his uncle's house in Akasaka in September, he had written Léonie that "autumn of Nippon (Yamato) is sweet and pensive," inquiring, in his customary playful-possessive manner, about "our dear Baby." Léonie had written back, enclosing a letter to deliver to Yone along with a letter of introduction.

"I thank you with all my heart for your first sistery voices across the Pacific Ocean," Miyake had written back on November 12. "I will soon see Oto-San [father, i.e., Yone]. I also thank you for your introducing note." Léonie had discussed with Miyake her idea to come to Japan and settle in Kyoto, away from Yone, and Miyake wrote her again on November 16, promising, "I will soon let you know of best schools in Kioto." He was still in Tokyo, however. On November 30, he finally visited Noguchi to deliver her letter. "Having talked with Mr. Noguchi," he wrote, "I wonder what he is going to do upon you."

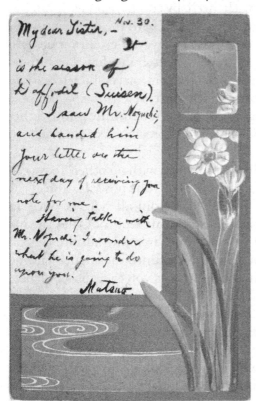

Matsuo Miyake's November 30 card. *Isamu Noguchi Foundation.*

Although Léonie and Isamu seemed happy to continue their tent life, it was only a matter of weeks before the next construction project was underway: a little house that was mainly to be used by Albiana.

A Little California House

Living Close to God and Nature In Sunland

The West-Coast Magazine, December 1906

When you say "California house" you mean something set close down to earth, smelling of new wood, seams all in sight, rough and homespun in appearance. No cellar, no plaster on the walls, few if any closets, no "modern conveniences." But your California settler isn't thinking of the inconveniences. The rough, board shanty in his "home," his house, a palace of luxury by comparison with—well, by comparison with "all out doors" as represented by an unimproved lot, or with the precarious tent which first sheltered his household gods. The way of evolution in California is from tent to "shack" and from shack to bungalow. The bungalow, charming epitome of elegance and solid comfort, is the affectation, or glorification of simplicity. Your "shack" or true California house is the real thing, the rude dwelling of the pioneer, painfully put together with his own hands, as a rule, out of timbers precious as gold bricks in the days of his poverty.

There is a charm about tent life comparable with no other. To waken in the morning with the smell of the mists in your nostrils, to feel the soft tide of light slowly flooding in on you from all sides at once, to watch for the dim shadows of birds' feet on your tent roof, and the lizard shadows that scamper up the walls, and dreamily admire the silhouetted picture of a swaying morning glory—until the sudden ending of a meadow lark's rapturous threnody wakens you to a consciousness of the world and Day—'tis a life ideal. Poetry, Nature, God—close, close beside you. Like other dreams, alas, the tent is perishable. Very soon it passes the way of dews and mists and mushrooms and small coins. It is liable to literally go up in smoke. The insurance companies won't touch a tent. So the provident settler, who is always looking forward to a bank account and "real" property, seldom tarries long in a tent.

We clung to our tent till it was threadbare, and longer, despite the inconvenience of frequent drenchings. "When the roof of your tent shows everywhere little pinholes where the light shines through, then prepare to abandon your tent," the neighbors told us. There were the pinholes. And the rain came in, as I have said. Still we clung to our threadbare flapping tent-house. Other considerations, chiefly the lack of space and closet room, and the need of some spot where needles and frying pans and flatirons wouldn't rust, induced us to build.

In that part of town where we live—it is "in town" though sparsely settled and without street lamps, without gas, without decent roads— the building of shacks goes on night and day. There is not a night when you may not hear the rhythmical tap, tap, of a hammer, or the wheezing of a saw, to show that some man's work is not done with sundown. But this home-building is "work that is play" as the cheery workers could tell you. And such contrivances! And such ingenuity! One of our neighbors is building a house out of packing boxes. Think of the labor of knocking them apart, and taking out the nails, and reinforcing the thin boards by doubling them. Another man is making his shack out of old lumber. The dealers in "second hand" lumber have put up their prices to anticipate the growing demand until it is as dear as new. There is one man who has laid a fine floor and reared a solid roof on uprights, and now he is going to fill in the walls with canvas until he gets money enough to buy some more boards, or until "San Francisco gets all built up again and leaves a little timber around at prices a poor man can look at." One ambitious carpenter built a two-story house, and mounts to the upper story by a ladder.

We had decided to have a "box house" with gable roof. That is the most usual kind. The redwood boards, one foot wide run straight up and down, the cracks between them being covered with battens. All these California houses have "mud-sills" by way of foundation. These are heavy redwood beams, say 2x6, which are laid flat on the ground. Above them are the floor joists, made of good Oregon pine, 2x4 in size, placed about thirty inches apart. The floor joists are raised to a "level" by the "underpinning," that is, blocks of wood of the proper sizes which are nailed with stout spikes to the mud-sills. On top of these blocks rest the joists, as I have said, and across these latter is laid the tongue and groove flooring.

Our little box house is a one-room affair, twelve by twelve in size, the walls eight feet in height "in the clear"—that is, above the floor level. To make a box house you make the corners first, by taking two redwood boards nailed at right angles along their edges for each corner. When these corners are in place, and secured by being nailed at the lower ends to the mud-sills or the joists, you have only to run a strip of 2x3 around the top of the walls inside the corners, and you have a firm support to which to nail the upper ends of your boards, which are set upright side by side. The roof is a more complicated affair. The rafters must be notched where they rest on the side walls, and cut to fit against each other at the top. Over the rafters are laid strips of board one inch thick called "sheeting." On top of the sheeting you place your shingles, if it is a shingle roof, or some waterproof roofing preparation which comes in rolls and is commonly used hereabouts. To calculate the length of your rafters from the width of your wall and the pitch of your roof is quite a little problem in mathematics, and I don't know how we ever should have managed it if Mr. Euclid hadn't thought of his little proposition about the hypotenuse of a right angled triangle. The gable ends of the walls are filled in with shorter lengths of boards which overlap the lower walls.

Some folks stain their shanties with creosote stain of a dark green color, which gives a "finished" look and is a pleasing contrast to the bare brown hills of the summer-time. And some folks don't because they can't afford it. We didn't. And some folks cover all over the inside with burlap. But we thought the natural finish of the redwood (surfaced inside), with its rich color and satin-like grain, very beautiful, so we have left it without adornment.

And we didn't put any ceiling in our house, because we like the look of the rafters pointing upward and the sense of space above. Two horizontal beams at right angles connecting the tops of the opposite walls (to keep things from springing apart) suggest interesting possibilities in the way of hanging fern baskets and Japanese lanterns and other things. We did ourselves proud in the matter of windows. Plain, primitive, ordinary—whatever epithet you may choose to apply to our shack—you cannot call our windows anything but distinguished. They swing sideways on hinges, a wide one opening to the south and the eucalyptus woods, a narrow one on the east inviting the morning sun. The hinges and the fasteners are in old copper effect. Think of such style in a shack! A fragment of old lace curtain embroidered with fleur-de-lys stretched across the window spaces keeps out some of the flies and buzzing things.

It is very warm and cosy in our little California house. Not too drafty in cold weather. Yet with just enough cracks to keep the air in circulation. In the hottest part of the day, when the glorious California sun is baking all the world to a crisp brown, we just open the windows and pull back the portiere that covers the screen door, and at once a splendid breeze blows from window to window and from window to door. Said one of our neighbor boys who works "in the fruit:" "Gee, but I'd like to sit in this house when we're pickin' berries. The sand gets so hot sometimes we have to climb up into an apricot tree to find a place to sit down on."

Our tent still stands—next door. Grey and weatherworn as an ancient sail, it still maintains its out-of-the-world charm, like an ancient fairy or a bearded witch. There I go to sit among the cobwebs and dream—of a ship that sails on the high seas, sailing near and nearer, and pretty soon e'll be "all aboard" and off for "far and far away."

Isamu, Leonie, and Albiana at the house, late 1906. *Isamu Noguchi Foundation.*

In January, Léonie suddenly informed Catharine she was "going to take Baby for a little trip across the Pacific Ocean about Feb. 1st." The causes of her sudden notion are unclear; she seems to have heard that a certain Mr. Kojima, whose wife she expected to meet at a church function, was to sail at that time, and thought she might travel under his protecting escort. The sudden arrival in California of her sister, Florence, might also have been a contributing factor. It is likely, however, that she was not as serious about the plan as she led Catharine to believe; perhaps she was merely exercising her Irish gift of gab, or testing Catharine's reaction to a plan that was not yet fully developed. She was, she confessed, getting bored of Los Angeles, where "the days are all sunshiny and very much the same, with nothing much in them."

Perhaps as a corrective for the weather, she had been reading Irish literature. In Lady Gregory's anthology, *Poets and Dreamers: Studies and*

Translations from the Irish (1903) she found four plays by Gaelic League founder Douglas Hyde which particularly fascinated her. In her next letter to Catharine, Léonie made an effort to imitate Hyde's style. She begins with mock-Irish gossip about two Bryn Mawr classmates who had settled in New Haven, Mary Moody, who had recently been in Los Angeles, and Alice Hammond, both of whom had ended up teaching in New Haven high schools.

To Catherine Bunnell, January 20, 1906

Los Angeles

My dearest Catherine:

A budget of news! A budget of news! But first let me ask: How is my Rose of Erin? And how are the folks in her house? And how are the neighbors of my acquaintance in the adjoining village of New Haven? Mary Moody promised me faithfully she would come back to Los Angeles. She is a promise-breaker, I suspect. Alice Hammond blew a few pipe-dreams in a similar direction. She is another, I daresay. You may give them both my opinion of themselves, with my undying love.

Now for the news: Firstly, Florence is in California. Don't say that you knew it! She has built a little room of her own, adjoining Mama's. A very small room, with a very big window. She has likewise planted onions, lettuce, spinach and other vegetables in various sunken gardens about the place to catch the feet of the unwary on darksome nights.

Secondly: Baby is now two years old, and is a wonderful conversationalist, singer, actor, story-teller, climber, dancer, jumper, and general stirrer up of things.

Thirdly: My friend Peter Georgis is staging his play of Golfo in St. Louis, and will himself act the part of the hero and villain, though afterwards repentant Tassos. You must go to see it if it comes your way, and shake hands with the young actor-author, and tell him that you are my chum.

Fourthly: The National Magazine printed the third of the series of my Mirabel and Dousabel stories this month. I wrote another one a few days ago which I like better than the others.

Fifthly: Yone San is in China.

Sixthly: I am going to take Baby for a little trip across the Pacific Ocean about Feb. 1st. Yes, we are really going to Japan, which is a fact that I can hardly realise though the time is so near. Yone is making all kinds of promises and I have been offered a position to teach in Tokyo, so that I shall be "on my own hook," and can make tracks if I don't like it. The horizon is very hazy to my view, though not without hope. I believe I have had enough of California for awhile, and will enjoy the misty-moist beauty of Japan by way of contrast.

Seventhly: I am invited to an entertainment at a Japanese church to-morrow, for the purpose of meeting a certain Mrs. Kojima, a lady who is the mother of six little Japs, and whose husband is going to Japan shortly on business and may take us under his protecting escort if it can be arranged.—

Seventhly: —Oh, I said seventhly, and it is a proper time to stop.

I am pegging away at a typewriter in a downtown office and the days are all sunshiny and very much the same, with nothing much in them. The only interesting book I read lately is Lady Gregory's book of stories and translations of Dr. Hyde's plays— which last are *splendid*—you must read them—and I think that as you are a lady of leisure it behooves you to learn the Irish language while I am imbibing the Japanese and we'll exchange inspirations.

Your faithful friend and admirer,
Léonichi Gilmourmiki Noguchi
Merry Xmas!

Before Florence had left New York, Catharine had taken up Léonie's suggestion that she might share Florence's West Village "eyrie" at 57 West 10th Street. She had arranged to do a brief stint at the Century Company, but it was "finishing up in a hurry," she reported to a family member on December 18. "Lots of us got walking papers today to take effect the first of January, very nice little notes they were too." The reason for the abrupt termination was the printers strike to begin on January 2, in which a thousand printers struck for an eight-hour work day. "The printers' strike has settled down to a long fight," Catharine explained to her brother, "so the Century Co. fired all but half a dozen of us and has decided to put the copy in shape at its leisure." In fact the strike dragged on until March and was unsuccessful, largely because the printers had given their employers four months' advance warning. Florence had wisely taken the opportunity to head off to California, and was so happy there she never went back. But Léonie and Florence had not relished the idea of living together in New York, and it could hardly have been mere coincidence that Florence's arrival in California coincided with Léonie's sudden decision to leave the state.

In the following letter to Sister Rosa Lima, written on the same day as the letter to Catharine, she said nothing of her new plan to go to Japan, though she did finally get around to asking her if she might secure for her a letter of recommendation.

To Sister Rosa Lima, January 20, 1906

Los Angeles, Cal.

Dear Sister Rosa Lima:— Baby received your postal and is very much ashamed of his mama for being such a slow-poke about writing. He is very much interested in all the letters that come to the house. He insists upon reading them aloud at the top of his voice, sitting on the floor, and after he has read for a few minutes he hands them over for me to read a while, then wants them back again, so you see they are much perused. The dear little Christkindlein delighted him—he is very fond of pictures, especially of babies.

Now about those autographs of famous Japs. I wrote to Japan immediately upon receipt of your letter. But I don't say that you'll get them. In the first place, Mr. Noguchi is an ardent hero-worshipper himself, and he keeps a scrapbook in which are pasted the letters that various great people have written to him. I'm sure he couldn't cut off a signature for the world. And as for getting new signatures,—let me tell you a little story about Admiral Togo. It seems that when he first came home after the war he was besieged by letters and telegrams from all over the world, and the good man sat down patiently to answer them all by hand himself, until he found that practically all of his time was taken up with letter writing. So he hung a placard at the entrance of his house which read something to this effect: Admiral Togo, owing to a sudden paralysis of his right hand, is unable to answer the kind letters of his friends or to write his signature, —so you see there are difficulties. However, I am sure Mr. N— will do his best, and I hope you'll get some. He went to China in December and I suppose will be returning to Japan in a few weeks when he will find my letter awaiting him.

That was a mighty nice letter you sent me, Sister, and I was glad to hear about my old girls—So Helen Somers—what's her new name?—has a boy too! Bless him! And Mary Haines I remember well—I suppose she is charming and pretty as ever. How does little Sister Inez keep up? Tell her when she wants to rest she should come to California, where life is a bit easier than back East. (And by the way, now I think of it, will you ask her to write me a letter of recommendation some day—at her leisure—forninst the day when I go back to teaching. I'll be greatly obliged.) We have been having a glorious shower—about three days of steady pour, which is the rarest treat in California—and my sweet peas have all popped their heads out of the ground—I have planted sweet peas and strawberries in my garden, likewise lettuce and onions and other luscious things.

Good-bye for to-day.

With love, Léonie Gilmour Noguchi

Léonie's initial plan for "a little trip across the Pacific Ocean" did not prove successful. Perhaps the meetings with the Kojimas were not satisfactory, or there were other unforeseen complications, perhaps her mother objected to her going; perhaps she found she and Florence could, after all, live in the same household. In any case, she most likely did not have the $150 necessary for even a second class ticket. Léonie had been unable to collect money *The Theatre Magazine* in New York owed Yone for two elaborately illustrated articles published in July 1904 and January 1905. Yone finally told her the magazine was "Dam" (the harshest word in his vocabulary) and that she should just give up. He continued to appeal to her to come to Japan, but he now recommended she wait until fall.

From Yone Noguchi, January 28, 1906

Koishikawa, Tokyo

Dear Leonie:

You must be wondering why I did not write you—I was in China as I told you, and had been at Shanghai. Alas me! I did not take my address book and unfortunately I forgot your address. Pray don't accuse me of my carelessness! I am always that. I wrote a letter from Shanghai but I could not mail it. On returning to Tokyo three days ago I received your letter with one cheque on amount of 39 yen. I thank you for that.

Leonie, this is a very important letter, and so you must consider carefully, and answer me. Some time ago I suggested you of your coming to Japan. And again I am thinking of it. And I believe it would be better for you and our baby of course. Why? Because I can help in bringing up the baby, and he can escape from being a fatherless child. And it is an important thing I believe. And also I believe it would be easier for you to make living here in Japan. You must be a school teacher and work as a company. School business is not hard here, and we respect a foreigner unduely to my thinking, and it is one advantage for you. Japan pays to a foreign teacher more than any Japanese teacher, and I think if you don't mind to teach, say, using your before-noons and it will be sufficient for your living. Don't you want to do that? The main thing to consider is about our baby. I wish he will grow brightly and happily. I was wrong in past, and I repent greatly, and I wish to do for him. Will you bring him over to Japan? And I will get a job in school or company for you,— oh, well, we will talk the matter over when you will come to Japan. You consider this thing carefully, and let me know. I have some influence among the schools, and it will be easy enough to get such a job for you. Remember, the main thing to consider is about the *Baby*. I am making money enough to support myself and a little house, but not enough to send money to you and keep the child in America. I am thinking that it would be better to bring up our child together. I think it would be wise to decide to come to Japan. Suppose you be in America? I think no good fortune will smile on you, and perhaps you are to live from hand to mouth, and—having the child as extra. Frank Putnam wrote me and said a bitter thinking of my turning out such a trifle newspaper stuff, and commanded that I will stop to do such a business. And I know that a writer's living is the most terrible thing—no matter to be a magazine writer or a book writer. I like to stop it—I must make money somewhere else. But it is not to say that I will stop to write anything, but I like to return to a poet, and to live in poetry. So you can not expect me to send you many articles hereafter, and naturally I will be far away from help- ing the child in a due form. If you come to Japan and don't mind to work four or five hours a day, we can solve our problem quite easily I think. We will work our salvation together. What do you think of it. I suffered enough, Leonie!

About the time when you should come? I should say anytime you are ready. But next Autumn—better. By that time our baby will speak some- thing, and he will be wiser than both of us. We have been fools, I think.

And about the transportation? Of course we cannot afford 1st class, and you come by so-called intermediate. It costs some one hundred dol- lars, and you get some money from the National for my articles and can you manage to get so much money? Write to me about this matter too. There's some time to exchange letter, and if you write me your decision, I will write you more immediately about the matter. I must get more money myself if you decide to come to Japan, and must furnish house, and buy some things. This is a serious letter, and you must think it over and over. Let me know—about your decision! If you think you can bring up the baby safely in America, and educate duely, and want to keep him yourself, I have nothing to say. You do what you please. But I wish I like to do something for him as his father. Answer me!

Yone

P.S. The Theater is Dam. Don't bother any more. The Theater is thief—that's all.

After writing Léonie, Yone turned his attention to Frank Putnam, whose December letter announcing the birth of his third son, Walter, he found on his return from China.

Yone Noguchi to Frank Putnam, January 29, 1906

81 Hisakata, Koishikawa, Tokyo

Dear Ever-hopeful Frank:

A few days ago I came back to Tokyo house from China. I believe I dropped a postcard to you from Shanghai—the maddest town of the Far East, the Chinese Chicago. And Behold! here is your letter dated Dec. 4th, which caused such a great joy. Another boy, Frank! My best wishes to Mrs Putnam as usual! Whenever I read your brief letter, I drink the wine of inspiration and courage. Write me as often as you can. I am weak sometimes, and must have your brotherly blessing and advise. How sane and how courageous you are, Frank! I trust in your opinion and in your heart. You are the Japanese Eastern wind which makes flower smile. And let that wind blow toward Japan—the Tokyo home! *Surely your letter makes me a better man.*

*   *   *   *   *   *

I must be thankful to you as you taught me many wisdom and a lesson of humanity. I was greatly mistaken in past. I am full of repentance nowaday. What you wrote about Mrs Noguchi is right to bottom. I must obey to what you think right, and I must follow gladly after which I must do according to Humanity. *I was young*, Frank! you forgive me, will you? I am afraid that you might think me worthless. That's another thing! If you think so, *let it go!* I am wiser and truer today. What I want to write you and ask your advice—is this. I want Mrs Noguchi come to Japan. I had been thinking about the matter for a long time. I must do something for the child to begin with. Mrs Noguchi must have suffering—perhaps more than she can bear. Yes, I know she is the best and true. I am beginning to appreciate her, and Frank, I was blind. In one word I was young, Frank. I like to join with Mrs Noguchi. Yesterday I wrote her saying whether she will come to Japan or not. And I hinted that she must work four or five hours a day till I will build myself solidly in Japan, and make money enough. Today my name is greater than my real income—here in Japan. I think there will be two or three years yet till I will see myself comfortably in financial affairs. And I don't think she mind that. As today she is working hard (in fact she was a hard worker in past) she will not mind to do that also in Tokyo. I returned to my senses and wisdom. Frank, what I want you to do is—will you be a go-between for my own sake. Mrs Noguchi might say "No", if I write her to join me abruptly, and so I wish you will tell her my own thought and determination. I believe that our re-union would be better for the child. Mrs Noguchi is a sweet woman, but she does not like any crooked action. I cannot force on her, and must respect her thought. I wrote her simply that it would be better for the child and her own living to come to Japan. But I mean that we will join our hands again if she will come to Tokyo. Will you write her about it? You are the best man to break such a new for my sake. I have no other good and trustful friend, and you know everything about the matter.

And I am sure you will endorse what I decided now. Only if such a decision did come earlier! You believe me—I suffered enough from my own action and nightmare. I like to be on the right road. Will you help me out about this matter? I am sure you will.

Write Mrs Noguchi immediately, will you?

*   *   *   *   *   *

As you say, I will devote myself for a better work hereafter. I will stop to turn out such a trifle newspaper stuff. If Mrs Noguchi will come to Japan and work a little bit, I believe that we can bring up the child splendidly. It would be better to unite our force together for the child. Don't you think so, Frank? My family don't speak English except myself, but have no objection. And on the contrary my brothers say that I must do what is right since I was a man in public. *They hate shame.* Tell Leonie that I am growing wiser and older!

I received notes from dear Paul and Thad. They must be happy and curious having a little baby-brother.

*   *   *   *   *   *

I am always asking you too much to do. But this thing you will do gladly, I dare believe. I hope you do it for humanity's sake, and also for your Yone's sake. Here in Japan Spring began already. We have the famous plum-blossoms already blossoming. A week ago we had such a great snow storm, I am told, but today the things are bright as can be.

Let me wish you again a happy New Year!

Yone

Léonie had written Yone on January 12 suggesting a way to sell his new volume of prose poems, *The Summer Cloud*, on commission. In his next letter, Noguchi rejected the suggestion, then returned to the question of Léonie's coming to Japan. It had been almost two weeks since his "very important letter"—not long enough to receive a reply. Perhaps under the influence of Putnam's inspiring letter, he was prepared to go a bit farther in his promises to Léonie. In his previous letter, he had spoken only of the practical benefits of their reconciliation, and the advantages to the baby. Now he was prepared to go farther: "I will be true to you, and be a good father to our baby, I promise that, Leonie," he declared.

Frank Putnam at home in East Milton. *Keio University.*

From Yone Noguchi, February 10, 1906

Dear Leonie: Your letter dated Jan. 12 here, and I think I must talk it over with my publisher—about sending the copies to Parker to have them sold on commission. The publisher does not like to send the copies on risk, and they wish the American store-keepers will buy them with cash money. I thank you for your taking much trouble for it.

* * * *

By this day when you receive this letter—you have read what I wrote to you in my last letter. And very likely Frank must have been writing to you what I wrote his about our future plan. I suggested that you must work a few hours every day if you come to you [*sic*], because I can only make money enough to keep me decently, that is to say, I make some eighty yen a month—but if you will come to Japan, you may not be able to stand our Japanese living immediately, and so it will be expensive. So I say you must try to make some money yourself to make our household go.—Of course, till the time when everything will be on the right road. I came home only one year ago—with a few disadvantage I cannot open the wings fully. So we will try to work together, and bring up our baby handsomely. What do you think? Come to Japan, will you? I will be true to you, and be a good father to our baby, I promise that, Leonie. I wish Frank did send you my letter to him—I wrote him everything I think about my matter today. If you come, when can you start—write me immediately.

Second-class passage—one hundred dollar, and some twenty dollars to San Francisco, and you must have some thirty dollars beside—I think. I am sure you may not be able to raise that mount [*sic*]—can you? Frank will give you some fifty for my article in three or four months—and then we have to consider the other one hundred.

And I wish you will come in August (but it is pretty hot in Japan). Well, any time when you are ready—I should say. Write me as soon as you can.

Yone

This second letter had not arrived when Léonie replied to Yone's "very important letter." At this point, when Yone had reached the apex of enthusiasm about the plan, Léonie began to have serious reservations. This was not just a casual jaunt with Baby across the Pacific. Her reply to Yone was nothing like the note she had sent to Catharine a month earlier with the casual comment that "yes, we are really going to Japan." She had been impressed by Yone's promises and attracted by the prospect of a return to teaching. But looking at the plan more critically now, from the new office at the top of the Slavin building in Pasadena, where she had recently been appointed assistant to the editor of *The Raven*, she could now think of a long list of arguments against the plan.

The editor of *The Raven* was Theo Lowe, a well-groomed youngish man who favored high-collared shirts and pince-nez spectacles. He had recently moved to the Southland area from San Jose, taking rooms at the posh Maryland Hotel, one of the social centers of Pasadena, and setting up his California Publishing Company in the new four-story Slavin Building. *The Raven* had run for several years in San Jose; Lowe believed it could be much more successful in the rapidly expanding new metropolis of Los Angeles. He was looking for talented staff and authors willing to work for a share of the profits, as he intended to run the magazine on a profit-sharing basis, having, he explained, invested all his money in it. Those who were interested in joining him as investors had a chance at even larger dividends when the magazine became profitable. Lowe was particularly looking for women contributors and staff, as the magazine would be designed to appeal to a growing population of women readers.

Theo Lowe. *The Raven.*, 1904.

The Maryland Hotel. *Illustrated Souvenir Book,* 1903.

From the office overlooking the pleasant town of Pasadena, composing her reply to Yone on *The Raven*'s crisp blue Editorial Department stationery, Léonie no longer felt the sense of urgency she had recently felt about the trip to Japan. Perhaps if she had received Yone's most recent letter, with its promises to "be true" to her and "a good father to our baby," and the supporting letter Yone had begged Frank Putnam to write, Léonie might have responded less emphatically to Yone's proposition. But the fact remained that Yone had never once said he loved her, and she felt she was doing them both a favor by turning down his invitation as decisively as possible.

Former Slavin building (now the Col-Fair Building). *Edward Marx.*

To Yone Noguchi, February 24, 1906

Pasadena, Cal.

My dear Yone—
I have read your letter—yes, several times. Of course you understand that I want to do the *very best* for baby, and as for wanting to keep him all to myself, why that is nonsense. I am only happy to share him with you. But whether it were wise to leave California at present and to go over to Japan—that is a question—I am *very doubtful* about it.

Listen: America is a good country, California in particular. Baby is well. He is happy. Though we be poor, he does not suffer from it. Maybe our way of living is not quite civilised—we live in a tent, where rains and wind come in at will—Baby has no shoes on his feet. He runs free as a squirrel on the hill side. Does it matter, our way of life? Roses are glowing on his cheeks. We built a little California house of one room beside the tent. There my Mother lives. And there I took Baby in on the day it was finished. He was like a caged bird lazily looking to door and windows for a way to escape. He does not like house: nor shoes.

He is growing like a flower under the sky. Shall I take him out of this beautiful green country to put in an ill-smelling city like Tokyo, where rains are incessant and winters are harsh? Wouldn't he turn into just a pale little Japanese boy? No, no, if I come to Japan, it must be to Kioto or some southern part of Japan. Such a change would not be too sudden. And education. Education is free here. I do not think much of "school" myself: I could myself teach him everything he would learn in school. I dare say the schools in Japan are not much better than those here. But there is an education *outside* of school; that I understand. As far as the aesthetic side of life is concerned, I suppose Japan may be far superior to here. For the moral training and character? I do not know. I believe there is much that is rarely lovely and precious in Japanese character (I have read "Bushido")—also some defects. No doubt you could help me to guide him aright. You will understand him. He is more like you than me.

Many a time I have thought, "Some day I will go over to Japan when Baby is five or six years old. Then I will have a little money, and better able to shape our life." I would like to put him to an Art school somewhere, where he will have eye and hand trained to express his idea—No matter if he become artist or not. I would like, if he shows ability, to train him as actor—something he must do different from our life. And still—all those things he could perhaps have here. What will my mother do if he goes away? She has become greatly attached to him. It would be the hardest thing to part now. And you talk of "social position" and "money." Let me tell you at once that everyone here is glad to make much of your son. And I can earn an existence wherever I be, I suppose, though it is different always to get a footing in a new place. Better in Japan? Oh, I don't know. And it is a minor question.

And you Yone! You like to return to be a poet, and to live in poetry. Very well! You will stop writing articles. Very well! And you must find some other business and then you will attend strictly to business, and be good man and citizen and father. And of course you will be happy(?) being so very good. Of course it is more important to be good than happy. But how about your poetry? Where will you find it? In business? In the crowding cares and responsibilities! In the companionship of a wife you *do not love*? Why? Because Frank Putnam thinks you should? Because of awakened thought of responsibility toward your boy? Maybe you think you will make amends for the past. Past is past, you *cannot* amend it. Maybe you think we, Baby and I, need you, we do not. Therefore I think it better we live apart. If I have chance to have work in Southern Japan someday I will come. And you can see Baby all you like. And we will have a proper separation when you get ready—and you will remarry according to your better and riper Judgement. Baby and I have each other to love. Yes, that's better.

(I am learning to be editor now. I'd like to start a magazine of my own when I come to Japan. That is more interesting than school.)

Léonie

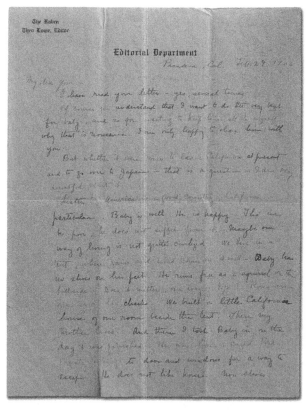

**First page
of Leonie's
letter to Yone.
*Isamu Noguchi
Foundation.***

In March, Léonie was surprised to receive a letter from Charles Warren Stoddard, who was hoping to visit her and "the little one" in the future:

From Charles Warren Stoddard, March 11, 1906

San Jose Sanitorium

Dear Mrs. Noguchi,

Yone has written to me, giving me your address and asking me to write to you. I am only too glad to do so, but you may not care to hear from me or perhaps will not care to acknowledge this, either, but I hope you will.

Did we meet in New York, I wonder? That whole experience was to me so distracting that most of it seems to me a horrible dream. Not for worlds would I live it over again. But I shall be glad to see you and know you and the little one, by and by when I go to Los Angeles. I wonder if I may—may I?

Yone's last letter to me is very sweet and sad. The tender spirit of fatherhood seems to have descended upon him and he writes as if he were lonely and regretful of much that has happened in the past. So are we all, I suppose, or so we should be. You know Yone and I were very close to one another. He was my "Kid," my "Poet-child." He called me "Dad"—and does so still. He says in this letter: "Since you are my father you must be a grandfather to my baby." Of course I shall be glad to. God bless it, and you!

I wonder if you have any thought of joining Yone in Japan? I have thought of it sometimes; I have hoped that perhaps next year I may be able to visit him and see a little of Japan and write of it—a book, it may be. Of course all is uncertain. I have no definite plans, but may go to Santa Barbara toward the end of April and to Los Angeles later on.

I wonder if you have a photograph of yourself and the little one? How I should love to have one! What is his name? The above address will reach me for a month. A permanent address is c/o Bohemian Club, San Francisco.

I am truly your friend, C.W. Stoddard

Léonie was amused by Stoddard's letter and wrote back encouragingly, but Stoddard never made it down to Los Angeles.

There was also a letter from Putnam, who had written at Yone's request that he act as a go-between. Yone's second letter had done little to alter Léonie's resolve, nor did Putnam's arguments. Putnam premised his case on the idea that any woman could make a man happy in marriage. Having read Yone's apparently sincere plea for help, Frank could not believe he had no feelings for her (in an earlier letter, Léonie had evidently complained of Yone's "bitter coldness"). Frank also hoped Yone's confession of weakness might elicit Léonie's sympathy and forgiveness. As for the Yone's other women, perhaps Léonie feared Ethel would haunt Yone, but Frank was sure that she was out of the picture. ("Poor Ethel," Stoddard had told him, "She once wrote me a letter which for hellish fury I never saw equalled. I turned it over to Yone, and he destroyed it.") Frank was worried, however, that Yone was already considering marriage with a Japanese woman. But for all these seemingly persuasive arguments, Léonie had an answer.

To Frank Putnam, March 14, 1906

414 Slavin Building, Pasadena, Cal.

Dear Mr. Putnam:—If I believed what you say I would go right over to Japan and shake Yone good and *make* him love me. But I mistrust any generalization beginning "Any woman—" Honestly I do love Yone (I don't mind telling you now you have promised not to bother him any more)—simply I wish to do what is the very best thing and for once in my life I believe I have decided wisely. It is a relief to have a thing definitely decided anyway. Really I am not "good enough" for him. Voila! Unnatural modesty? Do you say? I confess the remark springs from an ingrained pride.

When I spoke about "the bitter coldness" etc. you understand I was drawing on my imagination a little. I do not remember Yone to have ever been anything but charming to me, though I must have tried his patience by dissolving in tears every time he spoke to me for the last few weeks of our acquaintance—I couldn't help it and I suppose my condition had something to do with it. No, he is naturally gentle and forgiving, far more so than I , and I have no doubt he would try to be nice as possible and to make the best of a bad bargain. But I would like him to have something better in his life than that. And I am too proud, I daresay I am too much in love with him to undertake his "reclamation"—you know it makes one feel such an idiot—and I never was clever about managing people—

I think you don't quite understand Yone—he is not fickle nor weak—he is no woman's fool—never has been and never will be— His faults are not in that direction. (I believe he cares more for you than any of us.)

Now just one word about *her* (I am awfully tired of all this, but might as well go on now I have begun.) I don't quite understand your allusion. Do you mean she would "nag" him? Of course that would never do. Aren't you prejudiced? You see I happen to be acquainted with her friend in Los Angeles—the one who first came to me from her—and I know she is a high minded woman—she did exactly as I should have done in her place—I have been thinking she might come to forgive Yone some time. He was not true to her—it seems to me that is a thing a woman can forgive—once. I know perfectly well what she could not forgive was his treatment of *us*—Don't you think if she understood that Yone has tried constantly as best he could to make amends for that, she might grow more lenient in her judgement? And if she understood that I have withdrawn entirely? Won't you please be fair and honest and tell me about her? I haven't liked to ask anybody else.

You think he will eventually marry some Japanese woman—maybe that would be best—I should feel terribly for a little while, I suppose—but I guess baby can comfort me for anything.

I just received a letter from Mr. Stoddard—rather mournfully sounding—I will send him a picture of baby to cheer him up. (And when does Master Walter have his picture taken? That is a sweet name—glad he is a little gentleman—By-Bye   Léonie G Noguchi

P.S. I won't bother you any more with *such* personalities. Poor Frank, Yone draws on you—and I—I wonder you don't "shake" us.

Léonie's refusal of Yone's invitation had not yet arrived when Yone sent another appeal, but it held nothing likely to change her determination.

From Yone Noguchi, [March 1906?]

81 Hisakata, Koishikawa, Tokyo

Dear Leonie,

I had been expecting your reply for my letter which was written some time ago. How did you decide? Come to Japan? Or stay in California? Did Frank write you about my plan regarding to the baby and yourself? I wish he did. I had been thinking well and deeply about the matter, and I came to the conclusion that we will build home together in Japan, and it would be better for our baby. Today I received your brief note. So you joined with some magazine. Is it a good one? Surely it cannot be much since it came out from Pasadena. However, I like the place very much, sweet, quiet and luxurious. Think our matter soundly, and I wish you would come to Japan. And help me to build the home. We will not starve if our hands are joined and work together, I think. My position of the Keio gijuku University is high one, but not very high in material way. I am paid three yen per one hour. Today I attend only five hours in week, but from April my hours will be increased. And I get some money beside. So you see I have barely enough for my living. But if you come to Japan, things must be changed better. And it will surely.

About Parker? I wrote him that he will write to Brentano of New York. We made Brentano our American sale agent. Didn't I write you about it? And about your offer which wished to have fifty copies. The publisher has some orders from London too, and he may not be able to meet your demand. I will talk with his tomorrow. If he will be able to send so much copies you wish, I will let him send you right off. The book is meeting a good reception in London. The other day one London bookstore ordered fifty copies, and Duchess Sutherland thirty copies, and so on. Brentano bought 300 copies. And perhaps we have no right to send you the copies directly, since Brentano is our agent. I don't know about it. What do you think? Perhaps it would be better to write to Brentano about the copies, and if you incline to put the advertisement you must have Brentano's name in it. We sold one copy for 40 cents to him, and I do not know how he sells. You must make its price one. Anyhow I will try to send you some copies if the publisher could share. There would be no special harm done to the New York book-store. If Brentano know that we send you some copies directly, he may get angry. So you must not. Anyhow we sold only three copies, and there's hardly any profit in them. And we must try to sell some more somewhere else.

I will send you two or three articles soon. But meanwhile, you send Frank my Japanese Literary men article with these pictures. He will like the article, I am sure. Write me, will you? Of course, you must let me hear about your decision.

Yone

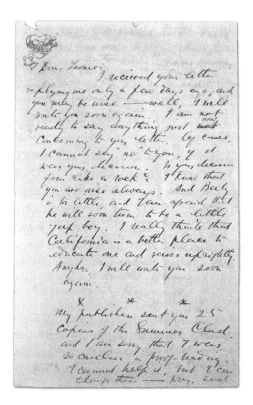

First page of Yone's letter.
Collection of Edward Marx.

After an unusually long delay, Léonie's letter of February 24 finally arrived in Tokyo. Though it must have seemed to Yone a slap in the face, he accepted it with Zen-like calm. It seemed that he could never amend the past; Léonie and the baby did not need him, and if she came to Japan, she did not wish to live with him. Though he had some doubt as to whether her decision was "firm like a rock," and thought it best to continue his efforts to persuade her, there was a palpable sense of relief that he had done his best and she had rebuffed him.

From Yone Noguchi, April 2, 1906

81 Hisakata, Koishikawa Tokyo

Dear Leonie:

I received your letter replying me only a few days ago, and you may be wise—well, I will write you soon again. I am not ready to say anything just now concerning to your letter. Of course, I cannot say "no" to you, if it was your decision. Is your decision firm like a rock? I know that you are wise always. And Baby is too little, and I am afraid that he will soon turn to be a little Jap boy. I really think that California is a better place to educate one and raise uprightly. Anyhow, I will write you soon again.

My publisher sent you 25 copies of the Summer Cloud. And I am sorry that I was so careless in proof-reading. I cannot help it, but I can change them—pray, send me your copy with pencil mark. I will send you one more copy, or keep one out of these 25. I was meaning to write you before, but I was in fact waiting for your reply. Here I have your answer. I will write you some again—so long, Just now.

Here is my article about China being the print of my journey. Will you send it to Frank? And also you send Sadda Yacco article to him with these illustration or pictures. The Japanese Literature article also. Frank will like the Chinese article, I am sure. You will approve it too. What magazine is it—you say you are going to edit? Raven—I never heard it—is it one of Pasadena magazine? I like Pasadena very much. Such a cozy and warm place. I like myself to be there again at Pasadena and other Southern Californian place. I like them immensely. I am glad that Baby is doing nicely. He will be a great boy, I am sure. Send me a copy of the Raven when you are ready! When my article will come up—the Girls University article? I expect to send you one or two more articles. I am tired by some other Japanese work nowaday. I am in the Spring holiday now. Write me soon, will you?

Yone

To Frank Putnam, April 3, 1906

414 Slavin Building, Pasadena

Dear Mr. Putnam:—

My mother says Walter is a remarkably beautiful child, and she is a connoisseur in babies, having assisted at the birth of several scores of them. (She is an ex-nurse.) He has certainly a most expressive little face— and he knows his papa, which is more than could be said of Yo San. May he and his daddy always be the good friends they look to be at present!

Thank you for the poem. Do you know I like it better than the one published in the April National. My mother also liked it—says there are *ideas* in it. I confess the sort of poetry I like best is that which makes me slightly drunk—and I find ideas to be not a necessary ingredient in producing the divine intoxication, in fact they have a sobering effect. I like your prose editorials *immensely.* "Isn't he somewhat of a socialist ?" queries Mama. "So is everybody who is not a pig," I retort. Me too, Mr. Putnam, tho I'm too lazy to work out anything.

Here is something of Yone's about the Japanese novelists. A whole lot of pictures to go with it under separate cover. By the way haven't you still something of his about the Younger Japanese poets? I don't want to swamp you.

Think I'll put in this sketch about a little girl who loved babies. You can send it back, you know.

By-bye

Léonie G. Noguchi

From Yone Noguchi, April 6, [1906]

Dear Leonie:

I received your letter of March 10th and I am glad Baby is all right. And about the copies of the Summer Cloud. The publishers sent you 25 copies the other day, by this time I am sure you got them all right. The publishers have not many copies left, but I will see them in a day or two, and if they can secure me more copies, I will let you have more of them. Our arrangement with Brentano you understand. It would be better. I think you would get the copies from the New York Store. It would be more honest, and business-like, I think.

Of course, you know, Leonie, you are wiser. You do what you think right and good. I cannot persuade you, this matter especially you know. Yes, you must consider about Mother, of course. Yes, you do what you think right. Or let the matter stand for some time as it was—I think. Then we can judge the things better, and we may have more wisdoms, and see our way clear.

I will send you more article. And you take some money out, and send me the rest. I am not living extravagantly, but always money is short. I must work little more, anyhow, but just now with money business I can not try to get the place where I found more money. That is not necessary to explain to you. It is pretty hard to stop at the higher place with a little money. Such a trouble is eternally same in any age and any place. It would be foolish to complain anyway. I like to see your magazine, how it does look like—is it good one? Stoddard wrote me that Nancy(?) O'Neel one of the famous actress will come to Japan in June and she will come to me. She is going to study the Japanese acting and other things, she likes to have some tragic drama of Japan, and doubtless think I can furnish here something. I will try if she will come. She is growing great in last few years. (I am giving one copy to you with my name in intending to give to Miss Randolph.) So long,

Yone

P.S. But Leonie, if you could come without feeling any trouble and pain, come to Japan. If Japan will not suit you and baby, in a year or so you can go back.

From Yone Noguchi, April 9, 1906

Dear Leonie:

You send this to the Boston Transcript and New York Globe. Can you print it in the Los Angeles Times? Doesn't it pay? I am hasty in writing, and have no time to read it over, but I am sure the article is all right. It is a good one for one sense.

Can't you send me a copy of your Raven or Black Crow? I like to see what a magazine it might be. I will send you my article whenever I feel and have something to write-up. And we will continue as it was, I think. I think it might be better. You do what you think right. Japan is a poor country to make money, as you know, but the foreigners are exception. The white people make two hundred while we Japs one. For the last thirty or forty years we had been treating them in that style, but we cannot change it now. Then they get benefit no matter who they are. Did you get the copies of the Summer Cloud? I remember that I forget to put "Pasadena" in the address. I wrote only this, I remember: "To the Pasadena Publicity Co. California". If the stokes [stocks?] did not reach to you, you might ask the postmaster of San Francisco. You attend it, will you?

I like to get some money every month from America, if possible, and so I will send you my article pretty regularly, I think.

Yours in haste,
Yone

On April 18, 1906, Los Angeles residents woke up with the shaking of a mild earthquake. It soon became known that the center of the quake had been more than three hundred miles north, near San Francisco, and that much of the city had been damaged. News of the earthquake was followed by news of the terrible fire that subsequently destroyed much of the city. The economic losses were staggering. San Francisco had been California's leading city; now much of it had been reduced to smoldering rubble. Noguchi, learning of the quake, wrote to Léonie again on April 22.

From Yone Noguchi, April 22, 1906

Dear Leonie:

Are you safe from the Earthquake? We hear much of suffering of S.F. but not about your town. I am sure you are all right. I am afraid that Mr. Stoddard might have been suffered, since he was in San Jose. Write me quick about the Earthquake matter.

And still I am thinking how to answer to you. I will write you in a few days my definite answer.

And meanwhile, here is my article for Frank. He asked me to write up Oyama, but I have no material. Some time ago I wrote for the Sun about Marchioness Oyama, and that article was good. I am sure Frank did not read it. And if he did, that's no matter. I made the article entirely new adding some head and tail to it, Marchioness Oyama is more interesting than Marquis himself. So my Marchioness article, here it is. Will you send it to him—typewrite—don't send it as it is! And you may change it as you please.

Send me a copy of your magazine I like to see it. Frank asked me to write up over Mikado. Then my work will be done for some time. Two days ago I sent you one article for Transcript and Globe. Did you get it? How Frank did like my Chinese article? Wasn't it good? I believe it was. How is Baby? I will write you soon. I feel terribly sleep just now. I go to bed.

Yone

I send Marchioness picture with the article. Send it too to Frank.

In May, *Good Housekeeping* magazine carried a short article Léonie had written back in January describing her views on feeding an infant. For a new mother, Léonie sounds remarkably authoritative.

Nursery Menus for a Week

Good Housekeeping, May 1906

In making these selections I have had an eye to the requirements of my own baby, now fourteen months old. There is nothing in the list that could injure a child of one year or older. I have chosen for breakfast such dishes as require little trouble in preparation.

Pure olive oil is a delicate and nutritious article of food whose use in feeding children is becoming recognized. A little poured on hot toast, or baked potato, is hugely relished by my baby.

I give honey to the baby in small quantities, spreading it thinly over a piece of bread that has been dipped in milk, or adding a half teaspoon to a bowl of cereal and milk.

Prune marmalade is made by straining well-cooked prunes through a colander. We live in a land of figs and honey, and I have found the pulp of fresh, ripe figs a light and digestible fruit. I do not recommend the dried figs as a substitute, though the juice of stewed figs is very good.

To make onion soup, put equal parts of butter and olive oil in the bottom of a saucepan. Slice an onion into this and fry a delicate brown. Add water and cook for one-half hour. Salt to taste.

Strain it over thin slices of stale bread.

A Scotch mother will tell you there is nothing like parsnips "to make bonny bairns plumps and fair." In preparing parsnips cut them lengthwise through the tough inner core, cook thoroughly and mash through a colander. Serve with olive oil or butter, or both.

It is best not to serve milk at the same meal with grape juice or orange juice. At other times when thirsty I give the baby a little hot water and milk (cambric tea). He drinks plenty of water between meals, and has a bottle of milk and water during the forenoon, with another in the afternoon.

The menus

Breakfast—Cereal with milk, buttered toast.

Dinner—Strained vegetable broth with bread steeped in it.

Supper—Baked potato with olive oil. Juice of orange, sugar and crumbled bread.

Breakfast—Cereal with honey and milk. Ripe fig.

Dinner—Soft cooked egg with crumbled bread. Grape juice and water.

Supper—Baked apple with cereal and cream. Bread and butter.

Breakfast—Toast with olive oil. Soft cooked egg.

Dinner—Barley soup and rye bread.

Supper—Bread dipped in milk and spread with honey. Boiled chestnut. Cambric tea.

Breakfast—Cereal with milk. Bread and prune marmalade.

Dinner—Soft cooked egg. Sweet apple sauce.

Supper—Mashed parsnips with olive oil. Bread dipped in milk.

Breakfast—Oatmeal with cream and sugar. Piece of ripe sweet apple.

Dinner—Strained spinach soup with crumbled bread. Prune marmalade.

Supper—Whole wheat bread spread with cream cheese. Sponge cake dipped in juice of stewed figs.

Breakfast—Cereal with milk. Bread. Ripe fig.

Dinner—Onion soup with crusty bread. Mashed potato with olive oil.

Supper—Boiled rice and milk. Crust of rye bread.

Breakfast—Oatmeal with milk. Toast with olive oil.

Dinner—Tomato bisque with crackers. Coffee cake.

Supper—Mashed parsnips with olive oil. Grape juice.

After some new advice from Frank, Yone, in his next letter, returned to the question of whether Léonie should come to Japan.

From Yone Noguchi, May 5, 1906

81 Hisakata, Koishikawa, Tokyo

Dear Leonie:

Yesterday was a great day in Tokyo. We welcomed the families of those dead soldiers in Manchuria, and we are trying to do the very best for their pleasure. Here is my article which should go to the Transcript and New York Globe. They would like it, I am sure. I sent you two articles for Frank's magazine, and also two articles for the Transcript and Globe, I am sure you got them. I must write up two more articles as soon as possible. The day before yesterday I received your letter and one copy of the Raven. What name? I do not quite like such name for the magazine. Never mind! Does the magazine go? I hope so.

I considered carefully over the matter which we have been talking lately. Frank Putnam wrote me that I must give you up. Really I do not know what I will answer to you. One thing is sure—I do not love Miss Armes today. She has been rather careless or mean to me for some time. She is clever, doubtless. She has no interest in me, and also I have not. Everything is done, and over. And about your coming over to Japan? And this matter is sure if you can build yourself up nicely, and be happy in California it would be useless and unwise to come over to Japan. I am rather doubtful to give you every comfort and pleasure in Japan. And you must understand that here you have no way to make living except in school for Americans. Everybody is doing that. We have no English paper in Tokyo, except one Japan Times. And two or three English papers in Yokohama. And they have not many circulation, and they are running between eight hundred and one thousand five hundred. There's no room for one to make a decent living in any English paper. The articles which were written for them are not paid. And so on. So to be a school-teacher is only one way here in Japan. If you do not like to do it—well, it would be a hard case to solve. I think, Leonie, it would be wise to wait—when we are doubtful. In due time, we may solve, I think, our problem better. Today I have no definite idea. I cannot ask you to come to Japan, when you are doubtful, and I am not positive in offering many opportunities and happiness. Wait! Only wait, when we are not sure to do things right. "Wait," as Miller used to say. We may come soon to a better wisdom. Meanwhile, we will love Baby, and try to do our best. And I think just now it, would be wiser to keep up things as before. I will send you articles which are salable and good. You will place them as I tell you, and get some money. The arrangement between you and me would be same as before. You keep some portion of the money we make, and send me the rest. I must tell you how I stand here in Japan. I am much honored—a great deal more than I deserve. But when I come to money matter, I am still far from satisfaction. Japan is a pretty hard country to make money. The pay which my school pays me is not enough for my living. Of course my hours I attend in school are only five hours a week. The budget of the school could not allow to increase my hours this time. I told you it would come so in my last letter. And no pay for the Summer vacation, you know. I must make some money somewhere else. But my name is too great, and I can not tackle any job which comes to my way from my present position. So it is too hard on me, but

I just stand bravely where I am today. I think it would be easier to make money in America, and I will return to my article writing. I wish you will send me money whenever you have for me, of course, taking out the part off it for yourself. I will try to send you three or four articles every month. Frank will take mine pretty regularly. Yours or mine, as he says always. And also the Transcript. And we will try to invade in the better literary magazine hereafter. I am going to make out some short stories, regular Japanese short stories, you know. If I can start well! In that way, some thirty-dollars, or even twenty would help me for my living. And if that (such an arrangement) would help you, it could be, then better for us both. I am sure, "wait", is wisdom, till we come to a better decision. I hope that we will keep up as we were before.

If you have money from Frank, send me before July, that is to say, when you get this letter. Our vacation will begin with July, and I need money. And also send me—send to *me* those book money, but not to the *publisher*. "We will wait—yes we will wait to do anything definite". What you say, Leonie? I like to read Miller's *City Beautiful*. If you have a copy of it will you send it to me? And also I like to be sent Harper's or Century's regularly. Can you attend to it? It is the hardest thing to get any American magazine here. I will send you a pretty good Japanese short story, pretty soon, you will see what it is. Wait, wait, only wait, when we are not positive with anything. "Wait" so Miller and Stoddard say. It would be better for us to wait. Meantime I will send you articles, and you send me money. I need some help from somewhere every month. Be happy, Leonie. I respect you.

Yone

P.S. Don't the Los Angeles papers pay for articles? If they do I like to write a regular Japanese letter for them. Will you talk it over with some paper?

There was still no resolution to the question of whether Léonie would come to Japan. "I wrote Leonie and she replied," he explained to Putnam on May 14, "and the matter between us is standing still,—I can assure you that it would not advance worse than it was. I believe that soon we will have settled it—better, I hope. I feel a great responsibility and I will take it over my shoulders."

Both Yone and Léonie were playing for time. Yone, for all his talk about shouldering responsibility, was content to have Léonie editing and managing his American literary projects again and did not actually press her to depart. "Only wait," he counseled, quoting his old mentor, Joaquin Miller. Léonie had said she was not interested to live with him, suggesting he might marry someone else. In the time it took her to decide, he would not be going against her stated wishes if he investigated other options. And Léonie was in no rush to leave her interesting new job at *The Raven*.

But Léonie's boss, Theo Lowe, was also playing for time. After two months there was still no sign of a paycheck. Léonie was content to go on waiting, but her coworkers were not so tolerant, and on May 23, 1906, one of them, a Mrs. Anna F. Martin, angry that Lowe "had taken the funds of the publishing concern and used them for personal adornment and hotel bills at the Maryland" while failing to pay his employees, had him arrested on charges of embezzlement.

As police and reporters began to investigate, it soon emerged that this was not the first time Lowe had run into trouble with the law. Theo Lowe had started *The Raven* in Oakland with a woman named Mary Lambert in 1899. Lambert had left in 1901, but Lowe continued running it until the spring of 1903. A few months later, allegations of financial irregularities began surfacing in San Francisco newspapers. In September 1903, he was arrested after a woman "alleged that Lowe obtained $200 from her by representing that the paper was a profitable investment." The case had been dismissed. The woman and her husband then threatened to kill Lowe, so he had them arrested, but the charges against them were also dismissed. The following June, another disgruntled former employee, an eighteen-year-old boy named Porter, was driven to extremes; this time Lowe was clever enough to have the boy arrested for a postal law violation when he sent an "insulting letter" to Lowe, addressed to "The thief editor of the Raven fake." At the hearing, Porter broke down in tears when told he would be sent to jail unless he posted a $500 bond. "Porter stated that he had worked for Lowe for six weeks as stenographer and typewriter and that Lowe had refused to pay him his salary, which was at the rate of $35 per month." A mere three weeks later, an Oakland woman had charged Lowe with swindling her. He had told her "if she paid him $150 he would appoint her his stenographer and proofreader at $35 per month and give her a share in the profits. He alleged that he had $2800 invested in the paper and had a large subscription list." A warrant had been issued for his arrest. Lowe left the city.

Lowe moved to San Jose, opened an office on Santa Clara Street, took rooms in the posh St. James Hotel, and brought *The Raven* back to life in Oct. 1904. Again, he found literary contributors willing to invest in the stock of the company and stenographers willing to work on promises of future pay. He canvassed local merchants and approached the San Jose Chamber of Commerce with schemes for regional development. But he eventually fell into disfavor once again, and came under threats of violence from an unpaid stenographer's father. Thus *The Raven* had ceased publication again in 1905, and Lowe had continued south to Pasadena, setting up shop again in early 1906.

The writers at the *Los Angeles Herald* laughed themselves silly telling how the "dapper little light of the Crown City's social world," unable to pay his bail, was led by a deputy constable from his "nice bed at the Maryland . . . to a bed of boards at the county jail." Nor could they spare much sympathy for the aspiring women writers and office assistants who had worked for months without pay. "Any woman who thought she was an author was eligible to enter the partnership" so Lowe had been "beseiged [*sic*] on all sides by women who wanted to show how they could wield the pencil."

Los Angeles County Jail. *California Historical Society.*

At the end of the *Herald*'s article, however, it was conceded that Lowe, "a convincing talker and apparently much in earnest in his schemes, . . . has worked hard for years to put his magazine on a paying basis, and so far as is known, never made any money for himself. Although always living at the best hotels and dressing well, Lowe has not reaped any profit by his literary ventures, and often told the dissatisfied stockholders that he stood to lose all his money as well as theirs. Some friends still cling to him and assert that the man is simply a victim of the game of business chance."

Léonie, of course, was one of the victims "who wanted to show how they could wield the pencil," and could not finally bring themselves to blame Lowe. Like the others, she lost a good deal of money which she would never recover. Yone's skepticism about *The Raven* had been justified. Lowe had not, in the final analysis, been the best person to teach her the business of running a magazine, except as a warning of some of its perils. Léonie had enjoyed the use of the Slavin Building, and the free stationery. But her financial situation was now dire, and the tent house would soon need to be replaced. Her comment to Frank that little Yo would have to go without strawberries for a while was a severe understatement.

Lowe's fall from grace had cast Putnam in a more favorable light: she now thought him "the best, truest friend, to take so much trouble" over Yone. In the *National Magazine* for May, Léonie had been interested to read Ethel Armes' article profiling a young newspaper illustrator named Haydon Jones. Ethel's journalism seemed out of Yone's league, she told Putnam, but perhaps Ethel had the qualities Yone lacked, and she still had thoughts of reconciling the two of them.

To Frank Putnam, May 27, 1906

> Letter box Cor. Stephenson Ave. and Camulos St.,
> Los Angeles, Cal.

Dear Mr Putnam:— I am glad you returned the China article directly to Yone (if it had to be returned) with your valuable suggestions.

I realize very well that his political essays are not what you might call the impartial judgement of the historian. He looks for the picturesque, and for effect. Also his style lacks the crispness, the terseness, the array of facts to set off his theories, which are considered proper to such journalistic work. I do not like to be always criticising, and how could I have the face to? since I have the same faults, and realize how difficult it is to change one's mentality. (Facts and figures always elude me, sorry to say.) Besides, I never know how criticism is going to effect [*sic*] him. He is quite capable of plunging headlong to the other extreme, and producing an awful list of dry facts. (Baby is like that, too. His zeal is something to reckon with. When I scold him for getting in the mud he is just as likely as not to jump into a washtub full of clothes with his own clothes all on.)

You are the best, truest friend, to take so much trouble.

I saw the very fine article of Miss Armes in your May National. She is a woman of big brain, undoubtedly. Her journalism must make Yone despair. How could he ever reach it? That is not his field. A few weeks ago I suggested to Yone to write an article on Japanese cartoonists, with some first rate illustrations. I had in mind somewhat such an article as that one upon Mr. Jones. Will he do it?

It may be she has the qualities which he lacks. I am sure she is a brave spirited woman, to rise above her own trouble. I have a certain scheme in my mind, to bring those two together—Now don't you interfere, you! (I admit that all the well-meant sophistries which you offered me to salve my wounded feelings went "in one ear, out the other.") I have my own ideas upon the matter, and Yone I think will understand me.

# # # #

This world is full of trouble. The other day I went to jail, to visit our editor, who has just been put in there on a charge of embezzling some of the company's money. Poor man! In just two days he had become an old man. His face was drawn and thin, and terrible wrinkles had formed across his forehead. Whether he is guilty or not I do not know. I know he has made a fearful struggle these last few weeks to meet his obligations. I would not have put him in prison for the $60. he owes me. Some member of the company did it, who is not poor. I have no idea that they will shoulder the obligations which they prevented him from paying. I miss the money which I had counted on for my salary—little Yo will have to go without strawberries for a while—I am selling the sweet peas out of my garden to make a little money—Those things do not worry me, however—but I dread the thought of going on a witness stand—Poor Mr. L—Even if he is a liar I really hope that he will wriggle out.

I am awfully busy these days—what with picking flowers for the market—and doing some typewriting for Mr. Georgis (He is a young Greek playwright whose play I have just revised—I will write you about him someday) and codgelling my brains for thoughts upon the subject of "Engaged Girls" in answer to a most polite request from "Good Housekeeping"—they said they were writing to the "brightest and most wide awake" among their contributors for material—ahem!—the days are flying away—carrying my youth, alas! Some gray hairs are shining among my brown.

Yours faithfully,

Léonie Gilmour Noguchi

Léonie must have had a good laugh over being targeted by *Good Housekeeping* as one of the "brightest and most wide awake" potential contributors on the subject of "Engaged Girls."

Sister Rosa Lima had sent several postcards addressed to "Master

Yone Noguchi." Around the beginning of the summer, Léonie wrote her to tell her of the failure of *The Raven* and her success at growing potatoes ("praties" in Irish parlance). She had been helping a local Greek immigrant playwright, Peter C. Georgis, with the English translation of a play, *Golfo*, she was confident would soon be in theaters. (The play, a conventional romantic tragedy, had a limited run in San Francisco three years later).

To Sister Rosa Lima, [June? 1906]

Box Cor. Stephenson Ave. and Camulos St.
Los Angeles, Cal.

Dear Sister—

Yo was very much amused by your postal cards. Evidently he thought you didn't know his mama if you thought she knew how to write letters. And he thinks all the pencils belong to him. Ink? You can't keep a bottle in reach at all at all.

I've been quite busy since I wrote you, helping to edit a magazine called The Raven. Unfortunately The Raven came to grief. Our editor was accused of misappropriating the funds of the company, was put in prison for a few days, and then the case was dismissed for lack of sufficient evidence. But it killed the bird. California is full of tricky people and business honesty is not understood here as it is in the East.

And still the question of my crossing the Pacific this summer is undecided. It is largely a matter of funds. Mr. Noguchi was disappointed in his expectation of obtaining a better position at the university where he lectures a few hours weekly—they are poor as every institution in Japan since the war, and he is feeling rather discouraged as the shabby remuneration in every line of work in beautiful but pathetically far Japan. So in the meantime we just stay in California and grow and grow, and water our garden and watch it grow and grow. It is very warm here now. A fierce wind from the desert blew all day yesterday. 99° in the shade. And the more it blew the hotter it grew. The garden drinks greedily all you give it. We have the finest praties you ever saw. And Yo eats praties more like an Irishman than a Jap.

I met recently the President of a Japanese orphan asylum who was traveling here for the purpose of raising some money. Would you believe it, Sister, $2.50 is considered a sufficient sum to keep a little Japanese orphan in food and clothes for *one month*. My boy drinks that amount of milk alone.

I meet some interesting people here—one young Greek playwright and poet, Peter Georgis by name, whose play "Golfo" you will probably see staged.

Excuse this scrawl. It's too hot to get at my typewriter. I'm glad you like the National. Frank Putnam, who does a good deal of the editing of that magazine, is a friend of my husband's and mine—a man of fine character and principles, I should judge.

Best love to the people of St. Aloysius

Your Friend

Léonie Gilmour Noguchi

While Léonie's *Raven* adventure was coming to its bitter end, Yone was organizing his own magazine project, a bilingual poetry magazine in book form, entitled *The Iris*. He sent Léonie a copy in June, thanking her for sending *The Dramatic Mirror* of February 17, which contained his "Sada Yacco" article.

From Yone Noguchi, June 8, 1906

Dear Leonie.

This is the first number of my magazine of poetry which has to be out quarterly. The Japanese part is filled with the best work of our best younger poets, and the English part is as you see. I like to know how you like my poems in it. A few days ago I received your letter which says of Baby's illness, and today your post-card (which was the view of Majestic Theater) and one copy of "Dramatic Mirror" and I suppose that our Baby had recovered entirely. Frank returned me (here in Tokyo) that Chinese article which I thought good and interesting. Frank is queer sometime, but never mind! He is the best soul which I came cross. We must be thankful for him always.

So happy dream yesterday I received letter from Duchess Sutherland and also from Rosetti [*sic*]. They are ever so kind to me, and give me suggestions and sympathy. Tell me what impression you have on this Iris. There are three pictures and many English poems and so some people might wish to buy it. Will you ask your Los Angeles book-seller about the magazine. The price is 50 cent., postpaid.

Why you sent me the Dramatic Mirror so late? Did you not see it before? Did the magazine pay you any? I feel that a magazine work is damnation as ever. You don't get money regularly, and it is so little when you get it. We must give it up sooner or later. Are you still connected with the Raven? It is not worth keeping with I think, but if you like such a magazine work you must find it somewhere else.

Summer is coming, and the vacation comes soon. The worse part is that I cannot get money from School during summer, since I am paid for hours. I must expand my business more, and if not, I cannot live decently. To have too high honor is entirely nuisance, isn't it? By the way, you remember that once I translated the Melon Thief, and it was acted by the students of my University the other night for an enticement, and it was such a success. I feel quite proud of it.

Write me some good news! I received letter from my San Francisco friends. And none of them got hurt. I am so glad of that. I will write you soon.

P. S. Send me the book money to me directly, when you are ready.

Yone wrote again on June 22: "I did not hear from you for some time, but I believe that you and Baby are all right." He hoped Léonie could send the money due him from his Sada Yacco. "I expect to be pretty hard-up in this summer vacation, since I do not get a cent from my school." The request came at an awkward time for Léonie, since she had recently lost her anticipated salary from *The Raven*. To make matters worse, Putnam, their only reliable source of income, had seemingly vanished.

It was August before Léonie heard from Putnam. A note among his letters states that he had been hospitalized for a hernia operation; he had also left the *National*. In his absence editor Joe Chapple, the editor and publisher, had accepted Noguchi's "Marquis Oyama and His Wife," which appeared in July 1907, and Léonie's children's story, "The Ways of Mirabel and Dousabel" which appeared in October 1906.

To Frank Putnam, August 8, 1906

American Engineering & Foundry Co.,
433 Mateo Street, Los Angeles, Cal.

Dear Mr. Putnam:—

I'm mighty glad you're getting along so well. One advantage of being sick is that you get a whole lot of time. I expect to see a crop of ballades fluttering among the autumn leaves—of the magazines. And you have time to get acquainted with Walter. (I hardly see Yo nowadays, as it's sleepy time when I get home from work.) Say, he got ahead of Yo in the matter of teeth. Why, Yo had his first tooth at nine months. I was rather worried about his slowness, until an ancient dame quoted an ancient nursery rhyme to the effect that our baby got his first tooth on the ninth day of the ninth month, or something like that. Yo has Twelve toofins now, all wonderfully strong and white. Yes, he is just as sturdy as his pictures, though they make him look bigger than he is. And far less handsome! Imagine a yellow peachy little face, with cheeks of brightest roses, browned with curly yellow hair, and lovely limpid brown eyes. That is Yo's coloring at present. A little boy said: "that" would be a pretty baby, if he hadn't such a funny nose. "What's the matter with his nose?" said I. "Why, don't you see, it goes into his face." He has a sweet little nose, just right I think.

I'm working in a big iron foundry, supposedly stenographer and assistant bookkeeper. The man asked me if I was quick at figures, and I said I was—So I am—I can slide down a column of figures as if it was a greased pole—Alas, I can slide down seven different times with seven different results. So I don't dare to leave a column until I get at least two results alike, Which makes it *seem* as if I was slow. And I do occasionally make mistakes after all. Yesterday I made three. One a trifling matter of $2000. The second was when I left $13.65 in a corner by itself and forgot to take it in. The third was a matter of 4 cents. The head bookkeeper endured all in patience until it came to the 4 cent one. "Those," said she, "are the errors that count." I expect every day to be fired on account of my lack of figurative ability.

My noon hour is pretty nearly up.

Yo has learned to throw kisses nicely, so you can imagine he is throwing you one. He frequently throws some to the moon, and if they can reach the moon I guess they can reach you.

Léonie G. Noguchi

My love to Walter and to *Mrs. Putnam*

Address: Box Stephenson Ave.& Camulos St., Los Angeles.

P.S.—By the way, Mr. Chapple wrote me nicely, and said he would print "Oyama" and also my little story which is to make you laugh—may it be soon, but not sooner than you are able to endure the cac-Hination (is that long enough for that word?).

Léonie had sent a picture to Matsuo Miyake, who, weary of waiting for Léonie's letter, was ecstatic. "My dearest Sister:—" he wrote on August 31, "Can you imagine how glad I have been extremely to-day on the arrival of the picture of my dearest sister and Babe smiling among the summer flowers? I have examined again and again to find out some note in the envelope, but in vain. But I consoled myself thinking there can be nothing as eloquent as the smiling picture." "In truth," he continued, "my heart, the all of my being, has been pulled to the warm Southern Califor-

nia where I might be a member of our smiling assossiation, whose president is charming Babe." He was surprised to see the new house. "When
did you leave your poetical tent life?," he wondered. He reported that
since entering the *Mainichi* newspaper office he had been "very busy with
the *Fude* (brush you remember)" and was well satisfied with his new occupation. In his apare time he was "intoxicated in continuing my course
in composing a novel named 'Tsuyu Gusa', the Flower of Dew. The novel
will come to the finis on the scene of the farewell of Tsuyu-ko and her
lover, an American youth[,] to Yamato, setting forth to sail to the Southern Ocean for seeking the ever-spring Islands, where they might live and
died in love, an eternal love."

"Are you not desirous of coming to Kyoto, fourty miles away from
Osaka?" Miyake inquired. "At present I may be able to assist you of your
getting some situation in a school or college. Will it not be delightful to
live in a Nippon no Iye, a Japanese residing house, together, you and I?!"
Miyake's last postcard, sent on June 17, had offered a glimpse of such a
house, with the explanation: "Such is the country cottage where Matsuo
writes. My wife Chrysanthemum on the *Engawa*. She loves Isamu too."

"Baby among the sweet peas enjoying the breeze and sunshine" (Léonie's
inscription), circa 1906. *Isamu Noguchi Foundation.*

Matsuo Miyake's June 17, 1906 postcard. *Isamu Noguchi Foundation.*

On August 29, Sister Inez at St. Aloysius wrote, "I am sending to you and to those you named the recommendations asked for." And in September, Stoddard finally replied to Léonie's December letter, which had been misaddressed and temporarily lost in the chaos of the earthquake.

From Charles Warren Stoddard, September 12, 1906

Monterey, Calif.

Dear Madam Leonie,

Your letter is so bright, so jolly, so hopeful—and so mis-addressed, I hasten to reply and put you on the right track. Tomorrow will be a month since I arrived in Monterey where I hope to make my home. Nothing could please me more than to see you and Yone and the wee one all together in Japan. What you write of the Boy makes me love him and covet him. I hope you are keeping one of those kid chronicles in which all the quaint and clever things he says or does are recorded. Are you? If you will, some day you can make a fascinating book of it. This Baby Boy is to be like no other Baby Boy in all the world. Mark my words and heed me! Please let me know, when you can, the day of your departure. Can you take with you some of Yone's scrap books, left behind?

Merry Christmas to you and Cheerio. Aloha

C.W. Stoddard

Sometimes I am not frivolous—perhaps.

**Charles Warren
Stoddard.** *Bancroft
Library, University of
California, Berkeley.*

It was probably a combination of many factors that finally overcame Léonie's reservations about going to Japan. Frank Putnam had continued to press the estranged couple to reconcile ever since becoming convinced of the truth of Léonie's story. Yone's attempts at persuasion, though not always convincing, were also continuing. If Yone's efforts were some- times lacking in warmth, the same could not be said for Matsuo Miyake. "Dearest Sister—" he wrote on October 10, "Why are you so lingering in your coming to Japan. Nara, the ancient Miyako, is waiting for you. It is a most poetical place. And Autumn is in her full dress there!" And then there was the situation in California. The earthquake had left lingering clouds in the land of sunshine, and it had also led to increasing racial tensions in the state.

In October 1906 the San Francisco school board acted to exclude Japanese and Japanese-American children from the city schools, setting off an international incident that dragged on for nearly a year. Boycotts of Japanese-owned restaurants and scattered acts of violence against Japa- nese visitors and immigrants were largely ignored by the police. The inci- dents set off angry reactions in Japan. The California exclusionists, more determined than ever, engaged in a frenzy of legal theorizing in search of a legal formula for Japanese exclusion that could withstand constitutional challenge. President Theodore Roosevelt's well-intentioned but heavy-handed interventions aimed at controlling the California state legislature helped fuel the controversy. In the end, Roosevelt had his way, making 1907 the watershed year in Japanese-American immigration policy by negotiating the so-called Gentlemen's Agreement, announced on February 15, in which he persuaded the Japanese government to voluntarily block the emigration of Japanese labor to the United States. In return, the San Francisco school board was persuaded to accept the Japanese students.

Although most of the actual agitation took place in the San Francisco bay area, it was much discussed in the Los Angeles press and, indeed, around the country. Although the *Los Angeles Times* took a moderate view, siding with Roosevelt, the other major papers of the city, the *Herald* and the *Tribune*, both supported the exclusionists. During the agitation, the Los Angeles school superintendent refused a request from San Francisco to institute a ban on Japanese students, which he thought "wholly unnecessary." If the city had adopted the policy, Isamu might have been forced to attend a segregated school for Asiatic children, as San Francisco's Chinese children were.

Although Los Angeles was as sunny as ever, Léonie must have been aware that the climate for Japanese immigrants had become considerably less welcoming. Enthusiasm for the "little brown men" in their valiant fight against the Russian bear had been succeeded by vague fears of Japan as a new Yellow Peril, threatening American interests in the Pacific and even the security of the west coast.

But it was a new, less widely-noticed law that would have the most devastating impact on Léonie and other women in international marriages like hers. Known as the Expatriation Act of 1907 or the Perkins Law (after the xenophobic California senator, George C. Perkins, who sponsored it), the bill, which passed the Senate in February, a week or two after the Gentlemen's Agreement was announced, was ostensibly aimed at resolving various problematic cases of international citizenship, including cases of international marriages. The law represented a belated attempt to bring cases under a single federal policy, where previously they had been left to the discretion of individual states. The applicable provision in the new law dictated that a woman's citizenship in such cases would be assumed to follow her husband's: that is, foreign women who married American men would become American citizens as long as they continued to live in the United States, and American women who married foreign nationals would be regarded as having expatriated themselves to their husband's nationality. Such women would therefore, automatically lose their American citizenship, and could regain it only by petition upon termination of the marriage. Though it had some advantages for foreign-born women and the American men they married, the new law was a clear reminder of the subservient status of American women, who still lacked the voting rights to voice their objection to it. The new policy would place Léonie in a very awkward position: as the supposed wife of Yone Noguchi, she was already in violation of the state's anti-miscegenation statute; under the new law she would also lose her American citizenship. Unless she could claim Japanese citizenship through her husband, a very doubtful proposition in her present situation, she would be left a woman without a country. Alternatively, she could admit that her marriage had no legal basis. If she did so, of course, she would lose any hope of social respectability. Perkins, an aggressive supporter of California's exclusionist laws, hoped the new policy would discourage the white women of California from marrying Asian immigrants.

Léonie's financial troubles had forced her to return to office work she disliked and for which she had little aptitude. The arrest of Theo Lowe had spoiled her dream of being an editor, and she had lost a much-needed $60. Frank Putnam's disappearance from the *National* also had dire effects on the extended Noguchi family, as editor Joe Chapple seemed to have no interest in maintaining Putnam's stable of contributors.

The letter in which Léonie conveyed her change of heart to Yone is now lost, but it was probably written in July, for on August 6, Yone casually mentioned to Putnam that "lately Léonie wrote me that she will come over to Japan." He added that he thought she was acting wisely and that he, too, would do his best.

Léonie had left Stoddard's letter unanswered for many weeks but finally got around to replying in December, after receiving the December *National Magazine* which contained her second women's section short story, "Of Pride and the Fall" as well as Stoddard's longer but equally whimsical "Half and Half."

To Charles Warren Stoddard, December 6, 1906

111 S. Broadway, Los Angeles,

Dear Mr. Stoddard:—

I have just read your delightful fantastical bit of nonsense in this month's National, and am minded to write you a little note. I'm glad to observe that you grow more rich and mellow with age, like the landlady in the story—Is it possible you were ever "tearful Charley"? as I heard a lady once aver who knew you in the long ago. However, I can easily understand how an over-serious youth may lead to a kiddish old age. I was sad and serious myself in my young days—I have not altogether outgrown the habit, but there is still a little time for improvement. Sometimes I have thought you too frivolous. Really, Mr. Stoddard, I have had my doubts about you sometimes.

Have you recognized the handwriting of your correspondent by this? Turn the page and see.

I suppose you may have heard from Yone San that we are going over to Japan pretty soon—that is, if poor Yone can ever scrape up the price of half a ticket via the way of the steerage people. (I anticipate a little fun out of the trip anyway)

I quite agree with you that poets—at least some of them—were not made for domestic uses. So I shall open the door of the cage as soon as I get over there. I am going to make a little Japanese boy out of my son. Can you imagine that he has a top-curl of burnished gold? The Japs will have to get over their antipathy to red-headed foreign devil [*sic*] when he comes along. (By the way, Japanese people in this city are being rather nice to us. And I will find one friend in Tokyo when I go there, that is Miss Tsuda, who went to the same college with me, and in whose school I shall teach when I go over.)

One thing I regret is the nice long scolding elder-brotherly letters I used to receive from Mr. Frank Putnam in the days when he thought me an incorigible. Since I decided to do what he would call the proper thing he doesn't write a word. It is funny that one's friends always take more interest when one is a sinner and a rebel.

I'm so glad your address is at the head of your article, as it will save me looking over a bushel of letters, vigorously assisted by Mr. Baby, of course.

Baby—of course I understand that you understand that he is the topic of interest, is developing a great imagination. He likes to tell your fortune in a tea-cup. This is a specimen of his story-telling (out of the tea-cup): "I see a boy, I see a man, I see a dog, I see a cow top house catch Mama. Cold day. Moon all whet."

Good-bye, Mr. Stoddard. I hope you are good in your heart if you are frivolous in your writings.

Sincerely,

Léonie Gilmour Noguchi

Gradually, it became apparent that Léonie and Yone would have to get along without the advice and financial support of Frank Putnam, who had left the *National* and had not been heard of in months. Léonie wrote him on January 23, 1907.

To Frank Putnam, January 23, 1907

Los Angeles

Dear Mr.Putnam:—

What has become of Frank Putnam? Yone is asking, and I am wondering. Now I have given you a little rest from letter writing, it is time to begin again. Take, take up your weary pen, and answer me truly. Where are you? What are you doing? And where's your family? And at just what stage of infancy has little Walter arrived? And are you-all well? And are the trees budding back East? Pussy-willow time? or crocuses? Here it is a summer day. The sunshine so white it seems unreal. The mountains are carved out of snow. It is 100 feet deep in spots on Mt Lowe. But we don't know it in town. The streets are gay with a fresh crop of spring bonnets. But I hunt in vain through the shops for a large white flapping leghorn hat for my little niece in Tokyo. I am going to start pretty soon. In the meantime I am pegging away at my typewriter, gathering up the precious pennies just to throw them into the sea again for a bit ticket to cross that same. Yo talks wisely about going on a big ship on the great wa-wa to see Papa. If you ask him what is a ship he smiles knowingly, or points over to a shadowy corner, saying: "See, cunning little ship!" He has the art of never being surprised or taken unawares. The funniest thing about telling a funny story before him is that he always laughs loudly before you get to the point of the story. He is "Johnnie on the spot" every time.

Do you know my address in Tokyo? I daresay you do. Am I glad or sorry? Really, I don't know. Call no man happy until he is dead. And I can't tell you if I like it till I get there. Yone's letters are ominous, to say the least. He warns me not to bring any "dreams" with me. Oh, well, I am tired of trying to do anything with him. I guess Baby Boy and I will take care of each other.

I've quit writing at your august command. Tho' the sequel to my tent story came out in the December number of the West Coast Magazine under the title "A Little California House." By the way, the West Coast folks are rather a nice sort. A Mr. McGroarty, who writes poetry that has the real flavor, is their biggest name and chief editor of the magazine. "Isn't Mr McGroarty a little bit Irish?" I asked. I like him so much it seems to me he must have some Irish in him." "McGroarty, a little bit Irish? Why, he's all Irish" said my friend, and that accounts for the feeling of kinship mingled with admiration of your humble servant for a more distinguished member of the clan.

I am sending this to East Milton, because I have always felt dubious about the New Orleans prospect, and you may be anywheres under the sun, so I guess you'll get it this way.

With love to you-all

Léonie Gilmour Noguchi

Léonie's passport photograph, 1907. *Isamu Noguchi Foundation.*

Tokyo, 1907-1911

In 1910, Noguchi sent off a story about Isamu's arrival in Japan to be published in two prominent magazines, California's *Sunset* and the London *Nation*. Frank Putnam also printed it in his *Southwestern Farmer* magazine with a preface recounting Noguchi's marriage with "an American woman of gentle birth," the romantic poverty of their marriage, and how Noguchi returned to Japan and "presently . . . sent for his wife." And Noguchi subsequently included the story in his 1914 collection of autobiographical essays, *The Story of Yone Noguchi*. The story was essentially the same in all of the versions, and can be considered the official account of Léonie and Isamu's arrival, at least outside of Japan: a public declaration of their relationship, serving as a literary proof of marriage in the absence of any legal documentation. Significantly, it did not appear until their formal separation, when Léonie moved south of Tokyo to Omori in 1910.

TOYO KISEN KAISHA, 6000 TON, TWIN SCREW, STEEL STEAMER "AMERICA MARU."

The *America Maru*.

Isamu's Arrival

The arrival of my two-year-old boy Isamu from America was anticipated, as it is said in America, with crane-neck-long longing. And this Mr. Courageous is now landed in Yokohama on a certain Sunday afternoon of early March, when the calm sunlight, extraordinarily yellow as it happens to be sometimes, gave a shower-bath to the little handful of a body half-sleeping in his "nurse carriage" and doubtless half-wondering with a baby's first impression of Japan, many-colored and ghostly. Now and then he opened a pair of large brown eyes.

"See papa," Leonie tried to make Isamu's face turn to me; however, he shut his eyes immediately without looking at me, as if he were born with no thought of father. In fact, he was born to my wife in California some time after I left America. Mrs. Noguchi attempted to save me from a sort of mortification by telling me how he used to sing and clap his hands for "papa to come" every evening. I thought, however, that I could not blame him after all for his indifference to father, as I did not feel, I confess, any fatherly feeling till I, half an hour ago, heard his crying voice for the first time by the cabin door of the steamer before I stepped in; I was nobody yet, but a stranger to him. He must have, to be sure, some time to get acquainted with me, I thought; and how wonderful a thing was a baby's cry. It is true that I almost cried when I heard Isamu's first cry. I and my wife slowly pushed his carriage toward the station, I looking down to his face and she talking at random. I felt in my heart a secret pride to be his father; but a moment later, really I was despising myself, thinking that I did not pay any attention to him at all for the last three years. "Man is selfish," I said in my heart, and again I had to despise me.

I learned that Isamu made the whole journey from Los Angeles sitting like a prince on the throne of his little carriage; he even went to sleep in it on the steamer. He was ready any time to cry out whenever he lost sight of it; it was the dearest thing to him, second only to the bottle of milk for which he minted a word of "Boo." We thought that it would be perfectly easy to take the carriage with us on board the train, as we could fold it up; but the conductor objected to our doing so as it belonged in the category of "breakables." And we had to exclaim, "Land of red tape, again." Isamu cried aloud for "baby's carriage" when the train reached the Shinbashi station of Tokyo; we put him again in his carriage and pushed it by Ginza, the main street. And there my wife and baby had their first supper in Japan; Baby could hardly finish one glass of milk.

It was after eight in the evening when we took the outer-moat car line toward my house in Hisakata Machi—quite poetical is this Far-beyond Street, at least in name—wrapping baby's carriage in a large *furoshiki*; it may have been from his kindness that the conductor did not raise his voice of objection. But afterward, when we had to change cars at Iida-bashi Bridge, we met again a flat denial to our bringing it in; and we had to push it some one mile more of somewhat hilly road under the darkness. A few stars in the high sky could not send their light to the earth; the road was pretty bad, as it was soon after the snow, though our Tokyo streets are hardly better at any other time. And it was a rather cold night. It goes without saying that my wife must have been tired nursing Isamu all the time through the whole voyage; he had been seasick, eaten almost nothing. Where was the fat baby which she used to speak of in her letters? It was sad indeed to see Isamu pale and thin, wrapped in a blanket; and now and then he opened his big eyes and silently questioned about the nature of the crowd which, though it was dark, gathered around us here and there. His little soul must have been wondering whither he was bound to be taken. And we must have appeared to people's eyes quite unusual. It was no larger than a dying voice of an autumn insect when baby suddenly asked mother where was his home. I am sure that not only Isamu, tired Leonie too wished to know where it was. I think that it was not altogether unreasonable for baby to keep up crying all the time; I was rather suspicious from looking at Leonie that her heart also wanted a heartful cry from the heavy exotic oppression whose novelty had passed some time ago. *"Karan, koron, karan, koron"*—a high-pitched song which was strung out endlessly from the Japanese wooden clogs on the pavement, especially in the station, had, I believe, the most forlorn kind of melody whose monotony makes you sad; and I dare say Isamu thought that the Japanese speech might be a devil's speech—in fact, it is, as one of the earliest Dutch missionaries proclaimed. I noticed he raised his ears at any chance to hear it. (By the way, he has come already to handle now this devil's speech so far. My writing was interrupted a while ago by his persistence in Japanese to take him to see his Japanese aunt; he is quite happy here as he can have aunts as many as he wishes.) And still he did not stop his cry even after his safe arrival to this Hisakata Machi home, and it tried my patience very much, and I did not know really what to do with him. He cried on seeing the new faces of the Japanese servant girls, and cried more when he was spoken to by them. I got a few Japanese toys ready for him, a cotton-made puppy among them as I was told a dog was his favorite; but he could not think that they were meant to amuse him and not to hurt him, and the dog did not appear to him like a dog at all, but as something ugly. And he cried terribly. *"Okashi!"* One of the servants brought a piece of Japanese cake, but he cried the more, exclaiming, "No, no!" The cake did not look to him like a cake, to be sure.

The night advanced; a blind shampooer passed before the house playing a bamboo flute. Isamu, though he was sleepy doubtless, caught its music, and jumped out from his little bed exclaiming: "Andrew, mama!" A man by the name of Andrew Anderson, Leonie explained, used to call at his California home almost every evening and sing to him in a sweet high Swedish voice. For the last month since the day of his departure from Los Angeles, his poor head had been whirring terribly through nightmare spectacles. Poor Isamu! But I felt happy in thinking that he was just beginning to feel at home even in Japan. "Baby, where are you going?" I asked him, when he was making his way toward the front door; he stood still by the door, and caught another note of the shampooer's flute, and again cried most happily: "Oh, Andrew, Andrew!" However, he was sad a few moments later, not seeing any Andrew come in; and he began to cry. But sleepiness overtook him immediately; and I found him soon sleeping soundly in his own bed.

When two or three days had passed, he stopped crying, although he was yet far from being acquainted with his Japanese home, of course. I found him trying to find something in the house which might interest his little mind. There are many *shojis*, or paper sliding doors, facing to the garden; they have a large piece of glass fixed up in their centers, over which two miniature *shojis* open and shut from right to left; and they caught his interest. He has been busy, I was told one day, opening them and shutting them again since morning; when I saw him doing it, he was just exclaiming: "Mama, see boat!" It was his imagination, I think, that he caught the sight of a certain ship; he was still thinking that he was sailing over the ocean on the steamer. Surely it was that. When he stepped in the house, I observed that he was quite cautious about tumbling down; it was very funny to see his way of walking.

It was the fifth day when he earnestly begged his mother to go home. "Where's Nanna?" he asked her. His grandmother, who still remains in Los Angeles, was called by Isamu "Nanna"; he began to miss her a great deal, as she was the dearest thing next to his mother. When Leonie answered him, "Far, far," in the baby's speech, he repeated it several times to make him understand, and he turned pale and silent at once. He was sad. "Baby, go and see papa," my wife said to him; he slowly stole toward my room, and slightly opened my *shoji*, when I looked back. He banged it at once, and ran away crying, "No, no!" I overheard him, a moment later, saying to Leonie that I was not there. I must have appeared to his eye as some piece of curiosity to look at once in a while, but never to come close to. However, I was not hopeless, and I thought that I must win him over, and then he would regard me as he did his mother. In fact, I was three years behind.

Isamu noticed that I clapped my hands to call my servant girls, and they would answer my clapping with "Hai!"; that is the way of a Japanese house. And he thought to himself it was proper for him to answer that "Hai" for my hand-clapping, and he began to run toward me before the girls, and kneel before me as they did, and wait for my words. I was much pleased to see that his growing familiar with me was quite rapid. And he even attempted to call me "Danna Sama"—Mr. Lord—catching the word which the servants respectfully addressed to me. It was too much, I thought; however, I could not help smiling delightedly at it. My wife could not be so wonderful as to be familiar with the Japanese food at once; but I found that baby was perfectly at home with it some time ago. I discovered when he quietly disappeared after our breakfast that he was enjoying his second Japanese table with the servants. When they objected to him one morning, I overheard him exclaiming: *"Gohan, gohan"* (honorable rice). His love of Japanese rice was really remarkable.

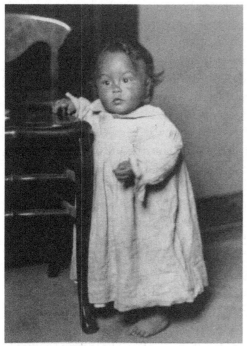

Isamu, circa 1907. *Isamu Noguchi Foundation.*

Every morning, when an *ameya,* or wheat gluten seller, the delight of Japanese children, passed by the house beating his drum musically, Isamu's heart would jump high, and he would dance wildly exclaiming, *"Donko, don, donko, don, don,"* and get on the back of a servant—any back he could find quickest—to be carried as a Japanese child. This *ameya* is indeed a wonderful man for children's eyes; he will make a miniature fox, dog, *tengu* or anything imaginable with wheat gluten for one *sen* or so.

At first Isamu seemed not pleased to ride on the girl's back; but soon it became the most indispensable carriage for him. It is ready for him any time to begin with; and the Japanese girl's large *obi* tied on her somewhat bended back makes a sort of comfortable seat. And the funniest part is that Isamu thinks that the girl's back is called *"Donko, don, donko, don."* As our servants did not know a word of English, they could not express their invitation to get on their backs, and it happened, when one *ameya* passed by, that one of them acted as if he were being carried on her back, repeating the sound of the ameya's drum *"Donko, don, donko, don."* Isamu caught the meaning on the spot and jumped on her back. And afterward, this *"Donko, don, donko, don,"* became a most useful word. When the girls say it, showing their backs, he thinks it proper, and even courteous, for him to get on them; and he will hunt a girl, repeating it, when he wishes to go out pick-a-back. And, again, its usefulness grew still more a day or two ago; he started to use it even when he wished only to go for a walk. I heard him saying a while ago to Leonie: "Oh, mamma, *donko, don, donko, don!*"

He showed a certain pride in learning even a few Japanese words which could be understood by the people round him. And he has made it his own office to sit down like a Japanese and say *"sayonara"* when a guest leaves the house, and he is happy to do it. He shouted *"banzai"* for the first time the day when my brother brought him two paper flags, one of them being, of course, Japanese, while the other was an American one. "You Japanese baby?" Leonie asked him. "Yes," he replied, turning to me. And when I asked him how he would like to remain as an American, he would turn to my wife and say "Yes." Indeed, I wish he will grow up as an American as well as a Japanese. He was the cause of no small sensation among the Japanese children of this Koishikawa district at least; his foreign manner and Western tint, and also the point of his having a Japanese father, made him a wonderful thing to look at for the children around here, while they felt some kinship with him. The fame of Isamu spread over many miles; even a *jinrikisha* man far away will tell you where "Baby San" lives, although Noguchi's name may mean nothing to his ear. The children think, I am sure, that "baby" is his own name, and whenever they pass by our house morning or evening, they will shout loudly "Baby San." And Isamu will rarely miss a chance to run out and show himself to answer. Why, this little fellow is quite vain already. And the children who caught the word of "Mama" spoken by Isamu to his mother, thought that it was Leonie's name. I am told by her that she was frequently startled by a shout of "Mamma San" from behind on the street. To be the mother of "Baby San" is not at all bad.

I feel happy to see that he began to play with the Japanese children. We have a little play called *Mekakushi;* many children will make a large ring with their joined hands and choose a child to let him stand in the middle of the ring with his eyes covered with his palms. *Mekakushi* means "eyes hidden." The child at the center will walk to the ring, and touch any child, and tell its right name; and then the child who was told its own name will take a turn to be in the middle. It happened one evening that our Isamu was obliged to stand in the center; it was clear to see his bewilderment, since he never knew the children's real names. But accidentally Leonie passed by on her way home; he took advantage of the chance at once and called out loudly: "Mama, mama!" I am not told whether my wife filled her duty to stand in the middle or not; however, we talked about it afterward, and laughed.

Our large oval wooden Japanese bathtub furnishes for Isamu one of the most pleasing objects. He will get in it even when the water is hardly warm; he does not mind cold water a bit. If I happen to see him in there, he will proudly let me admire his stomach, which is, in fact, big for such a little child; it is his proudest exhibit. He calls it "Baby's Bread-basket"; I cannot help smiling when I think that it was wisely named. And he will stay there such a long time playing that he is a tortoise. We have a little folk-lore story of a monkey and a tortoise; the latter was outwitted by the former when he attempted to get the monkey's liver. Isamu's mother told him of this story, changing the liver to stomach; the variation was effective, and it took his little heart by storm. A day or two later, when a monkey player dropped into our house, and made the monkey dance, he kept watching its stomach; and when it was gone, he was tremendously sorry that he could not get near enough to see it.

Isamu hates anything which does not move or makes no noise. When he has nothing new to play with he will begin to open and shut the *shojis;* when he tires of that, he will try to go around the house and hunt after the clocks, which I hid as they lost the right track of the time since he came. And presently I will send him away with a servant to the botanical garden to look at and feed the "Kwakwa," as he calls the ducks. He made a habit of playing with our shadows on the walls of the sitting-room after supper every evening. "Mama, shadow gone! Give baby shadow, mama," he will exclaim, sulkily, seeing his own shadow disappear. "Go to papa! He will give it to you," Leonie will say; then he will hunt for it, pushing his hand everywhere about my dress. "There it is, baby," I will say, seeing his shadow accidentally appear on the wall. How glad he will be. He is not pleased to go to bed if he does not see the moon. But I doubt if he has any real knowledge of the moon. When I say that he must go to bed, he will push a little outside door, and say that no moon is seen yet. Then I will quietly steal into the drawing-room and light a large hanging lamp with a blue-colored globe, and say to him: "Moon is come now. See it, baby!" He will be mightily pleased with it; a few minutes later, he will be found in bed soundly sleeping. Really his sleeping face looks like a miniature Buddha idol, as once Leonie wrote me long ago.

A while ago, our neighboring children passed by the house, calling loud: "Isamu San, Baby San, 'Merican San!" I felt quite proud, thinking that Isamu's popularity among the Japanese children was something wonderful. Isamu rushed out to the door to acknowledge their salutation, and I thought that he felt already some dignity as an American. And at the same time, he must feel quite at home with them. To be a Japanese-American is not a small thing here in Japan. To belong to two countries is far more fortunate than to belong to one; and if we have to choose one more country besides Japan, that country must be America. There is no other country like America, who we so admire and love with our sincerest hearts.

Any child appears wonderful to his father; so is Isamu to me. I confess that I made many new discoveries of life and beauty since the day of his arrival in Japan. I never pass by a store in the street without looking at the things which might belong to children.

No one reading the story of Isamu's arrival in its various American and British versions would have doubted that Isamu was the son of Yone Noguchi and his American wife—the woman named as "Leonie" and "Mrs. Noguchi" in the American magazine versions—though the latter name was changed to "Mrs. N—" in the British versions. In Japan, however—in contrast to most of Noguchi's autobiographical essays—the story was never published, either in English or Japanese.

The story of the arrival was publicized rather differently in Japan. Since his own arrival two and a half years earlier, Noguchi had been the subject of a good deal of attention in the Japanese press. "Those were the days of Noguchi's return to Japan," recalled an acquaintance who had witnessed Noguchi's much-discussed appearance at the funeral of Lafcadio Hearn: "the articles couldn't say enough, he practically monopolized the *Yomiuri*'s Sunday book page, and there was even some jealousy." Noguchi had left Japan as a penniless student and reentered as a literary star. His new friends, many of them prominent writers, were eager to find out what he had learned of the Western ways of love. In his poetry and essays, he wrote only in generalities, but he had been more open with friends. At least one of these friends was connected with the *Yorozu Choho* and managed to extract from him a fairly complete account of his love adventures by the time Léonie's ship docked at Yokohama. Meanwhile, reporters at the *Nichi-Nichi* and *Yomiuri* resorted to interrogating passengers on the *Amerika-maru* who had made Léonie's "love tale" a favorite subject of smoking-room gossip.

English Poet's Love Tale

American Woman Arrives, Yearning, Bringing Child

Yorozu Choho, March 5, 1907.

A rising literary star since his return from America a few years ago, the English poet known as Yone Noguchi, Mr. Yonejiro Noguchi, as everyone knows, spent more than a decade in places like San Francisco, Philadelphia, and New York. Tied together with a woman of a strange race, the eyes of another land also see only jealousy of seduction and gossip is also circulated and heard. But, be that as it may, among the passengers in an American ship that arrived in Yokohama port on the 3rd was an American woman carrying a single infant traveling the eternity of the great salt road without so much as a servant girl.

After the ship's departure from Seattle, the sight of Japanese fellow passengers seemed to make her very nostalgic. "Don't you know an English poet by the name of Yone Noguchi," she would ask every stranger she met, but having no guide and knowing little about the country's atmosphere, traveling the ocean road all the way hoping—these might also account for her passion. Such obedience of the heart brought out the pity.

Mr. Noguchi's friend, new-style poet Mr. Baba Kocho, in a conversation with our staff member, said, "I myself previously heard Noguchi was soon to greet his wife from America. And I've also heard his fiancée has a child, but whether the woman said to be coming this time is a different woman, or this other fiancée that I heard about, I don't really understand yet."

Then, to a staff member who called on him yesterday, Mr. Noguchi said:

"A telegram came on the morning of the third: 'Arriving at Yokohama: come quickly.' I looked in various places, asked various people whether this sort of woman hadn't yet come off the boat, then hired a small boat to go to the *Amerika-maru* and see. Embracing the child, I asked her, 'why on earth didn't you land?'

"'I thought it better to wait on the boat so as not to make a mistake,' she said, or words to that effect.

"Then we disembarked and took a train to Shinbashi station, arriving about five in the afternoon. We pushed the baby carriage with the child hungry for dinner, and returned home to 69 Koishikawa Hisakata machi.

"This lady born in New York, United States, is called Liyonie Biruma (31). Around the same time Ms. Umeko Tsuda was at Pru-Mawr University, she was at the same university. In 1900, I was in New York, when I issued a literary magazine, she (Biruma) was employed as a woman reporter. But since she has a style and manner not like an American lady, extremely plain like a Japanese woman, I also secretly admired her. Then one summer night for some strange reason I wrote Liyonie a marriage promise and went off to visit Washington. Returning to New York in November 1902 Biruma and I were together.

Yone Noguchi, Yoichi, Liyonie Biruma. *Yorozu Choho.*

"But at this time I developed a relationship with another woman who played music, Biruma and I finally had a discussion about separating, and going off to the newly-available mistress I concealed what happened with Biruma. After I returned home in 1904, however, the mistress, discovering the Biruma affair, became horribly angry and broke off her relationship with me."

"During that time, Biruma had moved to a back-country town deep in the mountains of California called St. Lucy [*sic*], gave birth to a child and lived there three years. When the child was born she notified me by telegram. We had once talked of divorce, but when the baby was born, there being no other way, I sent her a telegram calling her to come here. So, on the 7th of last month Biruma left San Francisco by boat with the intention of paying a visit, you know," he said.

And she also brought the child (a three-year-old boy called "Yoichi" for some reason). As for the tender-hearted poet, doesn't everyone do it this way?

Journey of Passion

Pining for Poet, American Woman Comes to Japan

Yomiuri Shinbun, March 5, 1907

On the morning previous to the fourth entered the port of Yokohama among the passengers of the *America Maru* the person of an American woman in the latter part of her youth carrying an infant of just three years. In spite of the public gaze that regarded with suspiciousness a young female leaving Seattle on such a long journey without even a servant girl to accompany her, her asking each Japanese fellow passenger one by one whether they could bestow on her some knowledge of an English language poet named Yone Noguchi quickly became the subject of conversation among all the passengers in the smoking room. There being nothing for it, approaching the time of arrival in Japan, among the Japanese, asking if there was any poet who could correctly write, even in katakana, the name of this person. And again among them the good people's gossip about whether the English poet had left the American woman could be heard, and furthermore, it was determined that this was indeed passion and "the horizon ten thousand leagues of distant waves," yearning for the Japanese person, came to be the subjects of various gossip. In any case, it appears likely that this woman was soon accompanied after the arrival at Yokohama to visit the home of Mr. Noguchi Yonejiro, or so it is said.

English Poet's Luck with the Ladies

Yone Noguchi and the American Woman

Tokyo Nichi-Nichi Shinbun, March 5, 1907

Poet prodigies, living for beauty, living for passion, have always everywhere been subject to slander for their immorality and dissipation; or on the contrary, this may be a complicated argument to escape the immorality of adultery. And as for that, even in the case of those who don't put on the air of a great poet, and are careless about the lack of flattery from closed mouths, there is something else. Yesterday (the 3rd) at the port of Yokohama on the Amerika-maru arrived from America one woman, a bit dark-haired but with one beautiful red-cheeked baby boy, and no other companion. On the way from Seattle, asking each Japanese in the ship, over-familiarly, at the first chance, such things as "is Japan a beautiful country" and "What sort of place is Yokohama?," it seemed that she was, with some embarrassment, trying to make sure that in the beautiful country of Japan there really was a poet named Yone Noguchi. Now those who know her and the curious are gossiping to each other. Had this woman, being shown the lines of Yone Noguchi's beautiful poetry, fallen even knowing that the brilliant poet was not sincere? Would the American rosebud blown by the east wind be shredded by the gale? Whether even the baby can possibly benefit, no one in the boat seems to believe. Someday won't a blonde beauty's shape turn up at the little brushwood fence of some "high-collar" writer in Yokohama?

Luckily, Léonie could not read Japanese, and was probably happily oblivious to this outpouring of salacious newspaper gossip.

After two and a half months in Japan, Léonie finally received a letter from Frank Putnam. Putnam, it seemed, had had enough of the east coast. He had burned his bridges by writing a long article entitled "What's the Matter with New England" for the *New England Magazine*, then packed up his family and headed south, where there was a job prospect in New Orleans. That had not worked out, so he continued southwest to Houston, where, impressed by the city's energy, he accepted an offer to work as an editor at the *Houston Chronicle*. Léonie was rather appalled by the idea of the Putnams living among Texas cotton fields ("Texas produces nearly one third of the total cotton crop of the United States," Putnam reported in another article for the *New England Magazine*). But Putnam liked Houston and the Texans liked Putnam, so the Putnams settled there, as it turned out, for good.

To Frank Putnam, May 19, 1907

69 Hisakata, Koishikawa, Tokyo

Dear Mr. Putnam

Your letter reached me today having been forwarded from America. It was about time you wrote. Yone and I were both worrying about you. Bad dear Frank! Now are you going to jump into a Texas cotton field? Don't you think at all about your poor wife and babies, who will be scorched if you take them, not to speak of homesickness, and sad if you don't. I'm sure the New England articles will be fine. We don't see the New England Magazine here. (I remember seeing your name in it in Los Angeles). Why don't you be its editor?

Yone and I don't fight. But as for Happiness with a capital "H" why I fear we are both too selfish, as you say. Yone changed so much I would hardly have known him—especially in the shape of his nose and the acquisition of a moustache. Yone seems to like the Boy tho he doesn't approve of his manners, which have suddenly flowered into a sort of wild Indian savagery amazing and dismaying (too much attention has turned his little head). Everybody calls him "Bo-chan" which is Baby-Lord, and I tell you he lords it over them.

It's rather lonesome here because everyone speaks a strange language which I fear I shall never learn. The mazy city streets (which are only dirt-roads) are all tangled up and I don't know which way is which. The trees are thickly planted and green things growing everywhere. There is an Exposition going on here and we have been. I like the old stone lanterns in Uyeno Park.

It is a snowy night—Baby is sleeping, so is Yone. I will send their love as I know they mean it. Good-night! Please write. And what about Bo-chan Walter?

Affectionately your friend
Léonie G. Noguchi

To Catharine Bunnell, Léonie affected a more cheerful manner, rarely revealing any sign that there might be anything amiss in her relationship with her husband. This must have been a strain, since Catharine was her closest friend, but Léonie could little afford unfavorable gossip among her Bryn Mawr circle.

To Catherine Bunnell, July 1907

Tokyo

My dear Catherine,
The sponge cake turned out splendidly. Omelet I haven't tried yet. Thank you for both—receipts I mean—collars too! Thanks!

We have just been to visit the Iwamura place, which is close by here. Fancy four acres in the city of Tokyo, part of it farm, part a veritable wilderness of forest trees and clambering vines, with a pond where the chorus of frogs sings loudly all the time, where the mournful cries of wild water birds rise frequently. The old Baron sits in his big house overlooking the city, crippled with paralysis, a devotee of iris culture and morning glory culture—he plants a thousand varieties of the latter every year. I am told that he is a heroic figure of the time of the Restoration War, and that he earned his title, not coming by it second hand. His son, Lieutenant Iwamura is my pupil in the study of English. Brave, chivalrous, yes also tall and fine looking from our Western standpoint, given to every athletic sport—and a lover of poetry, perhaps versed in the ancient Chinese poetry as your brother in Greek. I confess he is my favorite pupil. And why not? If I mention morning glory seed, they are forthcoming. Singing insects? Here is a cage. Goldfishes? He will bring his sleeves full of them tomorrow. With such arts he wins my indulgence toward his frequent remissness in the matter of getting his lesson. (By the way, the young man starts for America in a few weeks. If he is in your neighborhood I will give him a letter of introduction. He appears to be bound for Texas, however).

My other pupils are a Mr [Makita], professor of Electrical Engineering, a splendid mind and model student, 5 feet 8 inches, has to stoop to get in my door. Also Mr. Nakamura, a banker. Soon I shall have another pupil who is a member of a large drygoods firm of Tokyo. It is astonishing to find business men no longer young studying like schoolboys. I have promised to teach two mornings a week in the school of Mrs. Sakurai, beginning in September. Very small pay. Mrs. Sakurai was formerly a leader in the intellectual society of Tokyo, now is past her prime and has only a small school for girls, with which is connected a sort of home-boarding-house, where country girls are taken in who may wish to attend the city schools—also some American visitors who don't care to go to a hotel. How I run on! What wretched paper! Hard to get anything but rice paper, which blots abominably. I am growing old. If I could find a bonnet, I would wear it. Won't know where to find it. Wear the same things I brought from Amerikey. Children on the street call me "Mamma San." They think it's my name. Baby is learning Japanese very fast. Me? Nit! Easier to teach all Tokyo to speak English. Letters from America come in good. Had one from Peter Georges, now in New York. One from Suella B—, his divinity in Los Angeles, known all over town as a "fascinator". She's a peach—and by some anomaly she and I are fairly good chums—but she's not half good enough for Peter—so let's be thankful that she flips her fingers at him. Mama writes that Florence is busy in the garden. Inquired anxiously after you and was able to give her good news. My best love to Alice dear.

Your own
Léonie.
P.S. Yone sends best regards.

Léonie's hopes of landing a job at Umeko Tsuda's school, the Joshi Eigaku Juku or Women's Institute for English Studies, did not pan out. Perhaps, as Masayo Duus suggested, the scandal concerning her arrival had set off alarms, though this seems an unlikely speculation, for the moral atmosphere at Mrs. Sakurai's school, where Léonie had been offered a part-time position for the fall, was at least as stringent. More likely Tsuda's school proved less attractive than Léonie expected. Finances were dire, and Umeko already had a friend, Anna Hartshorne, teaching English. Though Anna had no college degree, her father was a local missionary, and her uncle a trustee of Bryn Mawr College. More importantly, as Tsuda's biographer Yoshiko Furuki notes, "Anna received no salary; on the contrary, she actually provided funds to pay for substitute teachers when she was away." In 1903, Fanny Greene had been hired as the school's first "properly salaried" teacher; having grown up in Japan as the daughter of a missionary couple, she was fluent in Japanese and a Wellesley graduate, and her mother taught singing at the school without pay.

Though Léonie described it as a "small school for girls," the Joshi Gakuin (which still exists as a junior and senior high school in its original location in Ichibancho, just west of the Imperial Palace) enrolled, at the time, more than two hundred students. The Joshi Gakuin was a merger of two schools, the Sakurai Girls' School, founded by a Japanese Christian woman, Chika Sakurai, with the financial support of her husband, a Christian naval officer, and the Graham Seminary, a Presbyterian missionary school originally located in Tokyo's foreign enclave of Tsukiji. The two schools had partially merged in 1889, but still maintained separate, adjacent buildings. The Graham Seminary housed the resident students (about half the student body) while the day students at the Sakurai school made up the other half. The school had a rather strongly evangelical Presbyterian orientation and was considered a model school by visiting Presbyterian missionaries. "Of all the schools for girls which I visited between Beirut and Yokohama," wrote one in 1903, "none more thoroughly commanded my confidence and admiration."

The private students Yone arranged for Léonie were a viable alternative to the low-paying school positions, and the students were often willing to come to the house, saving her the complications of commuting through the mazy city streets, most of which had not yet been paved, and that seemed to her "all tangled up." It was difficult to ask directions, since Tokyo, though a sprawling city of a million and a half people, had only recently begun its transformation into an international metropolis, and almost no one spoke English. Until 1899, foreigners had been required to live in a handful of treaty ports, which included Yokohama and a tiny outpost of Tokyo, Tsukiji (now the world's most famous fish market). Léonie's years of language study at Bryn Mawr had left her with little enthusiasm for learning Japanese.

Among her private students, her favorite, as she had noted, was Lieutenant Iwamura. Duus for some reason identifies this student as Tomoharu Iwakura, resulting in an extended role for actor So Yamanaka in Matsui's film, but it seems far more likely that this was one of the five sons of Baron Michitoshi Iwamura, a former samurai from Tosa (now Kochi prefecture in Shikoku) who had, along with his late brother Takatoshi, played a part in the Meiji Restoration back in the late 1860s. Since then, the Baron had served in various government posts, including a very brief stint as foreign minister.

Isamu, after his initial shock, found it easier than Léonie to adjust to Japan. Comfortable as object of fascination to the local children, "Babysan" would proudly present himself for inspection at their request and was soon taking part in their games, and even picking up some Japanese words.

Isamu Noguchi, *A Sculptor's World*

All I remember of my earliest time is being a child with his mother; that was the total of my existence all the time I was in Japan.

My earliest recollections are of a house in Tokyo where we arrived, myself aged two, from America, my mother a stranger. The house belonged to my father. Who was he? I dimly remember him sitting on the floor, to whom (I am told) I would bow respectfully, mimicking the maidservants crying 'Dannasama'. In the garden were two large cherry trees, and surrounding it was a high bamboo fence over which I could peer when riding the maid's back. The cherry blossoms came and then the wind that scattered them over the ground, so sadly.

Isamu and two women, probably maids, c. 1907. *Isamu Noguchi Foundation.*

For Mamma-san, as Léonie was known to the neighborhood, it was "rather lonesome," but there were a few bright spots: "green things growing everywhere," and the great exposition then in progress in Ueno

Park. And then there were the servants, a new and unfamiliar luxury to which she soon became accustomed. As she explained to an American visitor, "a faithful and industrious maid-servant, who will do cooking and house-cleaning, as well as serving and running errands, can be hired for a reasonable sum." In addition to the regular servants, there was also a young student "houseboy," such as Yone himself had once been. Hironobu Noguchi, "Hiro" for short, a student of Yone's priest-brother Yushin at the Jokoji temple, came to live in the Hisakata-machi house in 1907 when he enrolled at Shiba Junior High School. Hironobu's daily chores consisted of familiar tasks he had done at the temple—cleaning the entrance, living room, toilet, and the gas and oil lamps—and new responsibilities like shining shoes, caring for umbrellas, and polishing furniture. Occasionally he accompanied Léonie and Isamu on errands and excursions. To get the exotic foreign foods required by the family, such as butter, cheese, and pepper, it was necessary to go to specialty shops like Meidi-ya in Ginza.

The house was in a quiet neighborhood about twenty or thirty minutes on foot from the station, Hironobu recalled. There was a jinrikisha stable nearby, and Yone had a regular driver. Yone kept late hours, reading and writing on an oval shaped desk in his study after everyone else was asleep, until two or three in the morning.

Yone began to spend more time away from home in Kamakura, where he stayed in a Buddhist temple called *Zoroku-an*, or Tortoise Temple, a smaller temple surrounded by trees near the entrance of the great Zen temple-compound of Engakuji, founded in the thirteenth century. The still-unknown Natsume Soseki had stayed there after his return from London, before he replaced Lafcadio Hearn at Tokyo University. "Life here is very quiet, grey in tone, and sweet in atmosphere," Yone reported to Putnam in a letter dated May 19. "I found finally my ideal place in the Kamakura; and I will stay here as long as possible, and work."

Although increasingly lonesome, Léonie had stopped writing to Matsuo Miyake. "I have been imagining that there must have been around you something very, very happy things or some troublesome ones," he wrote her in October 1907. "And it must be reason you do not write me these day. And I made up my mind not to disturb you with writing when you are in a very happy condition and not to make you to tell me and increase your uneasiness if you are in the other state." She was most likely in "the other state." It cannot have been improved much by Matsuo's letter of two weeks later, where he pressed Léonie again to join him for an autumn visit to Kyoto, told her something about his work translating for the *Mainichi*, and then casually mentioned how happy his mother was living with him and his wife. "I have not told you before about my marriage," he confessed. "I will write you sometime of my venturing in my love affaire."

The house at Hisakata-machi was, as its name suggested, too far away from everything, and after a few months Noguchi located a house closer to transportation, at 40 Nishigoken-cho, Ushigome, not far from Koishikawa to the southwest. Friends like Inazo and Mary Nitobe could more easily visit, and houseboy Hironobu remembered a steady stream of visitors from among the Japanese intelligentsia. Léonie, however, did not find the new location made much difference in her access to the world. "Here we are shut up in Tokyo," she complained to Frank Putnam, "and likely to remain so for the rest of our natural lives, unless we happen to die off young, all because—well, for no reason on earth, I should say." She made no attempt to conceal her unhappiness and seemed on the verge of blaming Putnam. But at least she still had her sense of humor.

To Frank Putnam, February 2, 1908

40 Nishigokencho, Ushigome

My dear Frank:

Have you ever heard of the "Japanese Head?" Chiefly affects missionaries, I believe, but also other foreigners, as all we-uns are called over here. The poor things, being quite cut off from all their old associations, forget everything they ever knew, even the names of their best friends, and being debarred by their ignorance of the language, or the ossification of age, from acquiring new ones in the land of their adoption, their heads come, in the course of time, to be absolutely empty, like a blown eggshell. This may sound mythical to you. but I assure it is a dread reality. I myself have felt a touch of it. But not as regards Frank Putnam. No indeed. It is awful to think how long your last letter has remained unanswered. But it is all because Yone would insist on taking the responsibility of it on himself.

When many weeks went by and no answer from you came, I began to wonder. And then that wretched fellow confessed that he had never really answered it. And he's too ashamed to write now. Says he will wait till he has a book ready and send you that.

He has begun a book—prose sketches of Japanese life—childhood reminisces, etc., which he thinks will be done in a couple of months. If his typewriter doesn't get lazy. But that's a big "if."

I've been quite generally miserable in my innards this winter—too cold. Isamu, too, has a perpetual cold and needs lots of care. I'm home-sick for the country, Japanese country, American country, any country where there are fields and blossoms and breezes unscented by city odors. And a garden. I'm just crazy to dig.

But here we are shut up in Tokyo, and likely to remain so for the rest of our natural lives, unless we happen to die off young, all because—well, for no reason on earth, I should say. Country is just as near Tokyo as Boston. And there are chickens crowing and cows mooning as every-where else, I suppose.

There's quite a pretty garden to this house, with a picturesque little stagnant pool and some dwarf trees. But no place left to dig, alas. Very likely you don't sympathise with my mania for digging. But I'm sure Mrs. Putnam does. And the poor baby! "What are you doing, Baby?" I call out, seeing him bobble around on his wooden geta, trowel in hand. "Nussing, Mama, nussing," he answers, "Nussing to dig."

This is the season of plum blossoms and snow—such an ethereal beauty of both, like the delicate Japanese spring. And I have heard a nightingale more than a month ago.

I believe you are in Texas now—a cowboy? a cotton king? Don't say "editor." Are your boys riding wild ponies? And Mrs. Putnam making a clearing for her New England posies? I'm all in a fog as to your doings and whereabouts. It will be safest to send this to East Milton by a long road. If I ever hear from you I'll write again. In the meantime I send you all my dear love.

Yours sincerely
Léonie G. Noguchi

By April, they had moved again, and Léonie's spirits seem to have improved considerably, although it is difficult to know from her letters to Catharine exactly how much, since she tended to maintain in them a blithely cheerful tone. Perhaps the new house was an improvement: this time, it was "a tiny little house on a hilltop close by a grove of tall trees" at 90 Myogadani (just north-west of Koishikawa). And she had been to see a performance of the kabuki play, *The Precious Incense and Autumn Flowers of Sendai*, which she found deeply moving.

To Catherine Bunnell, April 4, 1908

90 Miogadani, Koishikawa, Tokyo

My dear Catherine

Imagine me seated on the floor before a ten inch high table (with a firebox beside me for company) trying to prove by my promptitude that I have no intention of cutting you as a correspondent. Oh how your thoughts do belittle me!

Your letter of Feb. 23 which arrived by this morning's post, is now being answered. Likewise the one which came about a week ago.

First item of news is that we have moved again, this time to a tiny little house on a hilltop close by a grove of tall trees where a Ho, Ho! Kikyo! (nightingale) sings to me daily. Isamu insists that the Ho Ho Ho Kikyo! is his brother and invites me to go and see him. He lives in the treetop, he explains, and I can take a train there any day. The child is developing a tendency toward imaginativeness. Yone calls it "lying." That for a poet!

Yone, by the way, is now at Kamakura, a seaside resort about 2 hours from here. he has engaged a room in a temple, where he may write in peace, far from the madding crowd of Babe and me. Incidentally this leaves me in something like your ideal of earthly bliss—a little house, one pretty little maidservant, and nobody to bother—Isamu thrown in by way of good measure. I'm quite enjoying it. Chance to get some work done—that means typing Yone's new book chiefly, with teaching, house-work etc. thrown in. Really awfully busy. Yone's plan is to spend about half of each week out there, the other half in town. Celebrated yesterday, however, by going to the theater with my friends the Fujiharas—mighty nice people, though rich, 'tis said. I saw "Masuoka." You know the story? A certain little prince comes to the throne at the age of eight. He is as-sessed by many counsellors and advisors, among them his governess Masuoka, a court lady who has a little son of the same age as the Prince. The court is divided into factions, one party, in the service of a wicked relative, plotting to assassinate the Prince. Masuoka, to throw sand in people's eyes, pretends to fall in with a plan of substituting her own boy for the Prince (nominally to put the letter in safety, really to make his assassination more easy). Masuoka's boy, who fully understands the case, gladly agrees to his mother's plan and dies to save his Prince. The two children are dear. The young Prince makes long speeches in a high childish treble. He is fully magnanimity, courage, and all princely qualities. The other boy does not show up so well until the end—when he jumps to his death with the utmost gaiety and sangfroid. I actually cried so at this part I couldn't see what came next. But everybody got revenged. Masuoka killed the woman who stabbed her child and the prince was saved.

There is one delicious scene where the two children are very hungry but Masuoka tells them they must not eat the food which is brought them as she fears poison—so they have to wait until she cooks their dinner herself. They sit down to play a game together, but every once in a while one jumps up and peeps behind the screen to see how things are progressing. When Masuoka brings her hand down on the floor with a whack (which sounds like "spank!") and tells them the son of a samurai should never show his hunger. When it happens to be the Prince who tiptoes up, Masuoka at once apologizes bowing to the ground. They feed some young sparrows to forget their own hunger. At last Masuoka cries from her sad thoughts. Her little son calls out "If you are crying because I asked you so often for dinner, I will wait until you and the Prince have finished." But the mother says she was not crying and dinner is ready at last. They clap their hands and shout for joy like any children.

Well, my paper is finished. Hard to write on rice paper. Good-bye, my dear, and don't get grumpy. I dreamed about you and that you had grown more beautiful than ever. Lovingly,

Léonie

An account of a spring outing, probably in 1908, with Isamu, the maid O Tei, and houseboy Hiro, also gives a happy picture.

Cherry Blossoms in Tokyo

Christian Science Monitor, 28 April 1921.

Tokyo on a day in April. The day for viewing the cherry flowers. Yesterday they were only half out. Tomorrow they will be gone. Hark to the boisterous wind! "Hasten to the flower viewing before I huddle the beauties away, lost forever to the laggards. Come now or come never!" My maid scuds along on her clogs, pushed by the wind. The baby shouts and digs his heels into his prancing steed. Which way? Yeddogawa? The banks of Yeddo River are lovely in cherry blossom season. Or the Botanical Gardens? Or templed Shiba Park? Or Kogane by the Jewel Pebble River? O Tei pleads for the Botanical Gardens. We go to Yeddogawa in the morning. In the afternoon O Tei has her way—she always has, this unobedient maid—and we go to the Botanical Gardens.

Yeddogawa is full of dancing boats. The little shallow turbid stream is in a great commotion. Why, this ditch is a river! Behold the rushing waves! The flat-bottomed boats leap, propelled by long bamboo poles. The navigators are boys, bare-legged from the thighs, with a sort of tunic caught and belted round the waist, barefooted or wearing straw sandals. There is a vista of misty bright blue sky caught in a net of blossoms and branches where the cherry trees lean from either side and interlace their fingers as if holding hands for a game of London Bridge. A good wise man planted the trees there many years ago—a hundred years, maybe, or more—purposing to strengthen the river banks with the deepreaching tenacious roots, cherishing, too, we may believe, a vision of a lovely bloom-bowered vista.

The river bank is thronged with people in their brightest spring dresses. Was ever a blue so blue as that girl's sash? Flame color and crimson and yellow, the whole gamut of purples and lavenders, mingle like strings of many colored jewels, brighter than flowers. Most of the people are on foot, indeed the brightest and cheeriest go afoot and laugh and chatter freely. Those in jinrikishas are more sober-toned, as a rule. "Americana!" cries O Tei, suddenly, pointing to the opposite river bank, where I see a long, heavy carriage of antique build drawn by two horses, with four liveried footmen, two in front and two in the rear, to clear the road. This carriage is occupied, not by Americans, but by a Japanese family, two women in showy silk blouses and impossible hats, a gentleman just perceptible beneath his silk hat, a small boy clad in red plush with large white buttons. They are the narikin, or newly rich.

O Tei was right in preferring the Botanical Gardens. There is not one discordant note. No carriages within, not even a go-cart on the pebbled walks. We climb a gentle slope from the gateway to a plateau outspread under the soft light of the cherry blossoms. The falling petals touch my cheek like small fingers. There a solitary butterfly dances, fantastically, to the inaudible music. The air is full of unheard melodies, under the sakura. There is an almost imperceptible fragrance, perfume of the flower. There is another fragrance of the mellow earth. In the distance I behold a band of golden daffodils. And Wordsworth's poem repeats itself inevitably:

> I wandered lonely as a cloud
> That floats on high o'er vales and hills,
> When suddenly I saw a crowd,
> A host, of golden daffodils.

An artist at his easel has caught the same glimpse of gold spilt between the clouds of bloom, and is making a little picture which we admire over his shoulder.

O Tei springs behind a cherry bole, nimble as a kitten. Baby follows suit, and around they go, tail and kitten. About the foot of the tree is a circle of green grass. They throw themselves headlong on it. Then up again and off for another tree. There are queer little sprites whirling under all the trees. Little girls in long plum-colored skirts, arm-pit high, which they wear over their flowery kimonos. They look like quaint dolls. Their hair is smoothly plaited, or hanging naturally, tied up from the forehead with a gorgeous bow of ribbon. They have wooden clogs on their feet. The babies, plenty of them tagging after their sisters, wear a little padded haori (coat), very gaudily flowered. Their heads are shaven, except for a top knot like some crested birds. Their elders are resting in a summer house near by. Thither we go. Thither all the children troop presently for a sweet cake and a tiny orange.

Pretty soon we start again, and presently we are in a shady grove, among thousands of tall slim bamboos. Tiny wild flowers glance up from the leaf mold, blue-eyed and starry-eyed little ones. We climb a winding pathway where stones set at irregular intervals serve as steps, we climb up and up to the very Castle of the Winds. We are almost blown off our feet when we reach the top. There, holding their skirts wide like sails, a group of little girls play they are ships in a storm and go careening and cavoorting, tacking and scudding, inviting shipwreck on the rocks, righting themselves again with little shrieks of laughter. Some have taken off their sashes and hold them to catch a bag of wind. Baby dashes into their midst and is thrown off his feet. They gather round him with cries of "kawaii koto" (dear baby), admire his golden curls and little fat hands. Nothing but the promise of seeing some "cunning ducks" will lure Baby from the spot. Down the other side of the hill we go to the edge of a pond where ducks are sitting amid the reeds. In a cage over another small pond are some beautiful specimens, brilliant feathered and small and plump. Baby pokes bits of leaves between the bars of the cage and the sociable little Japanese ducks eat from his hand. By the pond is a booth where a thriving business is done in "food for fishes." Special little biscuit, light as puff-balls, are sold to the people, who throw them on the water and watch for the fish to come and nibble. Sometimes a bunch of the biscuit tied together with a thread is flung from the end of a stick far out into the water. Then comes the fun of seeing the big carp jump out of the water and tug until one carries off the whole bunch.

Mercy on us, our carnival of spring is over and we are home again. We shall be glad to sleep tonight. But here comes O Tei, and kneels before me begging a boon. She says something about "teri, no tsuki," by which I understand that the moon is bright, and she makes a motion of her hands to indicate the whirling of the cherry blossoms. I know she longs to see the snow of blossoms under the moon. So I give permission for O Tei and our boy student, Hiro, to step out into the musical night.

"But," said my Japanese friend, "you should have gone to Sumida Gawa, not Yeddogawa, for the finest flower viewing. There, in the sparkling blue waters float clouds of bloom, clouds over and clouds under you, you as a mountain peak enwrapped in clouds, while against the adamantine gray walls near stand fantastically etched pines."

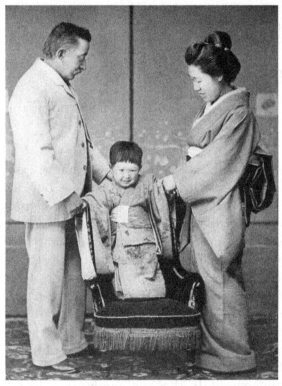

Lafcadio Hearn with Kazuo and Setsuko, 1895. *Ichida, Kobe*.

One of the more interesting additions to Léonie's list of private students was Kazuo Koizumi, fifteen-year-old son of the late Lafcadio Hearn (Yakumo Koizumi in Japan). Kazuo, along with his younger brothers, eleven-year-old Iwao and eight-year-old Kiyoshi, and a sister, Suzuko, then five, were being raised by Hearn's widow, Setsuko Koizumi, a samurai's daughter Hearn had met in his early days in the distant castle town of Matsue. In his lifetime, Hearn had been the most popular literary interpreter of Japan, and had been well loved as a teacher and professor. Yone, who returned to Japan just in time for Hearn's funeral, had cultivated an attachment with his widow and family. He became an energetic defender of Hearn's legacy, and thought of himself as a sort of successor to Hearn. Setsuko welcomed his help, and when the opportunity arose, Léonie took on the job of tutoring his eldest son Kazuo. She and Setsuko became friendly, though since neither could speak the other's language, they depended almost entirely on their children as interpreters. As Isamu was close in age to Suzuko and Kiyoshi, he often joined Léonie's visits to Nishi-Okubo in the capacity of playmate.

In June, a letter arrived for Yone from a certain Dr. Stopes who had read one of Yone's articles on Hearn and was curious to find out some additional information. Léonie, at the request of Yone, who was busy, replied, little suspecting that Dr. Stopes was, in fact, a woman.

To Dr. M.C. Stopes, June 27, [1908]

Koishikawa, 90 Miogadani

Dr. M.C. Stopes,
Dear Sir,
Your letter came while my husband was in Kamakura, and as I do not forward his letters it awaited his return a week. As he was only in town a couple of days and very much occupied, he asked me to write you in his place. As regards the attitude of the Japanese people toward Hearn, I believe he was quite widely appreciated as man and teacher, independently of his literary work. I myself have met Japanese people who were not literary or connected with the University in any way, who often did not recognize the name of Hearn but at once responded to the name of Koizumi San. It shows that he has another fame here than that of his books. I daresay it would be too much to expect any but a very few Japanese to have a real appreciation of his literary genius. They know him as the friend and interpreter of Japanese. They believe he understood them as they would want to be understood. In that sense only could he be called a "Japanese writer." I have seen some quaintly charming letters to his wife—some kind of "little language" in Japanese. Mr. Noguchi says they are exceedingly simple.

If you wish to meet Mrs. Hearn I daresay it would not be difficult to arrange. She would no doubt be glad of your appreciation of her husband. I have met her once. She has a very sympathetic face, but we could not speak each other's language.

Hoping that you will excuse Mr. Noguchi for not answering himself, and that we may have the pleasure of meeting you some day, I am—
Very truly yours

Léonie G. Noguchi.

At the time, Hearn's reputation was under attack as the result of the publication of George Gould's book *Concerning Lafcadio Hearn*. Noguchi wrote "A Japanese Defence of Hearn" for the press, and sent a copy to Frank Putnam.

Yone Noguchi to Frank Putnam, July 21, 1908

Keiogijuku University

Dear Frank:

I returned today from Kamakura; and in a day or two Mrs Noguchi and Isamu will go off to the seashore called Yaidzu where Lafcadio Hearn used to spend his summers. Did you read Dr Gould's *Concerning to Lafcadio Hearn*, a book with bad taste and unexcusable bitterness? This article, you will find, is my Japanese defence of Mr Hearn; you might be interested to read what I think about Gould's book and also Hearn. I do not know the nature of your Texas paper; and I did not send it to you when I sent it two or three American papers to be printed. But now I think that as you are, to be sure, one of the admirers of Hearn's writing, you might like to know my opinion on Gould's book; and I will simply glad if you can spare your column for my article. Of course you need not to pay me for it as it will appear in the other American papers.

The weather is getting very hot in Japan; Tokyo will be emptied in a week or so, but I expect to stay at home, at least, while Mrs Noguchi and Baby are living a week at Hearn's Yaidzu. For last few weeks, I was thinking of you and your family all the time.

Yone Noguchi

Do you hear sometimes from Mr Stoddard?

Yone wrote to Stoddard a few days later, on July 26. "Why don't you write me, Dad?" he complained. "You must not neglect me." He gave Stoddard a more detailed account of Léonie and Isamu's trip to Yaizu:

> I feel lonesome for you today being alone at home; my wife and boy (well, I wish you could see my boy, Dad!) went to a seashore last night, and they expect to stay for some two weeks. The place they went is called Yaidzu—the very place where Lafcadio Hearn used to go in summer. And the house where they were going to stop is the very house where Hearn used to stop. A month ago I made a special trip to Yaidzu to

study a bit of Hearn's Yaidzu landmark; Oh, what a glorious place it is! Such a sight of Fuji Mountain from there! And what a glory of water! It made me almost cry, and solemn. My wife took Hearn's eldest boy with her; he is studying English under her guidance. And now at Yaidzu he is acting as an interpreter for her. Isamu—that's my boy's name—is such a wonderful fellow; he speaks now perfect Japanese like any other Japanese boy, and handles English too. And he can make noise ten times louder than any Japanese boy; and he is such a handsome fellow, so many people flatter him. (You mustn't believe it!)

"I wish you will write me a long letter every week," Noguchi pleaded; "I can now promise you that I will not fail to write you everything which happened here with me." But there was evidently no reply. Stoddard was now 65, his health in decline; nine months later, he died of a heart attack in Monterey.

Frank Putnam no longer seemed to have time for the travails of Yone and Léonie; having achieved his goal of reuniting the estranged family he seemed to have no further suggestions as to how they might achieve "Happiness with a capital 'H.'" Yone, who depended on Putnam's "wine of inspiration and courage" and "brotherly blessing," returned to managing his affairs in his own way behind a façade of marital stability.

The Myogadani house, like the one in Koishikawa, proved short-lived. By October, they had moved again, a few blocks farther south to a house in Kohinata-daimachi. "I have moved away from Myogadani-machi to a little house at 71 Kobinatadai-machi Sanchome," Léonie wrote Kazuo Koizumi in October. "It is quite near the last car stop. After getting off the streetcar at Edogawabashi, cross the river, then climb a road up slope to the left, and just after the vegetable store near the top turn left on the next small alley and look for the house with the red gate."

Léonie neglected to send the address of the new house to Marie Stopes, who nevertheless was able to find it with the help of friendly neighbors when she paid a call in November. Stopes, a twenty-eight-year-old Englishwoman, was a botanist by profession; she had come to Japan ostensibly to study fossil plants, but in reality on the heels of a Japanese scientist, Kenjiro Fujii, with whom she had fallen in love while studying in Germany several years earlier. Fujii had declared his love and promised to divorce his Japanese wife, but Stopes' love journey was turning out as disastrously as Léonie's. Dr. Fujii proved unable to divorce his wife, and, fearing both scandal and confrontation, avoided the heartbroken Stopes.

One can only imagine the fascinating conversation about the perils of love with Japanese men that might have taken place between these two women, had they only been able to overcome the reticence of their generation. But such a breach of propriety remained unthinkable even for these two educated, independent women. In the 1920s, Stopes' pioneering books on birth control, in which she wrote openly about sexual relations, would bring her lasting fame as one of the most radical women of her generation. But in 1908, she was quite ignorant of sexual matters (a factor that probably contributed to her problems with Fujii). After her return to England, she pseudonymously published her correspondence with Fujii under the title *Love Letters of a Japanese*—part revenge, part genuine bafflement about what had actually gone wrong in their relationship. She and Léonie were in much the same predicament, but could find no way of approaching the topic.

Marie Stopes in her laboratory, 1904. *Marie Stopes International Australia.*

Journal of Marie Stopes, November 25, 1908

After working till it was dark, and worrying the laboratory attendants (for, nominally, we should all clear off at 4 now, but I can't get out of the habit of working later, particularly now that there is so much to do), I called on Mr. N—. She is the American wife of a Japanese journalist—a writer whose articles I have noticed. We started a correspondence, and she came to see me, but I was out. It was no easy job to find the house, for she had recently moved, so I went to the old house, but as it led to a little incident which illustrates the courtesy of the nice Japanese, I will relate it. I went to the house called No. 90, but as I have remarked before, there may be twenty houses of the same number. Of course it was the wrong one, but they told me the *N*—s had left the house, and gone to Kamakura. The little lady of the house at which I inquired sent her maid to fetch the address, and asked me to sit down while she went. Then, with gentle voice, she asked all the polite questions—where I lived? how long I had been in the country? what was my native land? All capped by compliments on my Japanese. She fetched a book of picture post cards to entertain me, and when her maid returned, sent her again to make sure if Mr. *N*— was not living in the neighbourhood. When she found out that she was, the lady herself came with me a little way to show me the road to follow, as if I had been an honoured guest.

As at last the gate was reached, a young lad came out in the dusk, and of him I inquired if it was really the house. He too had a soft voice and a courteous manner, and helped me to open the gate. After I had conversed with Mrs. *N*— a little while, I learned that he was Lafcadio Hearn's eldest son, the one he loved so, and wrote of so sweetly in many of his letters.

Mrs. *N*— was dressed in grey: perhaps it was the shadow of the lamp-light, but I received the impression that her life was in grey shadows. Her little son, however, was a bright contrast—round eyes, rosy cheeks, with a woollen cap with a long point and a dangling tassel—he was like a pixy. He was only four years old, but acted as an interpreter between his mother and the maid. There was also the merriest kitten I ever saw—round, soft, and tailless, with a scatter of claws and a jump like a grasshopper, as it dashed after the shadow of the tail it never had. The grey woman spoke with such a sad lifeless voice—slowly, as though it were rather troublesome to have to speak at all, but not in unfriendly fashion. I heard much of the Hearns, as Mr. *N*— is a very intimate friend of the family, and Mrs. *N*— has come close to the eldest lad, and teaches him.

I heard from her what I have heard from many people, that Mrs. Hearn can neither speak nor write a single word of English. That baby English at the end of the *Life and Letters* is either a translation or a concoction.

There are many letters of Hearn's to his wife in childish Japanese, that, since the appearance of Gould's atrocious book, Mrs. Hearn has placed in Mr. *N*—'s hands for publication, though before that she had not wished to make them public.

In Stopes' account, the contrast between the grey, seemingly lifeless Léonie and the bright, lively Isamu is very evident. Isamu, with his point-ed woolen cap, reminded Stopes at first of pixies: small, winged fairy-like creatures, fond of dancing, that are said to be the souls of unbaptized infants. But on further consideration she revised her judgment: he was, in fact, more like a brownie. (Brownies are small, brown sprites, mis-chievous but benevolent, popularized by the stories of Canadian writer Palmer Cox.)

Isamu in brownie mode.
Isamu Noguchi Foundation.

From K[azuo] Koizumi, December 3, 1908

Mrs. Y Noguchi.
On next sunday (6th) my mother and we are all at home and wait for you.
So please come with Isamu San.
little pupil
K. Koizume

Kazuo's letter ended up a souvenir of Marie Stopes, who invited Léonie and Isamu to lunch at her house in Azabu the following Sunday. Stopes adored her little house, with its veranda and garden and a bed-room "like an aesthetic dream." Her maid, a pretty and intelligent orphan girl named O Fuji san, managed everything with remarkable smoothness and thrift. "The way that maid manages a four-course dinner, with three saucepans and half a dozen bits of charcoal in the fivepenny stove, is nothing short of miraculous," she had noted in her journal. "It will break my heart to leave this house and garden, there is no doubt about it."

The Koizumi home, Nishi-Okubo. *Koizumi Yakumo zenshu*, 1937.

Journal of Marie Stopes, December 13, 1908

.—It has been a brilliant day with glowing sun, and at one Mrs. *N*— and the Brownie son of hers came to lunch. The Brownie looked and acted splendidly, and was a pleasure, and his eyes twinkled a keen appreciation rare in men of four years old when, after warning him to be good and not to spill anything, I tipped the pheasant's bread-crumbs into my own lap, and he got through the meal without a mishap of any sort. Almost immediately after lunch we went over to—Where do you think?—Lafcadio Hearn's house, to see his wife and family! A rare privilege, for the sanctum is unusually well guarded. But Mrs. *N*—'s friendship has won me the way in, for, as I said, the eldest boy learns English from her and is devoted to her.

The house is some way out of town, in pure Japanese style, with a Japanese name on the lamp, for you will remember Hearn became a Japanese and took a Japanese name, which is written in Chinese characters over his door. "Koizumi," we pronounce it.

There is a nice garden, visible partly from the entrance, where was the children's swing. As we entered we passed along an *engawa* (verandah) bounding a tiny internal square of garden on our way to the reception-room. This was in the purest Japanese style, well built, with pretty woodwork, a thing one learns to notice in this country. I immediately observed the *kakemono*, which was exceptionally beautiful, tall peaks of bare rock pillars standing up against a grey sky, where a moon half shone through a band of cloud. A picture that one could never forget and yet would ever wish to see instead of merely remembering. I remarked on it to Mrs. Hearn, who told me that "Lafcadio had very good taste in *kakemonos*," and always bought only what pleased him exactly (wise man!) when he had the cash. There was also a bronze in the room, the bent stalk of a fading lotus leaf with the collapsed blade of the leaf, and though there sounds no beauty in that, the bronze throbbed with it. Mrs. Hearn was very friendly: less shy and quiet than most Japanese women, she was yet distinctly Japanese in her shyness and quietness. Without beauty, she pleased.

She and the children were all in usual Japanese costume, and the only "foreign" things in the room were ourselves and the cakes and cups of tea she brought us. I inquired if she liked foreign food, and she told me that she did, *very* much, and that "Lafcadio" always ate it, for though he liked all the things to be pure Japanese, and would have nothing he could help that was not, Japanese food upset him, and he always had foreign food, but now she never prepared it. We chatted about many things, and she spoke freely of Hearn, of whom I did not dare at first to ask any questions till she had spoken voluntarily so much, to show that she liked to speak of him.

After the tea and cakes we went to Hearn's study, and got a sight of the real Japanese garden at the back of the house. The study was lined with low book-shelves filled with many charming volumes in French and English. There was a very high table made specially for him, for his extremely short sight, and the famous pipe box, with dozens of long tiny-bowled Japanese pipes.

The children were with us freely, and also a friend, a Mr. —, who was the first student Hearn had in Japan, and who has remained faithful through everything, and now acts as adviser and friend of the family, and lives in part of the house. He was bright and intellectual-looking, beyond the average, and speaks excellent English.

Mrs. Hearn *insisted* on us staying to a meal, which we could not avoid doing without positive rudeness, though we had only expected afternoon tea. It was a "first-class" Japanese meal, with nearly all the things I like (sometimes the things are quite uneatable, as, for example, the "sea-cucumbers" in a raw salad, which are also first-class things), and I enjoyed it, but I got home at 8 instead of 5 as I expected.

The children were with us most of the evening, showing Brownie picture-books, of which they had a fine stock. Hearn evidently liked Andrew Lang's fairy books, for they were nearly all there.

In his study, where we had supper, was the little family shrine, built rather like a miniature temple of plain wood; within was Hearn's photo, and before it burnt a tiny lamp and stood dainty vases of small flowers. According to Japanese ideas, the spirit of the departed inhabits this dwelling and needs the love and attention of his kindred, and takes part in their life. Is Christianity more consoling to the bereaved than this? From the window by the shrine could be seen the grove of the tall bamboo Hearn loved, and in the room floated one or two of the mosquitoes with which he had such sympathy.

To see the eldest son, after having read that tender, wonderful letter of Hearn's about his birth, was, I believe, a mistake. Hearn's words had made me love the child—but he isn't a child any longer, and is now a thin, lanky youth, shy of manner and slow in English speech. But per-haps—for there is promise in his face—I shall like him well as a man in the years to come. How Hearn wove words into an opalescent cobweb! I could imagine him feeling intoxicated with the beauty of words—nay, he must have been, for as a reader I am intoxicated by words of his, which must have affected him a thousand times more strongly.

Kazuo Koizumi, circa 1909. Nina Kennard, *Lafcadio Hearn* (1912).

A month later, as Stopes prepared to depart, she paid a farewell visit to the "grey lady" and "the Brownie" at the house in Kohinata.

Journal of Marie Stopes, January 17, 1909

At 1 o'clock I sallied forth with a long calling list. Fortunately, one can call early on Japanese ladies. Baron and Baroness *H—* were both in, and very gracious. It is difficult to say "good-bye."

There were several other short calls, and then my last visit to the *S—'s* pretty house, from which I saw the beautiful garden for the last time.

Afterwards I went to see the grey lady, Mrs. *N—*. Four-year-old Brownie remembered me and welcomed me in, doing the honours of the house and showing me all his toys. The grey lady is revealing herself a little—I am sorry I must go, and so will not see her again; people who really interest one are not too many on this earth. She started life as a scientist, but found chemistry so easy that it was no mental discipline, so she took to history, where dates have no reasons and are therefore hard to remember, but here, too, she came out top of the classes. She lies behind the poetry of that Japanese poet who wrote in English, and was so praised by Rossetti, the *N—* of American fame, if I am not much mistaken, though she does not tell one so consciously.

Isamu Noguchi, *A Sculptor's World*

Not far from the house I came to know a playground, or open space, that filled me with foreboding. My mother used to take me along with her to call on people. Among them was the family of Lafcadio Hearn, whose children she taught for a while. Thus cautiously did I come to know the world. My earliest memories are not happy. My first recollection of joy was going to a newly opened experimental kindergarten where there was a zoo, and, where children were taught to do things with their hands. My first sculpture was made there in the form of a sea wave, in clay and with a blue glaze.

It was probably during the early months of 1909 that Léonie and Isamu joined Léonie's unidentified friend on the midwinter trip to the hot spring resort of Ikao described in "Home, Sweet Home, in Japan." Ikao (now usually spelled Ikaho), could be reached from Tokyo in 7 ½ hours by a combination of train, tram-car, and jinrikisha. Though somewhat faded in glory today, it was, at the time, one of Japan's premier onsen towns, set picturesquely along a steep stairway ascending Mount Haruna in Gunma Prefecture. For a week, Léonie and her companions enjoyed "daily tramps over deep snow, accompanied by the silent fir trees, the sun above us swimming like a moon in the sea of mist, the world transmuted to a more ethereal one by the magic of snow and mist and silence," followed by luxurious plunges into the inn's steaming hot springs.

To Catherine Bunnell, March 13, 1909

My dear Catherine

I received the enclosed note from the P.O. at Washington, by which you see some friend has tried to send a Christmas present to Isamu, without knowing the ways of the post-officers. I have no idea who the sender may be, so am asking them to forward it to you. Will you inquire among the girls or of Florence if any of them sent such a parcel and ask her to fulfil the necessary formalities. I believe it is essential that the sender's name should be on the parcel. By the way, "speaking of praties" yourself are not exempt from error in the matter of postage. When you put a 2 center on a letter to me, I always have to pay 12 sen (just double the difference) at this end of the line. In course, darlint [sic], that's cheap anyway for a letter from you.

Your letter came a day or two ago, and I'm most sorry to hear of your father's poor health. Please tell him he has my most earnest wishes for his recovery.

Do you see anything of my Dad, and how is he keeping up? Yes, I fear Florence has undertaken more than she can manage—if there were any way to get Papa over here, I could take him off her hands. Isamu and he would be amusement and occupation for each other—and it might not be so difficult to find a small house with a garden attached where they could dig and grow vegetables. Florence is not the only one, however, who has to do two men's work. I have had only one week's vacation from teaching since I came here, that was last summer. And in spite of my best endeavors I can earn only some 85 yen a month, with which it is not easy to keep house, keep a girl to take Isamu to school, keep us all in clothes and shoes, and send 20 to mama every month. It takes as hard work to earn that 85 yen as to earn as many dollars in America, but it doesn't go nearly so far since most of the staples, bread, butter, sugar, chocolate, oatmeal etc., are imported from America.

Yone is in his temple in Kamakura and is happily oblivious of the cares and worries of this sordid world. There he spends his time, sleeping, working, writing divine poetry, emerging twice a week to lecture at Keio College. He contributes a part of his salary to our household expenses, of course, but generally speaking, I'm footing it alone here. End of this paper. Against my principles to start another—Goodbye with love, L.G.

[p.s.] Awfully obliged if you will attend to that business. L.G.
? — I see I have to return letters to Washington P.O. you will get the parcel.

**Yone Noguchi, Keio
University, 1909.** *Keio
University archives.*

In "Home, Sweet Home, in Japan" Léonie describes the unannounced visit of an inquisitive Mr. Kehoe whom she had met two years earlier in Los Angeles; since she left Los Angeles in March 1907, the visit probably took place in 1909.

Home, Sweet Home, in Japan

A Glimpse into a Japanese Interior

Japan, June 1922

"All things in blessed Mitsuho-no-kuni—the smallest ant also—bathed in sweet inspiring beams of beauty." The phrase from the "American Diary of a Japanese Girl" recurred to me as I lay loafing on the verandah of my Tokyo home one bright morning in May, a *zabuton* (square cushion) folded under my head for a pillow, the polished wooden floor my couch, the little world of the garden my book.

"*O Kyaku Sama*" (a caller). I heard my little maid's voice beside me without having noticed her soft footfall. I looked around.

Excitement shone from the girl's expressive face as she kneeled and awaited my permission to let out the torrent of news that threatened to burst her little soul.

"*O Kyaku Sama?*" I repeated.

"A foreigner."

We don't often have foreign visitors. And when they do call they are apt to choose the conventional afternoon hour. I frowned and speculated.

"Who can it be? A lady?"

"*I-ye.*" She answered in the negative. Then finally exploding, "He is very tall, very big, very handsome, very 'high-collar'—his nose very high. He is big, big. Just come from America, I think."

"The name?"

"*Ki-ho San.*"

"*Ki-ho San!*" I sat up. "That is not an American name."

"Yes, yes. He awaits at the entrance. Please come. Oh, your hair! Let me fix it, quick. Here, take one of my hairpins. Now your kimono" (pulling it straight in front). "All right. It's quite all right. He awaits."

O Chiyo's description was not far out. The caller about filled up our small outside entrance. He must have stooped to come in. He stood hat in hand, with a smile that looked confident of a welcome. I couldn't quite place him, though his face seemed familiar.

"I'm Kehoe, of Los Angeles. I hope you haven't forgotten me. Why, you're the only friend I've got in Japan. You wouldn't go back on me, now, when I don't know another soul in the whole country."

"Why! Mr. Kehoe! I believe I met you—er—?"

"Yes, in Los Angeles. Two years ago. Don't you remember I called on you for an interview? And we were both immensely interested in the Orient. Quite kindred spirits, don't you know? I told you then that I might turn up here some day. So here I am." Again that beaming, confident smile. I could do no less than ask him in, though I was a bit indignant at his claiming acquaintance on the strength of a half-hour interview. I absolutely didn't know a thing about the man.

"Do we take off our shoes?" he said, looking at my feet. I had on the white *tabi* (a sort of cotton shoes or socks) that are customarily worn in a Japanese house in the place of shoes.

"If you please. Shoes are hard on the tatami (mats). And my maid wouldn't stand for them anyhow. She's proud of her housekeeping. To have a bit of dust on the tatami would drive her to despair."

"Very pretty girl. Wouldn't make her mad for the world."

He sat down on the somewhat narrow ledge of our *genka* [genkan], bent over his fat knees, and began to unlace his boots, which he pulled off and replaced with a pair of woolen slippers which the little maid, kneeling beside me, pushed toward him. She brought her forehead down to the ground as he entered.

"Some kow-tow, that. Makes me feel like a high-brow."

"It's just ordinary courtesy," I smiled. "Don't take it for anything personal.

"We'll go out on the verandah. It's so pleasant in the sunshine after yesterday's rain. And there's a chair out there."

He gave a curious glance about the wide rooms without chairs or table or any of the usual "furniture" of an Occidental house through which we passed, our footfalls soundless on the soft mats. When we came out on the verandah I put a finger on my lips. "Don't speak." I pointed to the "spirit of the pond" as I was pleased to fancy a wee froggie in coat of emerald green, who sat on a fat stone by the garden pond, his brilliant eyes upturned in ecstasy.

I motioned Mr. Kehoe to the chair while I placed my *zabuton* near the edge of the verandah and squatted in Japanese fashion. I mischievously waited to see how long my injunction of silence could restrain him. It wasn't long. And let me say right here that Americans talk too much. Having been out of reach of it for some time I was quite carried off my feet by Kehoe's volubility. In fact, I must confess that I soon succumbed to the vulgar contagion of the thing and contributed my share to the torrent of chatter that drowned out all the beautiful silence and dreamy atmosphere of my Japanese home. First he told me all about himself, about his family, way back in Atlanta, Georgia, of his reasons for leaving that part of the country—some scrape and the toe of a parental boot were in it—he must have been a wild boy, to believe him, though to believe all his tales would have needed more credulity than I was endowed with. Then he went on to say how his interest in the Orient had been roused in "Frisco" by seeing a performance of "Madam Butterfly." (Shades of John Luther Long! Does he know that a Japanese called him Mr. Wrong? He is woefully wrong about everything Japanese.) And now he'd come to Japan to get some "copy," even as many another tourist, and perchance pay his traveling expenses by his writing, while economizing by living according to the simple standards of the country.

He had a good many preconceived ideas about Japan. One of them was that a person like himself could take off his American togs, put on a Japanese kimono, go out in the country somewhere (waving vaguely toward the distance) live in a temple in some romantic spot, eat like the country people and enjoy the simple life, for something like ten dollars a month.

"And where are you stopping now?" I interrupted.

"Imperial Hotel."

"Cheap?"

"Cheap! Confound it! Ten dollars a day. But that, of course, is what one might expect, coming in as a foreigner. It's the same everywhere. Look at the way they fleece Americans in Paris. I must admit the fare at the Imperial is good. They give you all your money's worth. That's not what you'd call the simple life. It's gilt-edged and velvet-cushioned. Of course, I expected I'd have to pay for that sort of thing at the start. But just wait until I get into the ways of the place. Don't think I'm planning to bury myself in the country right off. I'm going to do the sights first. But I'm keeping the temple and the simple life idea in the back of my head forninst the time I go broke," he guffawed.

My friend Kehoe wanted to know a whole lot of things. First, how I had learned to sit *à la belle Japonaise* and whether it was painful.

"Try it," I suggested. And clapping my hands to call O Chiyo, I told her to bring an extra huge and thick zabuton.

"*Zabuton*, you call it?" He caught the word easily. "Very pretty pattern, that cushion cover. What d'ye call the stuff? *To-chirimen?* I'll just jot that down. I'm going to get some to send a girl friend for a sofa cushion. Well, here goes." He bent his knees, he settled on the cushion with all the grace of a prize Jersey cow, flopping to one side.

"No. Put your feet straight. That's it, straighten out your feet under you, and sit on your heels."

A pained "ouch!" was his comment on this gymnastic feat with his feet, and he flopped to the other side.

"You may sit cross-legged. It was mean to put you down on the hard floor of the verandah at the first go. It's a whole lot easier on the *tatami*."

"I don't think it would be easy for me anywhere," he retorted, wiping the perspiration from a very red face. "Frankly, I guess I'm too fat. Now you are so slender and lithe I suppose it's just nothing to you."

"Just nothing to sit down. But all the aches in the world to get up. I'll do penance yet for this day's bravado. So now, if you'll excuse me, I'll just take a more natural posture," and leaning my back against a post I stretched my long-suffering limbs at full length before me, and in these postures we sipped our pale green tea from the tiny cups which O Chiyo set before us on a square red lacquer tray.

"What a beautiful thing that is!" he exclaimed, admiring the tray.

"It was given me by a pupil, a member of an evening class I was teaching. This young man was only twenty-one and had eight people to support, including his own parents, a grandfather, a widowed sister and her child, as well as his own wife and child, and finding it hard to raise the extra two yen needed for his tuition fee, was about to leave the class. That seemed a pity, as he was one of my best students, so I told him not to mind about the fee, he could pay me some day in the future, when he got rich. This lovely bit of lacquer-ware was made by his own grandfather, and he gave it to me as a 'small return for my kindness.' You can't do anything for a Japanese without his 'returning' it in some way or another."

"Grateful people, eh?"

"Grateful, certainly. Though this matter of 'the return' has also partly to do with pride, and is a matter of custom, of courtesy.

"You admired the tray. How do you like the tea-cups?"

"Very curious. Odd-looking. Don't they ever have handles to their cups?"

"Not to drink Japanese tea. These cups, that look as if they were roughly shaped by hand out of brown clay, are of Bizen ware, and considered very aesthetic. When you get to know Japan better you'll understand something of their ideas of nature and art."

"Got a long way to go, eh? I say, I feel guilty taking up such a lot of your time. Awfully good of you to take me in like this. My first glimpse of a Japanese house. Immensely interested, you know. I'll be going now. Will you let me come again?"

What could I say? Before I knew it I had invited him to drop in some afternoon and meet my husband, though I had a qualm as to how "Danna San" (the master of the house) would stand up under this young American's rapid-fire talk and questions.

"Would you like to go over the house?" I asked. "There isn't much to show you. But it's a typical Japanese house."

Our house is in fact just an ordinary Japanese house such as you may find occupied by people in the middle walks of life anywhere about Tokyo. There are seven rooms, two quite large ones upstairs which are practically one room, being separated only by *karakami* (Sliding doors made in the manner of Japanese screens by covering both sides of a frame with opaque paper printed with a delicate pattern) which we usually keep wide open. These rooms are very light, shut off from the outer air only by translucent white paper *shoji* along two sides of each room. On the south side these *shoji* come down to the floor in the fashion of French windows, and along that side a wide *egawa* [engawa] (verandah) extends the length of the two rooms and is continued by a narrower *egawa* around the west side of the two rooms. A great old cherry tree in the front yard makes a good bird-resting place. In blossom time it flings a carpet of perfumed petals over the whole verandah and even into the rooms when the shoji are left open. The downstairs verandah, directly beneath, is only half the length of the upstairs balcony, being cut off by a room that juts across the front end, making it a very secluded spot, hid from the street and from callers, who are usually taken directly upstairs. The *shoji* on the north side of this upper *zashiki* (parlor) come only half way to the floor, being more like windows, although they slide along grooves in the same way as the others. In some houses there are none of these half *shoji*, and this I suppose is the basis for the statement I remember reading in a geography that "A Japanese house has no windows," which might convey the impression that a Japanese house is a darksome place, when in reality the contrary is the case, a well-built Japanese house being in my opinion, the lightest place in the world.

My visitor was charmed with the light and airy effect as with the soft coloring of the rooms, the walls in sand color, the straw colored mats, the unpainted and unvarnished woodwork in the natural colors of the wood all blending to make a softly harmonious effect. There are no pictures on the walls, but on the wall space over the *karakami* hangs a framed Chinese poem done in bold beautiful characters, a picture in itself. Some open scroll work in this wall may correspond to the "transom" over an American door, and is infinitely more artistic. Of course the point of attraction of a *zashiki*, the shrine of beauty, if I may so speak, is the *tokunoma* [tokonoma], a sort of dais of polished wood raised a few inches from the floor. It is often framed by beautiful pieces of wood resembling the trunks of trees in their natural irregular shape, as though only the bark had been removed and the rest polished but not planed. The columns of our *tokunoma* are of ash wood. The *tokunoma* is the shelf where we may display something of beauty—not a mantel-piece cluttered with bric-a-brac—but the setting for a single beautiful object, which may be only a flower in a bamboo vase. "Things not qualified to convey charm are banished from the *tokunoma*."

The *kakemono* (decorative picture beautifully mounted on heavy paper that is unrolled from cylindrical bar from which it is suspended, usually hung at the back of the *tokunoma*) that met Kehoe's eye was a color print after Utamaru [Utamaro], representing a willowy lady of vaguely suggested features robed in a wonderful flowing gown all in faint lavender and faded persimmon color, with, one fancied, a delicate elusive scent of sandalwood clinging to the silken folds. The flower decoration for the day was an arrangement of tall iris in a straight bamboo vase. I blushed with pleasure when Kehoe pulled out a notebook to make a sketch of this, one of my first attempts at flower decoration without, of course, knowing that it had been done by the lady of the house. Our downstairs reception room is perhaps more showy than this upstairs one, though less used, as we are wont to entertain our dear intimate friends in the upstairs room, especially Danna San, who loves this room and in fact uses it as a study, as you might judge from the array of books to the right of the *tokunoma*, the deep space between the wee closets above and below having been filled in with bookshelves. His writing table with inkstone and brushes and paper is also in that room.

Of the five downstairs rooms one is a small entrance room, back of it a room we commonly use as a dining room, being easily heated and accessible to the kitchen, to the right a room where I sew or write or study when the weather drives me indoors, and where, too, I often receive my women friends over a cup of tea. Back of the dining room is the downstairs reception room, a large square room with very new mats, a deeper and more handsome *tokunoma* than the one upstairs, and boasting a beautiful screen painted with a silvery waterfall. Being in the brave month of May the *kakemona* hanging there appropriately showed two contending parties of warriors clad *cap-a-pie* in bright armor, waging battle under the flying blossoms of an orchard. Each side looks so dauntless, each thrust out their swords with such an irresistible elan that it was impossible to decide which side will win, and when I look at them I find myself continually changing sides in my allegiance to one or the other party. The flower decoration was one of gorgeous peonies in a handsome vase. As I have said, this room is not much used, being reserved for formal occasions. The maid's room, kitchen and bathroom take up the rest of the ground floor. Of course Kehoe had to poke his nose into the kitchen also, where we found O Chiyo with a blue and white towel around her hair, the skirt of her kimono tucked up into her *obi*, showing a glimpse of scarlet petticoat at her knees and two perfectly shapely bare legs. She was standing on the cement-floor part of the kitchen (sunk about two feet below the wooden floor, necessitating a good deal of agility in jumping up and down, into her sandals when she goes down, and out of them when she hops up), and was engaged in fanning up a charcoal fire in the two earthenware *shichirin* (kitchen fireboxes) we use for cooking. There is also a small gas plate for convenience in making hot water quickly, but for general cooking, especially for rice, which cannot be cooked in the true Japanese way over gas, we use the charcoal burners. To cook rice in the Japanese way you have to let it boil over and make a mess, and that would stop up the gas burner. Our kitchen sink is of new wood, shaped quite like an American one but larger, with a round hole in one corner into which is thrust a length of bamboo pipe that does not quite reach to the floor beneath, where the cement is slightly hollowed out and gives into a drain pipe. When the sink threatens to become clogged we work a stick around inside the bamboo pipe and the obstruction drops to the floor below. There is no ceiling in the kitchen, and the smoke is free to ascend to the beams and rafters which are coated with a layer of soot and ashes. Kehoe suggested that it would be a simple matter to convert this kitchen into an up-to-date American affair, as we had already gas, running water and electricity in the house.

"Instead of wasting time and energy over the tedious process of blowing up a charcoal fire, which makes a lot of dust, too, why not install a gas or electric range? I see a great future for electric household appliances in Japan. Do they use electric washing machines out here?"

"Perhaps they do, in the laundries, though I never saw one. Not in the homes, certainly. We have an electric flat-iron, however. It is O Chiyo's little wizard. I found her listening to the humming sound of it the other day as if it were a singing insect. See! Here it is. Made in Japan. Only six yen. As for installing a gas or electric range—well, the time will come, no doubt, when they will be made in Japan, and then we will think about it. The money it would take to buy even a small gas range—they run from 50 to 200 yen, while an earthenware firebox costs only 20 sen—would pay for such a lot of more interesting things. Several times we have thought of investing in one. I confess I too have a weakness for conveniences. Last winter I had laid by enough to buy one without pinching us, and then a friend suggested we make a mid-winter trip to Ikao. I'm glad I had sense enough to make the right choice. Fancy the exhilaration of daily tramps over deep snow, accompanied by the silent fir trees, the sun above us swimming like a moon in the sea of mist, the world transmuted to a more ethereal one by the magic of snow and mist and silence. Then when we came back to our inn to plunge luxuriously into a big tank of steaming hot water from a hot springs which has its source in some place of perennial warmth so far beneath the surface that it never knows winter's chill. All this joy we had for a whole week for the price of a gas range. O Chiyo got a week's holiday, too. And she's perfectly satisfied with her charcoal fire, even though she has to spend a few minutes kneeling before it with her kitchen fan, deftly putting the embers in place with a pair of steel sticks, or softly blowing a breath of life into a dying spark which turns and grows and grows into a blazing eye under her wise nursing.

"You see there are two ways of looking at this Oriental 'low standard of living.' Wasn't it Emerson who approved 'plain living and high think-ing?' Wasn't it an Occidental who wrote a book about the simple life? Here we live it."

"I see. I am argued down. But not yet convinced. However, we will pass that. And now, dear lady, will you pardon my curiosity if I ask 'Where do you sleep?' In all this your domain, which looks like a castle of dreams, I have seen nothing to remotely suggest that the people do ever sleep here."

"Sleep? Oh, anywheres!"

"Anywheres?"

"Don't look so mystified. Or do! I think, just to tease you, I'll leave you guessing. A Japanese house, though without lock or key, also has its secrets. If there are no keys, there are also no keyholes. Riddlemeree, Riddlemero! Why, what's the matter?" I broke off, seeing friend Kehoe looking extremely red and uncomfortable.

"Of course you couldn't know," he laughed off his discomfiture, "the fellows used to call me Keyhole Kehoe on account of my unhole-y curi-osity."

"Mr. Kehoe, you seem to have several failings. Next time you come I'll satisfy your curiosity, and answer some more questions, if you like. Have you managed to get any copy today?"

"I think I have enough for the day," he grinned. "No objection if I put you in?"

"Not in the least," I answered sweetly, "allow me to present you with a postcard as a souvenir of your call. Though it is a more pretentious interior than our own, the main features are the same."

Kehoe gazed at my postcard with interest. "What's that round thing in the middle of the room?"

"That's a charcoal burner, to keep us warm on a cold day."

"Why do they put it in the middle of the room?"

"Oh, it can be put anywhere. It's placed there beside the *zabuton* so you may sit and warm your hands over the fire."

"Where does the smoke go? Isn't it unhealthy?"

"There isn't any smoke. The fire is all a-glow before it is brought in. Good charcoal doesn't smoke after it is lighted. As for being unhealthy, do you observe the paper *shoji*? Air as well as light filters through them, just as it does through the walls of a tent. So long as we have only *shoji* to shelter us from the wind, a charcoal brazier, with the small fire that is deemed sufficient in a Japanese home, is not, I think, unhealthy. It is getting to be a modern fashion, however, to use a lot of glass about the house. Then the charcoal becomes a real menace."

"Isn't it cold in winter here? Don't you need some more heat than that?"

"It is cold. Japanese people have a very convenient and economical way of keeping warm, by means of padded clothing. You see everything is in keeping. You can't change one thing without changing another. Now do you want to know what these little things are that look like foot-rests? They are elbow rests, on which the awkward foreigner may prop himself up when he tries to sit in Japanese fashion. You will see them in the houses of the well-to-do."

Kehoe pocketed the postcard with the air of bottling an imp. "I'm not going to let out another question today."

"Before I go, may I ask one other question? 'Does everyone live in such a house as this? I mean in a dwelling of similar style and arrangement? Are there no "apartment houses" such as we have at home? Don't any of the Japanese live in hotels?'"

"For a 'single' question I think that takes the record," I answered, "but here are the facts. Japanese families invariably live in separate homes. There is not to my knowledge a single apartment house for Japanese in all the land—not one family living permanently in a hotel—except travelers—in the decidedly Occidental city of Tokyo.

"Japanese houses in cities are built closely together, and, with the exception of large business firms, business and dwelling occupy the same building, usually a large front room being devoted to business and the rear rooms and upper part of the house for living purposes. In residential districts in the outskirts of cities, houses are surrounded by spacious gardens, enclosed by wooden or bamboo fences, over which may be seen pine and maple trees carefully trimmed.

"Homes are of small size, made of wood, bamboo and tiles, built very light, so as to suffer the least damage from earthquakes. The most economic and practical size of a house, accordingly, is about eight rooms and is two stories high. This is the size of house most commonly used all over the country. It is just the right size for the average Japanese family, which consists of about five persons. Houses thus being invariably small and the members of each family large, the necessity of many families living in an apartment house is entirely unknown. Then, too, labor is comparatively cheap, and a faithful and industrious maid-servant, who will do cooking and house-cleaning, as well as serving and running errands, can be hired for a reasonable sum. There exists a cordial relationship between the master and the servant, who is treated as a member of the household."

Kehoe listened carefully to my explanation.

"I see," he said, when I finished. "Now I must be on my way. May I take advantage of your permission and come again for another visit? *Sayonara*, kind lady."

"*Mat-irashai*" (come again), I replied, with the customary formula, as he went away.

Yone and Léonie still made efforts to present themselves as a married couple, but the reality was that they had been living separate lives for some time. Yone gave the following account to Zona Gale, a writer friend he had known in New York.

Yone Noguchi to Zona Gale, March 25, 1909

... Mrs. Noguchi (originally Miss Leonie Gilmour of New York) and baby by name "Isamu" are in Japan now. You know I had one baby boy in Los Angeles; about that you wrote to me somehow vaguely in your last letter. And your letter came to me when I was rather up-set as it was the time they arrived in Japan. We live "separate," but I have to come up and see them whenever I am in Tokyo. It is a long story to go minutely how I married her, and at once we got separated with perfect understanding. I called them to Japan as she wished to live in Japan. The story is not interesting to you, so let us drop the matter for ever! But the baby is such an interesting and bright fellow. As I send you some of his photographs you will see. He speaks already Japanese as well as English; I am very proud of him. And I live here in the temple with my poetry and meditation. Mrs Noguchi, however, appears in public as my wife; I have no objection about that at all. Isamu lives with Mother and is exceeding happy; and he comes here in Kamakura quite often and sleeps with his father ...

To Catherine Bunnell, June 13, 1909

Koishikawa, Tokyo

My dear Catherine

The shirts from Florence arrived to-day (much obliged for your trouble). The book of Irish verse came yesterday. I am happy as seven kings at having a new book of Irish poetry. I'm no less Irish than ever—perhaps more so. Have you seen the plays of one John Synge? I am going to get some. Your letter with M.O. came several weeks ago, and I turned the latter over to Yone in exchange for a copy of his new book which you will receive about this time. You villain! . . . Isamu is out enjoying the street night-fair—probably bargaining for a toy at this moment. He took three large copper sen in his purse. He can buy a "kisha" (train) or a "densha" (trolley car) for that amount. Is he interested in locomotives? Well, I guess. And tunnels! All the sofa cushions, tables and other articles of furniture get turned into tunnels. And he likes a collision, when all the people get all smashed up. I don't think "locomotives" are especially an American child's delight. A popular street song, which every child here knows, has for its theme the electric trolley. And toy trains, trolley cars, and automobiles, which are wound up and made to run across the room, form the biggest part of the stock of every toy-shop. Isamu likes machinery of all sorts—my sewing machine and typewriter are not unknown to him. I should say he has a better head for that kind of thing than I. He also likes natural history. He has some silk cocoons hung on a bush and is watching for the moths to come out. Today he said "a butterfly can't see because it hasn't any eyes, so it is always bumping into things." I told him a butterfly *has* eyes, and he said: "How many?" which stumped me. Did I tell you about his planting some pussywillows and then inviting me to look at his "caterpillars" growing? "Very funny thing in my garden" he said. "Come and see what you think about it." I hear the clatter of his wooden geta. Wonder what he's got . . . . Well, he has bought a memorandum book, bound in green, cover decorated with the Japanese and American flags in gold and a looking glass let into the cover. Pretty good bargain. He is teazing me every day to teach him to read and write. I shall put that off as long as possible. He has the best eyes of any boy in his school, and I don't want him to spoil them.

Are you tired of all this chatter about the boy? In fact, he is everything to me. Now he wants to get on my lap, his favorite seat. "No cushion like this hard thing" he says, leaning his head on my shoulder. No, I am not anxious to invade Yone's temple. Glad to have him and his cigarette out of the way. Isamu and I can run this ranch. Must stop here. No school tonight and so *He* thinks I belong to *Him*. "Make story for me" he is saying. Goodnight. How is your dear mother? Write me of your doings. Léonie.

Léonie, still following the education program of the Workingman's School, had no intention of acceding to Isamu's craving for books. To the end of his life, Isamu never could spell properly.

On a California tour in February, Catharine Bunnell and her mother had arrived at the Gilmour home, and Catharine sent Léonie an illuminating account of the house and neighborhood:

From Catharine Bunnell, February 19, 1910

1144 Marietta St., Tokyo

beg pardon. I believe I'm still in America. You see where my thoughts are though. If your mother talks to me a little less busily than she has been doing, you may get a more coherent letter than otherwise.

The little place is very comfy; I judge there have been considerable many improvements since you last saw it. Boardwalks go from both doors to the front gate and the side fence, and Florence's tiny room is as pretty a spot of its size as I have often been in, with its tiny curtained windows, and the green-burlap-covered walls, and ceiling the color of brown linen. The pictures and bookshelves and some other odds and ends are so familiar I could fancy myself living somewhere with you and everything as it isn't at present. What gives one the greatest sense of time slipped by is that picture of Yone, the one in which he is holding Isamu. Has he really aged so in looks? I think of him always as such a boy with those big appealing eyes.

Mama Gilmour trots around springly as ever. I can see she prefers company across crowded streets and out in dark nights, though she never stays home for lack of it. She took me to a séance at the Canes' house one night, just they two and us two and a table, —and I sat by and swallowed everything, and the table wiggled just as her spirits decreed that it should till Mrs. Cane asked if she always told the truth. That was too much for me and I held the table down with an awful grip after the "no" rap; whereupon your mother brazenly accused me of tipping it myself. But the Canes were too wise to believe any of our insinuations concerning each other.

The Dutchman Dvorjak has been in for dinner brining free cauliflowers and enormous eggs. Wednesday we are to call on him and borrow his horse to drive home. Next Sunday he promises to dine here again. I've fallen in love with the next door neighbor, Mrs. Gyp Aten; you'd like her too; couldn't help yourself. And the rest of the Heights I've still to make the acquaintance of.

I had my first introduction yesterday to the soil when its name is mud. I thought Virginia was slippery, but Los Angeles certainly goes ahead of the rest of the Union in that particular too. Mama Gilmour and I went downtown and did the stores and a cafeteria (my first out here) and the Chamber of Commerce, where I used to address letters to you, and a moving picture show and got home at three just before the rain started. Pretty good time that, for my breakfast hour here averages ten o'clock. At least I think so; it was eleven this morning and it wasn't nine yesterday, not by no means.

Odd moments I practice the piano. You know there is one in Florence's room, and our "Old Lady" is paying for it by giving music lessons to two children twice a week. Solid pluck she is anyway. It's a good little instrument as far as I can judge of the matter. I think there's a family inside which has a passion for soap. I hear the patter of little feet around my washstand at night. At least the tracks are there in the morning. So far however the mice don't act like the story-book ones and come out to dance while we play.

How I run on! Excuse my not having sent the Bryn Mawr program. Your letter followed me out here, and I've been trotting about busily since. Mother wanted us both to see all the sights, and the whole of California is peppered with people whom we know. I went to Santa Barbara with her last week; then left her on her way north. I'm to join her at San José in ten days. What this paragraph started to say was that I'll take measures tomorrow to start the college program your way.

Fairy stories are home after two trials and no success. No hurry. Ganders still have a fatal fascination.

The Christmas gift that waited me here was a joyous surprise. I always did like frivolities,—and what pretty bits of workmanship the two pins are. Florence's was still here, you see, when I came. Thank you much.

Mama Gilmour wants to add something and we must go fairly early to bed after sitting up last night past eleven over fudge and gossip. We're quite a team, I assure you.

Goodnight, dear Brigitta. [Re] the postal correspondence with Mr. Ejiri—I'll think further of it. Most folk I know who would care about it live in too small places to procure postcards worth having. There's one little girl in Stratford I have chiefly in mind, an uncommonly bright little maiden of a dozen years. I'll suggest it when I see her.

Positively all. I'm afraid this will remind you of that famous old epistle I sent you years ago that took a month to wade through. 'Scuse me; I'm not often guilty, am I?

With much love your
Patricka

Nothing to add, says the Old Lady. Love from us both. Mama wants the boy kissed for her.

It must have been back in 1906 that Yone became romantically involved with Matsuko Takeda, most likely during the interval between February when Léonie turned down Yone's invitation, and July, when she informed him she had changed her mind and decided to come. Little is known about Matsuko's background, but according to the reasonably reliable account of son-in-law Usaburo Toyama, she was a seventeen-year-old domestic servant at the house in Hisakata-machi. On the day before Léonie's arrival (according to another family story recounted by Duus), Matsuko was whisked off with the other maid off to a second house in Yanaka Negishi, most likely already pregnant: she gave birth to a daughter, Hifumi, sometime in 1907. Yone stocked the Hisakata-machi house with new servants and found sanctuary from the question of his frequent absences by renting a third house at Engakuji in Kamakura.

How the relationship with Matsuko developed must be left to the imagination. Noguchi did publish a poem entitled "The Love of the Japanese Girl" in a Japanese magazine in December 1906 (it was later reprinted in *The Pilgrimage*) which might be taken as an indication:

O the oldest yet youngest love of the Japanese girl,
O her fading yet lingering scent of heart!
Let me kiss her ivory cheeks and let me die,—
In the kiss I taste the youngest soul out of the ages old,
I taste a rose out of the oldest brown earth.

Léonie had rather expected Yone would marry a Japanese woman: "maybe that would be best—I should feel terribly for a little while, I suppose," she had told Putnam, the implication being that she would soon get over it. If she had suspicions of Yone's infidelities, as she probably did, she did not tell them to Catharine. The perceptive Isamu was not far off when he told Léonie that the nightingale in the tree was his brother and that Léonie could "take a train there any day" and see him. More recently, he had become interested in playing trains and tunnels, taking a particular delight in collisions, "when all the people get all smashed up." A Freudian psychologist might suppose he was on to something.

On December 19, 1909, Yone wrote Frank Putnam after an interval of a year and a half, or "one century" as he jokingly put it. Noguchi thanked Putnam for reviewing his book, *The Pilgrimage*, and the obituary Putnam had written for Stoddard, which Putnam had sent along with a collection of poems by Noguchi's old friend Bliss Carman. Yone gave Putnam his usual cheerful account of his domestic life. "Mrs Noguchi always talks about you," he said, and "Isamu, our boy, is splendid in health and spirit; he goes everyday to his school, and is very happy here." But Yone was clearly holding something back that he could not say. "Oh, Frank, in fact, I do not know how to write to you." A few months later, he sent Putnam his article on Isamu's arrival in Japan, but after that, Yone could no longer manage anything more than a short note to his old friend. Putnam, too, was saddened by the waning of their friendship: a year or two later, asked by the editor of a local magazine called *The Stylus* to write something about Yone, he spent two hours "amid interruptions by politicians, planters, poker players and people in trouble . . . trying to find my way back into the lost atmosphere of romance we once inhabited, and from which I am now an outcast and a wanderer forever and forever."

The big smash-up occurred with the birth of Matsuko's second child, a son, Haruo, in February 1910. While the birth of Hifumi a few years earlier did not precipitate any great crisis, the birth of a son was a potentially more complicated matter, involving questions of inheritance and the future of the Noguchi name. There were few signs of affection between Yone and Léonie. Even her cheerful letters to Catharine were full of signs of impending separation: she was "not anxious to invade Yone's temple"; she was "glad to have him and his cigarette out of the way"; "Isamu and I can run this ranch." Yone had told Zona Gale he and Léonie lived separately.

At the time of Haruo's birth, Léonie wrote to her erstwhile intimate friend Matsuo Miyake, telling him in somewhat veiled terms of her sadness. Léonie had maintained an intimate correspondence with the young Miyake ever since arriving in Japan, although they had not seen each other until the previous May, Miyake was able to travel to Tokyo and Léonie cooked him a hearty dinner. "It is true I could not speak much that time, feeling my heart too much," he wrote her afterward. The 23-year-old Miyake had been through much, having been left a single father when his wife died shortly after giving birth. Now, on February 5, he alluded to Léonie's own expression of despair: "You say *you have a big sorrow in your heart*. Don't think your brother does not know of his sister's sorrow," he wrote, assuring her, "I am always thinking of you and of your circumstance. I sympathize you with all my heart." Léonie took no precipitous action following Haruo's birth, but did begin seriously thinking of leaving Noguchi to live on her own.

The two and a half years of supposed marriage had lent Isamu the desired air of legitimacy, and there was nothing really to be gained by continuing the pretense of living together. The last act of the marriage performance was the essay on Isamu's arrival, which was now belatedly sent out for publication. A literary acknowledgement of marriage and paternity, it featured unambiguous lines like "In fact, he was born to my wife in California some time after I left America." Frank Putnam proudly published the article in the *Southwestern Farmer*, though its appearance there would have left some Texan farmers scratching their heads. It was published also in California's prominent *Sunset* magazine and the London *Nation*, and subsequently appeared in *The Story of Yone Noguchi*.

"Isamu, son of Yone Noguchi and his American wife." *Sunset Magazine,* November, 1910.

In April 1910, Léonie took a job teaching English part time at the Kanagawa Prefecture Girls' Higher School in Yokohama, an important step toward independence.

Léonie, Isamu and four female colleagues, c. 1910. *Isamu Noguchi Foundation.*

To Catherine Bunnell, July 14, 1910

(Vive la république!)

My sweet Cherokee Rose,

Yes, I like your style—all in white, a glossy braid wound round your head, a few freckles on your nose (did you mention them?)—and I can imagine you eating ripe cherries, while you play tag with your conscience over the Lord knows what new mischief. Now I am dressed in a gray cotton—a curious gray with a tiny white pattern—I am told this dress reflects my eyes. My newest style of hair dressing is with a tress wound round the edge of my head, and a few escaping locks. But I am not distinguished enough to keep to one style. Sometimes I affect a princess sort of dress, which shows off my slender figure, and then people say "How young you look!" By the way, how do you like me in Japanese kimono? I am beginning to wear it with considerable ease—obi and all.

Speaking of fastidious in hair-dressing, I am sure you would admire Isamu's summer style—head completely shaved like an egg—he has the most splendidly shaped head you ever saw. I told him he should be careful about bumping his head now that he has no hair to protect it. So he promptly tried a bump—then said "why, it feels nice—It's much better this way."

It is a day of glorious sunshine—after a month of drizzly rainy season. All the umbrellas are taking a sun bath in the garden. There are also six wild little boys in the garden—Isamu and his friends—the place seems to belong to them. Tomorrow is my last day of school—Oh joy! Then for the pleasures of home—jam-making and sewing and mending and letter writing—then a month in August at the seashore—part play, part work—as I'm trying to write an English reader—to such uses is my genius bent.

So Helen Saunders is married? I'd send felicitations but am afraid they'd be rather late. I had a nice long letter from Kitty Dame one day. I'm sorry to hear that Bess got bubbly again. Wouldn't California be better for her? Or the Hawaiian islands—with their indescribably lovely changing atmosphere—she could make pictures of strange fishes and shells and seaweeds of the Pacific—and eat bananas and pineapples, and dress in a flower robe.

Is it true my family are to migrate to California? It is the first I heard of it. I wish it might be so. If they were all there in a bunch we might get over for a visit some day—well, after about seven years.

Now I have some work to do. So sayonara, my dear.

Léonie

Behold the address:
2 Kobinata dai machi Nichome Koishikawa, Tokyo.
(It means something like—the great street on the little hill in the district by the river)

"Where do you go all the time?" *Essen Communications Ltd.*

On September 23, 1910, Matsuo Miyake commented on Léonie's plan to move to Omori, casually mentioning that he had remarried. "During this vacation's leisure hours," he wrote, "I have succeeded in my love affair." His new bride Fumiko was also twenty-three and was a well-known musician in Osaka. The letter must have come as a shock to Léonie, who could not have easily forgotten the idyllic dream of Kyoto domestic life painted by the ardent young journalist. Now that dream, too, was lost. Shortly after receiving this letter, Léonie poured out her sorrows to Miyake in an urgent letter, the contents of which can be inferred from his October 6 response:

From Matsuo Miyake, October 6, [1910]

Osaka

My dear sister:—
I did not come to office last Sunday, and it was yesterday morning I received your note. To be sure I must have let you wait long. Please excuse me of it. I have, to say the truth, no words to console you, for my heart is full of sympathy to you.
Yet I can not understand your circumstances quite well, so will you let me know further more?

1. Are you going to separate for ever?

2. Is it effect of economical standpoint or affection? (How unhappy I feel to ask you such matter)

3. If you are going to separate will you return to America?

4. Or are you going to stay Japan forever or temporarily?

5. Are you going to look for a house to live there temporarily or for a long time?

6. Will Mr. Noguchi not give you some money on separation so that you may either go home or stay Japan being able to support yourself for two or three months?

7. Is Mr. Noguchi going to take *our Isamu* or are you. (I can not dare say thus without some any tears.)

8. If you are going to stay Japan will you come to Osaka (If I can get some good position for you) so that, if in need, you may keep household with me for saving the expenses?

9. If you stay Japan forever what are you going to do with your mother in America?

Those above are what I wish you to ask. Of course if I had enough money in hand I would send it to you before such asking. But I feel very unhappy that I could not do it. Yes I *will* help you as possible. Please write me soon,

Your brother for ever,

Matsuo

Léonie most likely told Matsuo that her separation—a matter of affection rather than economics—was permanent, that she planned to stay in Japan and would continue to care for Isamu, supporting herself by teaching (and the occasional contribution from Yone). She must have sensed that moving to Osaka to set up house with Matsuo—with or without his new wife and three children—was not the ideal solution to her problems. She chose to remain in the Tokyo-Yokohama area, where she already had work and connections.

In December 1910 Léonie and Isamu left central Tokyo where they had lived since their arrival and moved to Omori, a station on the Tokaido line just beyond the southern edge of the city. Yone's obligatory visits were now conveniently inconvenient, and the move served as public acknowledgment of their separation. Now more than ever, Isamu had to substitute for his father in his mother's affections. As Léonie recounted to Catharine Bunnell, "He told his papa the other day that he hoped to become a great man some day, but that he could not become *so* great as mama. Tonight he is busy making a book." But making books was not all there was to it. He lived in fear of losing his mother, beset with the classic Oedipal problem: inability to fill his absent father's shoes. He could not be quite everything to his mother: she sought emotional sustenance elsewhere, and had secrets she would never reveal to him or anyone. No longer feeling obligated to remain faithful to her estranged husband, she had a relationship with a man whose identity was unknown to Isamu. While living in Omori, Léonie and her lover conceived a child, a girl she named Ailes.

"Beauty's a Flower," the poem from which Léonie derived Ailes' name, was written by Moira O'Neill, the pseudonym of Agnes Nesta Shakespeare Higginson (1863-1955), a Northern Irish poet who wrote her *Songs of the Glens of Antrim* (1901) in an Ulster dialect. The poem had first appeared in *Blackwood's Magazine* (with the name rendered as "Ailish") in 1898, but Léonie probably found it in "A Little Garland of Celtic Verse," a special number of *The Bibelot*, a monthly literary anthology published by Yone's friend Thomas Mosher, to which Catharine gave her a subscription. "That and Shakespeare are the chief of my diet at present," Léonie told Catharine during her pregnancy. The poem was certainly a bold choice, as it tells the story of an extramarital romance.

> Youth's for an hour,
> Beauty's a flower,
> But love is the jewel that wins the world.

> Youth's for an hour, an' the taste o' life is sweet,
> Ailes was a girl that stepped on two bare feet;
> In all my days I never seen the one as fair as she,
> I'd have lost my life for Ailes, an' she never cared for me.

> Beauty's a flower, an' the days o' life are long,
> There's little knowin' who may live to sing another song;
> For Ailes was the fairest, but another is my wife,
> An' Mary—God be good to her!—is all I love in life.

> Youth's for an hour,
> Beauty's a flower,
> But love is the jewel that wins the world.

The passion that had led to Léonie's pregnancy may well have borne some relation to that of the singer, obsessed with the fair Ailes, though staunchly in love with his spouse.

Léonie took the secret of the father's identity to her grave. She had good reason for the secrecy: by refusing to divulge the identity of the (presumably Japanese) father, Ailes would take her mother's nationality, which, if she was no longer married to Noguchi, could revert to American. When Léonie applied for a passport to return to the United States in 1920, Ailes later explained, she "notified the American Consul that I was her daughter and was an American citizen through her, as she had never married." The laws of marriage and citizenship had not been written with women's interests in mind, but Léonie had found a way to work the system to live as she wished.

Léonie had also found a kindergarten for Isamu, an experimental one run by Ichizaemon Morimura, a wealthy Yokohama merchant, where children were taught to do things with their hands. "My first sculpture was made there in the form of a sea wave, in clay and with a blue glaze," Isamu Noguchi later recalled. To his great pride, it was "shown around." "Somehow or other I knew about waves. It was a kind of prophecy . . . On a boat, coming here, I saw waves." From the beginning, Isamu's artistic fame emerged from his conflicted identity, the space of separation between his American and Japanese selves. It borrowed something from his father, who hailed from a "town of purple waves," had blue waves on the cover of the Japanese edition of his most famous book, and had recently written, in an autobiographical essay published at that time, of his confrontation with "the threatening vastness of the ocean."

The success of Isamu's first sculpture, at the age of five, was of course no accident: Léonie had in effect been preparing for this first public exhibition for years. When Isamu was barely fourteen months old, Léonie had written Yone of her recurring thought to send Isamu to an art school. The idea became gradually fixed in her mind, and her determination was at times extraordinary. Nearly twenty years later, when a well-meaning friend tried to put Isamu through medical school, Léonie would raise an "awful row," accusing him of "turning a boy of artistic temperament toward a career for which he was entirely unsuited." Perhaps, as some have suggested, this determination stemmed from Léonie's own frustrated creative aspirations. Mainly, however, her determination came from the profound influence in her own childhood of Felix Adler's school.

To Catherine Bunnell, November 3, 1910

Tokyo

My dear Catherine,
    Today is the birthday of "everybody's papa" as Isamu calls His Majesty the Emperor of Japan. So I will celebrate by writing to you. This is the season when all schools hold "undokai" (athletic sports) and I'm

booked to attend the affair at Oriental College this afternoon. Isamu had his own school affair last Sunday, but the rain prevented the great bicycle race (Noguchi Isamu champion) from coming off. However, we attended and I saw many interesting things—one being a very high art sketch by Isamu—you had to look hard to see anything on the paper—and then you perceived some faint blue lines representing the waves of the sea, with a few pale yellow sails on it. He called it "Ibaraki ken by moonlight." He has about decided to become an artist instead of a soldier. "Why?" said I. "Because" said he "all the soldiers got to die, and I don't want to die." "Even a giniral has to die."

Thanks for your letter containing all the news. 'Twas entertaining, to be sure. Things do happen even in Amerikey. Here in Koishikawa it is very quiet. And I'm thinking of moving to an even more quiet spot just out of the city. Am house hunting now—tiresome job. Found a most ideal school for Isamu on the edge of the city—the side near my school. Rich old gentleman (Morimura) got a hobby for making an ideal school—turned his beautiful grounds over to the little ones and is getting the best teachers to be had for love or money. Goat, chickens, monkey, peacock, seesaws, swings etc. Very small, very high-toned, a trifle expensive. We visited there one day, and it seems all right. Isamu says he likes it "because it is such a beauty garden." And his own teacher Miss Koga (perhaps the best kindergartner in Japan) has also the charge of that school, so it will not be any break in his work. Got to economize on rent next go. I am very tired lately—too much railroading and rush. My fat all turns to lean. Sorry to hear that Bess is having a hard time. The last you wrote she was doing pictures for Sims and Co. and I thought it sounded like nice work. You don't say what she is doing now. Please give my love to Alice and tell her I'm thinking about writing. How is Mary? Now I must stop and make sponge cake—after your receipt. Company coming soon.

With best love
Your
Léonie
P.S. Better write next time to
Kotojo-gakko (Girls' School)
Hiranuma
Kanakawa [*sic*] ken, Japan

At Christmas Leonie wrote to thank Catharine for a gift of books and to inform her of her new address.

To Catherine Bunnell, December 23, 1910

Omori

My dear Catherine,
Your beloved vagabond wandered into my school yesterday about noon. And so it happened that I had a little chat with him then and there, with the result that when the bell rang I was utterly puzzled to think where I was. Surely I was in a school somewhere—in France? America?—Ah, Japan. And I was a teacher, and I had to teach—er—er—Oh English, to be sure, I was thinking it was French.

Well! A letter should have gone to you last week to escort a small ivory brooch (I thought of your rose that was burglarized when I bought it) which I sent you. But alas, the pen that should have penned the companion epistle was diverted to other uses at the moment. Last night of course I couldn't write, being deeply engrossed in my new acquaintance and the tales of his vagabondage.

Now why is it that all the charming erratic good for nothing heroes and heroines in fiction have an Irish father? And why is it that a fellow can't be a delightful vagabond (in fiction) and possessed of all noble and generous qualities without having also a taste for gin and gutters. I suspect that he, Irish father and gin and all, is merely a sort of stage tradition, and I wish, for the sake of Ireland and the dignity of noble freedom of thought and life, that someone would break loose from the tradition. There's a good old Walt Whitman looking down from his picture on the wall looks a healthy old chap if he was unconventional. And Meredith and others.

Change the subject. We have been to the circus, the Russian circus visiting Japan, and seen the Russian ladies performing thrilling feats on horseback, also some Russian village dances that were spirited and picturesque. Isamu was in ecstasies. There was one man Mr B— famous horse trainer—Isamu whispered to me: "He is a *Great man!*" Poor little Isamu. His hero worship is strangely placed. He told his papa the other day that he hoped to become a great man some day, but that he could not become *so* great as mama. Tonight he is busy making a book. His cheeks are red red roses. I think the country air does him good. Which reminds me to tell you that we are now living at Omori, a village which bears the same relation to Tokyo as New Rochelle to New York, and like that village, is by the water. But we are on a hill, away from the water, looking the other way. View of Mr. Fuji on clear days. This place is halfway between my former home and my school, and I spend alternate days riding on the train or trolley to school and to Tokyo, where I still have some pupils. My true address is 2737 Iriaraimura Araijiku San No, Omori, Japan. The meaning of it I don't know, except the last part which is "King of the mountain."

Now Isamu is getting mad with his needle and thread, so I will help him.

With love as ever and ever

Brigitta

P.S.—The Bibelot leaflet was a delightful surprise. I thought it was an ad, but I looked again and saw it was—something very nice.

To Catherine Bunnell, May 3, 1911

My dear Catherine,

Owing to something like a strike on the part of the graduate English class (a clash between the headmaster and one of the teachers) I am left without any class this hour. When the cats fight the mice will play, to vary the adage. I being the happy mouse, have rummaged through another teacher's desk to find this scrap of paper which I now use for my own amusement and yours. Well, what's the gossip? I received your peppery card from Africa and was thankful to Dr. Moody for stirring you up to send it, being as I never had the honor of a postcard from Africa. I had previously received a letter from the lady herself, full of questions and solicitude regarding Kotoku, the Japanese anarchist!!!! et. al. I think she is being converted from the ways of the Philistines. Well, I answered and gave her what information I could do. Anyway I have ten minutes to prepare my next lesson.

Gracious! I wrote this and forgot to finish it. Now it's Sunday. Rainy. Have just re-read the Bibelot about Leonardo da Vinci—Arthur Symons essay. It is one of my favourites. I enjoy having the Bibelot. That and Shakespeare are the chief of my diet at present. Spend much time watching for my seeds to sprout in the garden. It consoles me for the rain. Omori is, I daresay, a more quiet spot than Stratford. We know only one of our neighbors. But Isamu knows some more. Following is a specimen of his budding genius. It is meant to be Mama. Observe the foreign nose. I just told him it was time to go to bed. "I can't go now," said he, "because I told the neighbor's boy I would not go to bed so early, and *I have to* tell the truth."

With love,

Léonie

Kanagawa, 1911-1920

Léonie and Isamu had lived in Tokyo for four and a half years; they had been in Omori less than a year when they moved again in the fall of 1911, this time further south to Chigasaki, a seaside town beyond Yokohama.

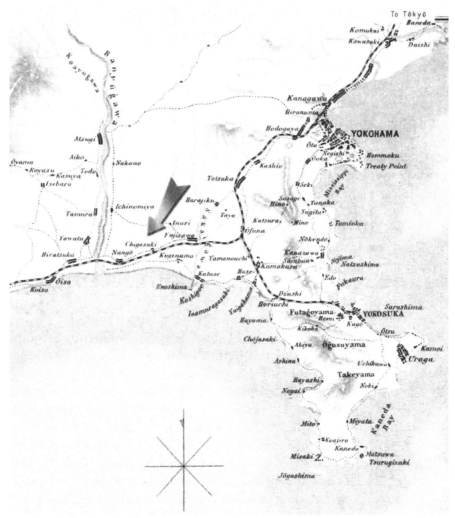

Chigasaki on a map of Kanagawa prefecture.

Chigasaki was "a place so small as to be unnoticed on the railway timetable, but rather famous for its clear air fragrant of the sea and pine woods which make it a resort for consumptives," Léonie explained to Catharine. "Don't be alarmed," she added, "I am not in that class." A 1914 guidebook notes that "Chigasaki was a solitary fishing village till a dozen years ago, when its sandy beach and extensive pine-grove began to attract people from Tokyo and Yokohama, and now, with its hundreds of villas, the place has become quite a fashionable resort." Yokohama, home to Japan's largest foreign community was near enough to be accessible, but far enough to feel comfortably distant. Chigasaki was part of Kanagawa, the prefecture extending southwest from Tokyo, which also included the former treaty port of Yokohama, as well as the old capital of Kamakura and the famed hot springs of Hakone. With its station on the Tokaido railway, Chigasaki was conveniently located but still remote and rustic. Today, it still has the relaxed atmosphere of a southern California beach town, complete with a substantial population of surfers drawn to Chigasaki's famous black-sand beaches.

Isamu Noguchi, *A Sculptor's World*

When I was four or five, my mother decided to move to the country, to Chigasaki, near the sea. There the land is a dark sand, covered with the small pines of the seashore, a place where sweet potatoes and watermelons do well. Through the village runs the Tokaido road with its magnificent pines of Hiroshige. At first we lived in the house of a farmer whose wife raised silkworms on trays of mulberry leaves in the house. It was there that I attended two years of the local school.

I had by then become a typical Japanese boy, knowledgeable in the ways of nature; such as how to skin the young willow twigs to make whistles, or where to find eels. There were all the festivals I delighted in, the Obon dancing in the streets, the kites in the wind, the many-coloured *mochi* 'rice cakes' roasted on forked branches over autumn bonfires. There was a travelling Kabuki troupe. There were the sunsets to which we sang 'Yu yake ko yake'.

Soon after her removal to Chigasaki, Léonie received word of the death of her mother. When she wrote to Catharine in November, she wrote about her new residence, the news about her mother, and her worries about her father, dropping only the vaguest hints about her pregnancy.

To Catherine Bunnell, November 3, 1911

My dear Catherine

Today being the birthday of Tenno Sama (the Emperor), all people are enjoying a holiday. I began it by going to sit out in the sun, spreading a straw mat on the dew-spangled grass, and crocheting on Isamu's winter sweater until I got sufficiently warmed up to come in and write to you. You see I am now in Chigasaki, a place so small as to be unnoticed on the railway timetable, but rather famous for its clear air fragrant of the sea and pine woods which make it a resort for consumptives. (Don't be alarmed, I am not in that class.) It is about one hour from my school, the same as Omori. (The newspaper just came, and I stopped a minute to note the rebel victories in China. Those people seem to know what they want, and are likely to get it.)

I can hardly realize that mama is no longer waiting for our visit to California, as I always hoped to get over once more in her lifetime. A letter from Florence last August told me of her illness, but that she was getting better. Strange to say, I have never had any word from Florence since then, and the news came to me indirectly, first through my aunt's letter, and then through yours. I suppose Florence must have misdirected her letter to me. To lose one parent makes one more anxious about the other, don't you think so? So now I am worried a bit about papa. I hope he will go to California or come here. I wrote once or twice to ask him to come here, but don't like to urge him as I fear the climate would be an endless source of discomfort. Old people are always a little cranky about the weather as the cold gets into their blood, just as with yours truly. I really must move to the porch, as inside is too cold. . . . well, this is better, with the sun on my back and Frye's geography for a table. I feel a bit disgruntled as a result of a visit yesterday from the head mistress of our school. You see I had asked for a holiday to rest up in, which the school seemed unwilling to give, so to clinch matters I played hooky day before yesterday. Result, the said visit. To convince the lady, I brought over my neighbor doctor to talk to her. Whereupon this wonderful doctor aired his theory that sick people should be kept busy, in order not to grow more weak, and that it was better for me to go to school. That man will never get rich. When people come to him he tells them that it is foolish to waste money for a doctor, and they had better go home and get busy. He even assured me that my toothache was not a toothache, but neuralgia, and there was nothing to be done about it. The gentleman himself is notoriously lazy, sleeps late in the morning, never walks when he can ride, and puts in his attendant leisure playing chess and eating sweet potatoes. Couldn't you put him in the Y.O.U. for a character?

Isamu says the fire is and good and it is time to start the bread pudding. So à tantot.

Affectionately your
Brigitta

氏ラライキ、スルアヤチ 人詩國米らせ朝來

Yone Noguchi and Charles
Keeler. *Taiyo*, 1911.

In the fall of 1911, Catharine's cousin by marriage, the writer Charles Keeler, visited Japan as part of what he called a "world tour of recitals." Keeler had married Catharine's cousin, Louise Mapes Bunnell in 1893, but Louise had died tragically of heart failure in 1907, at the age of thirty-four. Charles Keeler was a fixture in the San Francisco Bay Area literary scene; an ardent naturalist with interests in California history and architecture, he wrote poetry and plays, published in books that were beautifully printed, if seldom read. He and Yone had been acquainted during Yone's California days, though they had not been particularly close.

Léonie was entering her third trimester when Keeler arrived, so it is not surprising she did not join Yone and Charles on their Nikko trip. But she had not mentioned her pregnancy to Catharine, and continued to avoid the topic in the following letter, written in her ninth month.

To Catherine Bunnell, January 15, 1912

Chigasaki, Potamaooki [?], Kanagawa Ken, Japan, etc.

c/o Hamajiro [?] Ozawa

My dear Catherine,

It is indeed a pleasure to receive a letter directly, I mean without having been forwarded from place to place. You seem to be one of my few correspondents who can keep pace with my movements. My next address will be—well, I'll write you that later, as I don't know myself. Let me take this occasion to thank you for your Christmas letter, which reached me the day before Xmas, also for the promised book, which has not yet arrived. I know it will be a good one, relying on your well known taste in literature (ahem!)

Your distinguished cousin Mr. Keeler has come and gone like a comet and I believe made a brilliant sensation—a society sensation, I should say,—he was dined and wined, and his poems quoted in the Japan Times (alas for the distinction, the random utterances of every after dinner speaker are quoted with equal gusto). He and Mr. Hamilton Holt (of the Independent) shared equal honors during his short stay. Yone took him on a trip to Nikko, said he was glad to have seen him and glad it was over. He is not equal to the strenuosity of the average American, and C.K. may have an extra amount of the blizzard ingredient. By the way, I made C.K.'s acquaintance as a prose writer some years ago in his account of the San Francisco earthquake and found it splendid, vigorous writing. . . . now to return to this end of the string, as I look up I see Mr. Bear (you remember the dear little Teddy Ba-o you sent Isamu once in America? It is still his favorite plaything) wildly trying to climb a *dango* tree on the bureau. The *dango* are rice-cakes stuck on the bare twigs of a wintry branch, with tiny oranges similarly stuck on here and there. I think Eugene Field got his idea of the sugar plum tree from this same dango tree—yes, to be sure—there's a satisfaction in tracing the origins of things. Isamu's young mind is now intent on the problem of the first, firstest man. I gave him three theories for a choice—Adam and Eve and the garden, the Norse legend about the cow licking the stones, and the monkey's clever child. He promptly rejected the latter, saying, "Nowadays no monkeys turn into men, and even the most clever monkey's child is only a foolish monkey." He said he liked the one about God and Adam and Eve best.

Don't worry about Florence. She's always busy and finds it hard to keep up with correspondence like myself. She told me she has taken

to covering the letters to be answered with a newspaper, but still they haunt her. I go one step further, and leave them *unopened* for several weeks, until I feel in the mood for writing. Some letters have now been waiting their turn for three months. I wonder what's in them. But don't get ruffled, your letters are always read the day they arrive, though not always answered. This blot [ink blot] is not symbolic. Forever and forever
Léonie

Ailes Gilmour was born two weeks later, on January 27, 1912. According-ing to Duus, Léonie was at school in Yokohama when she went into early labor. It was another five months before Léonie got around to writing Catharine, in her characteristically breezy manner, about the new addi-tion to the family.

To Catherine Bunnell, July 2, 1912

Kowada, Chigasaki, Kanagawa ken

c/o Fukuoka San.

My dear Catherine,
Your letter came while I was convalescing from a headache—I smiled to think how often your letter had pulled me out of a valley of some sort or other. Behold me now retired to a hut in the pine forest—two tiny rooms, kitchen, bath—all so small I feel like Alice when she got into the rabbit's house. Why Viscount Fukuoka, my landlord, built such a small house right on the grounds of his summer villa I don't know. His own house is quite vast. I am waiting for him to put in an appearance these summer holidays to persuade him to annex another room, though he may consider the present size more in accord with the Japanese aesthet-ics of a hermit life. "I have cast the world and think me as nothing. Still I feel hot in summer and cold in winter," according to a Japanese poem.
Isamu is in the front garden, watering the morning-glories. Baby Ailes is rolling on the floor beside me. The maid is in the back garden, hanging up the baby's clothes. There are plenty of black birds (crows) about, but they never would think it worth while to pick off O Kan San's small nose. Alas, that jewel of a maid has given me notice as it is too "lonesome" here.
Yes, of course you could tell it was a boy at first glance. Anybody can. But in fact it is a girl. As to age, anybody can tell it is a two year old—judg-ing from appearance, size etc. Alas, the poor girl is only 5 months old

(born January 27, in opposition to the Doctor, who would have preferred another date. But I told him it was our family habit to be born on the 17th or 27th.) An American type, I should say—long legged—very long slim feet—grey eyes white skin, fine short brown hair. Well, I am rather overburdened, but I suppose it was her destiny to be born, poor thing. She's not so active as was Isamu. Puts in her energy in growing and talking—talks incessantly, and laughs out loud like a grown-up. Voice high and girlish. - - - - Just interrupted by an earthquake—guess it's quiet enough to go on writing—let me see—Baby's name? "Ailes Gilmour"— "Ailes was a girl that stepped on two bare feet" in Moira O'Neill's poem. Believe it's a Keltic version of Alice. I call her Ailes, but the neighbors have christened her "Mary San"—don't know which name will hold out—ouch! another earthquake!—It's proper to take refuge in a bamboo grove if the shocks keep up. There's a tiny clump of bamboos back of the house—but could a person stand therein?

Where's my letter paper? Now what was it I wanted to ask you? Ah, yes. Where's Florence? Hasn't she moved too? Letters are always going astray—but not yours, as a rule—you C.C. (careful correspondent)—your Xmas books being the inevitable exception. Say, I was interested in Arthur Symons' Prelude to Life—and I did enjoy Morris country walk—I kept thinking of you when I read it. Aren't you something like him? That your works don't finish up so roundly is only the evidence of your being a woman, and incomplete by nature ma chère.

With dear love

Léonie

P.S.—To be a maiden auntie and beautiful is lovely and romantic. Thanks for your picture.

Isamu Noguchi, View of Eboshi-iwa. *Isamu Noguchi Foundation.*

Isamu drew it. The Jap. characters are his name.

In Isamu's calligraphy the character for "Isamu" (勇) is recognizable beside an awkward attempt to write "Noguchi" (野口). The subject of the picture is easily recognizable to locals as the Eboshi-iwa ("hat rock"), a twenty-meter-high rock in a reef islet about a kilometer offshore, sometimes referred to as the symbol of Chigasaki.

The difficulties of Isamu's "process of self-manifestation," to use Felix Adler's phrase, became more apparent in the months after the birth of Ailes. Isamu was at the age when childhood freedom customarily gives way to powerful social constraints in Japan, but Léonie could not have known how to socialize Isamu to conform to Japanese norms even if she had wanted to—and she certainly did not want to. Her insistence on individualism insured that Isamu's relations with his new peer group started off badly and deteriorated quickly, as he found himself the subject of the merciless bullying customarily dished out to Japanese non-conformists. Since the previous year, Isamu had been enrolled in a Chigasaki elementary school where, as Duus notes, he was "surrounded by fishermen's and farmers' children with sunburned faces and rough ways . . . thrust into a milieu unimaginably harsher than Morimura Kindergarten." Perhaps Yone felt some sympathy for his son's plight, for in a rare moment of paternalism, he paid a visit when Isamu caught the measles in the spring.

**Ailes and
Isamu, 1912.**
*Isamu Noguchi
Foundation.*

Isamu's preadolescent troubles did not catch Léonie entirely unprepared. She had been teaching at a school in Yokohama, and in September 1913, she enrolled Isamu in a French Jesuit school there called St. Joseph's. The move offered Isamu a chance to escape his tormenting Japanese peers and develop his American side, but it was a move out of the frying pan and into the fire. Isamu was ill-suited for a Catholic school, even such a multicultural one as St. Joseph's. His mother had raised him on a good Adlerian diet of Greek and Irish mythology, William Blake, and Uncle Remus (fairy tales, Adler said, "reflect the unbroken communion of human life with the life universal," stimulating the imagination and quickening the moral sentiments). So it was hardly surprising that Isamu "became terribly confused" when he "learned later of God and Santa Claus." Moreover, the commute was grueling: after waking at four each morning to catch the train, Isamu had to walk two and a half miles from Yokohama station. After the novelty of the new school wore off, Isamu began to rebel. Léonie must have seen this coming, and she wisely continued to offer him alternative educational opportunities on the side. As Isamu later put it, "there came a reprieve. Mother decided to build a house, and insisted that we must do it together." She had found an oddly-shaped plot wedged between the palatial estates of the wealthier residents on Teppo-michi, a long road that runs parallel to the shore, at the edge of a pine grove. There, with Isamu assisting the carpenters and reporting to his mother on their daily progress, they built "a semi-Japanese house with a round window on the second floor, which on a clear day would frame Mount Fuji off to the west." Later, when Isamu refused to return to St. Joseph's, she apprenticed him to a Japanese carpenter.

Isamu Noguchi, *A Sculptor's World*

When I was eight my sister Ailes was born, and—to add to my distress—it was decided that I should commute to a French Jesuit school in Yokohama called St Joseph's College. But there came a reprieve. Mother decided to build a house, and insisted that we must do it together. She selected a spot closer to the sea on the edge of a pine grove overlooking potato fields. It must have been spring, for soon I was there constantly, following every detail. It was a semi-Japanese house with a round window on the second floor, which on a clear day would frame Mount Fuji off to the west. When I visited it in 1950 after the war, it was just as I had known it, though now surrounded by houses, and I was told that it was one of the few houses around there to withstand the ravages of earthquakes over the years. Its owners were most hospitable, and a little old lady who lived next door, remembering me, came running out with her apron filled with hot salted sweet potatoes, crying, 'Isamu san, welcome home. Have some sweet potatoes. Isa-amu,' she cried, imitating my mother.

My mother seemed always to be calling me. Frail and small, with grey-blue eyes, she would come home at evening to my infinite relief. How I lived in fear of losing her! My fondest recollection is of Mother reading to me. She read to me according to her taste. As a result I believed in Apollo and all the gods of Olympus long before I knew of any other. I remember often visiting temples and gardens. At one point she took up archery, which was conducted on a temple ground, and I was also given a small bow. I became terribly confused when I learned later of God and Santa Claus. My first awareness of poetry was Blake: 'Ah, sunflower'. Beyond that, Chaucer, Uncle Remus, and Lady Gregory are about equally mixed. I would say I was relatively happy in Chigasaki, though most often alone, while my mother was away working.

The house project was perhaps an attempt to keep up with the Noguchis, as Yone had begun building his own two-storey house in Higashi (East) Nakano, a gradually-developing suburb west of bustling Shinjuku.

From Yone Noguchi, January 12, [1913?]

Nakano, near Tokyo

Dear Leonie:
Are you well? I am still far from being quite well. And beside, two cheques I received from West were wrong, therefore I could not cash them. That is the reason for my delay in sending you money. I wish you will wait a few days more, I will raise money somewhere else if I do not get it by that time. Did you get my writing on Mr. Hara the Artist? Please send it to me when it is done. I hope you are well, health is everything.
Yours
Yone
My best love to Isamu; is it cold at your place? It is terrible here.

From Yone Noguchi, April 5, [1913]

So sorry to hear Isamu is ill. Hope he is well by this time. Yesterday your postcard came yesterday morning, when we were so busy—moving to our new house. So you two had been in town.

Here are cheque for some twenty five or six yen; the particular bank (International Banking Corporation, that is in the Main St. in Yamashi-tacho of Yokohama) is indicated, so you have to go to that bank. If you cannot cash it there, you might ask your English friend of Oiso to cash it. That is easy, I believe.

I received many good letters from England; but I might postpone one more year, I mean my going to England. I am somehow under a heavy debt; I think I must settle so far in some way when I leave here. I say I am under the debt; I built a house which was too expensive altogether. But I expect that I will be soon all well even in that money matter.

Herewith I send you one article called "My Own Poetry" (the old thing) which I wish you will typewrite at your earliest convenience. I need two sets of that article. I have a few communications from the English magazine. You know [Joaquin] Miller died some weeks ago.

Yone

Postcard to Catherine dated January 15, 1913. *Isamu Noguchi Foundation.*

To Catherine Bunnell, January 15, 1913

[postcard] Kowada, Chigasaki

I am so glad you sent him the Greek Heroes. He is a worshipper of Apollo, but does not know Kingsley's book. Have been reading "The Piper" to him (Miss Peabody) but a misery in my eyes stopped all reading and writing for a few weeks. Now better. Ailes has worn her pretty pin on her new bib and it was much admired. Of course the customs officer did not know what was in that card. I was puzzled myself. And there be thieves here too. But you would outwit Autolycus.

Yours lovingly

Léonie

To Catherine Bunnell, March 7, 1913

School

My dear Catherine—

Fire and devastation! I walked through the smoking ruins of a fire that destroyed 500 houses in Yokohama this morning. And I learned that a fire of equal extent occurred in Tokyo last night. It is only a few days since another great fire destroyed a large section of Tokyo and many schools and colleges. There seems to be a wave of incendiarism sweeping over Japan. And that when the country is pretty close to bankruptcy is really too bad.

Alas! I perceive it is near the green day of St. Patrick, and no appropriate token on hand. I should like to send you a doll, but it would break. And a broken doll is so sad. Ailes celebrated her second dolls' festival on the third of this month. I am sorry to say she walked right up to the tokonoma and stole some of the dolls' rice.

When are you coming to Japan, ma chère? It seems to me if you are coming this year it is now the proper season to arrive. Season of winds, cherry blossoms and the "Flower of Yedo" (that's what they call a big fire here, "flower of Tokyo.")

Well, we have read all the labours of Hercules, and the story of Perseus, and are half way through the story of the Argonauts. Isamu is an admirer of Hercules especially, though that has not ousted his beloved Apollo. And if you please, he prefers in future to be called "George Apollo"—a combination of George Washington and the sun-god. Did I tell you the disastrous outcome of the cherry-tree legend? You see Isamu told that story to his chum, Sho Morita. Sho-chan, being fired with emulation and desirous of taking the first steps to becoming a great man, promptly chopped down O Danna's (that's his lord and master Viscount Fukuoka) most precious bamboo. He promptly owned up, and was as promptly given the thrashing of his life by his grandfather. Furthermore, his grandmother told Isamu that before we came to the neighborhood Sho-taro had been a good boy, but owing to Isamu's pernicious influence he was becoming the worst kind of a boy. Isamu was so depressed he stayed in the house a whole day, occasionally muttering "am I a bad boy?" "Am I the worst boy in the world?" etc.

And here is one more page. Shall I tell one more on that precious monkey? It's like this:

Isamu—Mamma, when you die I get all the money, don't I?

Mamma—What money? (Oh, yes, yes, my money you mean).

Isamu—And when papa dies I get all his money? Eh? Eh? (nudging me playfully).

Mamma—See here, you young scallywag, are you waiting for us to die?

Isamu—Oh, no, no. Of co'se not. But of co'se, *if* you should fall sick, and—er—die (pulling a serious face)—why, no use to throw away money. Eh? (nudging again) And of course, Mamma, we must spend plenty money for your tooniform.

Mamma—My what?

Isamu—Why, your tooniform, you know. That's the stone you put over dead folks. You're going to have a splendid tooniform. (Beaming on me with the air of presenting a magnificent toy)

Time's up. Bell ringing!

Good bye with love. May your days all be green like the pine tree.

Léonie

To Catherine Bunnell, September 23, [1913]

Kowada, Chigasaki Sept. 23. (give you a day's start)

My dear Catherine,

So you were in the land of King Arthur and "dear Queen Vanilla," as Isamu would say. He draped himself in a sheet and a silken scarf one day and paraded in front of the looking glass saying "I do look just like Queen Vanilla" "Who's that?" says I. "Why, don't you know, mama, she was the most great Queen at King Arthur's court." My nice Englishman, Mr. Paget, was in England at the same time, at a place called Tumbridge Wells, where he took his Japanese wife and will leave her with his mother, to be initiated in the ways of the British — he to return to

Japan this month and to go and get her again after two years, if she has resolution to stick it out so long. And Yone is going over to England in a month or so where he will lecture at Oxford on the invitation of Sir Walter Raleigh (I say—in what age *are* we living? Where's Elizabeth and the daring Drake?) As for me, I'll just stay where I am and as I am, and I've taken back my old name of Léonie Gilmour as it simplifies some family complications. Isamu has started to attend an English school at Yokohama, St. Joseph's College, upon his own strenuous demand to be given all the rights of an *American*, as he pronounces himself. The Japanese schools have their good points, but they are overcrowded, to be sure. I daresay the change will be good for Isamu. Quite expensive, tho'—and means a good deal of effort to get up at half past four in time to catch the early train to Yokohama. And that's a mile's walk to the station at daybreak and another mile back when it's growing dark on the railroad track. I think we'll have to move—so I'm up against the house problem again. We like this Chigasaki ideal scenery, climate and beautiful loneliness. *But* no houses. If we want a house to suit ourselves in a place to suit ourselves we must build it. And whether it be of straw, of faggots or of bricks, and however little, it takes money to build, let alone the wolf at the door. [ink blot] (This blot is the wolf.) I understand that I can borrow money from Yone's elder brother and pay it back at 6%, but if I do I'm afraid that brother-in-law will want to have a finger in the pie and make a better house than I can afford. I've figured out that such a wee country house as I want would cost 600 or 700 yen. My annual income from school is just 840 yen (about the same as yours in dollars—if a yen here goes as far as a dollar in America, why is it that you are rich and I am poor, when we should be just even? But did you ever try to *live* on your income, my dear?) All this figuring makes me tired, so I'll quit. How's Alice's health? I do hope much improved. I feel sure trapesing around after hot scones and coffee carrying a few handbags and things should be an excellent sort of gymnastics, perhaps better than track-walking to catch the train, as I do. By the way, I've thinned down to 82 Japanese pounds, which is about 104 English ones I believe. Isamu is 58 Jap. pounds. But it makes light walking. I'm a better walker than I used to be.

Is the man in the woods a-mending? (of his heart, I mean) No doubt you do him an injustice and he may be a lot wiser than you—who seem to be unfamiliar with the doctrine of non-resistance—to follow the line of least resistance is to follow nature—nay, it is the way of evolution itself. But how could a Prejudiced Puritan ever assimilate with an Oriental Philosopher? I dare say it is the difference in mental attitude of the

P.P. and the O.P. that accounts for half the broken Americo-Japanese alliances (matrimonial). Ouch! I just caught my fourth flea today (and he escaped). I want a hardwood floor in my house—these straw mats are just flea-incubators.

Oh such a lovely day—doors all wide open right into the pine forest. Soon I'll put on a pair of straw sandals and stroll over the hill to look at Dr. I's empty house—he's just moved 17 miles away back into the mountains—new railroad goes there. By the way, he followed the line of least resistance and married his maidservant, a homely and ignorant little wench who cooked his meals. He might have gone further and fared better. In Japan marriage is chiefly a matter of convenience. And she was right there. But somehow I feel sorry—awfully sorry. He's a very good fellow.

Goodbye with love,
Léonie

"Mother, Isamu, Mr. Paget." *Isamu Noguchi Foundation.*

Léonie's "nice Englishman" was a Cambridge-educated merchant named Arthur Richard Paget, formerly co-director of a West African trading company, now agent for Sir Robert Hadfield, a Sheffield metallurgist whose super-hard manganese steel alloy, Hadfield steel, was used for machines, railways, and most lucratively, military materiel (torpedo-sized Hadfield projectiles could easily pierce armored warships, while helmets made of Hadfield's steel protected soldiers from shrapnel). The nice English arms dealer, six years younger than Léonie, had resided in Japan since 1909 (although he maintained an address in Tunbridge Wells); in 1911 he had married Ichi Watanabe. Léonie advised Isamu to seek out Arthur Paget when he returned to Japan in 1930; disappointed to discover he had recently passed away, she wrote, "I always thought that if I ever returned to Japan Mr. Paget would be one I most wished to see again."

Léonie's financial complaints did not go unheard by Catharine, who responded with an offer of financial assistance. She would loan Léonie 400 yen, a little over half of the amount Léonie had estimated she would need for the new house.

To Catherine Bunnell, November 29, 1913

Kowada, Chigasaki, Kanagawaken, Japan.

My dear Catherine,

I felt as if I had suddenly come into a fortune when I read your magnificent offer. I even grew a little extravagant on the strength of it. Let me tell you how the house business is getting on. I have bought a very small piece of land of 36 tsubo (about 1/10 of an acre) which is of a curious triangular shape, hence will take a three cornered house to fit into it. What's the odds? There's luck in odd numbers anyway. And I engaged a carpenter to make a little house of 3 rooms downstairs and one upstairs, in a fashion which I commanded should be cheap but not look so. The frame work will be set up tomorrow. And I didn't trouble my brother-in-law about money as I got a hint that he might ask an awful rate of interest. I just went to a neighboring banker, where it is my habit to regularly deposit my monthly salary and as regularly draw it out again. He said he would lend me a part of the cost of the house on a mortgage at 3 1/2% payable in two years. So that's what I decided to do and am doing extra work now trying to raise the rest. I will call upon him for his load when the house is done (some time in January). And I should be glad if you will set aside just $100 for my use in case I fall short, but I may be able to get on without it.

I have to go to the dentist this morning so I will cut this short. Isamu sends this message to you: "Please visit!" I hope you'll understand it as Pegotty did Barkis' equally significant one. He said "a man shouldn't marry till he's 20. That's about ten—'leven years. I'm growing pretty tall, and I might just suit her, you know." (This with a comical smirk of masculine conceit, and twirling an imaginary moustache.)

Yours with love,

Léonie

By the beginning of 1914, the new house was "a joy to behold," though the carpenters were still "whacking away at it." Léonie anticipated they would move in around the middle of the month.

To Catherine Bunnell, January 8, 1914

New address: Chigasaki Hamasuka Kanagawaken

My dear Catherine,

The baby has fallen asleep, the maid has gone to the station to fetch Isamu home with a lantern, and here's a quiet house and a good half hour to write you. Your Xmas gifts arrived a week ago—were you thinking your gold had been gobbled up in transit?—It's only a miracle it wasn't, in this land of poverty and thieves (more of my adventures with the latter gentry anon. A genuine burglar has fallen to my lot). Well, you see, it's been two weeks of holidays up to today, and every blessed time I thought I had a moment of leisure to take my pen in hand, a voice at my elbow would pipe up "now read some more Robin Hood!" Last night I read until my throat ached. There's one in this family still young enough to enjoy most any kind of writing that's sufficiently romantic and a bit *distingué*, and there's another with the voracious appetite of a young ostrich—being as he's my brood I'm not surprised.

The gold shall not turn to Japanese silver but shall be kept till Ailes is old enough to smile at its glitter, or until some grand occasion arises, like buying a ticket to America or the like. Now don't think a house of my own is going to prison your impatient Griselda forever and ever, nay, if there were not a chain around 'me fut' I might clap my wings and fly away even now. But that house is a joy to behold, and to hear the carpenters whacking away at it. You may have the best parlor (9 x 9 feet with a verandah) for your exclusive use any time you do be stopping in this country. Too bad I can't send you some buckwheat macaroni about ten days hence—I'll be sending it to all the neighbors to advise them of the event of my entering and taking possession. I daresay some of my Kodak owning friends'll be taking a picture of it and then you'll sure get one. There's a grand view of Mt Fuji to the westward, and from an upstairs window an equally grand view of the sea. Now I'll just send you a picture of myself. I'm smiling because I'm rowing in a boat on the Hanamizu gawa (flowery-water river) and remarking that it's the first time in ten years for me to have the pleasure of rowing in a proper rowboat—oh, time—I hear footsteps.

Goodbye, love and many thanks of children and me,
Léonie

For several years, Yone had been planning a second trip to England. Since the opening of a colossal Japanese-British Exhibition in May 1910, he had been busy writing articles for English periodicals and letters reviving connections he had made on his first visit. With the help of his "jolly companions" Laurence Binyon and Robert Bridges, Yone was invited to lecture at Oxford University where Bridges, the new Poet Laureate, was professor. "I might postpone one more year, I mean my going to England," he wrote Léonie in April 1913, but in the end he chose to go, leaving in November. This time his reception in England was all that he could have desired: he met everyone, lectured at prestigious venues, and arranged the publication of three books.

From Yone Noguchi, January 17, 1914

29 Montague Street, Russell Square, W.C.

Dear Leonie:

I am quite all right in London; people here show so much interest in myself. You might say that I am lionized in England. A few nights ago I gave a lecture at the Japan Society which turned out in quite a good shape. I will be a guest of honour at Poet's Club's dinner (Jan. 21st), and am hoping to read some poems of mine, or will lecture on Japanese poetry. Yesterday I was invited by Bernard Shaw and tonight am going to take a dinner together with Yeats. And so on—you see, I am splendid in condition,—but not financially. And that will be another matter altogether. I have been asked by quite many papers to write on something, but I am tremendously busy—drinking tea or eating English pudding, and have no time for my writing. But I hope that this strange rush will soon be over. Then—will London forget of me? Or I might forget London altogether. All the papers here are extremely kind to me, and say verily nice things about me. A few nights ago I dined with Robert Bridges, Poet Laureate, who was exceedingly interesting British type of poet: I am going to spend a day or two with him at his home near Oxford. And my Oxford lecture will begin on the 29th.

So you are building your house—that is a fine news. I hope that you will not be cheated by carpenters and other working men. How are Isamu and baby? I promised Isamu that he shall have picture-cards occasionally; please tell him: "His papa is tremendously busy, but tomorrow, no, the day after tomorrow, he will go to some shops and buy something for him". I do not know how long I shall stay here in London; but I hope that I shall hurry back to Japan when my work will be through—and that will be in May. Please write me whenever you have something to say. I left Garlant's Hotel which was quite high-toned; now am living at this place. But when you write me, it would be better to send your letter to Elkin Mathews, 4 Cork St. W.

Good-bye,
Yone Noguchi
P.S. Herewith 20 yen.

To Catherine Bunnell, March 1, 1914

Hamatsuka [*sic*], Chigasaki

My dearest Catherine,

Your last letter full of undeserved compliments shall receive no an-swer in kind, the fact of your being worth fifty of me being self-evident and needing no words. Now why didn't I write for a whole month? you might ask. Well, you see, the Providence that tempers the sunshine to the shorn sheep (or the devil that shadows him) was alooking after me, and just as I was feeling remarkably bumptious over my new house—gee-whiz—whak—I was laid low with the following quaint combination of maladies: acute bronchitis, acute intestinal catarrh, acute intesti-nal neuralgia. (Damp walls and unfinished house). I recovered slightly about a week after your draft came and went into town to cash it but being Saturday they were too busy to attend to it and advised me to come in after a few days. I relapsed home and never saw town again for several weeks.

Now getting better but bronchitis hangs on in the shape of a persis-tent cough. Carpenter sent his bill a few days ago with the intimation that there would be a few "extras" later. I paid him up with 200 yen of your money. The other 200 I have put in the bank (it's a comfort to have something there) and hope to return it intact after 6 months with inter-est (paid by the bank). As for the 200 I have already used, I'll return it when I'm able with thanks but no interest. You'd maybe like to see a plan of this triangular house, so here she is:

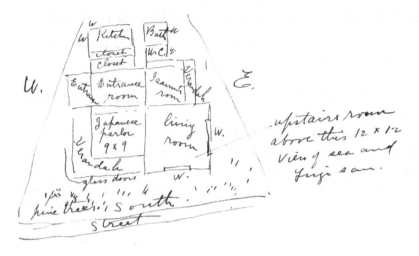

Children falling asleep.
Goodnight,
Léonie

The Chigasaki house in later years. *Collection of Edward Marx.*

Isamu Noguchi, Interview with Paul Cummings, 1973

PAUL CUMMINGS: But growing up as a child, because you lived in Japan until you were—what?

ISAMU NOGUCHI: Until I was thirteen.

PAUL CUMMINGS: So you had a chance to have kind of teen-age friends and school?

ISAMU NOGUCHI: That's right. Therefore I had a double background there, especially during the time that we were living in the country at Chigasaki from the time I was six years old or earlier—I'm not too sure—but maybe five or six years old, until I was ten certainly, we lived in this country place. There were no foreign children there at all so all my friends were Japanese children.

PAUL CUMMINGS: so you were really quite different from...?

ISAMU NOGUCHI: Yes. And, as to whether or not they accepted me, who knows. When I was about eight, I started to commute to a school in Yokohama which was a Jesuit school—St. Joseph's College.

PAUL CUMMINGS: Do you know why your mother sent you to that school?

ISAMU NOGUCHI: Prior to that, I was going to a Japanese school and she probably worried about my being a country boy in a Japanese school and thought I should have more European-type education, I suppose.

PAUL CUMMINGS: Did you speak English at home, or Japanese?

ISAMU NOGUCHI: I spoke English at home and Japanese outside. Well. When I started to commute to this school, which was frequented by foreigners, you know, the pupils were the children of the residents of Japan and also of other parts of the Orient came to the school. So, for a while I commuted, maybe for a year or so. And for one year my mother took me out of school and tutored me because she didn't particularly like that school and she thought maybe she could do better tutoring me herself. But that was only for a while. Then I boarded at that school for a while. Finally, she moved to Yokohama and then I went to that school from where we were in Yokohama. But that wasn't for very long, I don't think it could have lasted for more than a year. In any case, she was living in Yokohama then, you see. The reason was she was teaching in Yokohama then, you see. Therefore, I was kind of real waif, I would say.

PAUL CUMMINGS: You had no contact with your father at all during that time?

ISAMU NOGUCHI: None at all. None at all. So that you might say I'm a classical case of conditioning as a child in a not too fortunate way.

PAUL CUMMINGS: You know, it's curious from reading and everything how choppy it was and how broken up but, but it seems even more so. Was your mother's idea in sending you back to the United States again to get an education?

ISAMU NOGUCHI: Yes. Probably for the same reason that she sent me to St. Joseph's. Probably she wanted to protect me from the kind of half, you know...

PAUL CUMMINGS: Half in and half out.

ISAMU NOGUCHI: ...business of not belonging anywhere. She probably thought that I would have a better chance of belonging in society here that in Japan. But as to whether or not that was really so, other people are in a better position than I to know. She didn't know where to send me. She happened to read in a magazine about a school in Indiana—the Interlaken School—which was devoted to teaching children to learn by doing; that it, it had a kind of manual training approach. She sent me there in June 1917. As you can see from reading my book, I didn't stay there very long; in fact I never went to school there.

PAUL CUMMINGS: Right. But, before you came to this country, did you have a lot of friends as a student and as a young man in schools in Japan?

ISAMU NOGUCHI: No. I never had. I never had many friends; I don't have any recollection of them, or not much. Nor after coming here either, for that matter, did I develop great friendships with people. I'm a loner.

PAUL CUMMINGS: Your mother being an English teacher, did you have books around? Did you read? Did you read?

ISAMU NOGUCHI: Yes, there were plenty of books around.

PAUL CUMMINGS: Did you remember any of them?

ISAMU NOGUCHI: Well, you know, she was a rather literate person so we had books. I mention in my book William Blake, for instance. And there were books of poetry. She was fond of poetry. And my father was a poet. And my mother herself was a loner; I mean, it was not just me.

PAUL CUMMINGS: In what way?

ISAMU NOGUCHI: She was a very quiet person, a very retiring sort of person. She was not pushy at all. Therefore, I mean, her life was very lonely. She didn't have very many friends. So that also reflected on me, you see.

PAUL CUMMINGS: Did you ever talk to her about why she was so interested in Japan, what it was that—why she wanted to live there?

ISAMU NOGUCHI: Well, for one thing, she had fallen in love with my father and I was born and she took me over there, I think, somewhat to his surprise and maybe to his annoyance. And, having gotten over there and finding that by then he had gotten another family, there was nothing for her to do. For that matter, probably she couldn't afford to come back here, either.

PAUL CUMMINGS: So she started teaching?

ISAMU NOGUCHI: Yes, she started teaching there. It was a very mixed up and unfortunate situation.

PAUL CUMMINGS: Did you start drawing as a child the way so many children do?

ISAMU NOGUCHI: Well, after all, all children do draw. Yes, I drew. And I looked at pictures and magazines and so on. But I was not, you know—I would say that my mother wanted me to be something like an artist. For a while she thought I would be a forester or somebody like that, and she taught me botany. I have that in my book, by the way.

PAUL CUMMINGS: From this description and from what's in the book, it seems that there's been kind of a great searching that has gone on through your early years trying to find a place or a culture.

ISAMU NOGUCHI: After all, for one with a background like myself the question of identity is very uncertain. And I think it's only in art that it was ever possible for me to find any identity at all.

PAUL CUMMINGS: In what way, do you think?

ISAMU NOGUCHI: Well, after all, it is only in art that a person who does not belong with any social contact, you see, could find a viewpoint on life which is free of social contacts. One can be an artist and alone, for example. An artist's life is really a lonely life. It is only when he is lonely that he can really produce. If he is not lonely, he may be a social, nice, person, but you know, he might not be driven to it. After all, in a sense you're driven to art out of desperation. People are naturally lazy; they don't do things unless they are driven to it.

From Yone Noguchi, London, May 4, [1914]

Leonie—

I returned here from Paris for a few days to attend to some business— Then to Berlin & Moscow. I will arrive in Japan on about 15th of June. I am awfully tired of Europe—nothing in it. Japan is the better country to live.

Yone

Japan may have been a better country to live in some respects, but home security was not yet among them. In a little over a year the new house was visited by burglers on no less than three occasions. Some years later Léonie wrote up one of the incidents for the *New York Times*.

Dorobo, or the Japanese Burglar

New York Times, July 17, 1921.

The scene, a cottage set in a pine forest. The time, midnight. The only sound, the wind in the pines. The sea is near, near enough to make us fancy the waves breaking at our door, but it is always the waves of the green forest that we hear. Lonely? No, deliciously cozy in our pine nest. Some nights I have been awakened by the intimate call of an owl, or the screech of a train shooting between the hills, leaving its echo trailing in the mists of the forest. Only the nearness of the track, and the thought of track-walkers, ever disturbed our feeling of security. And that very little. We certainly didn't mind the track. By it came all our adventures, just as the yellow primroses had come with the railroad.

Well, on the night I write of I had awakened suddenly. Yet I heard no wailing echo of a train's shriek, no intimate call of a neighborly owl. I listened. Waves of the forest running on endlessly. The breathing of my two children, one on either side, was imperceptible. There was a tiny "bean lamp" on the tansu, which gave a glimmer of light in the room. I could see the wooden panels of the ceiling above me. I felt the comfort of the Japanese mats under me, like terra firma, so much more satisfactory than the uncertainties of spring bed. My children were by me, as I have said. We were warm, cozy, safe. Yet I was strangely awake, and listening. I put out a hand to touch the baby. All right. And still I listened. And then—I heard—a shoji sliding right above my head.

"That tiresome maid," I thought. "Hasn't she gone to bed? What does she want?"

I turned my head upward. The shoji, only a yard from my head, was half open and I perceived that there was a figure—a man's figure—in the aperture. I believe my first thought was that my maid had a sweetheart who had mistaken his way in getting out of the house. I remember that I leaped to my feet and stood facing the intruder in my night dress, and that I uttered a shrill and indignant "O Tami!" meaning to call the girl to account. At the very instant of giving the cry I realized that it was a "dorobo" (burglar) who stood before me. His make-up was perfect.

Exactly that of a stage robber. He was all in dusky brown. His kimono knee-length and with a sort of fringed apron in front. Brown leggings wound around his lower legs. Barefooted—the big toes showing white. Across his face and about his head there was drawn a brown scarf with fringed ends, and I felt that his dark eyes were glowing in the crack between the folds of the scarf. This was all the impression of an instant, for at the very instant of my cry he had drawn a knife—a murderous-looking thing—and was making a sort of sawing motion with it, holding it close down beside his thigh.

The blade of the knife was three or four inches wide and over a foot in length. Even at that moment it struck me as ridiculous. The thing was overdone. Probably a farmer had rigged himself up in this garb to frighten me. No doubt the blade was of wood covered with tinfoil. But, anyway, it was prudent to take no chances. Whether it was a professional burglar or peasant on a marauding expedition, he was threatening me—and the children—as I saw from his pointing the blade downward at the children sleeping on the floor, while he kept up his sawing motion. I didn't repeat my cry, as he evidently meant me to keep quiet.

The whole thing was rather absurd. But I waited, smiling a little inwardly at my perfect calm, to see what would be his next move. He spoke in husky whisper. "O Kane!" (money—honorable money!) making round with his forefinger and thumb, so that I should understand, "O Kane arimasen" (money have not), I answered. My self-possession made me smirk conceitedly. We never know our own courage until we are actually confronted with danger. I daresay I would have shown the same sangfroid in conversing with a ghost. But then that ridiculous knife was such a palpable giveaway I could hardly be expected to feel any thrills.

"Misite!" (Look) was his next utterance, pointing to the chest of drawers that stood against the wall. The little bean lamp was spluttering there.

I was beginning to feel impatient. To be sure, there was a little money in the top drawer—about a yen and a half. But then I didn't see why I should give it to him. If I turned aside he would have me at an advantage. Certainly he wouldn't be satisfied with such a paltry bit of money. I thought best to keep facing him as one does growling dog.

All the while I was wondering what I should do about it. After as it seemed some minutes of racking my brains I had an idea. I said slowly in Japanese: "All my money in Nitta-ya's bank."

My words spoken in very clear, though probably not quite correct, Japanese, seemed to make an impression on him, for he stopped the sawing motion of his knife and stood stock still. I felt encouraged to repeat the same remark.

"All—my—money—in—Nitta-ya's—bank."

And then I blinked to see the place where he had been was empty. He was gone, without a sound, like the witches in "Macbeth." I stood looking in wonder. Then I noticed that one of the sliding wooden doors which shut in the veranda was open about a foot. That way he had gone. He was surely gone. And then I ran to rouse my maid.

"O Tami! O Tami! O Tami!," I cried. My voice was strangely hoarse and far away. If I hadn't been right beside her it might not have roused her. She jumped up. "Okusan! [Madam.] What is the matter?"

My voice came in gasps, now loud, now low, like gusts of wind in a chimney. "O Tami! Dorobo!" And I dragged her to the veranda, pointing to the open door. She was very excited.

"Where? There? There!" She ran to the door to look out, then ran back in fright.

I kept on in my strangely gusty voice. "Shut—everything."

Both at once we ran to shut and bolt the door. Then all about the house to see that everything was shut. There was a barred window in my room and on account of the heat I had left the outer wooden shutter open. This I now tried to close. But my hand, strangely, was trembling so I found it impossible to clutch the shutter, and O Tami came to my assistance.

"Okusan is cold!" she cried.

"N-n-n-n-no. Ye-ye-ye-ye-ye-es-s-s-s-s." My teeth were chattering in such an absurd way it was impossible to speak, so I had to leave her to do the talking as well as the work.

At last we were safely locked in again and went to sleep. In the morning we notified the police. A policeman, not in uniform as it happened (perhaps he was on a detective job that day), wearing a flowing silken hakama (the divided skirt of the Japanese man that makes him look so much like a woman), came and sat on my cushions, while my maid served him with tea. He brought out a little notebook and leisurely took notes, while from time to time he sipped his tiny cup. He laughed with me as I described the burglar's knife. "So long—and so wide." He agreed that it was probably a toy knife, and the burglar a farmer dressed up to play the part. "This would serve his purpose," he said, drawing a slender sword from its scabbard somewhere among the folds of his skirt.

"Weren't you frightened?" he asked.

"How could I be frightened of a man with such a ridiculous theatrical kind of a rig and a monstrous bugaboo sword such as they use to frighten little boys?"

"Foreign ladies are very brave." he said admiringly, and went off, promising to let us know if he got track of the "dorobo."

A week later the policeman stopped in passing to tell me that my burglar had been caught.

"What it a real burglar?" I asked.

"Oh, yes. A particularly bad professional burglar. We've been trying to catch him for a year. He went down the railroad track and committed several burglaries. We were hot on his trail but didn't catch up with him till we got to Totsuka, where we caught him trying to get into a temple through the roof. He's in prison now."

"But are you sure it was my burglar?"

"Yes, he told about visiting the house of a foreign lady near the railroad track." There was a quiver of the policeman's nostril as he said this, and I wondered if the burglar's description of the foreign lady had been in any way funny.

"And the knife? Was it real?"

"Undoubtedly. It was by that knife we recognized him. Most burglars don't use a butcher's knife. But he did, you know."

"Did he ever use it?"

"He used it. But he will not use it again. Good morning, madam."

And the moral of this story is that some burglars are open to reason. You have only to keep perfectly cool and have your wits about you, and talk to the burglar as to a rational human being. Your Japanese burglar, now, is an intelligent and even chivalrous sort of person. He will not waste his metal on a defenseless but provident woman who keeps all her money in the bank. Another thing I may remark is that your Japanese is not much of a bluffer. When he shows a knife it is apt to be of cold steel.

Léonie recounted the third burglary incident in the following letter to Catharine.

To Catherine Bunnell, May 6, 1914

Hamasuka, Chigasaki, Kanagawaken, Japan.

My very dear Catharine

May Day's come and passed, and May 5th, the Boys' Day here, where every household that can boast a boy flies a gorgeous paper carp from the top of a pole (there are sometimes 10 carp for one house) has gone by, the barley is waist high, and here we are in flowery May, a-hugging our winter flannels ("Dinna doff your clout till May goes out" applies very well here). And so you're going to settle in California. That's interesting news indeed. I see a vista of "exchange visits." Seems to me as if I could reach a hand halfway across the Pacific Pond and shake yours say about Honolulu. When I get old and rich I'll maybe want to come and settle in California. When you begin to feel poor and want to change your dollars for yen, my house, my land, my job, I'll pass on to you for just a lease in California. You over there are so very far beyond us uns over here in riches that you cannot make a comparison. I living here in a quite real poverty am considered so rich that my house has been burgled three times in the course of a year. Night before last I was again subjected to such a sleep-disturbing nuisance. He came at midnight (the dolobo), seized 4 overcoats, a box of my letters, a box of machine fixings, Isamu's strapped up bundle of schoolbooks, an English song book and a tin of cornstarch, and a parasol. All of these things he dropped promiscuously in the neighbor's pinewoods in his hurried flight, with the exception of Isamu's winter overcoat and my summer parasol which he still retains. I awakened at the criticcal [*sic*] moment, as usual, and my voice I suppose, together with the return of my maid and her father from a nocturnal ramble, scared him off. Then for the policeman and his little book. No sleep till 3:30. Sent the maid again to police station today, but officer stated that *as he did not speak English* he would wait until he found a brother policeman who did before taking any further steps in the matter. Oh, yah, yah! (these being my prolonged yawns.) Pardon this digression anent the burglar and to return to your letter and California. You say you're to have a companion and that he's your true lover. I don't doubt it a bit. Of course, he must be. I am sure Bimbi (I don't know his other name, nor how he wears his beard—my preconceived impression calls for a beard and blue gray eyes) has a fastidious taste, since he would content himself with nothing short of my Catherine. I should like to send a host of gracious fairies, being my wishes, to attend the wedding. What shall I wish you? A house, not too small in a bee-loud glade. A child in the house. A woolly lamb and a flower starred lawn. A bubbling spring. A skiey view and a bit of forest shade. Hearthfire and books of course, not omitting Shakespeare (in 7 years I've not found a reader of him in Japan). A dainty cook (who may be the lady of the house). A wizard to kindle the fire o'mornings (who may be the man of the house). And that everything you touch may turn to fairy gold. As for Bimbi's ten years or more of loneliness etc., he may snap his fingers at it.

Speaking of burglars—about that loan of yours. There's 200 yen, as you know in the bank on a 6 months deposit. That means that I'll send it back sometime in July unless you wish to keep it there longer. I believe it's drawing interest at 5 or 5½%, better than an American bank. As for the rest, you'll please bide a wee.

Oh, say, have you decided where you're going to locate in California? Or is it some place more bright and more vague than Florence's Sunland. Just Sunland, Calif. is all I know about that.

Baby's going to wake.

Your loving

Brigitta

As Leonie's letter indicates, Florence Gilmour had by this time dispensed with the Marietta Street house and moved to Sunland, a small community situated along the southwestern edge of the San Gabriel mountains. Though less than ten miles from Burbank, it could take a full day to reach by automobile by the unpaved mountain roads. The relative inaccessibility of the area and its mountainous surroundings made it attractive over the years to reclusive and countercultural residents, including, during the 1960s, the Hell's Angels and the Hog Farm hippie commune. Florence acquired a small homestead where she took to raising goats and chickens, and later worked at the local library.

To Catherine Bunnell, August 23, 1914

Chigasaki, Hamasuka, Kanagawaken.

My dear Catherine,

"Where's the draft?" are you saying. Non est. On the 21st, that's day before yesterday, I went in town to the Shokin Ginko (Yokohama Specie Bank), demanded the privilege of withdrawing my money (which was granted, and was proceeding with slow, reluctant steps – they're very prompt about receiving moneys, however) and in the meantime went to another window to make out a draft. "Bad time to send money," remarks the clerk. "That so?" says I. "Rate of exchange extremely high." I asked whether he thought it might be better a month hence. He said he could not give any opinion on the matter as no one knew how this war was going. "How about 3 or 4 months hence?" says I. "Can't make any promises." "But just an unofficial opinion," urges I. "Well," says he, "I should say it's now at the very worst."

So I took the liberty of shoving it back in the bank, as I don't like throwing money into the maul of Monsieur Monster War Panic. But if you really want it, just drop a line, and you'll get it by return post. If you don't need it, I suggest that we leave it until Feb. 19th (one year from the date of my putting it in the bank) when it will be a bit larger—I guess by this time you'll be having carpenter's bills of your own coming in.

Very happy to make the better acquaintance of James McDougal Mitchell. Why didn't you mention the interesting facts about him before? I confess your remark about his enjoying Shakespeare didn't impress me much. I can do that same myself. But as for harvesting wheat, and being two inches taller than you,—I am overwhelmed. Sunland does seem a doubtful proposition for people who don't need to do it for their health. It might be on the whole a good thing for Florence who was fagged out and needed the tonic of open air work. To live there might be all right, but to try to make a living that is more than a mere existence out of the rocky soil itself,—well, you have a chance to demonstrate your pluck (which doesn't need demonstrating) and to admire Jim's.

We are now nearing the end of our brief, deliciously hot Japanese summer. The chorus of insect voices grows loud. The naked sinewy brown figures of farmers are hurrying by with their harvest of sweet potatoes (a huge basket at either end of a pole set over their shoulders). This is the land of sweet potatoes and watermelons, and peaches. We've been revelling in the last two fruits all summer. To see Isamu (naked except for a pair of white gauze tights) and burnt crisp) sitting cross-legged with a piece of watermelon, his startling green eyes reflecting the watermelon rind, is to get a glimpse into the poetry of savagery. Alas, on the 15th of September he will give up his liberty, don clothes ("foreign" clothes) even shoes, and catch the early train—5:52 a.m.—for school, and every day and every day and every day, as he says, it will be the same old thing. Adieu—it has occurred to me that I might send you a fan in lieu of the m—. I am tickled to have thought of this truly Japanese way of paying a dept.

Yours ever fondly
Léonie

Léonie's gifts of *hikkoshi soba* had probably helped smooth relations with the new neighbors: Masutaro Niida and Eiichi Makino (both Tokyo University law professors) and their families. Ailes played with Kazuko Makino, chasing cicadas and butterflies, while Isamu played with the eldest Makino boy.

Meanwhile, Catharine was preparing to embark on her own marital adventure with James McDougal Mitchell, a childhood friend of her parents involved in agriculture and oil businesses. Léonie offered her some encouragement.

To Catherine Bunnell, November 5, 1914

Chigasaki, Hamasuka, Kanagawaken, Japan

My dear Catherine,

Don't despair of your ability to qualify as a workingman's wife. Don't you remember your apprenticeship in our flat on 153d Street? And how cleverly you boiled an egg at the same time with the coffee? Or is that stroke of genius to be credited to me? It does sound more like me. But I sometimes forget which of us was which in those unforgettable days of auld lang syne. How you did put away the oatmeal and cream of a Sunday morn! Nowadays it's pancakes of a Sunday morning for us. And how the boy does put them away!

It's a real satisfaction to know you're going to have such an all round comfortable sort of man as Jim seems to be. ("Make plants grow?" quoth Isamu Why, that's just like me. And I'm fond of animals too, especially puppies." And still he can't quite see why you threw him over for Jim, who appears to be his twin in tastes—"I like Shakespeare too" says the boy) and I'm relieved that he didn't turn out to be a writer, which was what I most feared. No offense to the order of the plume, but you know they're apt to dawdle around the house and get in the way.

Nothing especial has happened since last I wrote—a sprained ankle is the only adventure I recall—now it's no more than a twinge of memory and a slight limp. I've been a little busy typewriting Y.N.'s new book on "Blessed England." Over here the school children sing God Save King George, by the way. But Isamu and Ailes joyously lift the roof with "Hail Columbia, Happy Land!" Isamu mercifully teases his sister: "you don't know what *is* Columbia, you foolish, ignorant thing!" "I do!" she asserts. "Then what is it?" "Over there" she points a fat finger vaguely to 'Columbia.'

I will send you something over $100 (about 125.00) in the latter part of this month, so you'll get it before the end of the year. I don't think Japan is so very much hurt by the war—America, going at high pressure, is more quick to strike a snag. Japan, like the tortoise, when hard times come, just takes a nap. Business is dull. But that's nothing unusual. By the way, did you see this? An alien suspect in London filled out a paper to this effect: Name—Leonisky. Born—Yes. Business—Rotten. No doubt it's a chestnut from an American tree. Have writ 5 letters and typed 3 articles today. I will put away my pen for another month.

Your ever loving
Brigitta

On January 23, 1915 Catharine and Jim Mitchell were married in the Los Angeles suburb of Torrance.

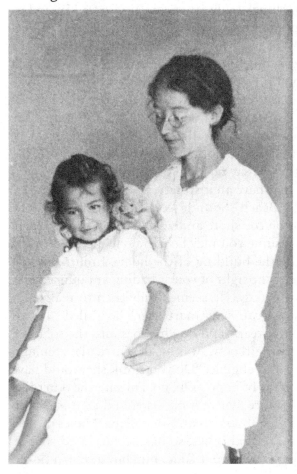

Léonie and Ailes, circa 1915. *Isamu Noguchi Foundation.*

To Catherine Bunnell, March 26, 1915

Chigasaki, Hamasuka, Kanagawaken, Japan.

Dear Madam Catherine,

You may have observed—or you may not—that I have not written for some time. The reason of that is that I have been considering—like the cow—considering and considering what would be a proper wedding present for a dear friend of mine. Now don't look as if you considered me an ill-bred guest to walk in after the party is over. There are reasons. You know I always hated a crowd. And I have imbibed enough of Japanese aesthetics to know that in solitariness itself there is distinction.

My poor offering, were it a weed, will gain something from being alone. And another reason. In Yokohama can be bought only things vulgar (I always shop there for myself—to buy cheap and serviceable things). But to Tokyo you must go for things truly Japanese—and there I intend to go this very Easter holiday and saunter along Ginza in search of *it*. Now my idea of a wedding present is a thing both useful and handsome—a lacquered dustpan or a vase made from the crooked root of an aged bamboo—something large I prefer—but alas, will it go by parcel post? Well, I may be reduced to sending you three carved ivory monkeys in a nutshell, but I hope not since neither you nor I are Lilliputians. My friend suggested a Japanese kimono of silk crepe with all the accessories—but would it fit? And if you're doing your own kitchen work the sleeves would be a nuisance—to say nothing of its being a trifle expensive. Well, you just wait. I may have an inspiration.

So you're at Redondo Beach. Sounds comfortably near. Quoth Isamu "She can just stand on the shore and wave her hand to us. We're just across the water." I presume you may be there only perched in the "temporary shack" abiding the building of the home. I must tell you that Isamu was staggered by the sight of your wedding announcement. The poor boy broke down utterly. He seemed only then to realize all that it meant to him. "Now I can *never* marry her," he wailed. "It's all over." And he shed real, bitter tears, and dug his toes into the sofa in a scandalous way. "I haven't any girl now," was his next articulate remark. I hinted that Florence was still eligible. "Do you think she would have me?" he queried with just a ray of hope. "Oh, no, I'm sure she don't like boys." And speaking of Florence, where *is* my sister and *what* is she up to? I haven't heard from her for about a year. Nor of Papa. Makes me feel like an orphan. I've written several times, so has Isamu. Dead silence. Isamu offered to go and look them up if I'd let him buy a return ticket. By the way, we've read the Talisman and Isamu thought it splendid. He wrote a postcard to thank you, long ago, but didn't send it for lack of your address. When it came, he said he couldn't send it because he had written "Dear Catherine" and he was afraid he ought to have written "Mrs." But I said you wouldn't mind a bit. "She mightn't," he said. "But how about James?"

I shall have to stop and warm my hands. It's snowing again today—that's the fourth or fifth time in this blessed month of March. Snow, rain, hail, wind, is all we get nowadays. And the strawberry blossoms are out. I'm covering them with straw mats, poor dears.

Now it's your turn to write.

Ever fondly yours,

Brigitta.

P.S. Enclose $37.00. Where are we at now?

To Catherine Bunnell, April 27, 1915

Chigasaki.

My dear Catherine,

Downstairs there's a fire and "my chair"—a wicker chair with broad, comfortable arms. Up here there's a little uneasy chair, my desk, and you. Let us home the animation of the company will make the lack of a stove an entirely unevident fact. (*Is* my English growing Japanesy?). I sent you, my dear, one day, "*mukashi, mukashi*" that's "once upon a time," a little lacquered cake-box with a pair of chop-sticks, which maybe will have reached you before you get this letter. The manufacturer advised me that you may put hot water in it, or alcoholic beverages (but don't!) without injury, but that you should be careful about scratching it. Therefore you'd best avoid, not only cats and pins, but even the innocent *bon ami* chicken. Just plain hot soapsuds is I believe the usual cleanser. You should put a few pieces of cake in the dish and offer to your caller, together with a tiny cup of Japanese tea. If your caller is bashful about helping himself to the cake, the hostess may lift up a piece or two with the chopsticks in a gingerly manner, and lay them on a plate (or folded piece of paper) before him with some hospitable words the purport of which is "set to." May your wedded happiness outlast even this "extremely durable" lacquer (a little caution about "scratching," if you please).

Any news in this part of the world? Everything is growing and "greening" under the April mist. Barley fields in front of me, barley fields to the right of me, and a pine forest to the left of me. Down in my garden are cabbages and lettuce. And I must not forget the strawberry patch which promises a feast next month. Isamu's garden is bright with pansies, yellow primroses, violets, English daisies and so on. And there is one white wisteria in full bloom, and a small magnolia tree with large purple flowers. Isamu is taken with "wanderlust" every Sunday lately, and tramps over the hills and far away, ten or twelve miles at a jaunt, in quest of rare blue flowers that grow "only at the tip top of the mountain," or wild azaleas or the like, which he laboriously carries home. "Why, Isamu," I complained the other day, "your shoes are full of mud." "Yes," responded the enthusiast, "there's such fine mud on that mountain, so rich and black and slippery—I wish we had our garden full of it." Ailes and I stay at home for the most part, not being blessed with mountain legs, but

Ailes promises to outdo her mother when she grows up.

Tomorrow is one of my busy days—school from 8 till 2, then a private pupil, this time the daughter of the mayor of Yokohama. I had the honor of riding in the Lord Mayor's carriage the other day—would you believe it, it was the *first* time for me to ride in a horse carriage since coming to Japan (we ride in jinrikishas you know). The sound of the iron shod hoofs on the road struck me as so very noisy, and I had a sort of feeling as if I had reverted to barbaric days and were riding in a chariot drawn by a lion and wild boar, for instance.

Time's up, and I'll be waiting for your next. Suppose we'll cross. "Yoroshiku" (that's best regards) to the man of the house, and my love to the lady.

Léonie

Léonie practicing *kyudo* (Japanese archery). *Isamu Noguchi Foundation.*

To Catherine Bunnell, August 29, 1915

My dear Catherine,

The enclosed letter of Isamu's, tho' dateless, I judge to have been written about a month ago, and the reason it did not go on its way was that I rashly promised to enclose it in one of my own, which for various reasons didn't get a-writing till this very minute. The "various reasons"

coming in the gay summertime, had to do with our usual summer oc-
cupations of swimming, eating and sewing. I have been feeling so well
this summer, that is ever since my holiday began on July 20th. Before
that date I have a vague recollection of being smitten with some sort of a
stroke one day at school and lying all day in a blazing hot room with my
head packed in ice, a doctor feeling my pulse, and several students fanning me. It wasn't till nine o'clock at night that I was able to go home.
You see I still have my same old headaches, only [worser] and more violent, but in the between times am stronger than I used to be. This is the
first summer that I have had a complete holiday with no private teaching to fill in. This means a slimness of my purse. But what's money,
as Ailes said. She has a habit of secreting her toys at night, for fear a
burglar might take a fancy to them. I told her she needn't be so anxious,
as the burglar only wanted money. "Money?" quoth she. "Why, money's
nothing I will give him all the money, I'll throw it at him, if that's all he
wants." Ailes has got the reputation this summer of being the bravest
baby on the beach. She can float alone, laughing and shaking like a jelly-
fish. Isamu has learned to swim, but not far yet. Speaking of Isamu, we
have come now to the critical point in the boy's education. He objects
strenuously to going to school and is begging me to teach him at home
this winter. Of course the long train journey every day is a strain upon
him. On the other hand, education at home with a busy mother for
teacher is apt to be desultory. He has decided to be a landscape gardiner
[*sic*] or horticulturist, and is quite an enthusiast on this his chosen specialty, but he don't see the use of arithmetic, spelling and all that [lim-
bo] for a gardiner. He thinks a man should begin his life work young. . .
Was just interrupted by a call. One of my boy friends wanting to try the
typewriter. . . Did your house party come off? And did ye hear a wailing
and a wailing as from the doormat, of one that was without and would
be in? It was me, me darlint. And how's Alice and her house that Jack
built? I predict that a year in California will put her out of tune for any
other clime and that she'll turn into a permanent inhabitant. If she still
yearns for adventures, let her try a trip around the world via Chigasaki.
Which puts me in mind of "my Adventure with the Lady." Met her in the
sand drift behind the station, wrestling with a Japanese phrase book
and the station men. Said they to me, "There's a poor soul footing it,
and she won't take a train, and we can't make out what she's saying."
I looked and saw her, bedraggled, sunburnt, barefooted, with a mass
of tangled red hair hanging about a small face with a preposterously
long prominent nose. On her bare feet she had tied a pair of the kind of
straw sandals worn by rickshaw coolies. And she carried a heavy bundle

which might be her worldly belongings. I addressed her in English, and she hailed me as her deliverer. She was an Englishwoman on a walking trip. Had tried to get a hotel at Oiso (two stations south) but was refused because they were full. Wanted to get to Katase before night but didn't know the road. "Now *why* must you get to Katase," said I. It's getting dark and it's a good three miles further." She said she didn't have where to lay her head for the night and she must get to some place where there was a hotel. Upshot was I took her home. After she'd had a bath and combed her hair turned into a proper English lady. Was making a trip around the world for her health and pleasure. Had started from London three years before and had no end of adventures to tell. Was to sail for America via Honolulu in a few days. Now what do you think of that? But I don't have to go anywheres to have adventures. They seem to come to me right at home. Why, it was only last night I had "my Adventure with a Rat." He was a huge beast, got into my mosquito net and couldn't get out. I chased him round and round in the moonlight, he hopping lightly over baby's head and Isamu's bare feet, I crawling after armed with a blanket and yelling for help at the top of my voice. At last, at last, came my maid with a lamp, and we caught and killed him. He lies buried beside a red rose bush that has never bloomed but we hope may now be moved do deck his grave. But let me cease this chatter and go and tend to supper. Roast pork it is after a week of vegetarianism. A watermelon lies cooling in a bucket of water which will save trouble for des[s]ert. Farewell, my love, must get to work. After supper, it's Puck o' Pook's Hill, reading aloud.

Your Brigitta.

To Catherine Bunnell, February 24, 1916

Chigasaki

Dear Catherine,

This finishes it up, I guess. $12.00. That's right, isn't it? And many thanks to you. You don't know what a lot of comfort we've got out of this little home. Isamu says there's no other house so cozy and comfortable. "Why not invite Alice over here," sezee, "if she wants to rest?" And that's not a bad idea, neither. Just pass it on to Alice that Japan, for all its erratic climate, is rather a nerve-resting sort of place, for the reason that the speed is lower than in America. But Isamu is not going in for rest himself. He prefers action, adventures. He is begging me to let him go over to America next winter, spend two or three years, perhaps returning when he is old enough to enter an art school here. He has 3 reasons for going. 1. Curiosity to see the unknown. 2. A desire to play baseball. 3. Emulation of Christopher Columbus. (Also 4. A wish to get letters from Mama). He wrote to the Yoyo Kisen Kaisha (steamship line) and found he could get passage by the South American route, Yokohama via Honolulu, San Francisco and Los Angeles (San Pedro) for 78 yen ($39) to Los Angeles, second class, so long as he is not yet twelve years old. Have you any ideas on the subject. How is Florence situated in regard to schools? And would she perchance welcome him as a cheap boarder? I believe his main idea of inviting Alice would be to take her back as a travelling companion. But that trip he selected would keep him a month at sea. And think of the German submarines probing around! He has already made a plan for a trunk which he intends to make himself, and is making a list (daily lengthening) of things to take; it includes a silver spoon, chopsticks, gold cup, tools, teddy bear, favorite books, and other of the appurtenances to an ideal bachelor den.

Here things are as usual, but being slowly starved out by the war. Kerosene oil has gone up to yen 3.10 ($1.50) a tin, so I refuse to buy any more and we're going to go to bed by candlelight. Mr. Paget says we soon shall not have soap to wash our hands. But thank heaven the sea is handy, and sand is a good substitute. Today if it clears we're going to visit a three year old friend of Ailes—German. She and Ailes play, each speaking her own language and each has a profound pity for the other's ineffectual attempts at speaking. "She tries to speak, but she *cannot*," says Ailes.

Hot bath is ready. Then dinner. Then da-da's.

With love,

Léonie

Around May, Léonie took a second part time job in a Yokohama Christian school run by Miss M.E. Mander, "an Englishwoman of robustious appearance," as she explained to Catharine a few months later.

To Catherine Bunnell, August 29, 1916

Chigasaki, Kanegawaken

My dear Catherine

When last I parted from you the wash was on the boil and if I remember rightly you were looking forward to a washerwoman's dinner of —corned beef and cabbage, was it? Would you believe it if I said that ever since I have been trying to find a moment to write you? Well, you needn't. In the meantime various things have happened. I have made the acquaintance of the inimitable Mrs. Green—read aloud with the proper English accent by Miss Mander. Do you know Miss Mander? She's an Englishwoman of robustious appearance, the kind I take to being entirely different to me, who had started a school for English children in Yokohama. Met her about May last, taught in her school for a couple of months and likewise during one month kept house for her while she had a bit of an operation on one eye. The school a seething mass of utterly irrepressible youngsters always on the bounce—a variety especially bred in Yokohama, I believe, and highly diverting. I expect to keep on with the Eng. Lit. there for two mornings a week next term. Still have my Japanese school—a weariness to the flesh. Putting in the summer with private teaching. Go in to the other edge of Yokohama three mornings a week (a four hour trip each time) to teach an American kid of ten, Isamu's classmate, the other three mornings have a pupil at home, likewise another two afternoons. And still my bank account is at ebb-tide (never a balance of more than 2 or 3 yen at the end of the month.) As the boy grows so do his needs—so do his father's financial delinquencies. I keep the sewing machine merrily humming all summer, while fanned by a delightful sea breeze that blows my sewing all about. And still I manage to get an occasional dip in the ocean, or to look after my tomatoes. May I remind you of your promise of "petit pois" for my garden? Now is the time to think of putting in seed in Japan. The summers are so short we must get everything in the year before.

Ever yours with love
Léonie

Ailes Gilmour's recollection of Chigasaki

Unpublished manuscript

Chigasaki is a small country village on the sea coast of Japan. I spent the first five years of my life there in a house that stood close to a dirt road that wandered fairly parallel to the shore and from which, about a half mile down, another smaller path made right angles with it and led directly to the sea. Our house was two stories high, European style, but the floors were covered with tatami (woven straw). There were three rooms downstairs and I can only remember one upstairs, the bedroom, although there may have been another. One floor connected with the other by a narrow wooden staircase, more like a ladder leading to an attic, dangerously exciting to climb and perhaps even more hazardous to descend. The kitten that I had usually turned somersaults down it and would invariably land at the bottom, fur ruffled, but feet down. I watched her rapid and seemingly comfortable flight down with enormous interest and finally, the temptation being too great to resist I gravely put my head down on the topmost stair and kicking my heels over my head followed suit. I arrived at the bottom in hurried painful bounces and screamed with all my lungs. My mother reached out and examined me carefully but since nothing seemed particularly wrong left me to howl loudly, now joined by the kitten who had seen my descent with amazement. That fall taught me that kitten and I were not the same size, a fact which hitherto had been completely overlooked.

I spent all my days outdoors, most often in the garden. There were about ten peach trees directly in front of our house and to the left we grew sweet peas and cosmos. At the back of the house, to one side, we had a small hothouse in which grew large red strawberries and to which a band of bees had taken a liking that they had built a hive for themselves right by the little door that was the entrance. Perhaps bees in Japan are more friendly—at least I can't recall a single sting. A small mound came just before the door to the house and purple and white wistaria trailed over the arbor. Our house was at the edge of a pine woods and I liked to hunt for caterpillars and would bring them home to our garden. Usually I would play games with them, mostly funereal ones. I dug little holes in the soft earth and with loud laments would drop my furry friends in and cover them over with earth and while I rocked back and forth singing to myself of their death, I would peek out between my fingers to see if any had wriggled from out the pleasant earth. Sometimes I played at house with them but I have a vague conviction that sooner or later I succumbed to the dramatic idea of a funeral. One caterpillar in particular, a bright apple green fellow with even yellow circles on his back and two villainous spikes on his back, was so handsome that I let him climb about the trees unmolested. Finally he too had an elegant funeral. We kept some rabbits for a while but I didn't pay much attention to them as somehow the rabbit hutch had a very strong odor and I didn't like their smell.

Another of my delights was to tie bamboo sticks to the rake and to go among the pines and poke it upwards at the moon. It *did* seem so close to the tops of the pines and it looked very easy to bring down. Once in my excitement I ran toward the hot house and my awkwardness in holding the rake aloft made me stumble and crash! The rake fell on the glass. My mother scolded me for getting so near the house and told me to try a little pulling on, and I solemnly poked and poked, talking and cajoling with the moon to catch itself in my rake.

Our nearest neighbors were about a mile away, a farmer living with family to the right of us. Between our house and theirs were many sweet potato fields and one mulberry patch. To our left were five woods and in the midst of these was a house belonging to Japanese friends of ours, the trees being the outer boundaries of their estate. They had an old woman for a servant then who had only one tooth which had a way of slipping forward so that when she talked she was always pushing it back with her hand or else sucking it in with a whistling breath. It was a little hard to understand her as she mumbled her words and then punctuated sentences or exclamations with the whistling intake of her tooth.

I went down to the shore every day cutting across the field instead of following the roads, jumping over the ditches dug for irrigation. Once I saw a thick black snake crawling sluggishly along the bottom of one of these ditches and after looking carefully at it to make sure it was a snake I picked up a stone and threw it at it and ran quickly away. I hope I didn't hurt it. The fields extended almost to the sand but just before that there was a fringe of tall pine, through which the sea could be seen. They grew on a slightly elevated bank of earth and I recall with vividness a pink carnation that grew at the foot of one of the trees. The beach itself was most beautiful and wild, its sands coarse and white. Few people swam there as it was a scattered village. The fishing was excellent and I saw the men, dragging in their heavy nets, in which hundreds of fish leapt and wriggled, clad only in their loin cloths, bodies gleaming with the sea water and sweat as they labored to bring in the nets. A man my mother knew gave her a bathing suit for me—it was canary yellow with the blue stripes across the chest—a boy's bathing suit. I objected strenuously to wearing it as I felt I might easily be mistaken for a goldfish. My mother got me to wear it a while by calling to me from the water—'yellow belly, yellow belly, come and take a swim!' and I would shout back, 'yes, by golly, when the tide comes in! and jump in with her. I don't yet know whether that was a nursery rhyme or something she'd invented. It was most satisfactory. During storms the waves would come rolling in, fifty feet high and crashing down on the shore. My mother would go in even when the waves were high and dive right into the heart of the most enormous wave and smile at me and I would ship in and spear them with her.

If a wave *had* hit us—but they never did. After a storm there would always be jelly fish, hundreds of them thrown up on the sands. I was warned not to pick them up but I disobeyed once and still remember the red tendril that shot out and about my little finger. It was swollen for days but as it was my own fault I said nothing.

Isamu Noguchi, *A Sculptor's World*

One season when I was about ten, my mother, who had her own ideas about education, decided to keep me out of school and teach me herself. She taught me botany as she thought I might become a forester, and semi-apprenticed me to the local cabinet-maker in Chigasaki. There I learned the basic uses of wood tools; to sharpen them, to plane, to saw, pulling in the Japanese way. Of the joining and interlocking of beams, I learned the simpler kinds. I also carved wood panels for above the sliding doors (*fusuma*), some of which were antiqued by burning and rubbing with straw and wet sand. And I made carvings in cherry wood of such traditional themes as rabbits in waves and dragons in clouds.

I had built a garden, to which I was devoted. The peach trees were not mine, but the flowers were. One of my mother's pupils named Iwasaki worked in a horticultural station nearby, and I used to go there all the time to beg for rose clippings, with the result that I had about fifty rose bushes.

The overflow from the pump I had formed into a brook. To this was attached my earliest feeling of guilt, for I stole a rock from a neighbour's wood to place there. Each time Haruhiko san came to call, I expected him to recognize his rock. He never did.

Close by there was always the sea, of which I was for a long while mortally afraid—a dangerous place of dark winds and typhoons. When it became warm enough, my mother would swim far out, farther than I could see, and I was in constant dread that she might never come back. But the summer also brought college boys to take me in tow, and I shared their swimming, and their watermelon parties and the ghost stories they told to keep cool. There were tales of transformation of foxes into ladies, ladies into ghosts—into badgers, into snakes, into watermelons.

When winter came, I commuted to St Joseph's. This was bearable because I still thought of myself as among my Japanese friends, even if I saw them only on the train. But then my mother decided to move to Yokohama. And there, living in a foreign—style house, attending a foreign school, I became a foreigner myself, a stranger in the land. I envied the Catholic children and their closeness to God, and I would surreptitiously join them in early morning Mass. Mr Griffin, the Scoutmaster, was the only person in Yokohama whom I felt really cared about me. He died during the earthquake of 1923 trying to help people.

In the fall of 1916, Isamu's long reprieve from school ended when Léonie reenrolled him at St. Joseph's. This time, to solve the problem of the long commute, she sent him to live in a school dormitory. But the dormitory was expensive, and she had heard "charges of immorality among the boys." Léonie herself was finding the commute to Yokohama exhausting. Finally, during the winter, she decided to rent a place in Yokohama, at the foot of the Bluff "where the swell foreigners live," using the Chigasaki house mainly for weekends and vacations.

To Catherine Bunnell, January 23, 1917

337 Kitagata cho, Yokohama

My dear Catherine,

The moving spirit seems to have seized us both at once. I am afraid I added to your woes by sending you a visitor at an inopportune moment. Forgive me! And *did* you move on Xmas day? (Your letter of Dec. 15 reached me yesterday. One from Los Angeles dated Dec. 31 came at the same time.) I moved for the sake of economizing time, money, health. Chigasaki is a delightfully breezy healthy place. But to face a mile of frozen mists and icy blasts at sunrise every morning was too much for us. The children called me Miss Cough. And I couldn't manage to talk enough to teach.

You wrote me that my father had been ill. So I'm sending $10.00 herewith which I hope you will get to him or to Florence for his use. Tell her I will send the same every month. I'm sorry to trouble you, but I don't know her exact address as she did not send it when she wrote last. I wish I could return your kindness in proper sort by lending you the money for your housebuilding without interest as you did me. But at this very moment I can't. Jobs have a way of expiring for lack of funds here as in California. Mine at Miss Mander's has half-expired for that reason. That is, I'm put in half pay for half work. And Miss M. seems to think I'd be glad to get a little needed rest. Perhaps I did need the rest too. I'm already much stronger after ten days in Yokohama with an hour longer in bed each morning. I've taken a little two room house at the foot of the Bluff. The Bluff is where the swell foreigners live. At the foot are the poor Japanese. But this house is quite new and cozy. Rent 8 yen. Water 1 yen. Electric light 1.10. I pay 10 yen to an old woman to keep the home in my absence. Isamu's schooling is 8.50 with extras for stationery, books, athletics and so forth, so that it amounts to about 11 yen. Ailes' schooling (she's just started in) 7.50. Carfares about 4 yen a month (used to be 20). We go back to Chigasaki on Sundays. Our food will come to about 40 a month. And clothes, especially stockings, is no small item in this cold weather. I'm using an oil stove and charcoal hibachi for heat, gas for cooking. Income is at present 70 yen from my Japanese girls' high school, 24 from Miss Mander's. And Yone contributes—irregularly—20 a month (1 yen is half a dollar). So you see that income and expenses balance pretty closely at this moment. However, tell Florence that she can count on the $10 all right, and I'll keep my eyes open for more work. I'm sitting on the floor while I write, hoping to draw a chair at next auction. Auctions are one of the attractions of Yokohama—you can get almost anything if you wait long enough. Now I've got some corrections to do so I'll have to stop. Ailes is in bed with Bronchitis—Isamu very well, his American ambitions soaring. May your household gods prove propitious and the new home be a place of joy.

Your ever loving
Brigitta
Please send my father's or Florence's address

To Catherine Bunnell, February 20, 1917

337 Kitagata machi, Yokohama, Japan

My dear Catherine,
Santa Claus arrived with books from Torrance on Feb. 7— and being long looked for was hailed with delight. Isamu likes Daddy Darwin's Dovecot the best in his'n. As I have not yet read all of mine—William Sharp I like to savour slowly—I can't tell which I like best in mine. The Passing of the Prince is charming. There's one about Lillith—I honestly like Lillith—especially as she didn't make a fuss about going. I always fancy her eyes to be like yours—that is, no ring about the iris—to symbol her lack of a soul.

Ailes took hers to school—Miss Mander's kindergarden—and let it be read aloud to her little friends. We're now in Yokohama, as I think I wrote you—under the bluff—I enjoy lovely lonely week-ends at Chigasaki. Isamu is a boy-scout and carries a string in his pocket in which he ties mysterious knots. He wants to go to America. And he wants to know if you would have him—and if there's a school in the neighborhood. I believe it would be high school soon. He wishes me to inform you that he is an American, not a Japanese. In fact, so far as appearance, speech and habits are concerned he would pass far more easily for a foreigner American than for a Jap. He has been going to a foreign school since he was eight—but he can neither read nor write Japanese, sorry to say. He could take my name in America, if it seemed desirable. I have been seeing the American consul, as there was a notice to American residents to do so. And it seems there may be difficulty in establishing my American nationality as a woman takes her husband's nationality. And I have put in a plea of irregularity in my marriage on the score of not being registered in Japan. The papers have been forwarded to Washington to be considered as a special case. If my plea doesn't hold I should be unable to get a passport from the Consul to leave this country—tho' I might get one—with difficulty, from the Japanese government. The reason Yone didn't register us was for the sake of evading the military service for Isamu. But Mr. Consul thinks that as various police reports have been signed by me and Mr. Noguchi together it is equivalent to a registration. Anyway there is nothing to be done but to await word from Washington.

As to Isamu, having been born in America, if by the time he is 21, he can show that he has lived some years in America, he can claim American citizenship. But if he is here when he is 18 years old the Japanese government may seize him for military service—a brutalizing and demoralizing service, I am told by Japanese who have been through it. Yone is opposed to sending Isamu to America so soon—but he is ever averse to doing anything in a hurry.

If you are not so situated you could take him. or if it would bother you, I believe Mrs. Donald, our old neighbor on Marietta Street, might take him as a boarder. They are a Scotch family, no particular culture—somewhat high tempered—one son a little older than Isamu—a very pretty daughter a year older than he, who sometimes writes to him. As I remember Miss Katy, she was as high strung a little vixen as you'll find—probably a result of her mother's over indulgence in giving the child strong tea etc.

Well, anyway, tell me what you think about it. We can only afford about $20 a month for his board. Isamu has some leanings toward being an architect or ship architect. Pity your father's not alive to advise him.

With best love and thanks for Xmas,
Léonie

To Catherine Bunnell, March 10, 1917

337 Kitagata machi, Yokohama, Japan

My dear Catherine,

I suppose you received ten dollars that I sent about six weeks ago for Florence, but the mails are so slow I will send another without waiting to hear from that. If Florence doesn't want it, please do not return it, but use it for paying off the debt on your own house, if you still owe any of it, or if not, put it in the bank to keep for my father when he may need it.

Spring weather arrived today—the first warm day. I'm going out to Chigasaki by next train to see things sprout. My peas—alas—were mostly killed by the heavy frosts and cold—the coldest winter here in 20 years—but a few survived, and I put in some more seed last week. Jim's plan is quite right—put in a lot to allow for weaklings dying off, also for varmint—here the ground is full of young cicadas who regale themselves on the roots of things all winter. We have—at least Isamu has—lots of roses—his present fad—white and red and cream and tea with high sounding names—and a pink Dorothy Perkins that rambles over an entrance arbour. Of course they will not bloom till May. English violets here have begun to bloom on the verandah—they get watered once a week. Our little house in Yokohama is all right in itself, but a bit too slummy for the good of Ailes. It is awfully hard in this country to keep children from the contagion of eye and skin diseases. She goes to Miss Mander's school every morning, but afternoons runs wild—a remarkably long-legged youngster, with curls about 6 inches long. Isamu also grows apace. I shall have to get his picture taken in his scout suit I suppose. He is broad and solid. I send you one of Ailes. It'll be too late for your birthday—but I never can think as long ahead as the mails. Have one more pupil—a Chinese gentleman—missionary—who will go to America to college shortly. He's thirty three and has two children in China and has still the English language to acquire—*rather* an undertaking I should say. Spring holidays for the two schools are not simultaneous, so I'll only get away a few days.

Sayonara

Your devoted

Brigitta

In 1917, Léonie found her first opportunity to edit a magazine since the *Raven* fiasco of 1906. Her new editor was Scottish journalist John W. Robertson Scott, who was spending the war years in Japan, and had launched a magazine called *The New East.* "I was aided by . . . as secretary, a gallant young American woman who was once the wife of Yone Noguchi," he noted in his memoir, *Faith and Works in Fleet Street* (1947). Since the magazine was based in Tokyo, Léonie brought the neighboring Makinos a jar of strawberry jam and asked if they wouldn't mind taking Ailes for a month or so, and, leaving Isamu at home with the maid, went up to Tokyo. Léonie said she sometimes wrote for *The New East,* but her contributions were unsigned, and her stint as secretary was not acknowledged in the pages of the magazine itself.

It was around this time that Léonie began investigating an experimental school in Indiana she had read about in the November 3, 1916 *Scientific American.* Called Interlaken, it was run by a German immigrant named Edward Rumely.

To Catherine Bunnell, July 31, [1917]

Dearest Catherine,

Your birthday letter came on the 16th—so did guests—my "villa" at Chigasaki being rather popular—and I put your letter in my bag, to be answered "at leisure." The leisure came Sunday and yesterday, the 30th, anniversary of the death of the glorious Meiji Emperor which is remembered with great rejoicing over the land, being a holiday—and that leisure was shamelessly spent in gamboling in the waves at Chigasaki, with Miss Wills as my guest, a lady of about my age and more than your proportions who, clad in my bathing suit, turned somersaults on the strand. Now back in Tokyo, where I am putting in time this summer as temporary secretary to Mr. Robertson Scott, editor of the New East (magazine). The children are at Chigasaki, with a very incompetent little country maid to get their meals—but they can always fill in on watermelons. I go out every Sunday—share Miss Wills' house in Tokyo during the week. My garden has turned to a wilderness of sunflowers. Your farming and Florence's bee keeping sound fascinating—now those ought to be my jobs, while you could better do the literary act, not that I'm saying anything to belittle your farm work—I'm sure you'd be efficient in anything you do. I'm still worried about Isamu. Want to get him to America—want to get him away from his present school—there are charges of immorality among the boys of St. Joseph's—it is said that the majority of the boys over 14 are immoral—so you see why I'd like to get him away before he reaches that age. I wrote to a school in Indiana where the boys spend some time every day in shop or garden. Prospectus was ideal—expense only $600 a year—with extras. Well—I'm working up shorthand and may get a better job—in fact am getting 150 yen a month this summer. If I could only find some place where Isamu could earn part of his expense—I am sure there are such schools, but it is hard to find them from this end of the line. He is really clever with tools—does a sort of woodcarving—makes boats and aeroplanes after Art Smith's models and the like. Splendidly strong and healthy—but blissfully void of aspirations, quixotic standards, democratic ideas and all that sort of thing that are supposed to be in the atmosphere of America. (And I believe they truly are.) Dr. Nitobe's son has recently come back from America—a fine American type by education, born Japanese, and in my opinion with a good deal more solidity of character than the average Japanese youth—he's also at The New East. Isamu was quite disgusted that you took the picture of a 4 year old girl for him—He's up to my shoulder—That first photo was for my father, the second for you.

Heigho—must go to bed if I'm to get in an hours practice of shorthand before going to the office. Goodnight and love—

Léonie

The war news sounds real in your letters. Here we are touched by high prices—try to keep to war rations—but the big demonstrations—women taking up the men's jobs and so forth, have not the faintest echo here. L.

It was only a matter of time before Léonie's presence in Yokohama began to stir up gossip. When Yone published a critique of American civilization in the *Chuo koron*, the Yokohama-based *Japan Advertiser* found the irony too rich to ignore. Among Yone's complaints was his belief that "American civilization is throughout a feminine civilization—as American literature is a feminine literature." American men were unable to escape from "woman worship." "Will America's participation in the war help Americans find their true selves?" he wondered. "Or will it leave them as haughty as before, childish optimists?" The *Japan Advertiser*, taking a swipe at the Tokyo-based *Japan Times* which published Yone's weekly column, ran an unauthorized translation on September 21 with the headline "AMERICAN MEN MERE RUSTICS—WOMEN SENTIMENTAL, SAYS POET," followed by the subhead: "Yone Noguchi Flays the Country Which Helped Him Get His Start as 'Undeveloped' and 'Woman-Ridden.'" The translation was preceded by an introductory paragraph which explained that the article was "all the more interesting because the author was the recipient of many kindnesses in America, where he married an American girl whom he brought to live in Japan. His moral conduct and treatment of his wife led to a separation. His former wife is living in Japan and is supporting herself and her child by teaching. Mr. Noguchi is now married to a Japanese." Léonie, though she might well have sympathized with some of the writer's arguments against Noguchi, found the piece offensive and wrote a letter to the editor to say so.

Regarding Yone Noguchi

Japan Advertiser, October 7, 1917.

To the Editor of The Japan Advertiser

Sir,—I beg to call your attention to a gross misstatement of facts which appeared in your paper recently, in the headlines over an article written by Yone Noguchi. The position in which this statement appeared, no less than the substance of it, seemed designed to hurt Mr. Noguchi. I refer to the words, "His moral conduct and treatment of his wife led to a separation." Your correspondent has been misinformed. I, as the former wife of Mr. Noguchi, who know the facts, assure you that this statement is utterly untrue. Though I was not happy as Mr. Noguchi's wife, I did not consider myself to be ill-used. On the contrary, he used such courtesy toward me as I should expect from one of my own countrymen. Nor was the moral conduct of either of us the cause of our separation, though this is usually assumed to be the most obvious cause of separation. We separated upon a mutual understanding.

(It is possible that a thoughtful reader of Mr. Noguchi's article in The Advertiser might find in the author's own mental attitude and inability of appreciation of Western ideals a clue to the hopelessness of a union between such a thinker and an American woman.)

As I have some regard for justice I cannot but feel indignant at your unjust attack, and most earnestly desire that you will publicly retract the erroneous statements which appeared in your paper of September 21.

I beg to add that Mr. Noguchi contributes regularly toward our support. That I am making my living by teaching is hardly a matter for commiseration, since teaching was my chosen profession for many years before I met Mr. Noguchi.

Sincerely,

THE AMERICAN WIFE OF YONE NOGUCHI

Chigasaki, Sept. 29.

To Catherine Bunnell, December 6, 1917

School

My dear Catherine,

This is the only paper I can find to write on. And if I don't seize this moment to write, you mightn't get this letter for Xmas. But I believe you don't mind my coming in after the crush. I sent you a calendar yesterday which I got in a Japanese store. You see how English we are becoming. The picture reminds me of Chigasaki. Our little Chigasaki house is standing lone and empty at present. It has been "through the wars" of late. A typhoon which occurred October 2 lifted off half the roof, broke all the windows, carried the stovepipe into a neighbor's field, burst open doors, etc. We took refuge in your little Japanese parlour, the only dry spot in the house, and waited for daylight to show us the extent of the damage. Impossible to light a lamp of course, with the wind roaring through the house in a way that I have never heard or felt wind in my life. Isamu and I with our united strength were unable to hold shut a door that had blown in. I dare say you've read about it in the papers. Many people lost their lives. Well, we moved the next day. The Chigasaki house has been repaired, almost. And we are living in a palatial foreign house on the Bluff. Rent 35 yen. Plenty of work—now very busy. Teach every night. Did I tell you that I spent the summer in Tokyo, as secretary to Mr. Robertson Scott, editor of the New East? Have gone back to teaching, as I am able to be more at home. Still do some writing for the "New East." Mr. Scott is kind enough to encourage me to write. He thinks I know something about Japan. But time is too short to do more than make a bluff at it.

Children are both at school in Yokohama. Isamu now 13 years old, 4 feet 10 inches, broadshouldered and husky. Ailes is in the "Intermediate class" of Miss Mander's School (between kindergarten and school). Shows talent for Arithmetic and talking. The Catholic school which Isamu attends (there is no other for boys in Yokohama) is not good for developing character or originality. I am always anxious about him.

I hear nothing from Florence or papa. Depending on you for a word now and then. If any of your friends come this way I'd be glad to see them and hear of you at first hand. I dreamed of you the other night, but couldn't picture you in any other way than in the blue dress you wore at eighteen—some pink about the yoke. I thought you might have changed and would look older, but couldn't for the life of me imagine how you would look if older.

How's the farm. I *wish* you and Jim would get enough to take a holiday off to Japan. Our papers are full of war news, but except for the influx of Russian refugees, see nothing of it directly. Was invited to sew on pajamas for soldiers one morning at Union Church. Made 8 buttonholes and put on 8 buttons in 2 hours—decided I might be worth more in other lines.

I hear a noise of many feet. The bell has rung—examination over.

I want you to give my love and Xmas greetings to all our dear friends. Alice and Kitty and Dolly and Mary.

With best love to you and Jim.

Léonie.

Address: 1492 (Columbus discovered America) Nakamura-cho, Yokohama.

To [Ollie Polk Pitts] Superintendent of the Interlaken School, April 5, 1918

1492 Nakamura cho, Yokohama, Japan.

Dear Sir,

I have your letter of July 4, 1917, in answer to my inquiry about your school. It has not taken me all this time to decide upon the merits of the school. The splendid catalogue is sufficient to convince me. Mr. Griffin, scoutmaster of the Yokohama Boy Scouts, is also enthusiastic over the idea of it—says it should be the place to make a man of a boy. Only the expense of it brought despair upon me. Even at the reduced rate of $400 which you offered. You see we in Japan earn in *Yen*, and expenses here are in yen. The best boarding school in Yokohama (St. Joseph's College) attended by the sons of ambassadors, is 400 yen a year. But in America we must pay dollars, and a dollar is only half a yen.

Your school, however, seems so exactly the thing, that I take the liberty of writing once more, to ask whether it would be possible for the boy to earn a small part of his expense at school, say 50 to $100 a year, and also to earn his keep during holidays. Of course I know there is plenty of work in America for a strong boy—what I mean to ask is whether you could put him in the way of getting the work.

Another thing I wish to ask. Supposing I sent the boy over at the end of May or early part of June (some friends are going over then and could take him with them) could he earn his keep this summer? That is, in your part of the country. Or would it be better to let him stop in California or Vancouver, try to do something there during the summer, and go on to you in September?

He has not a good supply of clothing for such a cold country. That might be remedied during the summer, however. Could you give me an estimate of the cost of the entire outfit in America?

Now supposing you, after consideration of his case, think your school not quite the place for a boy whose backing is mainly the daily earning of his mother (I am a teacher in a Government School here, supplementing this work by secretarial work, as English and French correspondent to a business house) could you advise me of a place to send the boy? He has a very strong inclination for manual work, in fact rather a surplus of motor energy. Canada might offer a chance for an education within my means. I should be most grateful for any suggestion.

Regarding the character and temperament of the boy. He has a tendency to be very absorbed in the thing he is interested in for the moment, to the exclusion of all else; to ignore other people and their claims; to be domineering and self-willed. Is very impressionable. Will imitate those whom he admires. Very sensitive to beauty. He is the son of Yone Noguchi, a Japanese author and poet, who is somewhat known in America, especially in California, where he spent some years with Joaquin Miller. Since my separation from him, I have taken my own name, and the boy also has taken my name. He inclines to admire all things American, and slight his Japanese ancestry. I am an American, of Scotch-Irish and New England ancestry, educated at the Felix Adler School in New York, and at Bryn Mawr.

The boy's health has always been good, but this year is not up to the mark, and he has been ordered to take cod liver oil. I dare say he is at a critical age. I am sending this letter without the application form, as I wish it to go by today's steamer. Will send application by next steamer.

Very sincerely yours,

Léonie Gilmour

Enclosure. Photograph.

In April, Léonie sent the application form, along with Isamu's school report, a letter from his scout master, and the $25 application fee. On the application she listed Isamu's favorite subjects as "art, manual work, and arithmetic"; his least favorite: "grammar." His strong points were "enthusiasm and capacity for taking pains"; his weak points: "truthfulness and politeness"; asked to choose from a list of "qualities my son seems to lack most," she chose "Habits of Order" and "Willingness to Do for Others." She wished to encourage his interests in "art craft, gardening, [and] manual work," adding "Some of mother's family were shipbuilders. The boy is keenly interested in boats." On the back, she noted that Isamu's marks "were usually a little above the middle of the class," but "when he formerly attended a Japanese Kindergarten and school where more importance was given to art work, he was at the head of his class. His Japanese ancestry and environment would undoubtedly make him superior to the average American boy along these lines."

In June, Isamu was ready to depart.

To [Ollie Polk] Pitts, [Superintendent of the Interlaken School], June 24, 1918

1492 Nakamura-cho, Yokohama., Japan.

My dear Mr. Pitts,

My son Isamu will leave Japan on the 27th of this month and reach you by the middle of July. I could not get passage for him earlier, and as your letter did not reach me till some time in June I was glad it turned out so.

I note that you offer me a rate of $350 a year, to be paid in three instalments. I am quite able to do this, and thank you sincerely for the reduction.

The summer camp you say is $165, of which you thought he would be able to earn $70. As he will not come so soon as he expected I believe these figures will want revising. I will remit the amount for the summer upon receipt of your next letter.

Isamu is taking some money with him for expenses of his trip and I believe there will be some left over when he arrives which I have advised him to turn over to you.

He is looking forward with the greatest interest to his new adventure, and so are many of his friends on this side of the Pacific.

Yours sincerely,

Léonie Gilmour

By June 1918, Léonie had received approval from the school and prepared Isamu for a hasty departure.

Isamu Noguchi, *A Sculptor's World*

When I was thirteen years old, my mother decided that I must go to America to continue my education. She had selected a school in Indiana that she had read about in, I think, the *National Geographic*. I am sure that she must also have been concerned about the unfortunate situation of children of mixed blood growing up in the Japan of those days—half in and half out. She decided that I had better become completely American, and took me to the American consul, who performed a ritual, mumbling over a Bible, which I believe was my renunciation of Japanese citizenship.

At this crucial moment I was again made aware of my father; whom I had not seen in many years. He came to the boat to try to stop my going. For my part, there wasn't much choice. I was to be an American, banished as my mother had decided. No more Japan and the sands of Chigasaki.

To Miss Rumely, September 14, 1918

1492 Nakamura-cho, Yokohama, Japan.

Dear Miss Rumely,

It was a very kind thought that made you write to me. Isamu's letters are too brief, Mr. Pitt's too business-like, so if you will write me once in awhile about Isamu I should be grateful.

Are you interested in Japan? I think you would find it in some ways different from your impressions—if you came to live here. Some folks get "disillusioned." But I know the people as few foreigners do, in fact in a sense have become one of them, and cannot look on them with the critical mind of an outsider. I have taught Japanese girls for the past ten years, also many men and boys privately, whom I got to know individually better than the girls in large classes. I have lived for years in a Japanese house in the Japanese way, have lived in a country village four years—and tho' I've reverted to my American ways I still feel very much at home in Japanese surroundings. Isamu went through a Japanese kindergarten. The best kindergartens here are ideal—but the schools sadly groping along antiquated ways. I hope to visit your lovely lake country some day. I wish a few of the future educators of Japan could be educated over there. If you wish any information about things here I will get it for you.

Isamu I suppose wants many things that I cannot get for him. But the most necessary things I wish you would let me know about.

With much appreciation of your kind interest in my boy,

I am,

Sincerely yours,

Léonie Gilmour

P.S. I will send you a copy of "The New East", a magazine published in Tokyo for which I sometimes write. I was at one time secretary to the editor.

Léonie's plans for Isamu's schooling did not go as expected. The United States was at war, and, unknown to Léonie, a few days before Isamu's had arrived in La Porte, the school's founder, Edward Rumely, had been arrested for "trading with the enemy" (specifically, using undeclared German money to fund the New York *Evening Mail*, which he owned). As a result, at the end of the summer, the Interlaken School was closed and transformed into an army training camp. In early October, Léonie received an unexpected telegram from the headmaster: "SCHOOL CLOSED SEND MONEY ADVICE." At a loss, she replied: "In the emergency I wish Isamu to go to public High School in LaPorte and will be obliged if you will consult with the secretary of the Y.M.C.A. about finding a home for him. If there is a Boy Scouts organization the scout master might be interested in helping to place him."

On October 14, she wrote again: "My first thought on hearing of the closing of the school, was that I must take the first opportunity to go to America myself, and I am now trying to make an engagement over there. If you hear of an opening I should be glad to know of it. I have been advised that I might get a secretaryship to one of the faculty of my college, Bryn Mawr, at a salary of $100 for half time, with the chance of putting in the rest of the time at tutoring or writing. But although this is fair pay I do not feel that I can undertake the expense of a long journey to settle in a high-priced place like Bryn Mawr. I rather look to the Pacific Coast or the Middle West."

In November armistice was declared but Isamu was still living at the school as "a kind of mascot" to the soldiers. Finally, in January 1919, Léonie was notified that Isamu had been enrolled in a public school in nearby Rolling Prairie. It was only the following summer that Isamu "was discovered by Dr Edward A. Rumely" who rescued him from his "wild existence" by placing him in the home of a Swedenborgian minister.

As Léonie organized her plans, Yone provided some assistance, but it was not much. In a fragment of a letter dated September 7, 1919, Yone seems to state that he had lost interest in Léonie and Isamu. The brief fragment refers to an inquiry by Léonie about an insurance policy she and Yone had evidently discussed, a photograph taken at the Mitsukoshi department store, and the address of Genjiro Kataoka (formerly known as Genjiro Yeto) the artist who had illustrated *The American Diary of a Japanese Girl*, who had been a neighbor when they lived in Koishikawa.

From Yone Noguchi, September 7, 1919

. . . . Since then I lost my interest in you and even in Isamu. So I did not put the matter of insurance into practice.

—

Mr Kataoka's address:
57 Hayashi Cho
Koishikawa, Tokyo

—

I will see about the picture Mitsukoshi had taken, when I have time to go there.
[second page top missing]
Yone Noguchi
Sep. 7th, 1919

It may be surmised all of these topics are related to Léonie's announcement that she planned to return soon to the United States; the photograph may be the one she used for her passport, and she may have needed Kataoka as a reference, perhaps with regard to her supposed marriage. It is difficult to imagine what the insurance plan might have been. Yone's "since then I lost my interest" may have referred to the Isamu boat incident when Yone felt slighted by Léonie's unilateral decision to send Isamu to the United States.

On January 16, Leonie submitted the paperwork for her emergency passport to the American embassy in Tokyo. The documents contained no mention of her marriage, only of her American relations. As a witness, Leonie brought along one of Yokohama's oldest foreign residents, the seventy-four-year-old missionary, Jane Herring Loomis. Léonie must have been feeling a bit elderly herself, as she took the opportunity to trim two years off her age, claiming her birth date as June 17, 1875 and reporting her age as 44 rather than 46. She is described as being 5 feet, 5 inches, with brown (slightly grey) hair, and grey eyes.

Léonie and
Ailes' passport
photo. *Isamu
Noguchi
Foundation.*

Return to America,
1920-1933

Léonie and Ailes left Yokohama on the China Mail Steamship Company's *Nanking* on January 25, 1920, arriving at San Francisco on February 11. Léonie's letters to Catharine from 1918 to 1926 are missing, so relatively little is known about this important period in her life. However, some of her correspondence with Isamu survives, and several of the autobiographical essays she began to write more seriously during this period offer revealing glimpses of her life and thoughts.

Léonie knew something of San Francisco from Yone, who had lived in the Bay Area for more than six years before moving to New York. *The American Diary of a Japanese Girl*, which she had helped Yone write, was set mainly in San Francisco. But much of Yone's San Francisco had been destroyed in the great earthquake, and other parts of the city undamaged by the quake—notably the Western Addition—now housed much of the expanding city's population. Léonie was attracted by the neighborhoods surrounding Golden Gate Park, an ideal haven for eight-year-old Ailes. By March, they had moved into the Bon Air Apartments on Stanyan Street at the northwest corner of the park, despite the expense and inadequate space, and enrolled Ailes at the Andrew Jackson Elementary School (now the New Traditions Alternative School) two blocks up Grove Street. The comfortable middle-class neighborhood, later host to San Francisco's countercultural revival, proved congenial, and they soon found a more comfortable apartment a few blocks away at 1310 Haight Street.

Hoping to profit from her fifteen-year residence in Japan, Léonie had made plans to start a small import-export business. She had brought cheap Japanese needles she could sell at a profit, silk kimonos, and samples of Japanese paper she thought she could sell through American paper companies. She had ideas about importing and exporting chemicals as well.

She made no immediate plan to see Isamu. Now sixteen, Sam Gilmour was halfway through his sophomore year in high school. Having survived the ordeal of his wartime arrival, he was living comfortably in the home of a Swedenborgian minister, Samuel Mack, his wife Fanny, and their three children. "Sam" Gilmour was attending an ordinary public high school, not the Interlaken School (which remained closed while Dr. Rumely awaited trial in New York). Isamu might have rejoined Léonie and Ailes easily enough. But when she wrote him, it was to suggest he collaborate with her on one of her business ventures.

To Isamu Gilmour, March 14, 1920

Bon Air Apts. Room 35, San Francisco.

My dear Isamu,

It is very nice to get letters from you so quickly nowadays. It's quicker to get an answer from you than even to get one by cable from Japan. I was getting discouraged about getting any reply to my inquiry on Strawboard, and was even on the point of cabling again, when an answer came last Saturday, just 12 days after I had cabled. Unfortunately the price has gone up, so I feel dubious about the result. Anyway I have managed to get in touch with all the largest paper companies here, and next week am to meet the president of the biggest one and show him all my samples of Japanese paper.

In regard to the fibre needles. As I believe I told you, I had figured on a price of $8 per 10000 on unoiled needles, and $8.50 on oiled needles, f. o. b. San Francisco. If you add fifty cents more on each it would pay the cost of carriage to you. Now you ask what you think you can get for them. There is a man in San Francisco who is also selling them, being supplied by the same company. I should like to find him and see what he is asking. If you think you could take care of the selling of these needles for your section of the country I will put them in your hands, but if it takes too much of your time will give them to a travelling salesman. Better ask Dr. Rumely's advice and if you really could take them it would be better than newspapers.

If you have any money of your own earning I should be glad to have you send it on, as my expenses have been very heavy and I cannot expect to receive any from Japan until the first week in April. I was counting that I'd just pull through, when some silk kimonos from Miss Wills called for a duty of $30.50, so I am that much short. This apartment house is rather high toned and expensive and we have hardly room to turn around in, but I have not yet been able to find anything cheaper or larger that did not have some drawback. So I have taken it for one month longer. I shall get the rest of my baggage from the ferry tomorrow and put it in the basement store room.

That is all for today from your loving
Mother

"Sam" Gilmour, Indiana, 1919. *Isamu
Noguchi Foundation.*

The Interlaken School reopened in the fall of 1920, and Edward Rumely, though still awaiting trial in New York, again made special arrangements for Isamu. Léonie wrote to thank him, and also to explain her
reasons for not attempting to reunite the family.

To Edward Rumely, August 29, 1920

L. GILMOUR EXPORT AND IMPORT

1492 NAKAMURA-CHO, YOKOHAMA, JAPAN.

1868 Page St. San Francisco

My dear Dr. Rumely,

I hear from Isamu that he is now at Interlaken upon your invitation
and I thank you sincerely for looking after him so well. I believe it is
now about time for school to open and I enclose my cheek No.18 on the
French American Bank for $40 to start him in.

I came here at a rather unfortunate time for business with Japan,
but in spite of everything am beginning to make some headway. As I

presume you have business connections in your neighborhood I will ask you to keep me in mind for anything in my line, whether American manufacturers wishing to export their goods to Japan or buyers for Japanese goods. I am concentrating on PAPER and CHEMICALS. Now I have connections with three of the largest Paper mills in Japan—the samples I have in hand include Printing Paper, Wrapping Paper, Tissue Paper, Crepe Paper. Paper Napkins, Wall Paper, GRASSCLOTH, Paper Cloth, Imitation leather, Veneer Paper, Celluloid Paper, Match Paper, Coloured paper etc. Of course I only take import orders. For Chemicals I have good connections on both sides. I am already receiving inquiries and orders by cable from Japan. A Dutch firm of this city (friends of a very good friend of mine in Yokohama) are desirous of having me join in with them to help them sell their herrings, cheeses, tea etc. Although I should prefer to keep to my own business, still if Dutch cheeses and herrings are going to bring in any bread and butter I may decide to give part of my time to that work. It takes so much time to get things started. I should like very well to be nearer to Isamu, but as I have already put so much time and energy into working up things here I don't like to lose it all by moving, so think the best plan will be for me to stay here for the present, and have Isamu continue where he is. He is probably much better off than his little sister, who runs wild while her mother is all around town on business.

With cordial regards, I remain
Sincerely,
Léonie Gilmour
Encl.

To Edward Rumely, October 11, 1920

L. GILMOUR EXPORT AND IMPORT

1492 NAKAMURA-CHO, YOKOHAMA, JAPAN.

1868 Page St., San Francisco

My dear Dr. Rumely,
On August 29 I sent you a check for $40 on Isamu's account, which I trust is in your possession, and today I enclose $50 more. Isamu writes me that he is going to an evening school by your advice, but I am afraid this extra work may be too much for him. He is always an eager worker, ready to go to the full limit of his endurance. When he was about eight

years old I had to keep him out of school a year on account of nervous strain—In that case the strain came from having to make a long train journey back and forth every day, together with long hours at school. I taught him at home only two hours a day, and when he went back to school he was ahead of his class, which showed that the shorter hours made for better efficiency. He is so far from me that I must trust to you to look after him in every way, and while his health may not actually suffer, you know that all work and no play makes a dull boy. Isamu's play—a bit of gardening, making pictures or carving on wood or the like, was always entered into with so much zest I thought it quite as much worth while as his regular studies. I am quite willing to trust the matter to your good judgement, only I want to put in a word of warning. My family are all inclined to overdo. My sister is now incapacitated for any regular work on account of having stuck too long and too steadily at her job on the Century dictionary . . . . I suppose Isamu has told you that I am with the EAST & WEST EXPORT Company of this city, in charge of their Paper Import Dept.—am working very hard and hope for some results soon.

Yours Sincerely,
L. Gilmour

In addition to her import-export business, Léonie was making some efforts at writing for publication. One of her first efforts, written in the fall of 1920 when the presidential election was underway, was an ostensibly first-hand account of Ailes' acclimation to San Francisco. Léonie found humor in Ailes' experiences of travel, school, and recreation, making the most of her misconceptions of American culture, and poking fun at nationalistic ideas on both sides. The story was apparently never published. Léonie had difficulty finding the right tone: adults would have found jokes about "hot dogs" too silly, while humorous allusions to *The Golden Whales of California* (a recent collection of poems by Vachel Lindsay) would have gone over the heads of children. Moreover, editors of the day would have had a hard time accommodating Léonie's cheerful depiction of the life of the "little Eurasian girl"—so different from stereotypical images of Eurasian children as degenerate orphans and social outcastes, the pitiful offspring of sinful liaisons between lustful white adventurers and victimized Asian women. In a state like California, where interracial marriages between whites and Asians were illegal, her story had little hope of publication. Still, for Léonie and Ailes, it was a nice memento of their San Francisco days.

Ai-Chan Goes to Frisco

(A little Eurasian girl writes to her friend in Japan)

Unpublished typescript.

My native country! Although I was born in Yokohama, I always thought of America as my native country. I used to tell the other children stories about my country. It seemed almost as if I knew more about my country then than even now when I know it better. When anyone said anything mean about America I felt a burning rage. But my little Japanese children didn't say anything mean about my country, because they *knew* how wonderful it was from my stories. "Land of sweet Liberty!" I taught them that. We used to take hands in a ring and all sing together. They all said they wanted to go with me when I returned to my country. And I promised to take them all.

Suddenly my dream came true. Mother got two tickets for her and me to go on the boat. But there were no tickets for my little Japanese children.

When the boat sailed away and away till we couldn't see Japan any more suddenly I wanted to go back. Because all my friends were in Japan. "Stop the boat," I cried. "I want to go back." "We can't stop the boat," said mother. "Now we have started we must go on till we reach America." "You may go on if you like," said I, "but I am going to get off at the next station." Mother only laughed. Sometimes mother laughs in such a way I feel a burning rage at her.

At last we came to America. It's not so big as I thought. Quite a little place. But very interesting. And there is Golden Gate Park, with wild woods and wild animals and everything. Do you know what a buffalo is? I will send you a nickel and you can see it for yourself, I mean a little image of him. I have seen the real ones in the Park. I thought it was an extinct animal but I found out it is not. He sits in the dirt just like a Yokohama drunk. There are no drunks here. I believe they are extinct. I am keeping my eyes open for the Golden Whales of California. I guess they'll be over at Neptune beach some day. The Three Bears live in Golden Gate Park. They have a tub, not three, but only one, and I couldn't see their bowls or their Three Chairs. I suppose that living in this climate they just sit on the ground and eat out of their hands like everybody else. It's awfully jolly in the Park, especially on Sunday when everybody is having a picnic on the Green. Perky little birdies hop about and pick up the crumbs. If you sit near the trees dear little squirrels come and eat peanuts out of your hand, then whisk about, and scurry up their tree. Oh, if you could see those funny little frisky things! I did so want to sleep one night in the Park with them and pretend I was a squirrel myself. There's one lawn only for Mothers and Babies. Those babies are tumbling about and trying to dance to the music of the Merry-Go-Round. The Merry-Go-Round is going round and round all the time. Some kind ladies have their pockets full of tickets. "Have you a ticket for the Merry-Go-Round, little girl?" they will say. "No? Then here's a ticket for you."

The first time I went on the Merry-Go-Round I felt like an enchanted Princess being carried through the air on a winged steed. I shut my eyes and thought maybe I would be somebody else when I got off. But I found I was the same person. There are Donkeys too, and we may ride on them. There are rings and swings, and children and monkeys swinging on them. The children here wear Over-Alls, and sometimes they are quite dirty. I thought at first they were very poor. But Mother says no, it's because there is no hard-working Amah-San to wash their clothes and faces and be always telling them to keep out of the dirt. A good riddance, I say. I do love to grub in the dirt myself. Mother says I needn't go the Whole Hog, but I say, Do in America as the Americans, and more too. They eat sticky popcorn and other delicious things. Right in the street! Mercy on us! And sometimes they eat Dogs, I believe, because I saw a sign at the Beach, "HOT DOGS!" but my friend said, "It's too cold to stop and eat those Hot Dogs. We'd better be getting home." And one day the Minister at Church said the Knights of King Arthur (they belong to our Church) would be going on a hike, and everybody should bring as many dogs as he could eat. I have seen the Smallest Dog in the World, in the museum. About as long as your finger. I didn't have a chance to taste a dog yet. But I get Suckers and Ice Cream Cones. Oh, Boy! I am sending you a picture of me and my pals eating Cones.

The children in Yokohama used to say there was Gold in the ground in America. But I found out it's a lie. There's lots of earthworms though. I dug some up in our school yard and took them home for pets. I do love pets. Mother doesn't. One evening she was late getting home and I found a little lonely Cat in the street. We was both lonely, so we comforted each other, and I taught him how to dance, as I learned it at the Movies. And I sang to him, "You're my swe-ee-t-hear-rt," giving him a hearty hug, as they do in the Movies. And he said "Me-you!" in an unutterable tone of voice. Then Mother came along and said "Come along to bed." So I bade him a regretful farewell, and he cried piteously to come along too, but Mother says there isn't room for him. I was sure he was an Enchanted Prince. No room for my poor little Prince, alas! We live in an Apartment, with a Disappearing Bed. We can't go to bed, of course, till it appears. And it can't appear while there's Company, because there would be no room for the Company. Likewise we can't eat while it's there, because there's no place for the Table. Unless we eat in the Kitchen, which we often do, because it's so convenient to get the toast. It's a mercy there are no servants around to criticize our ways.

There's something new to see here every day. And pictures, pictures everywhere. Great high fences all covered with lovely pictures—nymphs dancing around a pool where floats a cake of snow-white soap like a water lily, and travellers with seven league boots stepping blithely over blue mountains, and Teddy-bears eating chocolates, and a man looking at a camel and saying "I'd walk a mile for a camel." So would I, the old hunch-backed dear! And there are the Presidential Candidates, who are Great Men. My school is named after a Great Man, Andrew Jackson. He is nicknamed "Stonewall Jackson," because when he used to play *judo* with the boys they couldn't throw him any more than if he was a stone wall. I bet I could have thrown him. When I think of the way I used to butt into the Yokohama kids—well, it makes me smile. There is a sign on our school fence, "WAR GARDEN. KEEP OFF." I thought it was dangerous at first. But I found out there aren't any Bombs or anything. Just dirt, very nice for digging.

At school one day the teacher showed the American flag. We used to think it so beautiful with all the shining stars on it, didn't we? All made of silk. This was a little cotton one. Pretty, of course. But that day I couldn't help thinking of the Japanese flag all soft white wool with just the big red Sun in the middle—the beautiful great big flag we used to put out on holidays at the end of a bamboo pole with a gold knob at the end. It seemed as if a lump came in by throat as big as the red sun on our old flag. So when all the other children bowed down their heads as if the Emperor was passing by I didn't bow down my head a bit, but kept looking straight ahead and seeing the flag of Japan. "Why don't you bow down your head?" said the teacher. "Because I think the Japanese flag is prettier," I said.

And at recess the other children said, "Why do you stick up for Japan? That's only a little bit of a country, not great like America." "It is, too." I cried. The most wonderful, most beautiful country in the world! It's great! It's big! Oh, far bigger than this country, I can tell you." Then one of the big boys got a map and said, "Look at this big picture, that's America. With the Rocky Mountains, and the Great Lakes each one big enough to swallow your little Japan, and the mighty Mississippi rolling down the middle of the world. And here on this page is your little Japan." "What do I care what you say?" said I. "My mother has a picture of me as big as the geography book. And she has a teeny little one of herself that was taken for our passport. But my mother is bigger than I." Then they all began to talk at once, and I got mad. I felt such a burning rage because I *knew* Japan was greater, but how can you argue if everybody is against you? So then I rolled up my sleeves, and I said "Come on! Come on! I'll show you which country is bigger. If any kid says Japan is not as big as America I'll wipe the floor with him." (You mightn't know what that means but I think you can guess. I learned to speak American since I came here because they laughed at my English—said I talked like an old-fashioned story book — so I learned American and I like it because you sure can say some thing in this language). Well, do you know those children all backed away. And now they don't say anything mean about Japan, and I tell them stories about the land where I was born. I tell them about how much room there is there, and how every family has their own house and their own garden, with a pond and fishes, trees and flowers and pleasant walks. And how nice it is to have so much room, not having to be crowded in apartment houses with so many decks as in Frisco with people above you and below you. And how we had our own servants in Japan. Oh yes, of course. And they treat me like a Princess, and sit around and listen while I weave a magic web of fancy. And I think it's really great and lovely here. But I hope some day to go back to my native country of Japan.

Even when Léonie avoided controversial topics like "little Eurasian girls," she still had limited success with her literary efforts. A "little story" entitled "The Butterfly" submitted to *Today's Housewife* was rejected on May 31, 1921 by Children's Page editor, Constance Cooke, who liked it, but lacked space to use it. She invited Léonie to send more of her work, noting that stories should be kept to around 500 words. The *San Francisco Chronicle* rejected an unidentified manuscript on June 7. (From one of the rejection notes, we know that in May 1921, Léonie was living in a house at 1310 Haight Street). Léonie had better luck with the *Christian Science Monitor*, which published "Cherry Blossoms in Tokyo" in April 1921 and the following piece, "Glory of the Morning in Japan," in July 1922.

Glory of the Morning in Japan

Christian Science Monitor, July 24, 1922.

Getting up early is a Japanese habit. Your true Japanese of right old-fashioned sort will cheerfully turn out at any hour of the night or morning when occasion calls for it, such as seeing a friend off on the midnight train, when he will make his way by the light of a paper lantern as he hobbles over the frozen ground to the station; or stealing forth in the gray twilight of a summer morn to stand on the bridge of Shinobazu pond awaiting the crack of dawn, heralded by a loud report from a thousand lotus blossoms bursting at once; or joyously setting out to the morning glory mart at Iriya to view these frail beauties in their pristine dewy freshness.

I remember well the day we went to Iriya. We arose at four. Had we been an hour earlier we might have seen and heard the lotus flowers open. Alas! the great white and pink flowers were basking in the morning light by the time we got to Shinobazu pond. What did it matter? It was enough to have seen their pure faces washed in morning dew. Then on we jog to Iriya.

+   +   +

We are not alone. We find ourselves in a stream of people, a stream swollen by other little streams from side streets, and tributary to another stream flowing along a more populous street. We converge upon Iriya. There the flower vendors have gardens, booths, tea-houses, where the flowers are displayed to the best advantage. Already a few early-comers are returning. See that girl in shabby cotton dress, hatless like all the girls in Japan, without a bit of ornament for her hair, holding her pot of morning glories to her bosom as she hurries home to be in time for her work. An old dame follows, bent double over her stick, a little flower pot in one hand. It is surely morning glory day. Hardly another flower is to be seen. Each plant is in a pot by itself, some with only one bloom of exquisite shape and color, perhaps four inches in diameter, like a diaphanous canopy, like a crystal goblet, like a chalice brimful of moonshine, like a thousand fancies snared in dreams. Others with two or more contrasting blooms making a color chord, perhaps a shining white one and a dull mulberry one, deep blue with faint lavender, or blush of dawn starred in white companioned with fawn color. Most of them seem to have been trained to leave off their trick of climbing and spend their whole soul in the art of a perfect bloom. Some, however, lift their charming plebian heads on little bamboo trellises set up in the pots.

How many pots of morning glories did we buy that day? More than we could carry. A rickshaw man was engaged to help take them home. And some exquisite little porcelain cups, shaped and tinted like the flowers, we bought for a few cents at the same place, to remind us of their prototypes when these should have faded away.

As we sat down to breakfast, happy with our treasures set out in a row on the verandah, still sweetly blooming like little maids in crisp cool dresses, my eyes suddenly fastened on my blue and white rice bowl, of the shape called in Japan the morning glory shape. You know it? It is small at the base and quickly flaring, the symbol of all that is airy, delicate, soaring, ready to spring away from this earth, just as the pyramids with broad base, or the mountains of similar shape, are the symbol of what is solid, everlasting, world without end or change. It is in Asia that we find the colossal gods of stone or bronze sitting like images of indestructibility, and in Asia that we find the cult of the morning glory. I believe the latter is somehow symbolic of Japan and Japanese art, which is above all others insubstantial and mutable.

In April 1922, Léonie had an office in the prestigious Mills Building on Montgomery Street (a beautiful pre-earthquake building where Yone used to visit a lady admirer, Mrs. Nelly Smith). Evidently Léonie had an office in Yokohama as well: her letterhead "L. GILMOUR EXPORT AND IMPORT" carries the address 1492 Nakamura-cho. But her focus was not entirely on business. In a note to the director of the Sequoia Little Theater, she inquires about the availability of dramatic texts, explaining "I have a small Dramatic club of Japanese young men who practice for the sake of improving their English."

On graduating high school in June of 1922, Isamu had declared his intention to become an artist, and was sent as an apprentice to Gutzon Borglum, a Connecticut sculptor who worked on large memorials. Had their pairing proved successful, Isamu might well have found himself carving the presidential faces of Mount Rushmore. But Borglum said he would never be a sculptor, so Isamu, with the encouragement and promised support of Dr. Rumely, turned his thoughts to medicine and prepared to enroll in Columbia University's premedical program in the fall of 1922.

Some clues about Léonie's eastward journey may be found in two July 1923 letters from Léonie to Ailes, who was left temporarily with friends in San Francisco. In the first, written from La Porte on July 1, Léonie gives Ailes instructions to see various people, and ends with the postscript, "I will stay here to help Isamu celebrate the Fourth." The second, from New York, is dated the 27th:

To Ailes Gilmour, July 27, 1923

39 E. 10 St., New York

Dear Ailes,

The other day someone telephoned from Dr. Rumely's office that there was a letter on pink paper and a package for me. So I went up to get it. But the clerk had already dropped them in the letter box. As they never came here I tried to find out about them. The girl then remembered she had written 10 E. 39 St. instead of 39 E. 10 Street. What a mistake! I think the letter must have been from you, and that it has gone back to you. Isn't that a shame? Did you send a package too? I am still treasuring the little blue handkerchief you made for me. I have not used it.

I hope you are happy and having a good time. I hope you go to the U.S. Grant school still. It is such a good school. Don't be in a hurry to come to this horrid city.

What do you think I came upon the other day? The house where I lived when I was just your age. And I got some cake at the bakery where my mother used to send me for bread. Well, well.

I am working just as hard as in S.F. Have to string beads tonight. The lady with whom I live is making me a new dress. And she is making over my grey silk one. The dress I wore on the train got all ragged. So I fixed that over.

I ride up and down on the bus on Fifth Avenue. Everybody is rushing around, and the dust is flying around, and gets in my mouth and tickles my throat. Brother is far away in La Porte. I wish I could stay there.

Did you see Mrs. Toluboff? Give her my love and tell her I did not see her daughter. I hope Mrs. Bailey and the children keep well. I will write her again soon.

With love to all

Mother

The wealthy Rumely family had invited Isamu to stay at their New

York apartment at Riverside Drive and 103rd Street, just a few blocks from the Columbia campus. But Isamu told Rumely he preferred to live with his mother. Leonie had taken rooms in an upscale apartment building on East 10th Street between Fifth Avenue and Broadway. She made efforts to reconnect with her Bryn Mawr classmates, the October 1923 *Bryn Mawr Alumnae Bulletin* listing her 10th Street address with the note that she was "spending the winter" there.

Isamu Noguchi, *A Sculptor's World*

About this time my mother managed to come to America. She had reached San Francisco, and shortly afterward arrived in New York, with the idea of importing specialized Japanese goods such as color prints, pearls, and other small objects. She took an apartment on East Tenth Street, and I went to live there.

My mother had come home, returned from a life's voyage, to Greenwich Village where she had been born. She had loved Japan, as she was much loved there, staying for seventeen years, making her way alone. Of my father's eight children by his Japanese wife, the eldest was but two years younger than I. How many times must she have felt defeated as she left Japan, for my sake, my sister's, or her own?

If she had thought to break my dependence in sending me away, my own reaction had been to feel deserted. My extreme attachment never returned, and now the more motherly she became, the more I resented her. I was at this time still known as Isamu Gilmour, and I had become completely acclimatized as an American. There was no hint of Japan about me. Yet when I finally became conscious that I was to be a sculptor, I decided almost involuntarily to change my name, adopting one that perhaps I had no right to. I could see my mother's consternation, but she did not object, helping me rather in my travail, away from her, toward Japan, and the way that I had chosen.

Thwarting Dr. Rumely's plans for Isamu may not have been the primary reason for Léonie's move to New York City, but it was certainly on her list of things to do. A few years later, after Rumely had graciously admitted defeat, he recalled "how [Isamu's] mother turned up one day at [his] office and hotly denounced him for turning a boy of artistic temperament toward a career for which he was entirely unsuited." "It is quite true," Léonie told Catharine, "that Dr. Rumely and I had an awful row on that score, and the Doctor, then Isamu's best friend and advisor, persisted in his opinion, so that Isamu, as you know, took a year and a half at Columbia at a pre-medical course." Isamu, now accustomed to the middle class life of the Rumely and Mack homes, had grown skeptical of his mother's artistic plans. But Léonie had been right, after all, about her son's unsuitability for medical school, which he hated.

Another reason for the move to New York was Léonie's wish to send Ailes to the Ethical Culture School, where she could receive a scholarship. In later years Ailes recalled that she had "moved to the East to attend the Ethical Culture School; their educational philosophy influenced my mother." Felix Adler, now bald but still energetic, continued to preside over his society and cast a watchful eye over the school, though he devoted much of his energy to his lectures at Columbia University, where he had held the chair of Political and Social Ethics since 1902. Fanny Schwedler and Gabriel Bamberger were long gone. The school had changed character considerably since it began to admit paying students a few years after Léonie's graduation. In 1904 it had moved to its own impressive building at 33 Central Park West, beside the new building of the Ethical Culture Society at 2 West 64st Street, the same buildings the School and Society occupy today. In 1912, the school had added the latest German educational development: an Open Air Department; it was specially designed for "anemic and nervous children," but the objective was for all the students to study and recite in the open air the year round. In 1922, the Elementary, Open Air, and High School enrolled a total of 759 students.

To turn Isamu back toward his artistic destiny, the first step was to get him into an art school. In 1924 Léonie heard about one she thought might attract Isamu: the Leonardo da Vinci Art School, which had opened in December 1923. It was a charity school organized by local Italian community leaders including congressman (and future mayor) Fiorello La Guardia, and the Piccirilli Brothers, marble sculptors responsible for the city's best-known landmarks—the Washington Square arch, the lions of the New York Public Library, the Columbus Circle USS Maine statue—not to mention such Washington, D.C. masterworks as the Lincoln Memorial. A critical supporting role was played by William Norman Guthrie (the rector who made St. Mark's-in-the-Bowery Church into the fabled center of East Village cultural radicalism that it remains today) who allowed the school to occupy the basement of a church building at the northwest corner of Tompkins Square. The school's director was Onorio Ruotolo, a thirty-six year old Italian immigrant best known as a portrait sculptor, though he was also an editor, poet, playwright, and political commentator.

In the summer of 1924, Léonie "took a business trip to the summer places along the coast of Cape Cod and Cape Ann for several weeks," as the November 1924 Bryn Mawr Alumnae Bulletin noted. Though the plaster was scarcely dry on Isamu's first sculptures, Léonie wasted no time touting his success to her classmates: "Her son, Isamu Noguchi, has suddenly come into notice as a sculptor, one of the Sunday papers having recently shown a picture of him in his studio."

Isamu Noguchi, *A Sculptor's World*

One evening she told me that she had noticed the Leonardo da Vinci Art School in a converted church on Avenue A. Why didn't I go there? So I walked there and looked around, rather disdainfully. The director, Onorio Ruotolo, spotted me and asked, 'Wouldn't you like to study here!' I said I wasn't interested in sculpture. Finally I copied a plaster foot, whereupon I was offered a scholarship. I began attending evening school but then announced that I couldn't go on because I had a job and also went to college. Ruotolo suggested that I should work for him and give up the restaurant job, and he would pay me the equivalent. How could I resist? I became a sculptor, even against my will. I shall always be grateful to him and the Italian community in New York.

Even Hideyo Noguchi, the famous bacteriologist, advised Isamu it would be better to "become an artist as your father is," and the dancer Michio Ito also encouraged him. Within months Isamu's work was appearing in regular shows; a few months after that, he was rebelling against the "slick and quick way of doing academic sculpture" and setting out on his own, reclaiming his former name of Isamu Noguchi as an artistic necessity.

There is only one surviving letter from Yone to Léonie written after her return the United States. Yone was now concentrating his diminishing English writing efforts on art books. The first, *Hiroshige*, had appeared in 1921. As was his usual practice, Yone arranged the printing in Japan, then sold the books overseas through local publisher-booksellers. The arrangement worked well with Elkin Mathews, who acted as his London publisher, but less well with Ananda Coomaraswamy, who was to handle the American distribution through his Orientalia bookshop on East 60th Street. Léonie visited the shop toward the end of 1925, and was able to obtain some payment, and sent Yone a check.

From Yone Noguchi, December 10, 1925

865 Nakano in Tokyo

Dear Leonie:

I was away from home—travelling for lecture.

Many thanks for the cheque you sent me!

But I am tired with Orientalia—Of course the first arrangement was that I will be paid 2.50 per copy of Hiroshige on the spot. But when the arrangement was not realized, I have my own terms.

Perhaps I sent 250 copies of "Japan & America" to Orientalia,—but I forgot the exact number of copies of the said book. This matter should be written correctly in the shop book of Orientalia. I have nothing to quarrel with them about it.

Hurriedly,

Yone Noguchi

Yone subsequently gave up on Orientalia, listing only Elkin Mathews as publisher for the other four books in the series. He sent Léonie some of the books, which she sold as part of her Japanese import business.

In an essay she apparently never published, Léonie attempted to grapple with the question of intercultural marriage. The essay is undated, but Gilmour mentions that the topic was suggested by *Liberty* magazine (an adjunct of the *Chicago Tribune*) which began publication on May 10, 1924. Léonie describes the essay as a second attempt to grapple with the topic: after her first effort was dismissed by *Liberty*'s editor as too flippant and cursory, she "put out a few feelers to find out what he would consider the more serious aspects of the question," and then, in the new essay, proceeded to politely but firmly deconstruct his stereotypical assumptions of Japanese and American "types" and intermarriages. "The ethical code is the same in Japan as here," she argued in the spirit of Felix Adler; "ethical codes all over the world, whether promulgated by Moses or Confucius or Buddha, have a strong similarity, based on human nature and the needs of community life." She found East and West more similar than different; just as there was no "American type," the "Japanese type" was constantly changing its form, like the Old Man of the Sea in Homer's *Odyssey*.

Though she did specifically address her own marriage, she did make an effort to accommodate the editor's request that she write from her "own observations and experience." Getting to the core of the matter, she attacked the implicit suggestion that that her own Japanese-American marriage, which had evidently failed, could be taken as a proof that all such intermarriages were doomed to failure. Divorce, she argued, was not "a sure sign that a marriage was not successful and desirable while it lasted." Marriage could be judged—like a tree—by its fruits. Her own children (though she modestly avoid saying so) were her proof. Moreover, divorce was now an accepted feature of American life. She regarded it as "salutary," offering as support the great English writer John Milton's 1643 tract on "The Doctrine and Discipline of Divorce," aimed at abolishing the "unwarranted law" against divorce. Legalizing divorce, Milton had argued, was necessary to eliminate the "open vice and frantic heresy" committed by prisoners of some unhappy marriages, as well as the "repining and blasphemous thoughts" that affected others (including his own).

It is not clear for whom Léonie was writing the essay: clearly not the *Liberty* editor approaching the "very serious subject" in a "serious spirit" so different from her own "flippant" attitude. Despite her self-criticism and the missing ending, the essay remains a forceful statement of Gilmour's view on the topic of intercultural marriage, views that anticipate a day when everyone might regard interracial relationships in a spirit as cursory as her own. Perhaps she was writing for the future.

Inside Looking On
When East Weds West

Unpublished typescript.

When the Editor of Liberty asked me to write an article, based on my own observations and experience, on the subject of marriage between Europeans and Japanese, I promptly responded that I would make a few little sketches from life among my friends in Japan. Alas, my trifling sketches seemed to him too flippant, too cursory, not to attack the problem in the serious spirit due to a very serious subject. "And where," said he, "are your conclusions?" Conclusions? Where, indeed? He talked in such an earnest way that I felt sure I ought to go to the bottom of something. So I put out a few feelers to find out what he would consider the more serious aspects of the question.

He assumed, to start with, that there were certain fundamental differences between Japanese and Europeans, differences in their philosophy of life, differences in religion, differences in customs, and that these differences might easily become a source of that "incompatibility" which is the frequent excuse for a broken marriage. (Incompatibility is sometimes pieced out to make quite a decent cloak). He assumed that there was a Japanese "type," with variations to be sure, just as there is an American type, or types, pretty clearly recognized in literature—sometimes we recognize traits of the type here and there among our friends, tho a complete type is pretty hard to find. (The literary "type" is largely a vogue, the persistence of a type depending largely on the brilliancy, or popularity, of his originator. The American type having been studied at first hand, at least, the features are fairly clear. The Japanese type has hardly emerged in literature, because few have taken the trouble to study the Japanese through the medium of their own language and literature, or through personal contact. Lafcadio Hearn is a notable exception. He has been able to portray something of the delicacy, the restraint, the poetic and tragic turn of mind that are sympathetic to his own temperament. His pictures are true, not idealized, as is sometimes claimed. There is not one of his exquisite delineations that has not its prototype in life. Those characterizations are just. There are such Japanese. And then there are others. Among Japanese types you may run the gamut from refinement to vulgarity. It is quite as far from a gentleman to a rowdy in Tokyo as it is in New York. And the differences between these two extremes, whether in Tokyo or New York, is far greater [than that] between New York and Tokyo, an American and a Japanese.

"The fundamental differences between the East and the West" is one of those stock phrases that, once accepted and adjusted to one's vision like a pair of imperfect magnifying glasses, discover, exaggerate and distort all the minutest differences on which they are focussed. How far more true to speak of the "fundamental likenesses" between East and West. The likenesses are fundamental. The differences rather superficial and extraneous. It is true that a Japanese laps the left side of his kimono over his right, turns out to the left in encountering a person walking in the opposite direction, gives a present when he marries, writes from the top to the bottom of the page, holds his closed umbrella upside down and so forth and so on, while we do all those things in the reverse. He "worships his ancestors" to use another erroneous phrase, that is, he tries to live in such a way as not to shame his ancestors. I have yet to meet a well born American who fails to bring his grandfather into the conversation if the old gentleman has done anything to be proud of. I guess he likes to live up to his forbears too. (Though sometimes his pride takes the form of digging up pirates whose bones had better be left in the mold). A Japanese, walking with his wife, goes a step or two ahead. An American walks on the outside of the street. In both cases their masculine vanity probably leads to his condescending attitude of "protecting" the weaker vessel from imminent danger, whether from devouring demons in front, or from fiery steeds or chortling automobiles at the side. Japanese are taught filial obedience, their duty toward their parents. We talk more of parental obligations to children. Do you think that Japanese are less devoted to their children, or that their efforts for their welfare are more slight? How many a poor Japanese family keep their boys at school until they are nineteen or twenty, and even manage to send one to college, when the average American boy in similar circumstances would be earning his way at fifteen, getting his education in the school of hard knocks, which may after all be quite as good for him.

Religion is not taught in the schools of Japan, for much the same reasons that we have cut out the subject from our school curriculum. That is to say, neither the Buddhistic nor the Christian dogma (two leading creeds in Japan today) is allowed in the government schools. But ethics is taught in every school. The ethical code is the same in Japan as here. I fancy that ethical codes all over the world, whether promulgated by Moses or Confucius or Buddha, have a strong similarity, based on human nature and the needs of community life. Human nature is greedy, wants to take things it has no right to, to the vast disturbance of community life, hence "Thou shalt not steal." Human nature is cowardly, prone to evade consequences with a lie, and lies are a pest in social intercourse. "Thou shalt not lie" becomes one of the first lessons in good manners. There is a social evil in Japan, as here. They have tried a different method of controlling it, by restricting it to localities and subjecting it to governmental considering perhaps that what can't be cured may be alleviated. We raid any locality, and scatter the evil. Both methods are conspicuously ineffectual, as would be any method of control other than self-control.

If the general conceptions of what is right, moral, proper, are so similar, it follows that Japanese and Europeans are fundamentally the same, just as we may assume that when different religions teach the same virtues, the religions are fundamentally the same. But civilization in Japan and civilization in the West have advanced along somewhat divergent paths. These divergences may make for friction when extremes meet. And yet we learned at school that divergent forces will exert a resultant pull in a direction midway between the two divergent forces. Let us consider, for a moment, the divergence of Eastern and Western civilizations.

We have heard the word "dynamic" applied to American civilization, in contrast to "static" applied to the civilizations of China and Japan. Here we have two excellent catchwords; expressing a truth, and useful, if not overworked. You, as an American, prefer to be "dynamic" do you not? It swells your national complacency. From "dynamic" and "static" your mind jumps to "stagnation" and "progress," does it not? Not so fast, good sir. In Norman Douglas' brilliant book "South Wind" the old Greek Count Caloveglia also uses the words "static" and "dynamic" to contrast different societies, and again applies the word "dynamic" to America, reserving "static" for the status of the old world peoples, especially the Latino-Greek culture bordering on the Mediterranean. And he insists that only in *static* society can civilization emerge. That in "dynamic" societies we find *progress* but not civilization. He defines the terms thus: progress is a centripetal movement, obliterating man in the mess. Civilization is centrifugal: it permits, it postulates, the assertion of personality. The terms are not synonymous. They stand for hostile and divergent movements. Progress subordinates. Civilization coordinates. The individual emerges in civilization. He is submerged in progress. To quote further: "Democracy has substituted progress for civilization. To appreciate things of beauty, as do the Americans, a man requires intelligence. To *create* them, as did the Greeks, he requires intelligence and something else as well: time."

Time! There, in a word, is the gist of the divergence of the Far Eastern from the Western, and more particularly from the American civilization. The difference between Japanese and American conditions are then similar to the differences between the older European culture and our own, that is between an older, more established order, "static" if you will, where the slow growth of culture has its place,—and a more "dynamic" world where culture is replaced by 100% Americanism or the product of the "melting pot." Of course it seems very sad to be an American if you look at it in that light. Bluster and progress are not really the things after all. I don't know how many Americans have written books to tell us that we don't know how to live. I don't know how many have migrated to the old world, Europe, or to the still older world of Japan and China, and are finding their lives more satisfactorily filled there. May not this very chorus of protest against our American ways show that the germs of civilization have started to sprout even here! And are the others, after all, so very static? It seems to me there is a lot of dynamic leaven in Japan today—quite too much for comfort.

Comparisons like this are really odious. It makes us mad to be told we are "uncivilized" and it rather riles a Japanese to be told he is "un-progressive." All such generalizations, containing a modicum of truth, become false when turned to universal application. It is the injustice of the falsehood that rankles. And the truth of today is the falsehood of tomorrow. The customs of yesterday are not those of today, either in Japan or here. Europe too, is becoming quite *bouleversée*. The laboring classes, the uncultured ones, are coming up, and a lot of civilization is getting scattered and shattered, in Europe and in Japan. *Shikatanai!* ("It can't be helped." This useful expression contains a good deal of Orien-tal philosophy. God's will be done! a pious Christian would say.)

In the present fluid conditions of humanity, no generalizations on the divergences between peoples and races can hold. We are like shifting sands. And modern education is rolling us flat, rolling over the world, now here, now there. To generalize on the probabilities of happiness in marriage between Japanese and Americans (or Europeans), and to base your conclusions on the general characteristics of the peoples seems to me a waste of time. Where is your typical Japanese? Put your finger on him. Catch him and hold him up. Presto! He changes like the old man of the sea. He is an old world aristocrat, a man of leisure and fine taste. No, he is a bustling, hustling business man. No, he is a professor search-ing for microbes. No, he is a cosmopolitan speaking another language better than his own. Like your typical American. You remember that to-bacco-spitting type which Dickens held up to shock or amuse the world and hurt our feelings? And the miner all bristling with pistols and car-tridges of another writer? And the cowboy? The Chicago pork-packer we have often met in books. The millionaire collector (leaning on an expert staff) seems now to be a favorite type. Who knows but we may come to see him as a creator of real values? Geniuses indeed we have already. Best leave out of account the sport of nature, without nationality, that springs sporadic in any soil.

To return to those Japanese–American marriages. How to tell if they are happy or likely to be? To judge by the statistics of divorce there are more unhappy marriages made right here in America between Ameri-cans than anywhere else in the world. Is that a criterion? Many married people ought to be divorced who are not. Didn't Milton write about the salutary "discipline of divorce?" The figures of divorce are also high in Japan. What does it show? What are the causes? People will tell you that one cause of divorce in Japan is that marriages are too often arranged by parents, and that these "glued" unions are apt to break. (Old fash-ioned Japanese say it is the spread of Americanism that makes divorce more frequent.) And we are told that in America there is not enough forethought, we are guided too much by impulse. Perhaps we both err by going to opposite extremes. I am not sure, either, that a divorce is a sure sign that a marriage was not successful and desirable while it lasted. What is the test of marriage, anyway? Judge a tree by its fruits. My friend Mr. John Robertson Scot made quite a study of the statistics of inter-racial marriage in Japan. His conclusions? I can only hazard a guess from some of his remarks. Seeing a five year old girl playing at the sea-shore one day, he exclaimed: "What splendid legs that child has! She is a fine type of what can be done by the blending of Japanese and European. You tell me she goes to a British school in Yokohama? How does she compare with the other children?" I was able to tell him that Miss Mander, head mistress of the school in question, where I was a teacher, had found her to be the tallest of her age in the school (where the others were all British with the [*typescript ends here*]

It is uncertain whether Léonie left the essay unfinished, or whether part of the essay has been lost.

Léonie evidently spent the summer of 1925 in summer resorts along the coast of Maine and Massachusetts. In August, having left Ogunquit, Maine, for Kennebunk, she sent Isamu a postcard with directions in case he might visit.

To Isamu Noguchi, August 11, 1925

Kennybunk port, Me.

Came here from Ogunquit in a bus along the shore. Wonderful sky and sea and mists on the meadows. Return to Magnolia tomorrow and stay there till the end of the week. May come again to this vicinity before going home. Do you know you can take a bus from 34th St. N.Y. to Boston via Hartford & Springfield, run by N.Y. & New Haven R.R. makes good time. They will check your baggage by train.

Love, Mother.

From Boston to Magnolia is about 35 Miles from North Station

A few days later she sent the following postcard from Magnolia, a small coastal village in Gloucester, Massachusetts.

To Isamu Noguchi, August 14, 1925

Back at Magnolia. If any packages come please *hold* them. There will be one package from Ogunquit, (Winifred Irwin) containing Droste's Dutch Cocoa. You open that and have some cocoa. How are you? You can take a bus from Boston to Portland, Me. for $4.00.

Love,
Mother

In 1925 Ailes was approaching her fourteenth birthday. Léonie had been fourteen when she left home to for high school in Baltimore, and Isamu had been fourteen when Léonie had sent him off to Indiana. Now she was thinking to send Ailes away as well. The school she had in mind was the Cherry Lawn School in Darien, Connecticut: another open air school project connected with the Ethical Culture Society. The origins of the school went back to the great Polio epidemic of 1916, which began in Brooklyn, New York, and eventually spread around the country, leading to twenty-seven thousand reported cases, six thousand of them fatal. When Beatrice Stein, the daughter of a prominent Ethical Culture Society member, starch-manufacturer Leo Stein, was paralyzed by the disease, Stein's brother-in-law, Frederick Goldmark, a Harvard-trained pediatrician, quit his practice to set up a school for the Stein children at the family's home, Cherry Lawn, in Stamford. As the Cherry Lawn School became known among the Ethical Culture community, where Leo Stein was elected chairman of the finance committee in 1917, other parents began to send their children. In 1918, the 53-year-old Stein suddenly contracted pneumonia and died, but the school continued, and in 1920, a 28 acre plot was purchased in nearby Darien. By this point, Uncle Fred, as Goldfrank was known, had become an extreme believer in open air schooling. Classes were held on the porches, as long as the temperature did not dip too far below freezing, and the students "slept outside on special screened-in porches, often with only ponchos for a roof." "The idea was this would protect you from anything," recalled an alumnus. The educational style was "sort of casual." All this simple living did not come cheap: tuition in 1926 was a stunning $1350. (At the Bryn Mawr School, in comparison, it was a comparatively reasonable $400). At such prices, a scholarship to Cherry Lawn was too good to pass up. But after Ailes departed for Darien, she and Léonie only rarely had opportunities to spend extended time together.

While Ailes was taking her first steps toward independence, her brother's art studies were advancing with amazing speed. Soon after Isamu began studying with Onorio Ruotolo in 1924, his admiring teacher had recommended him for membership in local artists' societies. Isamu's first portrait sculptures were mainly of friends. Dr. Rumely commissioned a portrait bust of his late father-in-law, Emmet Scott. After his arrival in New York, Isamu had been taken under the wing of two of his father's Japanese friends, dancer Michio Ito and the famous bacteriologist Hideyo Noguchi. Both encouraged him to drop medicine and take up art. Ito sat for a portrait in 1925—Isamu's first work to break away from the academic style of his teachers—and in 1926 he commissioned Isamu to create papier-mâché masks for a production of Yeats's Noh-inspired play, *At the Hawk's Well*. Ito also arranged for Isamu to sculpt a portrait of Russian dancer, Michel Fokine.

Isamu made his first appearance in the pages of the *New York Times* on May 5, 1926, having received honorable mention the previous day at the Grand Prix de Rome competition at the Grand Central Art Galleries. The article focused on the two artists who had won fellowships, but also noted the three honorable mentions, including "Isamu Noguchi, a naturalized Japanese of Los Angeles, at present residing in New York." Léonie was anxious to correct the erroneous description of Isamu's nationality, and wrote the following letter to the editor:

Noguchi an American

New York Times, 8 May 1926.

To the Editor of The New York Times: Will you kindly correct a misstatement made in yesterday's Times? My son, Isamu Noguchi, is spoken of as a "naturalized Japanese from Los Angeles." He is in fact an American by birth. He is the son of the distinguished Japanese poet Yone Noguchi (who writes, by the way, in English) and myself, an American college woman. He was born in Los Angeles and spent the first two years of his life there. Then I took him to Japan, where he lived until he was thirteen, and then returned to America.

LEONIE GLENOUR [*sic*].

New York, May 6, 1926.

The summer of 1926 saw Léonie in Bar Harbor exhibiting her collection of Japanese prints. The summer colony with its scenic coastline and lively port bringing a steady stream of wealthy tourists would become Léonie's favored summer destination.

In January of 1927 Léonie was to be found plying her wares in two of the most prestigious locations in Miami Beach. The opportunity probably had something to do with the massive hurricane that had damaged the Miami coastline in September, destroying many local businesses. Miami developer N.B.T. Roney brought in Léonie and others setting her up at his newly built Spanish Village on Espanola Way (still one of South Beach's most pleasant streets) and offering her a retail space in the luxurious Roney Plaza Hotel, a few blocks up Collins Avenue.

Postcard from the Roney Plaza Hotel, Miami.

To Ailes Gilmour, January 19, 1927

Spanish Village at Espanola Way, Miami Beach, Florida

Dear Ailes,

Am in the land of cocoanut palms, sunny skies and summer in winter. It seems incredible that you should be having snow now. I left New York in a snowstorm, which followed us for about a day. The decks were covered with snow and ice and it was hard to keep warm. That was Saturday, the 15th. Monday Evening we danced on deck, under the summer moon, the ladies in their dresses.

I expect to have a place at the Roney Plaza Hotel, Miami Beach, and will be very busy to fix it up to get ready. Got to hustle, tho I'd rather go swimming. Address me as above.

Lovingly
Léonie Mother

The following week, after receiving Ailes' letter, she wrote again:

To Ailes Gilmour, January 27, 1927

Spanish Village at Espanola Way, Miami Beach, Florida

My Dear Ailes,

Today I received a bunch of mail—the first since I came here—and your letter forwarded by Mrs. Farrell was among them. Then I sat down to write you and asked the date of someone. January 27! Sounds sort of auspicious and happy. One small girl baby opened her eyes on her mother way off in Yokohama on that day just 15 years ago, and then wrinkled up her forehead in such a fearful way that her mother had to shut hers quick, thinking, "What a pity, it's a girl if she's got to be so homely!" Well, my dear old sweetness, how do you like growing old? I wish I had a cocoanut to throw at you. Saw something that looked like them growing sky-high on a palm-tree. But I am not a monkey, alas. And no good at throwing. So I throw you fifteen kisses instead. They will probably descend on you in the shape of snowflakes. Let me know if they reach you all right.

Here the wind blows and blows from the sea—always warm—and the windows are all wide open—and in the morning you hear a meadowlark. The public school is nearby and we see the children playing in their cotton dresses. Now this is the kind of place for an open air school. They could sit and study from September to June—no need to run about to keep warm—then go north for their summer holiday in the *cool* of the year (cool to them by comparison). Suggest it to Dr. G.

Much love,
Mother

Next time you better write: The Roney-Plaza, Shop no. 69, Miami Beach, Fla., as I may change my room.

This funny flower grows here.

Flower enclosed in letter to Ailes. *Isamu Noguchi Foundation.*

There are several stories about Isamu's first meeting with dancer Martha Graham. "I introduced Isamu to Graham in 1929," Ailes Gilmour recalled in a 1988 interview. But Graham's biographers generally see it differently: Alice Helpern dates it to 1925, while Agnes De Mille says that "Martha had met Noguchi when he came around the Greenwich Village Follies, and later, at her studio in Carnegie Hall, with Michio Ito." Ito had choreographed Graham's breakout performance of *The Garden of Kama* at the *Greenwich Village Follies* of 1923, but if Isamu met Graham at the ongoing *Follies*, it would likely have been later. Graham herself says in her autobiography, *Blood Memory*: "I met Isamu when I had a studio in Carnegie Hall, and his mother, who was Irish, was doing costumes for me. His sister, Ailes Gilmour, danced in my company." In a later memorial of Isamu she wrote for the *New York Times*, Graham explained: "Isamu's mother had helped with the costumes for my company then; soon his sister Ailes came to study at my school and to enter my company. It was through that association that Isamu entered my life." Isamu Noguchi scholars have concluded that Graham "met Noguchi through his mother," as Nancy Grove says, or as the *Isamu Noguchi: Sculptural Design* catalog puts it, "Noguchi and Graham met in the late 1920s when his mother made costumes"; thus, it is now a common assumption that Léonie "worked as a seamstress for Graham." But Graham's rather vague statement may be somewhat misleading. Léonie never seems to have worked as a professional seamstress or costume designer (though she did sew clothes for herself and her family); if Léonie "did costumes" for Graham, that most likely meant that Graham was a customer for her kimono import business; if so, Léonie, who had long been wearing kimono "with considerable ease—obi and all," was no doubt happy to advise Graham on their use. Any such help would have been welcomed by Graham, whose battle against her mentor, Ruth St. Denis, had been over costume preparation. "Miss Ruth, either I am to be a dancer or a seamstress. I cannot do both,'" she had declared; St. Denis was shocked, but Graham "never had to sew again." When Graham started her own company in 1926, she would have needed to stock up on kimono for the Japanese dances she had performed with Denishawn. And she did not exempt the dancers in her own company from sewing. "We made our own costumes," Ailes recalled. "Even the leotards used in class were cut from a yard of old jersey, split like a diamond where we sewed the crotch."

Graham had a studio in Carnegie Hall from 1926 to 1933, and it is entirely possible that she met Isamu there, independently of Léonie, through Michio Ito. In 1929, when Isamu returned from his Guggenheim travels, he took his own studio in Carnegie Hall, and made two portrait heads of Martha Graham. It was around this time, as well, that Ailes began dancing with Graham, her brief career in the company lasting from 1930 to 1933. It was after that, in 1935, that Isamu began creating sets for Graham, an extraordinary collaboration that lasted half a century.

All this was in the future in 1926, when Isamu, intrigued by occasional exhibitions of modern art, became a frequenter of Alfred Stieglitz's newly opened Intimate Gallery, a small exhibition space in which Stieglitz promoted the work of his estranged wife, Georgia O'Keefe, and other modernist artists. Stieglitz encouraged him to apply for one of the recently-established Guggenheim Fellowships. Isamu's application outlined an ambitious three year plan: the first year to be spent in Paris, the latter two on an extended journey through Asia, from India through China and then to Japan, where he would hold "an initial exhibition prior to one to be given in New York." He explained, "I have selected the Orient as the location for my productive activities for the reason that I feel a great attachment for it, having spent half my life there. My father, Yone Noguchi, is Japanese and has long been known as an interpreter of the East to the West, through poetry. I wish to do the same with sculpture." The Guggenheim committee heard his plea sympathetically, and in March 1927, Isamu was ready to depart for France.

By this time Isamu had an international cohort of friends. At his farewell party Léonie met some she knew—the German Rumelys and Isamu's

Italian teacher Ruotolo—and some she didn't—Majdrakoff Ivan Boris, a Romanian portrait photographer who had come to the United States in 1922 to escape retribution for a murder he had committed, Dimitri Romanovsky, a Russian painter who taught at the Art Students League, Isamu's deaf Russian model Nadia Nikolaiova, and another beautiful model named Nita, who seemed to be Isamu's girlfriend.

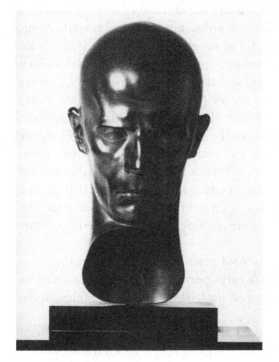

Isamu Noguchi, *Portrait of Boris Ivan Majdrakoff,* **1927. Photo:** *Isamu Noguchi Foundation.*

To Isamu Noguchi, March 21, [1927]

127 University Place

My dear Isamu,

Rain, rain! The rain is raining all around. It rains on the umbrellas here, but does it rain upon the ships at sea? You *would* go at the equinox. Though the heavens weep, your thoughts may be roseate as this ink. What became of you when you disappeared that night, at the drop of the iron curtain? We all ran to the end of the pier, and shouted "Banzai" with all our might, hoping you would hear it and answer. Not a sign of you. Poor Dimietri Romanovsky was overcome. "What a tragedy!" he exclaimed again and again. I tried to cheer him up. Then he said it was on my account he felt so bad. We all walked home together. First we took Nita to her home. She kept assuring me that you were "the nicest boy she ever knew," a "wonderful boy" and so on, and gave me her address and telephone number and I promised to call her up and let her know where I was. Then we went to Seventh Avenue, and parted from Boris. Romanovsky took me home. On the way he told me all his ambitions and his family troubles about the dear woman whom he cannot marry because he is too poor. Arrived at the Albert Hotel we found the chairs turned over for the night, but we found two, sat down and he discoursed on music. He should be a novelist. Saturday, alas! the real tragedy came, when Ailes turned up at the studio at seven in the evening. Poor child! She was quite taken aback to find you gone. She said that at 3 o'clock she wanted to commit suicide, and at 4 she happily started to N.Y. to see you off, after unheard-of efforts to get permission. We met Mr. Boris and his wife Sunday (Ailes and I both slept at your studio). He said she looked like a girl who always lived in the open air. Quite true. When she went back she took your picture, and your paint box, and your brown suit, and a pair of white trousers (to work in her garden) also several neckties. She wants me to send the fixative and some other things. She wanted to take the statue of Clair but I would not let her and anyway she could not carry it. Mr. Boris and I are considering what to do about this statue. I can't bear to destroy it.

I hope you soon get a studio. And get some woman to come every day for an hour to make it clean & tidy—perhaps cook your breakfast or lunch too. They are so clever. Be well nourished and enjoy yourself. Go to the country on Sunday.

I found many pictures scattered around and in the little drawer of the desk. I have gathered all together and will keep them. I found a room at No. 70 Irving Place, rather small, but there is some place in the cellar to keep things. Rent $32. A very good house and neighborhood, close to Gramercy Park. The window looks out on a wide garden in back. There is a basin with running water in the room, and in the hall just outside a good bathroom which I can use. I will move over by the 1st of April. Just now I am camping in your studio. Mr. Pavone came to see your furniture again and offered me $25 for everything. I agreed to that, but now I think I would like one or two things, as the room is so small my larger pieces of furniture would not fit in, so I want to take your desk. I will see if he will make a compromise.

Write often, though the letters be short—but prefer them long. In French if you wish.

I was so glad to meet all your friends. I want to keep up with them. Mr. Boris and I get along famously. I am putting all my thoughts on you, and some day I will glide on a dark river right into your room.

Sometimes I feel myself gliding that way to some other place. So I don't worry if you are rather far away.

Much love from
Mother

A few days later Léonie described Isamu's farewell party in detail in a letter to Catharine:

To Catherine Bunnell, March 27, 1927

My dear Catherine,

Excuse the typewriter but there isn't a pen in Isamu's room that will work. Yes, I made it. Not by the romantic way of jumping a baggage car, but by a Pullman express, the only thing that would go fast enough. I did even eat one meal in the diner. Helped Isamu pack, accompanied him to a dinner at the little Armenian restaurant on Thursday where I met his good friend Boris, and on Friday evening to a party at the Japanese restaurant where I met a good many of his friends. There were fifteen in all—Dr. Rumeley and his family (it was the Doctor's party), Boris (Bulgarian), Dimietri Romanovsky, a Russian artist, another artist whom he called Maurice, a young girl artist named Miss Johan, a pretty girl model called Nita, Mr. Onorio Ruotolo, Italian, Isamu's teacher, and others. I sat at the head of the table. There were a lot of speeches. I made one too. Ruotolo took the lead, with a lengthy peroration, beginning with his reasons for considering Isamu a genius—apparently his contradictoriness helped to this conclusion, since he was always going smack against Ruotolo's advice—and, quoth Ruotolo "I recognized that it is the prerogative of the great to speak their mind out freely, and to be so full of themselves that they will follow their own bent against every opposition and advice" and ending with wise words of admonition and advice and affection. The admonitions included also warning against ladies, after profuse Italian bows and flatteries to the ladies present, saying that the ladies, while undoubtedly the source of all inspiration in every art were, it must be acknowledged, also a source of danger. Isamu winked at Nita and she threw him a kiss. Then Dr. Rumely made a speech telling how Isamu arrived from Japan and turned up at his school at Interlaken. How he went through High School and decided on a medical career. How his mother turned up one day at Dr. Rumely's office and hotly denounced him for turning a boy of artistic temperament toward a career for which he was entirely unsuited. It is quite true that Dr. Rumely and I had an awful row on that score, and the Doctor, then Isamu's best friend and advisor, persisted in his opinion, so that Isamu, as you know, took a year and a half at Columbia at a pre-medical course. I have just found a note book of Isamu's, neatly labeled "Chemistry and Biology." Inside is nothing but sketches of vagaries, fishes, rabbits, nude ladies etc. Not one word of any science. Dimietri Romanovsky also made a long speech, in which he said that genius had no age, and remarked that the three greatest artists of his acquaintance were, respectively, aged 54, 40, and 22. (You can imagine who was the 22 year old.) I took exception to so much adulation and tried to tone it down a bit and told Isamu to keep his head, but he answered "what's the use of putting water in the soup?" Isamu was called on for a speech, but all he did was to get up and grin all around and say that he hadn't a thing that he wished to say but that he felt fine and hoped they all did the same and he drank their health in saké. We had a regular Japanese meal, raw fish and sake and everything. When we were going out one of the waitresses spoke to Isamu, saying she used to live in Chigasaki, and knew there such a little boy, name of Isamu-san, and was he that little boy? Well, a lot of us went with Isamu to the boat, which sailed at midnight Friday, not Saturday as he had told me at first. The boat was a floating palace. Isamu had a room to himself, as there are not so many passengers at this time of the year. Nita wanted to smuggle herself under his berth, and Scotty (Dr. Rumely's little boy) said the top berth would do for him. Dimietri went off and had a talk with the Captain, and returned satisfied, saying "I fixed it all right with the Captain—I told him this was a great artist, and he must take special care of him." Everybody hugged and kissed and handshook all around. Isamu and Nita went about with their arms around each other (Ruotolo was not there) and Nita skipped like a lamb, and every once in awhile remarked plaintively "I can't cry, I can't cry." When we were going to be put off she kissed him on the mouth. I suspect there's a romance there, and wonder how long it will take them [to] cure the ache of parting, and perhaps, probably, find other loves. She is a Russian girl, and deaf, so she speaks with a slow drawl, not so very distinctly. She posed for several of his studies, but not for Undine. That was Nadia.

Now you ask about "Undine." It is at present on exhibition at the Grand Central Art Galleries. In bronze it has a somewhat different effect from the picture, which was taken before it was cast. It looks more warm and alive. The price marked on it is $4500. The art gallery gets 20% of the selling price, $1500 goes to Mr. Albee, who put up the money for the casting, and Isamu promised 10% to his model, Nadia, who heroically posed for over a period of 8 months without accepting any return. I went to see Mr. Albee the other day, told him of Isamu's circumstances, and how he had gone to Europe and it was left to us, his friends, to sell the statue and pay Isamu's debt. I asked either for an extension of time, or, if he really wanted the statue, that he should pay a fair price. Told him about Nadia, who must be recompensed. Also how Isamu had worked for 8 months, and had been helped by friends not much better off than himself to live during that time. Mr. Albee listened with interest, said he had not known Isamu was so poor. Said we might take some more time to pay, and that he would go and look at the statue in the Art Galleries. He also asked about Nadia. Said if I would send her to him he would give her a job. Now I'm trying to find Nadia, but she has completely *disappeared*.

Isamu's fellowship is for *one* year, not three, as I said, and amounts to $2500. It may, however, be renewed, for a second and a third year, each time to be won again. Or, at the end of a year, Isamu might try for the Prix de Rome, which is for 3 years. The Guggenheim fellowship is considered higher than the Prix de Rome. Isamu wants to spend four years abroad, to complete his work—then he says he will be a real artist. His first thought was to give me a part of the fellowship money every month. But of course that cannot be. He will need it all, especially as the materials for sculpture are so dear. But he says I may retire after 4 years.

This is a very long letter. If you see Florence pass it on. She will be glad too.

I am camping in Isamu's studio for the present. It's pretty awful. No heat but gas, which makes me sick, so I have to turn it off. Cold as a barn. No convenience whatever. Ice cold running water outside the room. Smells of the toilet in the hall? Noisy, dusty—rats running about. I move next Wednesday (March 30) to No. 70 Irving Place. Small studio room, running hot and cold water, steam heat, bath just outside my room, place in cellar to put some things, rent $32 a month. Very good house, near Gramercy Park. I'd be glad to see you, but can't see why anybody should come to New York if they've got any other place to stay.

Write me how Jim is getting along, and I am interested in Eloise Keeler's career. My own daughter is still "in the making" growing handsome and efficient. The poor child had such a disappointment when, with the greatest difficulty, she escaped school and came in to see her brother off a *day late* (he had told us he would go on Saturday and didn't write her of the change as he thought she could not come anyway).

Well, enough for the day.

With love,

Brigitta

P.S. Did I tell you I have to talk on Japanese prints at the Brooklyn Mu-

seum next Sunday?
Will send photo of Undine.

Isamu Noguchi with *Undine*. *Isamu Noguchi Foundation*.

Léonie even managed to gain a bit of recognition as an artistic authority in her own right. As she told Catharine, the Brooklyn Museum offered, on April 3, "'Japanese Prints', conducted by Mrs. Léonie Gilmour, writer, lecturer and former resident of Japan. . . . illustrated by prints and the implements used in their production," as *The Brooklyn Museum Quarterly* noted.

In late April, Léonie received Isamu's first postcard and letters from Europe. After a brief stop in London, Isamu had arrived in Paris where, at the Café de Flore, a day after his arrival, he met American expatriate poet Robert McAlmon, who introduced him to Constantin Brancusi, the Romanian sculptor whose abstract works had fascinated him in New York. Isamu was delighted with his good fortune when Brancusi accepted his spur-of-the-moment offer to work as his assistant. He began work at Brancusi's studio in Montparnasse the next morning. Then, with the help of Japanese artist Tsuguharu Foujita, he had the good luck to find a nearby studio for rent at 7 Rue Belloni.

To Isamu Noguchi, April 21, 1927

70 Irving Place, New York

My dear Isamu,

To-day your card from France came. Is the Mr. Fujita you speak of the artist who illustrated "Legendes Japonaises," a beautiful book I have lately seen? I am glad you know him.

Your other letters, two written on the steamer and one in London, reached me all at once last Saturday, through the hand of Mr. Boris. Did you meet Epstein while you were in London?

I took the first occasion after you were gone to go to the Grand Central Galleries and see Undine. She is most lovely and witch-like. Have you read Fouqué's Undine? I could not see Madonna and Child because it was out on a loan exhibition. Have not even a photo of it. I decided, with the approval of Mr. Boris, to call on Mr. Albee, to ask for an extension of the time of payment of the loan, in view of the fact of your being away. He was very interested in all I told him about you and your work. He said we might have more time to pay back the loan. I told him also about Nadia, and just as I was leaving he called me back, saying that if I would send Nadia to him he would like to help her, to give her a job. Well, I tried my best to locate Nadia, but I didn't know where to look. Nita said she never knew her address. If you know Nadia's address *please send it to me*. If not, send me her former address and I will write her, hoping that she may have left a forwarding address. I feel myself an interest in her, first because she helped you greatly, and second because she can tell interesting stories and perhaps live them.

Last Sunday we met Romanovsky and Mrs. Chadwick's daughter Barbara at church (Ailes was with me)—at Grace Church where the music is very good. Then they made us go home with them to see the birds and the cat and the dog. That dog is just like one we had in Japan named Peter, who used to eat sweet potatoes.

Write *soon*—in fact right away—as it takes a month to get your letters.

I like your new address. No. 7 is our family number. Then Beloni I think has something to do with war. I like you to be valiant. I was myself born under a conjunction of Venus and Mars. I hope you emulate the martial part of your mother. She is your

Proud and loving
Mother.

From Isamu Noguchi, May 1, [1927]

7 Rue Beloni

Dear Mother,

I was mighty glad to receive your second letter.

However I was disturbed about what you said regarding Albee and Nadia. You must understand that [I] have left everything in N.Y. just as I wished them to remain. First of all I know that Albee can not help Nadia and secondly that she does not need help. I do not know her adress [*sic*] and I wish you would kindly stop poking around in my graveyard.

Now let us change the subject, as the foregoing is rather disagreable [sic] and stupid.

The other day who should I bump into but young Fukuoka from Chigasaki who is now an artist. We had many reminiscences to exchange. He is living at a castle in St. Gratien.

Well I have been working hard but today is Sunday May the first and I am taking a promenade with some muguet in my button-hole.

Rue Beloni runs into Rue d'Amerique half a block from my place.

Much love
Isamu
P.S. The Guggenheim Foundation is also to be left alone.

To Isamu Noguchi, May 4, 1927

Bryn Mawr

My dear Isamu,

I have been so wrapt in delight with your various postcards and letters that I forgot to answer. That one from the musée Guimet with long legs and long arms took my fancy. I shall put them in your album. The Guimet collection is I understand one of the finest Oriental collections in the world. I hear there is a smaller collection in Paris with especially carvings in jade and other stone that is beautiful. Have you flowers on your balcony? And a woman to come and tidy up. Those French women are so clever. They will wax your floor or make an omelette or do your marketing without any fuss. And how they can mend shirts etc. with fine stitches that can't be seen!

I had a very nice letter from your friend Mr. A. E. Hamilton. You see I had written him for advice in regard to Ailes' summer. She just heard from her former teacher that she could not get her a scholarship at the Ethical Culture Camp this year. As Ailes has had two years at Camp I think she may be qualified to act as junior counsellor or do something to earn her way in the summer. She is very anxious to go to Camp. I have written to several people Unfortunately it is already a little late in the season. By the advice of Dr. Goldfrank she will stay at school until June 25 and take two college entrance examinations. For the month of June I must pay again $65.—, covering cost of examinations also—but this is a month longer than I had counted on. I am now at Bryn Mawr and will perhaps go to Princeton.

Tell me what you are doing.

With much love

Mother

Isamu in Paris.
Isamu Noguchi Foundation.

Léonie spent most of the summer of 1927 in Dark Harbor, a summer retreat on a Maine islet, living in a barn. She was reading Guy de Pourtalès' *La vie de Franz Liszt* (Paris: Gallimard, 1925), which must have suggested an interesting contrast with her rustic lifestyle. Ailes, having escaped from a summer camp she hadn't cared for, joined her in July.

To Isamu Noguchi, July 28, 1927

Dear Isamu—
The ink is getting low so pencil is easier. I am in the midst of packing. Received your two letters, one with the check—thanks awfully—and one about the weather in Paris. Wish I didn't need to take the former. I will blow on it and maybe it will glow and grow. I know expenses are not low anywhere. I note what you say about the weather. Exactly what I observed in 1893. If the French climate is so constant I presume the French temperament is likewise unchanged. If either of them pall on you—well, maybe Ireland would be an antidote,—but I suppose it takes fares to go there too. They say the mists of Ireland and Scotland are quite different from the damp of Paris. They are island mists, refreshing. Like those in Maine where I am going. What did you say you had at Brie? Couldn't make out your writing. Did you see the three islands in the river? L'isle d'amour, l'isle du loup, and l'Isle de Beauté they were called.

Ailes is here, and will go again in a couple of days. You find her letters fantastic? She is in the phase of grand ebulition. I enclose 2 of hers received on the same day, my birthday.

Boris has a boy, but I haven't seen him yet. Mr. Kasai in San Francisco also has a boy.

I enclose the certificate of birth of a boy you may remember. Keep it with your documents. You may find it useful in travelling about—especially if you want to return to America.

With much love
Mother
Tell me *what* you are doing. I can imagine the weather, but not your creations.

From Isamu Noguchi, [August 1927]

7 Rue Belloni, Paris XVe.

My Dear Mother,
I am affraid [sic] that you have almost convinced me that I was born on the 17th and not on the 18th. Anyway I was glad to get the birth certificate and will keep it safely so that I will never forget myself.

No I did not see your three islands but the river was beautiful there. The word which you could not read was circus—they were having a sort of circus there in Brie when I got there.

Thank you also for those letters of Ailes which show considerable talent, I think.

Really both you and Mr. Boris are hard on me in pumping me with questions as to what I am sculping [*sic*] for the very simple reason that I am not. All I do during the day is cut marble for somebody else. Have not made a thing for myself. Anyway I am sending Mr. Boris a copy of my quarterly report to the foundation which you may get—but it is realy [*sic*] very uninteresting. I will not do any creative work for a long time until I am completely orientated to my new medium and method of thought. Ahem.

Lovingly
Isamu

Now you might tell me what you are doing.

To Isamu Noguchi, August 3, 1927

Dark Harbor, Maine

My dear Isamu,

I presume you are learning to cut marble as the longest way round to learning to cut wood, or trying the hardest thing first. Be careful not to breathe any marble dust, as it is injurious to the lungs. You said I might see your report to the Guggenheim foundation, but where? I did see your Madonna and Child, after its return from Chicago. It is lovely— I like the way the hand slides under the baby—that is the real mother touch. Wish the baby didn't look so like the Rumely children, but anyway it's a fine child. I still think Undine is so far your masterpiece, if one may make such discriminations which I don't believe in, as each one is a masterpiece considered by itself. There is an audacity, a sort of defiant impudence about Undine—you know she is defying life and is going to suffer for it.

What am I doing? Why, living in a barn, making up bracelets and things and trying to sell them. Incidentally reading the life of Liszt in French and enjoying it immensely. He had certainly a full life. There is a life of Chopin by the same author, Guy de Pourtales, which I hope to read some time.

I have mastered the art of living in true hermit style, without cooking. I had brought an electric grill with me, hoping to have electricity in the barn, but alas, there is neither water nor electricity. I munch bread and Gruyere Swiss cheese, or sardines, drink milk, have berries and peaches, honey, cans of California walnuts all shelled. Go swimming before breakfast for a bath, tho' I have the privilege of washing up in my landlady's house. Ailes came up here about the middle of July. She didn't like Camp Darien, so I got her a job to wait on table at the Inn. She seems to be having a pretty good time, what with swimming and dancing. I had to buy uniforms for her, raincoat and sundries, and her fare up—so far she has not got any money, but she will have a little something in her pocket at the end of the season, and if you know Ailes you know she has ways of spending it.

Mrs. Porter called today, together with Pauline Goldmark (Felix Adler's sister-in-law). Mrs. Porter's son Fairfield is spending the summer in France. I hope you get a little holiday. The mosquitoes are eating me up alive. I really can't go on. Goodbye and bless you.

Your loving
Mother

In the fall, Léonie was in White Sulphur Springs, the "queen of the watering places," where the wealthy came to escape the summer heat. Patrons of the exclusive Greenbrier resort, "just overnight from New York . . . America's health-giving resort in the High Alleganies," were her target, and she opened a little shop on Main Street just down the road.

To Isamu Noguchi, October 9, 1927

White Sulphur Springs, West Virginia, U.S.A.

Well, old boy—here am I, perched on a ridge of the Allegheny mountains, in West Virginia. Do you know where that is? It seems funny that I should be planted here, and Ailes in Connecticut, and you across the big water in France.

I got your letter just before leaving New York, and sent the draft to the bank at once. I was in the throes of moving as well as getting ready to come here. Our landlord in New York began to assert his landlordship—wanted a lease, and no cooking, and so on. So I felt impelled to move around the corner to

141 East 17th Street

Note well for future reference. A young woman who lived in the same house, a Miss McCormick, found me in the move, and we took two rooms in an old fashioned house, top floor up a spiral stairway which would not admit my "high boy" so I traded it for a small bureau. Have a little more room, and less expense, so I can go away more. Our next door neighbor is an English girl named Erica Brooks, an artist and teacher of manual training at the "Friends School"—very big and bluff and breezy.

Our landlady is also an artist—theatrical decorations. I saw Boris just before I left. He gave me a lovely picture of you, and I fell in love with you all over again. He says his boy is wonderfully good—"because he has a good mother" to take care of him.

I went from New York first to Hot Springs, Va., but could find no location there, so I went 50 miles further to White Sulphur Springs. We are 2300 feet above the sea—the hills are all around—and old tumbling houses, and darkies fat and happy. The smoky smell of autumn is in the air, and big autumn leaves drift down with outspread wings and alight very softly. I engaged a little shop until November 15, on Main Street, ¼ mile from the big hotel where rich folks go for the baths and to drink the water from a bubbling spring that smells of rotten eggs. "Some it makes sick to their stomach, and some say they like it" I am told. The water supplied to the town is good enough for me, sparkling clear and odorless, tasteless etc. Went for a long walk today and saw the state fish hatcheries, full of big speckled trout, and "a kind of goldfish" that looked like the red carp of Japan.

Write me the news and don't say I'm no newsmonger.

With love which can't be measured in a bushel basket, as Ailes does hers—

Your mother dear.

To Isamu Noguchi, October 30, 1927

White Sulphur Springs, West Virginia

My dear Isamu,

I took a walk early in the morning up to Graveyard Hill, where there is such a fine view of the country all around. People in all countries seem bent on giving the dead a good view of the world they have left. Shrouded mountains were rising from blue mists and it was beautifully quiet and lonely. Now is the season a sort of Indian summer here. Most of the leaves have blown from the trees, and the effect is much more aesthetically arranged thus. You see the separate leaves hanging, golden brown on one side and silver on the other, like the drooping hands of aristocratic ladies. There are just enough of them to make an exquisite brocade against the gray bark of trees and the misty blue of the sky. I went regretfully to my shop, to sit and weave phantasies in beads all day and dream of the leaves.

For your birthday what can I send you that will feel at home in your studio better than a peacock of Toyohiro's which I remember you admired. He is elegant enough to walk alone in a Parisian garden or in your studio where the sparrows on the balcony cannot disturb the serene quiet within.

Are you twenty-three? Alas, you are nearing the age when you will be half as old as I. That will be in seven years. And then you will go on getting nearer and nearer and before you know it we will be twins.

I had a letter from Mr. Boris—very nice. And one from Zinaida who wished to be remembered to you. I shall be home by Thanksgiving or sooner.

Take care of your little charcoal stove. Remember that charcoal has to be used sparingly if you care for your health. The autumn of Paris has a penetrating chill. Those woolen shirts of gray or khaki are the thing. Do you wear a blouse and a beret? I feel quite French here. My landlady is French—her name Mrs. Léonie Mackay, a French-Scotch combination. Remember to address your next letter to 141 East 17 St. N.Y.

With love
Mother

In the half-year since his arrival Isamu had become friendly with the American artists Alexander "Sandy" Calder and Andrée Ruellan. He wrote Léonie on November 8: "As I have not yet received any letter in reply to my last, I take it that you are still perched on top of the mountains. Anyway, I am writing this in case you are in NY this winter—because—a young girl artist friend and her mother have recently left for the States and would be able to give you considered information concerning your son." He was referring to Ruellan, who was returning to New York to organize an exhibition of her work. "You know I have a prejudice about mixing female friends and mothers—however, I am giving this case a special dispensation. She is a nice girl, intelligent, etc.—judge for yourself." Ruellan did look up Léonie in New York, as she told Masayo Duus. "She was living in a very poor apartment, and she had a very pale face. She was soft-spoken and seemed to be a very reserved person." Ruellan probably said little about Isamu's love troubles, which (she told Duus) included one of his New York girlfriends following him to Paris, getting pregnant, and having a near-fatal abortion. She probably did tell Léonie about Isamu's artistic activities: the mornings spent working in Brancusi's studio, the afternoons sketching at the Académie Grande Chaumière, where Ruellan also studied, and the Académie Collarosi. She and Isamu had fallen into the habit of taking walks around the city visiting galleries, museums, and cafes.

To Isamu Noguchi, December 4, 1927

Princeton, N.J.

My dear Isamu,

I left White Sulphur on November 15, went home via Baltimore and Philadelphia reaching there just before Thanksgiving. Got your letter about Andrée. Mr. Boris and I are on the lookout for her. He tried to find her at the address you gave but had not succeeded when I came away November 29. We are going to bombard her with questions—at least I think he will, but I shall perhaps follow my usual tactics and keep quiet, and perhaps as usual confidences will flow out over me. It's funny the way that works. One evening Miss McCormick (we share the place on 17th street) and I were sitting before the little Franklin stove, when she started to sing some charming darkie melodies, crooning them over and over. I found that our English neighbor, Erica Brook, had begged and begged her to go with her to spend the evening with a collector of folk songs. "I won't go," said Miss McCormick, "because they will surely ask me to sing or play, and I don't do either, and never sing for anybody." "Why, you are singing for me," I said. "O, You're different, you never asked me to sing."

We have two pretty good sized rooms on the top floor, far from modern. There is a small stove in one, with a bulging eye, in the other a little gas range for cooking. A bathroom adjoins which we share with Erica Brook—I wonder how she squeezes in, she is bigger than either of us. We have to light the gas under a very small tank that overhangs the bath at one side every time we want a bath. I burned my elbow twice, just like in a Japanese bath. There is considerable wall space in the larger room and I am thinking of having an exhibition right there before Xmas. Some folks may like climbing up the bare stairs among the musty odors (it is like an office and studio building) to ye garret, as they did to the barn last summer—maybe they'll think they're slumming. Just fancy!

O, about your friend the jeweler. I should be interested to see some of his work. Ask him if he will send a few things, giving the price *to me* in his invoice, on which I will pay duty and then add enough to make my profit. Does he do *enamel*?

I think I will not send you a Xmas present, but give it to myself instead, for you and me, and from you and me. Now guess what.

Saw Ailes at Thanksgiving. She took the part of a man, in a French play. Did it to perfection. Walked and sat like a man—slapped her thigh and snapped her fingers—completely filled her teacher's evening suit of clothes. Her French was intelligible to all. We are thinking of college and I suggested her trying for a scholarship at Bryn Mawr. Her teacher thinks there is not enough *art* at B.M. but you know the atmosphere is good, and a college is not the place to go for an art education anyway. If there is art in her it will probably come out in the course of a year or two. What do you think?

Must pack up now and start on my way to the next place.

With all love

Mother

From Isamu Noguchi, [Dec. 1927]

Museum Hotel, 56 & 58 Bloomsbury Street, London

Dear Mother,

I was so happy to get your two letters the day I left Paris. It was like a blessing as I left that infernal place.

Here all is quiet and pieceful [*sic*] and I am indeed happy.

I am and will be up to my ears in books upon Oriental sculpture for a month at the library of the British Museum. After that I will go to Italy, there to work untill next Fall when I will go to India.

I have made these changes in plans first because I felt that I had not yet gotten all that I should out of Europe, secondly because I wanted to do some studying at the British Museum and thirdly because I wanted to do some work in Italy. Also I was told that one must go to India only at the end of the extreme heat if one is to avoid fever.

My financial situation is not altogether in a happy state and I would like to postpone sending you the final $100 until next April if you can spare it—otherwise please cable and I will cable it to you.

You ask what I think would be the best course for Ailes to follow as regards college. Well, I think that depends entirely on her. If she thinks she should I think she should. Or rather, should I say that, if she is not sufficiently advanced mentally to search out and pick up knowledge and read books by her self, she should. Or if she wishes to have a scientific training she should. But if she wishes to write, and she knows her English grammar, spelling, and composition, which I do not, I don't see what particular advantage college might have for her. A few knocks in journalism might be better. But then again she may not be mature enough to take care of herself or she may not be sufficiently energetically idealistic enough to be creative. I am afraid after all the desision [*sic*] is up to you—college is, of course a nice place to meet people—but

I am rather skeptical about its advantages unless one has that college fraternal spirit, which I did not.

In any case I think she will become a writer of note.

This place in which I am staying is like some country inn—quiet—and the open fire by which I am writing makes me feel sleepy.

Much love, from

Isamu

As a birthday gift, Léonie had sent Isamu a peacock print by Toyohiro Utagawa, teacher of the great Hiroshige. Since her talk at the Brooklyn Museum the previous year, she had established some reputation as an authority on Japanese prints. A note in the *New York Times* on April 22, 1928, stated that "Japanese prints (the collection of Leonie Gilmour" were being shown for a week at The Galleon, a Madison Avenue gallery of art objects and interior decoration.

In the summer of 1928 Léonie returned to Bar Harbor, Maine. "Visitors to Bar Harbor two years ago," the *Bar Harbor Times* wrote on August 22, "will remember the interesting collection of Japanese prints shown by Leonie Gilmour at that time, and will be delighted to renew their impressions at the 1928 exhibition, opened on August 17 at the Jesup Memorial Library." The collection was evidently substantial; among the prints not displayed previously were "a couple of fine examples by Yeishi, a Kiyonaga of quality, some small Harunobu, and some excellent impressions by Hiroshige." "Miss Gilmour, better known in Japan as Mrs. Yone Noguchi, clings to the beauty of the Orient in all things," the article noted, noting, but politely downplaying, the less sophisticated side of her business: "Besides exhibiting and lecturing on Japanese Art, she amuses herself by making up jewelry with semi-precious stones and intricate 'Chinese' knotting, and these things will also be shown at the library this week." Léonie was also making money selling trendy Asian clothing imports like the Chinese "coolie coats" favored by Florida beachgoers in the late twenties to wealthy customers like the wife of yacht designer Clinton Crane.

To Ailes Gilmour, November 11, [1928]

My dear Ailes—

Guess who was here. Nell Dayton! She spent the night here, sleeping in your bed, and went back to New Haven today. She said she had a lovely restful time (she had got all tired out going around New York—says New Haven is much nicer). She slept till 10 o'clock, then we had brunch, and she got the 1 o'clock bus. She is quite pretty. I feel rather sorry for her. Says she "wasted" six years being married, when she might have educated herself to be fit for something. And she regretted her husband didn't have old fashioned ideas about women. *She* thought a woman should stay at home, and the man go out and earn a living. *He* apparently thought otherwise, so now they are separated, and she is working in a tea room. I don't see much before her but to find some other man, who *has* old fashioned ideas. Shouldn't be a bit surprised if it wasn't the men who started the New Woman idea. Maybe they got tired of having the women hanging on their necks.

Nell brought back the green coolie coat, and now wants a red one, so I have the black on my hands and must get another red one like that I took to Mrs. Clinton Crane. She was wearing the bathing suit blouse, and looked awfully well in it. Just wore it without sleeves, with a black skirt. It's pretty cold here. Do you keep warm? I shall look for your Wednesday letter.

Lovingly
Mother

There is an article on Japan by Paul Claudel in the Dial. Do you see that magazine, or shall I send it to you?

Paul Claudel's "A Glance at the Soul of Japan" appeared in the November *Dial*. Yone, who had befriended Claudel during the French poet's recent tenure as ambassador to Japan, was probably also impressed by it, for later that month he began sending his own articles to the *Dial*'s editor, Marianne Moore.

Isamu's Guggenheim fellowship had been renewed for a second year, and in the spring of 1928, Tsuguharu Foujita helped him find a studio in Gentilly, on the outskirts of Paris. Isamu hoped the Guggenheim Foundation would renew his fellowship for a third year, in which case he would use the money to travel to Asia. But his application this time was not approved, so he was forced him to return to the United States in February of 1929.

Back in New York, Isamu rented a studio on the top floor of Carnegie Hall and organized a small exhibition of his Brancusi-influenced abstract works at the Eugene Shoen Gallery. It was reviewed respectfully in the *New York Times*, but nothing sold. To make money, and also as a way of socializing, Isamu returned to making portrait sculptures.

Isamu Noguchi, Interview with Paul Cummings, 1973

PAUL CUMMINGS: Anyway, we have you working in Paris in 1928. That was where your first one-man show was—right?

ISAMU NOGUCHI: No, not in Paris; it was here at a place called Eugene Shoen's. You see, I brought a number of the things back here with me, including these that you saw in here, and they were shown at Eugene Shoen's. He had a kind of furniture shop—not exactly a furniture—I don't know what he had—things like that. It was, I think, on 61st Street between Lexington and Park, around there. Eugene Shoen was his name and I had an exhibition there.

PAUL CUMMINGS: Was that successful in any way?

ISAMU NOGUCHI: No. I didn't sell anything. And I needed money badly. So that's when I started doing heads again.

PAUL CUMMINGS: Right. That's the Carnegie Hall Studio. The heads have always been useful?

ISAMU NOGUCHI: Useful because I could make money and meet people.

PAUL CUMMINGS: [After interruption] Anyway, we have you back here in the Carnegie Hall studio.

ISAMU NOGUCHI: Yes. Well, I tell you the Carnegie Hall studio—

PAUL CUMMINGS: How did you find that?

ISAMU NOGUCHI: How did I find it?

PAUL CUMMINGS: You know, there are some artists who have been there but usually it's dancers and musicians.

ISAMU NOGUCHI: There was a penthouse there, you know, at the top. Dorothy Maynor had it for a while. How the devil did I get in there? I must have gotten in there in the very beginning, I mean when I came back here. I needed a place and I got that. I did all my first heads there.

PAUL CUMMINGS: But how did you meet people?

ISAMU NOGUCHI: Well, by then I was a kind of social character, you see. I had become an artist. I don't know how I met people. For instance, Michio Ito I had known before. He was this Japanese dancer, very handsome. I had done a head of Michio Ito in 1926, maybe before I went to Paris. [Addressing Ms. X] Have you got a head of Michio Ito there?

PAUL CUMMINGS: You know, there were people who you met who had other studios in Carnegie Hall.

ISAMU NOGUCHI: Well, I didn't know anybody in Carnegie Hall. I used to go there and listen to music but .... Here's the head of Michio Ito that I did in 1935 in my academic period.

Ms. X: 1925?

ISAMU NOGUCHI: Or 1926—I'm not sure. I really don't know. I mean it's in that time. So, as I say, I had letters to various people in Paris, from him. He had a studio in the John Murray Anderson studio building, the dance studio building. He had a dance class there, and so did Martha Graham. I think I met Martha Graham there. So subsequently, when she moved to a studio near Carnegie Hall right a few doors away on 56th Street, I used to go there and watch her dance, or rather watch the kids dancing anyway. That was my entry into the dance world that way. And various other worlds that compose New York. One meets them, you know.

PAUL CUMMINGS: But where did somebody like Buckminster Fuller appear?

ISAMU NOGUCHI: In 1929 I used to go down to Romany Marie's in the Village. A lot of people went down there. I met him there. And one met a lot of people down there. It was sort of a transfer of the Paris café life to New York in Romany Marie's. She had a real function.

PAUL CUMMINGS: I'm very curious about your association with that place because so many people have mentioned it with different groups of people. It seems like each corner had its own group and once in a while somebody would go back and forth.

ISAMU NOGUCHI: Yes. Sure

PAUL CUMMINGS: Who are the people that you met there generally? Or who would you see when you went there?

ISAMU NOGUCHI: Well, I mean everybody went there. For instance, Stuart Davis went there. Or anybody you can think of in those days went there, I mean in the early days. I remember when I was doing Bucky Fuller's head in 1929, she had a place on Minetta Street.

In the course of a year, Isamu earned over five thousand dollars from his portraits. He chose many subjects himself from among the notable members of New York's lively arts scene with whom he came into contact on his rise to fame: the photographer Berenice Abbott and the painter Marion Greenwood, both of whom he had met in Paris, fellow Carnegie Hall occupant Martha Graham (who, displeased with his first effort, demanded a second sitting), composer George Gershwin, future ballet impresario Lincoln Kirstein (then a Harvard senior whose art society organized a Noguchi show), architect Harvey Corbett, Harlem blues singer Gladys Bentley, fashion model Marion Morehouse (who later married e.e. Cummings) and even a waitress, Ruth Parks. The portraits were done with remarkable facility in a range of styles, but all, except for the cast iron Morehouse, were cast in bronze.

Isamu working on portrait of Mary Poole. *Isamu Noguchi Foundation.*

Among Isamu's new friends, none proved more influential than the brilliant and eccentric Buckminster Fuller. Isamu met him in 1929 at Romany Marie's, a Greenwich Village restaurant where Fuller often held court, expounding his futuristic ideas on all manner of topics. Isamu was soon a disciple of "Mr Fuller," as he respectfully called him. When Isamu moved to a studio in a former laundry atop a building at Madison Avenue and Twenty Ninth Street, Fuller persuaded him to paint the whole interior silver to make it even brighter. The blinding result made the studio unusable until Isamu repainted, and probably served as a useful warning of the practical limits of Fuller's brilliance. Most of Fuller's ideas, like his revolutionary Dymaxion car and house designs, and the myriad structures made from geodesic domes, fell short of Fuller's revolutionary objectives. Appropriately, when Isamu sculpted Fuller's head, he gave it a chrome plate.

Ailes graduated from Cherry Lawn in the spring of 1929. As she later explained, "I was graduated from a boarding school in Connecticut in 1929 and then applied to the Neighborhood Playhouse in New York City for a 'living scholarship'—a fifteen-dollar-a-week stipend for food, lodging, and free tuition. At that time, fifteen dollars was sufficient living money and enabled the students at the playhouse to study the arts of speech, drama, and dance. It was there that I studied under the direction of a brilliant and blazing new dancer Martha Graham." Ailes' talent so impressed Graham that before the year was out, she was invited to join Graham's professional Dance Group. "I took classes with Martha at the Neighborhood Playhouse by day and again at her studio at night. We would rehearse until one or two in the morning and Martha would give us rye bread and cheese to eat at the end of rehearsal. We never got paid."

Graham was developing her first major work, entitled *Heretic*. In it, Graham, dressed in white, repeatedly advances against a double row of hostile women clad in black puritan garb until her spirit is finally broken, and she sinks to the floor, defeated. The *New York Times* review of the season finale on April 14 called it "at once strikingly original and glowing with vitality." But audiences did not always share the critics' enthusiasm. "The public was not used to the starkness and simplicity of movement in her work. It was not 'pretty' and contained none of the conventions of ballet. It was a complete break from tradition. People unused to the bare bones of dance were often repelled." But Ailes loved it. "There, it seemed, was truth."

Isamu's portrait show at the Marie Sterner Gallery in the first two weeks of February 1930 was a great success; by this point, the portrait sculptures had earned Isamu enough money to resume his plan to travel to Asia. Before his departure, he organized a portrait exhibition at the Arts Club in Chicago, and drove there with Fuller (in his station wagon), stopping over in Cambridge, Massachusetts, where Fuller was promoting his Dymaxion House. Isamu returned only briefly to New York before embarking for Europe on April 16; from Paris, he would travel from Russia by rail to Beijing.

Arriving in Paris, Isamu sent Léonie a note, enclosing an Easter lily. He had asked her to pick up his laundry and to write to various Japanese connections informing them of his plan to visit Japan. Léonie's connections were not exactly numerous: there was Yone, who was less than thrilled to hear the news, the nice English arms dealer Mr. Paget, who, it turned out, was no longer of this world, and Viscount Fukuoka. (The old Viscount having died in 1919, this was his Roanoke-educated son, Hidei). Isamu had also asked Léonie to contact his Greenwich Village artist friends the Ishigakis (Eitaro, an eccentric socialist artist connected with Yone) and his young wife Ayako.

Léonie was enjoying the company of Ailes, who had been rapidly climbing the ranks in Martha Graham's dance company. They continued to spend time with Boris Majdrakof, occasionally joining him for dinner at Arakel's, an Armenian restaurant on Lexington Avenue. In May, Léonie made a brief trip to Bryn Mawr, where she wrote Isamu.

To Isamu Noguchi, May 6, 1930

Bryn Mawr

My dear Isamu,
Your Easter lily still fresh and shining white as the day you plucked it to send me. In return I send you a branch of the pink dogwood whose large blooms are the radiant glory at Bryn Mawr in this season.

Your commissions I have attended to as far as possible. The laundry did not materialize. The man insisted he had given you back your last laundry just before you left—on Tuesday I think he said—that you had paid for it and he had nothing more of yours.

Letters I have written to your father and to Mr. Paget, giving your address c/o Guarantee Trust. Will next write to Fukuoka. Ishizaki [*sic*] I have not yet located—went to the address you gave on 14th Street—there was a Grand Rapids Furniture—no one knew Ishigaki. Called up the Japanese consulate—they gave me an address to which I wrote, but the letter was returned "not found"—I shall get on his track soon by inquiring among Japanese artists.

I have come to Bryn Mawr and the heat did not agree with me—will get off to Maine as soon as possible after returning to New York, say about May 17—so you will be safe to address your next letter just "Bar Harbor, Maine."

The latest news of Ailes is that she has been chosen to belong to Martha Graham's special group next year. Pleased as Punch. Boris says Ailes is a wonderful girl. Certainly she has done well with the dancing in the short time she has had. I think you might *loaf* a little in Paris. Boris says no! When you go to Japan I hope you learn the special technique of Japanese *wood carving!* Take all your wood carving tools.

Your loving mother.

In the summer, Léonie and Ailes headed north to Bar Harbor, Maine, heading up well before the beginning of the tourist season with the aid of a check from Isamu. The stock market had crashed in October. Léonie, undaunted, set up her summer shop at 83 Mt Desert Street, advertising color prints, jewelry, bead restringing, Chinese knotting, and repairs.

To Isamu Noguchi, June 14, 1930

83 Mt. Desert Street, Bar Harbor, Me.

Dearest Isamu,

I have been savoring the savor of your last letter. I am so glad you are happy and pleased with yourself. Don't hurry on to India in the very hot weather. People have been telling me dreadful stories of Malaria bugs, typhoid, enteric and what not. Anyway we know what the terrible heat of New York is even with the relief of soda fountains, salads, and suitable foods. Japan of course is another question. It is a summer resort for people from those warmer climes. And there are the watermelons of Chigasaki. When you do go I believe you could get passage on the Osaka Shosen Kaisha line from Marseilles. You could also ship your carvings, tools etc. more reasonably that way, as *freight*. Freight goes by the ton, and 40 cubic feet of space is rated as a ton. I believe the cost between Europe and New York is about $5 a ton. A packing case about 4 x 4 x 3 feet makes nearly a shipping ton. You can get marine insurance on freight. Japanese officials open every box and make themselves a nuisance over the customs. It would be wise to get some business man used to shipping, like Mr. Paget, to help in getting your things out of the customs. As you know, Chigasaki is about 50 minutes by train from Yokohama, and I think you'll find Paget at the old Danjuro besso, and the Fujiis near by.

We are now in Bar Harbor, happily escaped from New York. Could not have done it without your money, as there are two of us, and business won't start up before July. We got a little store this time, have put up two camp cots (one being yours) in the rear of the building (partitioned off from the store) set up an electric grill, and are keeping house with great complacency. Ailes goes mountain climbing and swimming every morning before breakfast. She is looking fine. I have had two dips in the icy cold Maine water myself.

We saw Boris just before we left—one of those little dinners at Arakel's where Boris' enthusiasm runs riot. This time he advised Ailes to turn into a fortune teller—said he would coach her, and they'd have a partnership, he to provide the mystery and she the charm—he was quite serious, and got excited over the millions they would get from a gullible public, especially big business men, who do nothing without consulting the stars, it seems. He told Ailes she would never be a dancer, that it was a shame to waste her fine intellect in mere physical exercise—he said in the fortune telling business also she would come up on lots of material for writing, see the insides of people's minds etc.—then she could become a famous writer—he adroitly shook the shekels and the fame before her in turns, but she was immune. I notice Boris inclines to be carried off his feet by thoughts of lots of money. That's a dangerous sign, as he is apt to make imprudent investments, as he did the summer before last, while you were away.

Ailes practices her dancing on the beach, early morning, after her swim, and can do some things she could not before. I don't think it will hurt her intellect.

Now be wise, foresighted, careful of your health, be your own god and your own star.

Your loving mother

Léonie's closing advice, "be your own god and your own star," seems clear enough, but where did it come from? One possibility is Ralph Waldo Emerson: "follow your own star," he had once said, "and it will lead you to that which none other can attain. Imitation is suicide." But Léonie, like Emerson, may also have been thinking of Hindu philosophy. "We believe that every being is divine, is God," said Swami Vivekananda. "Stand as a rock; you are indestructible. You are the Self (atman), the God of the universe." Isamu was, after all, planning to visit India. In her next letter, Léonie, after giving further advice about Isamu's visit to Japan, suggested he contact Yone's Indian writer friends, Rabindranath Tagore and Sarojini Naidu.

To Isamu Noguchi, June 17, 1930

83 Mt. Desert Street, Bar Harbor, Me.

My dear Isamu,

I just received a letter from Mrs. Paget telling me of the death of Mr. Paget on February 10 from heart failure. She said he often spoke of us and had sent something for remembrance last Xmas, but of course we didn't get it. She says she will be very glad to see you. I am sure you will find her kind and hospitable. Her address is 476 Sanno-cho, Oiso. I always thought that if I ever returned to Japan Mr. Paget would be one I most wished to see again. Mrs. Paget will be able to give you news of our other friends—for instance Mishima's who had a villa at Oiso, with a beautiful plum garden.

Before you start, write to Tagore and Mme. Naidu, and await their reply. The latter may not receive her letter, and anyway it would be censored. Tagore is hospitable. He knew your father, also Mrs. Wm. Vaughan Moody. And he manages to keep away from politics, or has so far.

I will not write more just now, just this note to tell you of Mr. Paget.

I have had a feeling that something would happen, but my uneasiness centers about you. However, Japanese seers tell me this should be a lucky year for you, beginning from the beginning of the year they said all your ventures would be prosperous and happy.

With a hearty kiss and a loving heart
Mother

When the census takers came around that summer, Léonie and Ailes were back at the 141 East 17th Street apartment Léonie had taken three years earlier. She gave the census taker her true age (56) but identified herself as a widow. She gave her profession as jeweler and said she was presently working; Ailes' occupation is given as "none." The rent on the apartment is listed as $45.

Isamu remained in Paris for several months, seeing old friends and waiting for a visa to travel over the Trans-Siberian Railroad. "But a shock had come to me before leaving, in the form of a letter from my father, suggesting that I should not come to Japan using his name," Isamu wrote in *A Sculptor's World*. As he clarified to Yoshinobu Hakutani, "before I left Paris I had received a letter from my father which said, 'Don't come. Don't use the name Noguchi.'" Isamu later concluded that Yone's Japanese wife had objected to his using the Noguchi name "because I'm the oldest, you see." Matsuko may have feared Isamu was positioning himself as *chonan* or eldest son in order to inherit his father's property according to Japanese custom.

Toward the end of July, Isamu arrived in Harbin after the ten-day trans-Siberian train journey; after his luggage caught up, it would be another two days to Peking. "May stay there, may go to Kyoto, depending," he wrote Léonie around the end of July. He found Peking congenial, and ended up staying.

Léonie mounted another Japanese art exhibition at the library in August. This time she went to the trouble of writing an article about the show for the *Bar Harbor Times* on August 20. Readers might not be familiar with the work of the late print artist Hashiguchi Goyo, but she explained that the Goyo print, exhibited in the show, had been singled out for praise by noted collector Howard Mansfield, who had been among the first to visit the exhibition.

To Isamu Noguchi, October 24, 1930

On Board Steamship Portsmouth, Boston to New York

My dear Isamu,

I carry your letter with me for the address, as I haven't yet learned it by heart. I expect to reach New York tomorrow morning, to spend two days looking for an apartment, and then to go to Princeton for a couple of days, afterward to a place near Philadelphia called Upper Darby, as Grasberger writes me I might do a little business there. This day I spent in Boston with Mme. Bournat, a charming little French dressmaker I met in Bar Harbor. She treated me fine, and insisted on accompanying me to the boat in all the rain and mire (Boston in its usual drizzly garb) carrying a large paper bag of apples as a parting gift. Of course the rain melted the paper and we were lucky to reach my stateroom with arms full of apples, hatbags, handbags, umbrellas etc. Such is the life of a voyager. It got very cold in Bar Harbor before I left, at first with beautiful autumn foliage and lovely skies, then storms and even a flurry of snow. I stayed in the little room back of the shop until it was impossible to stay longer in an unheated place, so for the last two days took a room in a regular house, with a proper bed which seemed so strange after the summer on your camp cot to which I had become accustomed. This summer was not good for business, and it was a good thing we had your money to fall back on. It was a dear little shop, however, and maybe I'll make good at it next summer. If I need anything special from China I will let you know. At present I seem to have so many boxes I don't know where to put them all, so want to reduce stock all I can. Packing is a painful job. Had a letter from Mrs. Close that she is back in America, and did not go either to Russia or India this time as she is not very strong and it would have been too much for her. I hope you keep well and take all precautions of sanitation—get plenty of fresh air and avoid trachoma by wearing white cotton gloves and frequently washing your hands, as that eye trouble comes chiefly from touching things and then putting your hands to your eyes.

I hope you have made some friends by this time, and don't get lonely or homesick. If there is any fighting going on in Peiping you better pass as a Frenchman, that is better than being either Japanese or American.

The wind is moaning and shrieking around this boat in the most melancholy way—like a banshee—I seem to feel very much at home in this kind of weather, as if in my native element. I suppose that is my celtic temperament, or an inheritance from seafaring ancestors. Now I am going back to that strange city where I was born and where the only homelike thing is the sound of fog horns and bell buoys in the East River.

I look for a letter from you soon and will write you again as soon as we find a place to live.

Lovingly
Mother

Have seen Ailes, found apt., everything all right.
New address 119 E. 17

Isamu Noguchi, Interview with Paul Cummings, 1973

ISAMU NOGUCHI: I was in Peking for eight months. I hate to go over this again because it is in my book. But a letter was sent to me from my father—from my mother enclosing a letter from my father—asking me not to come to Japan.

PAUL CUMMINGS: Oh, I see.

ISAMU NOGUCHI: So I didn't want to go to Japan. That is, I was very ambivalent about it; I wanted to go, and I didn't want to go. But I was already on my way, so I went to Peking, my money was running out and I might as well go back to the States but I thought I'd better stop in Japan anyway. I had no intention of seeing my father; I was just going to stop by. It was only because of newspaper reporters that I got to meet him.

After eight months in China, Isamu overcame his ambivalence about visiting Japan. He thought he might make a brief, incognito visit, as a "temporary absence from Peking," but his plan to travel quietly was foiled by a *Mainichi shinbun* reporter to whom he unwittingly told his tale while on the boat. Yone was now a well-known public figure who wrote frequently for the newspapers and even read his poetry on the radio. The newspaper played the story for all it was worth, publishing, on January 26, even before the ship arrived, an article headlined "Yearning for his father the poet." It gave no suggestion of Isamu's resentment toward his father, only hopeful feelings about their reunion. "I remember my father's face very well. I never forgot him for a moment and I always talked about him with my mother. I never got out of my head the idea of going to Japan, where my father was, and now I am finally realizing my hopes."

When the ship arrived two days later, the press was waiting. A *Mainichi* reporter wondered why his father had not come to meet him. "I have not come to Japan to meet my father," Isamu explained. "I have come to Japan not as the son of the poet Yone Noguchi. I have come as the American Isamu Noguchi to see Japan for my own sculpture." He wanted to see how Japanese culture had progressed, to see "the splendid sculpture of ancient Japan in Kyoto and Nara," and "to work here under their inspiration." "I have come to Japan only for work," he reiterated. "I will not meet my father."

The newspaper also sent reporters to the Noguchi house in Higashi Nakano. "I really want to see my son. I want to do what I can for him," Yone told them. "I did not know that he was coming to Japan. The first I knew about it was when I read the newspaper yesterday." He did not deny that Isamu was his son. "There is no connection between the big public fuss that happened twenty years ago and what is happening now," he added, somewhat mysteriously. (He was probably alluding to the controversial "Analysis of the Americans" and subsequent exchange of letters the year before Isamu had left for the United States.) "Now that he has come to Tokyo, to this land, I want to help him. I want to explain the misunderstandings, but he may not accept my feelings."

Faced with the well-publicized fact of Isamu's appearance, Yone arranged a meeting and did his best to be helpful, short of actually inviting him to stay at the house. Isamu later recalled the meeting as "trying." Isamu was angry not only for his father's recent rejection, but also Yone's earlier treatment of Léonie. "I did not think he treated her fairly," he would later tell Yoshinobu Hakutani. At their meeting, Yone "didn't say anything," and while Isamu had "no quarrels with him at all," it "was not exactly pleasant."

Yone's brother Totaro Takagi was willing to let Isamu use a new house he had just built in Tokyo's central Nihonbashi district. Isamu found that Takagi "showered me with kindness, as did other relatives who gave me to understand that they favored my mother." Nor did his father remain entirely distant, if he did remain inscrutable. "My father would come to call on me, and we would hold long silent conversations," Isamu recalled. "Then he would take me around to introduce me to various artists he thought I should meet, such as Kotaro Takamura and his father Koun." The elderly Takamura was still, at age seventy-nine, carving large wooden Buddhas, while his Rodin-influenced poet-sculptor son took Isamu to a bronze foundry; neither interested him much. When Isamu thought he might try to find a practitioner of the T'ang style figurines seen in Peking and said to be still produced in Japan, Yone introduced him to the American-educated National Museum director, Jiro Harada. Harada, referred him to a Celadon potter in Kyoto, Uno Jimmatsu. Before leaving Tokyo he made portrait sculptures of "Uncle Takagi" and the Takagis' maid,

"Tsuneko san," but, as he put it, "two months of this was enough," and he "fled to Uno san and his kilns," spending the last five months of his stay living in the cottage of a ditch-digger in Higashiyama while applying himself "to making terracottas and to discovering the beauty of gardens and the Japanese countryside."

The *Bryn Mawr Alumnae Bulletin* noted in February 1931 that Léonie had "moved her studio of Japanese Art and Jewelry to 119 East 17th Street, New York City" (the "new address" she had sent to Isamu the previous October with the note that she would write again "as soon as we find a place to live").

In September 1931, Isamu sailed for the United States without returning to Tokyo to see his father, though he did send a letter soon after his return to New York. "I wish to tell you that I have no regrets about my trip to Japan," he wrote. "I believe it to have been all for the best. I feel grateful for whatever you were able to do for me there. I feel great attachment for Japan. I love it as much as I would some person for its faults as well as its virtues. I feel there a great humanity—the foundations of my earliest dreams." The letter was signed, "Affectionately, Isamu."

By November Isamu was back in New York. During his absence, Ailes had made great strides in her dance career. Toward the end of 1930, Graham gave Ailes and another eighteen-year-old dancer, fresh from Seattle, significant parts in *Primitive Mysteries*. "Martha often pointed to Ailes Gilmore as the model for the way we should move our hands," Dorothy Bird later recalled. "See how Ailes presses the air down with her hands as she rises. It is as if she carves her own body's shape out of the air, like a Rodin figure emerging from marble." Martha paired the two again in *Chorus of Youth*. "It must have been quite startling to see the contrast between Ailes, the exotic, dark-haired Oriental One, and me, the sunny, fair-haired, Blue-eyed One. We walked and ran softly, side by side, like a team of horses, with our long hair loose, brushed out like manes." In addition to her dancing, Ailes also occasionally worked as an artist's model: she appears partially unclothed in Walt Kuhn's 1931 painting, "Miss A."

Ailes Gilmour in dance costume. *Isamu Noguchi Foundation.*

On January 4, 1932, Léonie brought Ailes to a tea given by Bryn Mawr classmate Mary Swope. The tea was in honor of Masa Dogura Uchida's daughter, Sumako, who was was attending a small school in Massachussetts. Her father, Count Yasuya Uchida had been appointed president of the South Manchurian Railway the previous year. Having served twice as Japan's foreign minister, he would fill the position again later in the year.

In February Isamu exhibited the fruits of his "pilgrimage to the East" at the John Becker and Demotte Galleries. Afterwards, he took the new works and a number of portrait busts on tour to Chicago, the West Coast, and Hawaii. In his absence, Léonie looked after his studio, forwarding his mail, and making some effort to deal with his unpaid bills.

The May 1932 *Bryn Mawr Alumnae Bulletin* noted that Isamu's exhibitions had been a success and that Ailes was now "one of Martha Graham's dance group and has appeared with them on various occasions this season." "Leonie says of herself: 'I am endeavoring to carry on what appears to be a 'frozen business.' I expect to go to Bar Harbor again this summer, if I can raise the fare, and open my little shop at 83 Mt. Desert Street."

To Isamu Noguchi, Easter, 1932

What lovely Easter love! Better than orchids. Far more abstract and symbolic of your splendid work as if every bit of it was pure gold. Means more than a million got some other way. Don't know if you will get this letter in Chicago. There are *heaps* of letters in your studio. Shall I forward them? Where?

Starting an exhibition tomorrow in the big studio downstairs. Persuaded the landlord to lend it to me.

Love

Mother

Sorry to tell you, Mary Rivoire had an accident to her ankle. It may be broken. Ailes had to dance in her place last night.

To Isamu Noguchi, April 7, 1932

119 East 17th Street, New York City

My dear Isamu,

I went up to your studio this morning. There was a notice pasted on the door. I believe legal notice of eviction and claim for $210 rent. I left it on, but if you like I will tear it off.

Then I gathered up the letters I saw around and sent them in a package. I left out Romeike's press notices, also many letters from tel. and Edison Cos. The telephone co. sent a letter from a lawyer threatening to sue you for 27.95. So I called them up to see if we can't make a compromise—the man was out but they said someone will call on me. Don't think it can be reinstalled for less than full payment, and the girl said an additional deposit might also be required, unless it were put on *my* bill, which might make a difference. Will see what I can do Monday. Called up Mr. Armstrong—he said he will do his best to sublet your studio, but there have been no summer rentals yet, and don't expect any before May, the time when summer artists come to the city for 4 months.

The Edison Co. said if bill of $6.55 was not paid by April 1 it would be cut off. Don't know if they have done so but will attend to it.

Saw two letters from you to Mary Rivoire, and have forwarded them to her, as her leg is broken and she is confined to the house. She's studying French with her grandmother and is snowed under with scraps of paper with French exercises.

Also saw a stamped letter addressed to you, perhaps by Mary and forgotten to post, so I have mailed it.

I tried having an exhibition in the empty studio downstairs, but am not lucky. However, someone has now rented it, and will come in at the end of the week, when I give up. The landlord should thank me. Have had an awful cold and flu for two weeks—same as you had, not so good. Ailes danced in Mary's place last Sunday and got a little press notice "rendered able assistance to Martha G." They go to Boston today and will be back Sunday.

I hope you are having a good time and get some fresh air in La Porte. How are the Rumely's? Give them my regards. I'll look for you some time next week.

Your loving Mother

They say it is lovely outdoors today. Must be Spring in La Porte.

HUNTERS' BEACH HEAD   BAR HARBOR, ME.

Postcard of Bar Harbor, Maine. *Isamu Noguchi Foundation.*

In June, Léonie returned to Bar Harbor, Maine.

To Isamu Noguchi, June 28, 1932

My dear Isamu,

I will now tell you all about my journey here. As you might like to come the same way some day, I will go into some detail. I took the Providence boat in the late afternoon, getting a ticket through to Boston for $5.00. That was a beautiful trip, and the boat very home-like and pleasant. Coming up the sound the sailboats showed the most lovely studies in abstract form, the forms of the sails evidently created by a master artist. They would hold one form for awhile, then slowly change to another. I kept thinking of them. When I see anything of sheer beauty, like that I hold on to the memory, and every time I recall it, get a thrill of delight. So I recall things you have done, with a deep delight.

We reached Providence at 4:30 (Eastern Standard time, I believe) about 5 was transferred by motor coach to the railway station, waited there for a train, got out at Back Bay Station, Boston, and took a taxi for a very short distance to No. 10 Park Square, where they said the B. and W. (Boston and Worcester) bus would start in 2 minutes (8:15). Suddenly a man seized my baggage and began throwing it into a Pierce Arrow car that stood there. "Stop," I said. "I go by bus."

"All right, lady."

"It's not all right. I told you I am going by bus."

"We're the bus," said the driver of the Pierce Arrow limousine. "Hop right in."

There were six passengers in all, and the ride smooth and comfortable. We got to Portland an hour ahead of the Greyhound bus which had started before us. That car went as far as Lewiston, Maine, reaching there about 12:30. There was half an hour to wait for the next bus, so I went upstairs to an Italian restaurant and had a fine Italian salad.

The next lap of the journey, to Waterville, was in a small bus with wicker seats—also quite comfortable. At Waterville they stopped at a hotel, and I was told there would be an hour and a half to wait for the next bus. So I took a walk; came back and had afternoon tea at the hotel cafeteria, and about 5 o'clock started in a larger bus to Bangor. The roads on this lap were in a most frightful condition, we were thrown and tossed about, and left passing signs which said "Pass at your risk."

Reached Bangor shortly before 7, and at seven took the Staples Motor Coach, a small rickety car, to Bar Harbor. The roads consisted mostly of mud holes and sand piles. Awful. Reached Bar Harbor at 9 o'clock, left my bags in the office of the doctor across the street from my shop and found a place to stop for the night.

The fare from Boston to Bangor was $5.50 and from Bangor to Bar Harbor $2.50. The journey was lovely as far as Lewiston, even to Waterville, after that abominable. It might be an idea to ride to Lewiston, then trek and hitchhike east and get to Bar Harbor somehow without going up to Bangor. I'll look up the map.

I long to hear from you. Write soon. About *everything*.

Great love,

Mother

To Isamu Noguchi, July 5, [1932]

The Eastern Sea, 83 Mt. Desert St., Bar Harbor, Me

Dear Isamu,

Made my first sale today. Small pickings but hurrah just the same! I enclose a dollar of it for a swim. Why don't you write? How's the carpenter shop? Going into the exhibition room of the library saw a large picture of Benjamin Franklin. He must be the fashion now.

Enclose a map of the vicinity. The best way, I should say, if you incline to come up, would be by bus from New York to *Portland*, Me. Cost $5.50 leave Hotel Cadillac, N.Y.C. at midnight, arrive Portland at noon the next day. *Walk* from Portland to *Rockland* along the coast—about 77 miles—chance of your life to be a hobo—at Rockland take a boat for Bar Harbor—leaves Rockland 6 a.m. arrives at noon. I *think* it costs $3.50.

So far very cold and some horrid storms.

Take care of your health and *breathe* fully. The reason you stoop is because you do not sufficiently expand your lungs in breathing. A little weakness in the upper lungs. Several times a day you should breathe slowly and quietly, first expanding the abdomen and continuing to breathe in until your upper lungs are full of air, also try to feel your breath against your backbone. My father practiced slow full breathing on the way to and from work—He had a wonderful chest expansion, and always erect and alert. Buck up. Swim. Get out in the air.

Write to Your loving mother.

To Isamu Noguchi, July 9, 1932

83 Mt. Desert St., Bar Harbor, Me

It would be a lovely surprise if you and Mr. Fuller should drop in on me. But if coming by car beware of the roads. They are awful, it would be better to walk. You know his island is within rowing distance of the Porters. They'd probably write you. Do come and see how your mother sleeps on a shelf, eats off her lap and hangs by her toes from the ceiling to save space.

Lovingly
Mother

PULPIT ROCK   BAR HARBOR, MAINE

Léonie's postcard from Bar Harbor, July 9, 1932. *Isamu Noguchi Foundation.*

Bar Harbor adjoined Mount Desert Island, a favorite summer resort of some of America's wealthiest families: the Morgans, Vanderbilts, Fords, Carnegies, and, especially the Rockefellers. John D. Rockefeller, Jr. had bought up as much as he could of Mount Desert Island in hopes of preserving its scenic beauty. Léonie was aware that Rockefeller and his wife, Abby, were avid collectors of Japanese art. After visiting China and Japan in 1921, they began acquiring Japanese furnishings for their homes in New York and Maine, relying mainly on the Osaka-based importing firm, Yamanaka and Company, which conveniently had galleries in both cities, as well as Boston, Chicago, London, Newport, and Atlantic City. For decades, the Yamanaka galleries had supplied artifacts for wealthy Americans smitten with Japonisme, as well as more serious collectors like Ernest Fenollosa and Charles Lang Freer. The Yamanaka shop was clearly in a different league from her own, and she thought Isamu might sell his recent Asian works there, rather than in her own modest shop. She became friendly with Mr. Nakagawa, the Yamanakas' local manager. There were not many Japanese in the area, but there were rumors that Inazo Nitobe was visiting friends nearby, and the Rockefellers' favored portrait photographer, H. T. Koshiba, would be arriving later in the summer. Léonie was still hopeful Isamu would come for a visit, but as the summer wore on and Isamu sent no word, her hopes diminished.

To Isamu Noguchi, July 24, 1932

The Eastern Sea, 83 Mt. Desert St., Bar Harbor, Me

My dear Isamu,

My crane-necked longing to see you seems not destined to be satisfied. No sail on the horizon. No letter in port. Does that mean you haven't come or aren't coming? So I'll just continue the correspondence and hope you keep up your end of it. For news I will begin with something nice. A letter from "ASIA" tells me they accept my article. They also ask if I have any photographs for illustration. I haven't anything handy, so have written one or two friends. Wonder if you have any photo of the following:

Zashiki with *tokonoma*

Japanese garden with *stones*

Japanese screen

Fence

Plum tree.

Any of them, I mean.

Next news. I have paid Dr. Weber's bill he sent last May, amounting to $15 so that is off my mind.

How are you getting on? Have you breakfasted since then?

Yamanakas here have a very beautiful place, with little garden at the side in which are good stone carvings. It has occurred to me they might be good people to sell something of yours for you—for instance, girl reclining on elbow. The manager is on very friendly terms with Mr. Rockefeller. If you should be around I will introduce you to Mr. Nakagawa.

Next news: Dr. Nitobe is, or was, at Southwest Harbor, about 18 miles from here, visiting someone there.

Have not heard from Ailes since she first went to the farm. Perhaps she is back by now. Had a letter from the Olivers saying that on October 1st they will start a 3-months trip to Texas in a car, and offering me their East-River-view apartment at $20 a month in their absence. It is at

442 E. 23d St., corner Ave. A., top floor, 4 light rooms, furnished. Maybe you know someone wants it. Would not do for me on account of the W.C. being down three flights. A good buy, I should say, however. 2 beds, gas range etc. No heat or bath.

Have had no word from Yamamoto. Do you see him?

I hope tomorrow will bring me some little crop of letters, as it's getting lonely without them.

It is still very cold here. No swim yet. Took a walk today by a lovely mossy brook, Duck Brook path, to Witch Hold Pond, thence to Hull's Cove, had supper there, then someone drove me back in their car.

Best love and write soon. Don't forget about the photos, if you have any.

Mother.

Léonie's article for *Asia* (journal of the Yokohama-based American Asiatic Association) appeared three years later with illustrations by German-Algerian-American photographer Zaida Ben-Yusuf.

House and Garden in Beauty-Loving Japan

Asia, June 1935

I have often thought that, if the world without is to be the object of your contemplation, there is no abiding place equal to a tent, preferably one set on an eminence in command of the country around. The Japanese house has in effect always met this need for a place of vantage. It is a house that must be, it is true, a home, a shelter in a climate embracing all weathers from frigid mists to sultry typhoons, with an everyday pattern of dripping rain to wear away the very roof tiles. But in obedience to Japanese traditional canons of fitness and good taste, the house resembles a tent, the translucent white paper *shoji* serving instead of canvas walls and suffusing the rooms with gentle light and tremulous shade, the grass-covered mats strewing the floors like rushes. The credit belongs to oriental conservatism if the dwelling characteristic of an advanced civilization keeps something of the charm of its nomad ancestor.

In the process of civilization Nature also has been in a measure tamed, never quite subdued. Nature is no longer the free Amazon; nor is she the poor thing that she sometimes becomes where men attempt to conquer her. In the little intimate garden of Japan she sits like a wife in a happy captivity, a captivity so gentle that the very fence hedging her about looks not like a fence but more like a lattice—of slender bamboo sticks or irregular bundles of twigs lightly tied with bark-stained hempen cords—made to shut out curious eyes.

That the Japanese architect recognizes the subordinate character of interior decorations is shown by his care that these decorations, although distinguished, shall be of such tones and textures as serve best for a background. The mat-covered floor, the sand-colored walls, the white paper shoji, the low ceiling in warmer wood brown, seem like a frame awaiting a picture. What is the picture, what the show for which the stage is set? The show is indeed a picture, a moving picture, if you will, changing seasonally, a picture hung, not against the wall, but just without. I mean, of course, the garden.

You may say that in all western architectural plans also the view is important. I am not speaking of the Japanese garden as a view in quite that sense. Such a view is rather of the hills and reaches of country that Nature unrolls in a vast panorama. The Japanese garden is more like a picture, a privately owned picture for the esthetic pleasure of the owners, only hung just outside the room in such a way that, sitting on the floor by the open shoji or on the veranda, they have displayed before their eyes a work of art in which the artist has won over Nature as an ally and not merely used her as a model or an inspiration.

This living picture is peculiarly happy in fulfilling the Japanese idea of dualism in art. For a picture or a poem may be considered from two points of view. What the artist or poet is thinking of is one thing; what it evokes in the mind of the beholder or reader is another. A poem or a picture is great precisely in proportion to its effect in making the beholder also an artist or a poet, evoking creative power in him to supply what is not in the picture or poem. Nature is full of transient allusions and suggestions. Take away what is redundant, leave what is necessary for subtle effects, and you have, with a minimum of effort, produced a picture with the maximum of suggestive power. It is significant that we are more responsive when the artist does not obtrude his personality. The artist must indeed show a due reverence in undertaking this work. Bend Nature gently to his will he may. He dare not violate the secret laws of her soul.

Since the garden picture is one that must hold its charm throughout the year, it depends not much on the fleeting beauty of flowers—more on trees, stones, ponds and bridges. Of trees, evergreens have the first rank. Sometimes they are dwarfed, so that you may get the effect of overlooking them (as from a tent on a hilltop) or, while sitting on the floor, may still see under and through them (as if in a wood). A ruby-decked maple (you know the slender Japanese maple with small, seven-fingered scarlet leaves), a pearl-strung plum tree (it blooms in January under the snow), a cherry tree under clouds of bloom or in a maze of flying petals, add their seasonal touch. Bamboos rustle beside the pond, speaking a strange language, and the pond itself harbors another world, a mirage of watery beauty.

And there are the stones. Stones are the most important thing in a Japanese garden. In the garden of the famous actor Danjuro at Chigasaki I saw a stone, a not remarkable stone, about four feet long by two feet wide, a water-worn obloid mass, brought, I was told, from Ise Province, at a cost of three hundred *yen*. There it lies in the garden by the sandy shore of Chigasaki, where no stones are found—a monument to the extravagance of the actor in satisfying his whim. I remember an unfinished Yokohama garden in which, at the end of about eight months' work, there was still nothing to be seen but stones. "When will your garden be done?" I asked. "It will never be perfectly done," was the answer, "but, once the stones are right, the rest is easy." We shall take two weeks now to put in trees, shrubs and flowers. Then come and see us."

But do the Japanese live on the veranda? Is there nothing in the house to satisfy the esthetic sense? Well, suppose we close the shoji and turn our faces the other way, to look at the room before which the garden picture has been hung. You will note the mats of the color of dried grasses, greenish in tint if new, more tawny with age; the walls finished with dull, rough-surfaced plaster, in some shade of stone color varying from warm brown to cool gray; the low ceiling paneled in wood, polished to bring out the grain. You will perceive with approval that any wooden surface, as the *tokonoma*, a table, a passageway, is fastidiously polished and free from dust. The Japanese are not afraid of new wood; a newly built house of plain white pine, which may look crude and unfinished to some, is rather pleasing to them. Besides, they know how soon time and the weather and the *zokin*, or housecloth, will get in their work. Though there are many attractive woods in Japan, with subtle gradations in color, this ordinary pine is most in use; without staining it takes on a fine patina and rich tone when treated in the Japanese way, that is, simply wiped daily with the zokin, wrung out in cold water.

There is almost no furniture in a Japanese room, beyond the fire box, which with its glowing eye of fire amid the feathery ashes gives a very homelike effect, like a purring cat or a singing kettle. The kettle too is usually there, of old iron or bronze, and musical as only a kettle can be. In such a milieu, you have at first only a sense of peace. There seems to be not one thing that is striking. Then out of the gray quiet emerges the graceful arrangement of a few flowers or leaves in a vase, or some other trifle of simplicity, which grows and grows on you until you catch your breath over the touching loveliness of it.

Where are the pictures, the color prints, the bronze pieces, the carved ivories, lacquers, jades, porcelain vases, incense burners, lanterns, which Westerners, from their familiarity with oriental shops, are wont to associate with the East? Where, indeed? Why, in the shops. You will look in vain for such a medley of bric-a-brac in a Japanese home. Carved ivory? Yes, the master of the house may wear a small *netsuke* on his tobacco pouch. Lacquer? Ah, to be sure, the soup bowls in the kitchen closet are of lacquer. Color prints? You may find one of them adorning the walls of a tea-house. The best are in portfolios, brought out on occasion to give pleasure to some friend. For a picture, observe the bold ideographs of a poem framed and hung up over the *karakami*, or wall-paper. For gods, candlesticks, incense burners—bronze, silver, golden, brass—look in the Buddhist temples, where these things belong.

In their homes, to be sure, the Japanese have their treasures, and a special place for showing them. This is the tokonoma, or dais of polished wood, raised a few inches from the floor and set in a sort of alcove, two or three feet deep, four to six feet wide, framed by the limbs or trunks of trees, bared of bark and polished, but keeping their own knotted and twisted shapes. You may see a fine bronze piece—perhaps an ancient warrior in armor astride a fiery steed—alone on the tokonoma, with nothing to draw attention from his august self. The next time you call at that house, you may see on the tokonoma only a potted plant or flowers arranged in a bamboo vase, but seldom more than one such object at a time. Against the wall at the back of the tokonoma is hung a *kakemono*, a scroll which may be rolled up and put away. Flower and kakemono often will be changed, just as the garden varies its aspect from season to season.

Objects that do not form an essential part of the decorative scheme in a Japanese room are never left lying about, however beautiful they may be in themselves. For instance, the square *zabuton*, or cushion, that is placed on the floor for you to sit on, is removed when you depart. The table is brought out at mealtime and afterward removed. A large dining table stolidly sitting all day in the middle of a room would be to

Japanese eyes unesthetic, because inappropriate. The function of such a table is utilitarian, and therefore, if kept in a room when not in use, it would detract from the economy of line and economy of form that are first principles in the Japanese philosophy of taste. Even the fire box is moved from place to place, never left standing in the zashiki, or drawing-room, in Japan when no one is there. Beds of course are shut away in the closet and appear only at "bedtime."

There is indeed sometimes a piece of furniture, so classed by Westerners who have it for practical purposes, that is purely decorative in a Japanese house—namely, the screen. Some of the greatest Japanese artists—Korin, in the late seventeenth century, for instance—have been pleased to leave their title to fame chiefly to the pictures on a screen. In the homes of rich men, I have seen some fine six-folded and eight-folded screens, perhaps a gold background with wonderful deep blue waves running across it so as to make a continuous picture. Or others, more to my liking, of simple white *hanshi* paper, two-folded, with a design of India ink, say of wild geese rising above the waves to soar into infinity. Or a silvery waterfall in the corner of a quiet room, seeming to break the silence with its suggestion of music.

Japanese art brings something of the elusive beauty of Nature into the home. The fresh voice of the waterfall, the *élan* of a flight of birds, the descent of flower petals or snow, the somber mystery of a pine, the spectral swaying of a willow—these are the subjects that engage the artist's as they do the poet's thoughts. For such fantasies the color scheme of the Japanese house is most suitable and harmonious. Perhaps I should say the absence of color; for the hues of straw and wood and sand are not in the rainbow, nor is yet the touch of black seen in the written poem that hangs like a picture high on the wall. For color there is the flower in the vase or the dress of the young girl, herself a flower or a butterfly. If you think that space is less important for a Japanese designer than is the thing to be put into it, consider Korin. "Modern" art spans two centuries back to him. Have you seen an aged Japanese plum tree, its trunk gnarled and bizarre with hoary antiquity, hoary antiquity, putting out slender new shoots of bloom at abrupt angles? Korin is that aged trunk still putting out new shoots, spiritual shoots that bloom in Japan, in Europe, wherever new life is stirring. Do you think that Korin merely ignored background? He left things out of the background because he wanted the space. Every object of art that exists, requires a certain space, where nothing exists, to bring out its special quality. It is upon the intuitive understanding of this fact that the charm of the Japanese house depends.

To Isamu Noguchi, August 15, 1932

The Eastern Sea, 83 Mt. Desert St., Bar Harbor, Me

Dear Isamu—Got the letter—got the check—bless you. Have paid my water tax (8.50) and have ordered from Sears Roebuck a one dollar stove which with the pipe etc. will come to 3.50. Warm weather now, but the roof leaks like the dickens in seven places, takes days to dry out, and makes a musty mouldy smell. So I thought it a good idea to get the stove, burn my rubbish in it (saving the 50 cents I have to pay the rubbish man every time he takes it away) and be prepared for cold weather. Have a sore throat now from the last wetting. One day the toilet overflowed and there was suddenly two inches of water all over the floor[;] got in a plumber post haste who found the main pipe clogged up with the small roots of trees—I don't mean the pipe in the street but the one in the road beside the house. This happens every summer. In spite of everything it's quite a darling little place. Have moved my camp cot to the other side of the room where it is not under a shelf. I can just sit up without bumping. If the roof falls there's always the shelf to protect me.

It's extremely quiet. More than a touch of autumn in the air. Mr. Koshiba (photographer) and his wife have just arrived, so I suppose I'll be invited on a picnic next with them by Yamanaka's man. Met the French photographer—he does wonderful color work—Lives and works in a trailer on the public camping ground—he also complains of lack of business—he goes from place to place—Newport, Palm Beach etc. He is the grandfather of a 3 year old child, who is with him, also his wife, the grandmother, and his son, the young father of the grandchild. I found the old lady sitting on the running board, calmly knitting, there was a stove under the trees and a puppy tied to a string who frantically tried to get close enough to undo my shoes.

Glad you had a trip to Providence and only wish it had been on the lovely boat that I went on.

What is Ailes doing? She wrote asking whether she should go to Hunter College next year, or work at Cherry Lawn for her keep, or take a job in a sweatshop, or—or—Maybe Cherry Lawn would be a starter—she'd get a little experience teaching, and maybe some more self-reliance.

What is Isamu doing?

What shall we all do next?

lots of love

Mother

To Isamu Noguchi, August 20, 1932

The Eastern Sea, 83 Mt. Desert St., Bar Harbor, Me

My dear Isamu,

Will you do something for me? That is to send me some of your father's books—the Hiroshige and Korin ones. They are over at Yamamoto's, in a good sized corrugated board box, and marked on the outside "Noguchi" or books by Noguchi, or something like that, or "Korin" "Hiroshige."

I brought two of each with me, and have been writing to people offering them at $5 so now I have only one left. You could either take out half a dozen of each, wrap carefully with extra wrapping over the ivory hasps, then in corrugated board. Or if it is easier, you could ship the box as it is by Express Collect—I think it is pretty well packed. In that case you'd have to go there on a week day, and take them by taxi to the nearest express office in Brooklyn, as you wouldn't want to wait for the express man. If you send only a few you could send by parcel post.

Am sending this in haste. If you are out of town you might get Yamamoto to send them. Would have asked him but am never quite sure of his understanding.

Best love

Mother

I didn't ask Ailes because she is no good at packing.

To Isamu Noguchi, September 3, 1932

The Eastern Sea, 83 Mt. Desert St., Bar Harbor, Me

My dear Isamu,

I received the books you sent. They were all right except the Hiroshige, of which the hasp was broken. That was the only one that did not have extra folds of newspaper over the hasp. Perhaps it was broken already, I could not find the other piece of the hasp among the wrappings.

Ailes writes me that you went out to Borglum's place. Was it just for a trip, or did you stay awhile? It has been suggested to me that if I went to some place like Westport, Conn. for the winter I might do as much as in New York, with less rent. What do you think about that? A man was in here said a friend of his had a house in Westport, on the Boston Post Road, for $200 for the year.

It's quite hard to make sales this year. I am only hoping that by staying late I may catch the last crumbs. Anne Doyle says their sales have been only 500 dollars so far—their rent is 1500.

I sold one of your Chinese paintings for $20. It was one of the best.

A man took photographs of the shop, and I got some on a trade for some goods. Perhaps I will send you a couple. Then you give one—or both if you prefer to Ailes—they don't amount to much. I hope you ...

Sept. 6—This letter was interrupted by three days sickness. Living is too painful sometimes. Do take care of your health. Without it we can do nothing. Just got a letter from Miss Matsushita. She says she has moved to 249 W.109 St. She says to come for our things. Didn't know we still had anything there—perhaps some old clothes—will write her to give them away.

Write me what you are doing. I still feel very punk.

Much love,

Mother

Consider the Westport idea. Probably I'll stay here some time and try to get some strength after the people are gone.

Enclose letter for you.

To Isamu Noguchi, September 24, 1932

The Eastern Sea, 83 Mt. Desert St., Bar Harbor, Me

My dear Isamu,

I keep looking for a letter from you, but the days pass and none come. A Danish lady whom I met here told me today that she has been in Westport, that it is a delightful place in winter, and the rent Miss Stokes asks is very low. So unless I hear from you or Ailes in a few days I will write Miss Stokes that I want to come, if it is still available. That will give me a chance to escape a New York rent and whole year's lease, and have a place to stay until I come back here next year. There is a possibility of my getting a better place for a lower rent next summer in Bar Harbor.

Maybe in Westport I could really see more of you and Ailes than in New York, as you would make trips out for a change of air. Or maybe you could use the garage for a studio. ? ? ?

Today Mr. Mansfield came in for a minute, and said he would come again before I go. Mrs. Rockefeller sent her chauffeur to fetch two of your father's books for her to see. I think I am beginning to get established in Bar Harbor.

Have just been for a drive to the top of Cadillac Mountain. Marvelous view of sea and islands, with lovely lakes among the mountains.

Mrs. F—, the Danish lady, will be driving to New York about Oct. 20—Could go with her if I want.

I hope everything is going all right with you and Ailes and would love to have letters.

Ever your loving mother.

Léonie did evidently hear from Isamu shortly after sending the previous letter; he had been invited to exhibit at the California Palace of the Legion of Honor in San Francisco, and Pasadena Fine Arts Society.

To Isamu Noguchi, September 29, 1932

The Eastern Sea, 83 Mt. Desert St., Bar Harbor, Me.

My dear Isamu,

I enclose a letter from Catherine which you may enjoy reading. The letters she speaks of are those I wrote to her from Japan, mostly about you. Here is one story "Isamu planted some pussy willows in the garden. Then he came in and said "Something funny about my garden. Seems to be caterpillars growing there." The letters are quite entertaining. They are supposed to be to help on "the book" which I haven't yet had time even to start.

I was disappointed to lose the chance to get Miss Stokes' house— someone else took it while we delayed.

You will note from C—'s letter that stoves and coal are needed even in Southern California. Apartments in San Francisco are all steam heated—rents about like Brooklyn. You might get a job in S.F. to teach in the Calif. School of Fine Arts—very low pay, I hear. The most beautiful place I know in California is Santa Barbara—sea and mountains—pleasant people—many rich Easterners spend the winter there. If you go to California look up my sister Florence. She is at Tujunga (pronounced "To-hunger," very appropriately, quoth my sister) near Los Angeles. California has lovely scenery—a few people rattling around in a lot of scenery—and those few have a large proportion of nitwits and rapscallions, the former encouraging the latter. There are also the invalids putting up a brave fight, and the hard working farmers. Grand place for gardening.

Love,

Mother

Return C—'s letter, after taking her address.

When Léonie returned to New York City in the fall of 1932, she found the city in a political uproar in the wake of a massive corruption scandal that had forced popular mayor Jimmy Walker to resign on September 1. The interim mayor, Joseph McKee, a former high school teacher turned politician, failed to gain the support of Tammany Hall, and was ousted by the Tammany-backed candidate in a special election in November. The unpopularity of Tammany's machinations paved the way for the victory of Fiorello La Guardia in the regular election of 1933. Amid the scandal, Léonie was reminded of an eccentric Tokyo mayor who had once championed fiscal efficiency by advocating the eating of *kara*, the skins removed from soy beans in the production of tofu and other soy products. The recollection brought her to her typewriter to write a short piece evidently meant for a newspaper or magazine.

Léonie's memories of Japan were none too clear at this point: the Mayor's name was not Tajima, as she thought, but Tajiri. Inajiro Tajiri, who had served a term as mayor in 1918-19, may have been a bit eccentric, but, aside from his fascination with *kara*, his ideas had a decidedly American tilt. Like Yone, Tajiri had been inspired to go the United States after studying at Keio Gijuku. After graduating high school in Hartford, he enrolled at Yale, studying diligently with financial support from the Japanese government. Graduating in 1878, he completed a year of graduate study before returning to work in various Japanese government financial agencies, eventually rising to Vice-Minister of Finance. Before his brief term as mayor, he spent sixteen years as president of the Imperial Board of Auditors, which kept tabs on government spending.

A Mayor of Tokyo

Unpublished typescript

It has of late become the fashion to scrutinize the ways of mayors. In fact, they have always been much in the public eye. From Dick Whittington, thrice Lord Mayor of London Town, remembered for his cat, to John Burns of London County Council fame, from Jimmy Walker to Mayor McKee, there has been quite a variety of fashions in mayors.

Viscount Tajima, who was elected Mayor of Tokyo in 1918, will be remembered, I suppose, for his bean-husk banquet. There is in Japan a kind of cheese made from beans, an inexpensive delicacy of daily consumption. In the manufacture of this product the skins of the beans are discarded. Not thrown away, Since in Japan everything is utilized, but sold as "*Kara*" for food for rabbits or pigs. Some very poor people also use it, trying to disguise its tough tastelessness by the addition of chopped carrots or greens. The scientists say that it is highly nutritious and urge the people to use it more. You might as well tell them to eat peanut shells. Mayor Tajima tried to make it fashionable. Or rather, he tried to make economy fashionable. He gave a banquet, inviting many important personages, at which every course consisted of *kara* prepared in various ways. The guests appeared in frock coats, the mayor in his "official uniform" which consisted of his son's cast-off school uniform, patched at one elbow. That would have been enough to make the guests feel foolish at the start. Then those bean skins! They had to keep exclaiming "Kekko!!" (delicious) or "Oishi!" (very nice) as they endeavoured to look delighted over their fare, for such is Japanese custom. They could not just leave it on the plate, because that would have been an insult to their host, and the mayor's watchful eye was on them.

I can't say whether these gentlemen on their return home ordered bean skins to be added to their customary fare. The Mayor didn't stop there. He had handbills printed and distributed in the schools. Not just haphazard. Printing costs money. One was found neatly laid on every teacher's desk as he entered his classroom. And the lesson thereon the teacher was expected to teach to his pupils. One day the virtues of *kara* were extolled. Another day the low price and dietetic value of barley were set forth. Another day they were urged to add potatoes to their rice, as they were so much cheaper. Recipes for making palatable dishes of cheap foods were given.

Mayor Tajima also ran a large boarding house, where the charge was extremely low. It was his way of helping poor students. Many of the boarders were even given free accommodations.

I think that the MacFadden one cent restaurants are the sort of thing that would have delighted this Mayor of Tokyo. Does anyone rise to nominate Bernarr MacFadden for Mayor of New York?

Léonie's proposal of eccentric physical culture guru Bernarr Macfadden for the mayoralty was not as strange as it might seem; having made a fortune from a seemingly endless series of health books and a magazine empire that included *True Story, True Romances, Movie Mirror*, etc., Macfadden was the Arnold Schwarzenegger of his day, and had proposed himself as the nation's first Secretary of Health, if his friend Franklin Delano Roosevelt would create the position for him. Roosevelt refused (the position was created by his successor, Harry Truman in 1953) and the disappointed Macfadden was driven to make his own failed bid for the presidency in 1936. Perhaps he might have had better luck running for mayor of New York. Macfadden's vegetarian One Cent Restaurants were by this time a popular chain.

It is not clear where Léonie intended to send "A Mayor of Tokyo," or whether she actually did so. The typescript gives her address as 149 East 36 Street, a pleasant four-story residential building two blocks east of J.P. Morgan's mansion in the expensive Murray Hill neighborhood. In a December letter to Isamu, she gives "Hotel White, Lexington Ave. at 37th Street," just around the corner. The Hotel White, now the Shelburne, at 303 Lexington, offered rates from $3.50 a night "to those who seek the accessible residential hotel home, whether for an overnight stay in New York or longer." It is difficult to see how she would have afforded the rent in either location.

Léonie's sister Florence was continuing to live in a primitive manner in California; though she rarely wrote, Léonie had periodic updates from Catharine. On October 30, 1932, Catharine wrote that Florence had turned down an opportunity to go gold mining because she felt that she couldn't abandon her family of cats and goats. "I too feel sad not to be able to help her. Course I can see to it that the cupboard isn't bare or the coal-bin empty; but to rescue her from the rocky hillside and the lack of all conveniences is something beyond your power or mine. After all we each have to choose our own ways of living, and freedom to go our own way is the dearest thing we have." On December 20, she mentioned that "Florence ... is working hard freeing up the pens for goats, hens and self. Wish I could persuade her to have some plumbing and electric lights..."

There is no indication in Catharine's letters that Isamu made it to Tujunga to visit his aunt Florence. In the spring, around the time his Chicago exhibition opened, he had met a beautiful, married dancer, Ruth Page. Attracted to each other, they began a collaboration: Isamu stayed on in Chicago, designing costumes for Page's dance, *The Expanding Universe*, which premiered in November, and also made an abstract sculpture modeled on Page, which Buckminster Fuller cleverly suggested he call *Miss Expanding Universe*. The affair went on for nearly a year, keeping Isamu in Chicago longer than he had originally planned. But the California exhibition was a great success: on October 10th, *Time Magazine* praised it as "an exhibition of much local importance, the first California showing of a native though wandering son." Isamu exhibited fifteen of his "huge Kakemono-like drawings" made in Beijing and "about twenty of his well-known portrait heads." Absent was "Miss Expanding Universe" which the writer described as "a great white plaster shape something like

a starfish and something like a woman." Isamu had tried "not very intel-
ligibly, but with contagious enthusiasm . . . to explain . . . how much she
meant to him. "So much modern stuff is so bitter, so hopeless," he said.
"To me, at least, *Miss Expanding Universe* is full of hope." Critics who saw
the piece at New York's Reinhardt Gallery in December did not generally
share his enthusiasm, though the portrait sculptures and brush drawings
continued to garner praise. Léonie, who visited the show in mid-Decem-
ber, was herself interested mainly in the brush drawings.

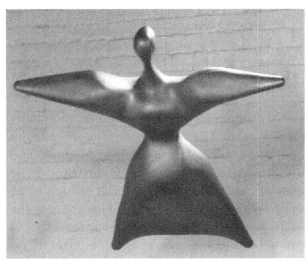

**Miss Expanding
Universe, 1932,
Isamu Noguchi
Garden Museum.
Edward Marx.**

Ailes was still dancing for Graham's company, which was gaining
fame, though it was not yet securely established. In 1932, Graham choreographed a wild *Dance of the Furies* for the grand opening of Radio City
Music Hall. "When we danced on the enormous stage, the *New Yorker*
magazine described us as looking like mice racing across the vast ex-
panse," Ailes recalled. They were cut from the show soon after the December 27 opening, but Graham made sure the dancers came to the
hall each night, ready to dance, so they could claim their much-needed
paychecks.

Léonie's letters to Catharine from 1933 are missing, but Catharine's
and Isamu's survive. On February 11, Catharine wrote that Mary Moody
had suffered a stroke and was near her end. "It is a shock to have one of
our group dying of an old-age disease." Alice Hammond, now teaching in
Los Angeles, was "having nightmares of being fired from her job." Catharine was unscathed by the March 10 Long Beach earthquake. "'Twas
really quite like being alive to enjoy one's funeral, to get all the nice mes-
sages, and people's ideas that they'd be after missin' me if I stepped off,"
she wrote Léonie on the 23rd. In June Catharine sent birthday wishes to

Léonie, who was about to turn sixty-one on the 17th. "Here's to you and to Ailes and to Paradise Alley."

Paradise Alley was a notorious East Village tenement courtyard at 11th street and Avenue A, somewhat infamous as a colony for indigent poets, writers and artists. In the 1950s, Allen Ginsberg famously wrote of the "angelheaded hipsters" who, among other things, "drank turpentine in Paradise Alley." During the depression years, Paradise Alley was the frequent site of evictions and resulting protests that were often featured in the papers. Léonie and Ailes evidently lived here while Léonie spent most of her time managing her store, occasionally assisted by a certain Mr. Wood.

To Isamu Noguchi, December 17, 1932

Hotel White, Lexington Ave. at 37th Street, New York City

My dear Isamu—

We have had a great fall of snow today, and I have wondered whether you got through to Chicago ahead of the storm. It's beautiful to look out and see the whiteness—not so bad to walk out in it, but it gets down your neck and the wind drifts in your eyes. Yesterday—or was it the day before?—I went to your exhibition. I thought the figure of a man—brush work—something like Don Quixote, very clever. Liked the draped figure—thought it was marble at first. And that small baby on the big scroll more important than a skyscraper. Am surprised you still have those two beautiful scrolls of mother and baby—they are *great* you know. Heard you had a couple of commissions. Haven't seen Fuller. Had a letter from Mrs. Lewis. Everything as usual.

Best regards to the Rumeleys, and hope you have a good time making a "Yuki-Daruma" or snowballing.

Great love,
Mother

Léonie's words of encouragement were no doubt intended to salve Isamu's wounded pride. His return to New York had not been the triumph he had expected, he was deeply in debt, and although he later remembered these exhibitions as the "most successful of all my shows," he had not gained approval for his abstract efforts; moreover, with the economic depression deepening, even portrait commissions were difficult to find. In June of 1933, Isamu departed for England, ostensibly to arrange an exhibition, but at least in part, to flee his creditors.

Ailes was also having life complications. Léonie attempted to advise her on her love life as well as her dance career in the following undated letter.

To Ailes Gilmour, [1933]

My darling child,

I had a fairly comfortable night and left Bloomington at 8 o'clock, arriving home at 12:20, only one stop for gasoline, and had to slow up for a mean rain storm. But on the whole, it was pleasant driving as there was no glare on the road to hurt my eyes. I wonder what time you got home. I fear you are a wreck today, after such a strenuous performance. I am so glad that I came over. I think you are making "strides" in your art. Some things please my personal taste, some not. "Lament" [*Lamentation*] I thought very interesting & moving. It has a good many of the same step movements as "Possessed"—I would never again use them on the same program. I think "Possessed" really a good dance—much more to it than any of the others.

"Hope" is certainly unique, very original and intriguing, but it does not appeal to my taste, though I can see its merits. The Casella numbers are really very funny and are nice for contrast. I liked "Vagabond" too—the costume is interesting. [*The Coming*]—I like the music and *some* parts of the dance. You could work it out much better. I could see that you were not very interested in it yourself. It is a number which the general public will like.

I actively dislike the Cuban number. I can't bear to have that really beautiful music treated in such a manner. I think the costume grotesque without any idea behind it, and the mask feeble. (I thought all the other masks wonderful). To that music I should like to see you do a Cuban dance of real grace and beauty (there are some) with an artistic and beautiful costume. If you must use that costume and dance, do it [to some] tawdry music. You do the Balinese dances stunningly. I think your version really much more interesting and arresting than the real thing. You give them more fire and vividness.

It was altogether a stirring concert, and I feel very proud of your work. How you are physically able to give such a long strenuous program is beyond belief. Don't see how you do it.

Naturally I am thinking a lot about the complications of your life.

One of the strangest phenomena of life is a sudden violent love affair, generally taking one absolutely unawares and "out of the blue." No one is to blame. They come and go, leaving their poor victims absolutely powerless to help themselves. All through the ages this has occurred and no solution has ever been found. If people are free to marry and do so, this violent passion subsides, usually in a year or so, and perhaps the lovers find they have absolutely nothing in common. In pain and hampered in every way, disaster is certain.

If they cannot marry and are separated, they idealize each other, and are terribly unhappy apart—and this may last several years, though if either person is doing creative work, or has some interesting outlet for emotion, the reentry is much quicker—but the one certain thing is that *people get over it.* The real problem is to find the best mode of conduct when the need is greatest. It is *very* difficult to keep one's balance and good judgement and deliberately decide what is best to be done, and then do it. To divorce one husband and then marry another seldom works. In a few years you are with no. 2, just where you stood with no. 1. Sometimes I think the Russian and French way is better: either partner to just go on a vacation and live with their beloved and get it out of their systems. It is surprising how the gratification of sex—opens the eyes of lovers—even the Anglo-Saxon world approves of this for men—and women do this more and more—being *very* discreet about it. I see why artists do not marry, as the ties of marriage do hamper any career, and I am convinced that the possessiveness of marriage is what is bringing about so many divorces today.

You do not realize how dependent you are upon physical comfort, [unreadable], good food, comfortable and charming surroundings, you think you would not feel the loss of all these things, but you would. Cheap clothes, restaurant food, cheap ugly rooms, no place to keep your costumes, work hard to get and badly paid, these things can wreck a life, no matter how much love there is back of it all. And you are not physically strong—it really frightens me to death to think of my beautiful little girl being brought bang up against all the ugly, sordid conditions of life.

Then too, one idealizes the beloved beyond all semblance of fact, and when disappointment and disillusion come, life is too terrible. One hardly has the strength to go on. I know only too well. What an ecstasy of joy being in love brings, but it is as unstable and evanescent as the froth on champagne.

I see I am growing eloquent—forgive me, my darling. I wish I could help you, but no one can—you have to work it out for yourself. Well, remember that whatever you do, or do not do, you will always have a devoted and loving *friend* in your mother.

P.S. So tell me freely your plans and ideas. I do not censure or blame.

I only hope for some reasonable solution and I feel terribly sorry for you, and also I am,

[Signature omitted]

From Isamu Noguchi, June 30, 1933

Dear Mother,

This is my 5th day in London—it takes time for me to get adjusted to any place and London is especially difficult—however, I seem so far well off, established in this Hotel called the Eiffel tower Restaurant 1 Percy St. London W.1. with a studio up above. So please write me here—write me how things are—hot and stifling I am afraid, not altogether uninteresting I hope—the weather in any case could not be worse than here.

Lots of love
Your loving son
Isamu

From Isamu Noguchi, July 9, 1933

Dear Mother,

I am sad to hear of Ailes's trouble—however I hope by now all is well and that she has been able to have a small vacation—give her my love, tell her have courage.

Things are still very unsettled for me over here—next week I must go over to Paris to see how the stone-cutting progresses—upon my return here I think to take a studio for a month—should I make sufficient contact to be able to afford it I will stay—otherwise I will then return to the states.

London is not easy to get used to—it is expensive and inconvenient—yet undoubtedly there are a surplus of interesting people here once one can reach them.

This is the end of a dull Sunday. Tomorrow again starts me on my wild career.

I am as always full of expectations.

My lots of love
Dear mother
Isamu

From Isamu Noguchi, July 27, 1933

Dear Mother,

I have just got back from Paris to find your letter—of course I am sorry to be such a forever bad letter writer—but then I find myself in such a turmoil doing this and that and just now busy looking for a place to work in like a dog making a bed for himself. I am determined to settel [*sic*] in a studio by the end of the week—to work very hard for at least a month or two.

I'm very happy to hear Ailes finally got away to the country—quiet and green things are very necessary surely—I am made aware so the more I hear noises unfamiliar as they are here—houses that appear ugly to me in this section of London—with the cars all going the wrong direction. So I do hope Ailes is rested—to once more enjoy life—or am I wrong in guessing her main trouble as fatigue?

A delicious breeze blows in my window. But as I said I detest this hotel and will move into a studio in a day or so—then I will send you an adress [*sic*] where I trust you will write many many letters.

I will write a real letter the moment I am settled.

My best love

Mother

Isamu.

Léonie remained in New York City tending her shop for most of the summer. Ailes, after recovering from an illness, had spent some pleasant weeks in Woods Hole, a village at the tip of Cape Cod where ferries departed for Martha's Vineyard. In August, she returned to New York to mind the store while Léonie visited the same town.

Bell tower, St. Joseph's Rectory, Woods Hole, September 2012.
Edward Marx.

Mary Garden, St. Joseph's Rectory, Woods Hole. *Edward Marx.*

Vinol M.S. Hannell's concrete *Virgin***, St. Joseph's Rectory.** *Edward Marx.*

To Isamu Noguchi, August 9, 1933

Wood's Hole, Mass.

My dear Isamu,

I am sitting on the grass in the garden of a beautiful little bell-tower—a shrine to St. Joseph. Before me the smooth water of Eel Pond, with little boats at anchor. Beside me a charming and naive Madonna sculptured in stone emerges from a clump of flowers yellow and white, with one lovely big blue Japanese morning glory. I hear the voices of the people singing in the church across the street. I am very fond of church services from the outside. In the tiny room at the foot of the tower are some fine bas reliefs in bronze—very good—I wonder who is the artist,—and a table of books of poetry and philosophy, among them Nitobe's Bushido. No door whatever, so I take it the elements do not enter the stone doorway. I hope you may be loitering in some such pleasant spot in England. This is the place where Ailes spent a few weeks, then returned to New York to take my place there while I came away. Catherine Mitchell sent $20 to pay Ailes doctors bill, but Ailes insisted on my using it to take a needed holiday. I had been in the city all summer, and got knocked up—it was 100° in the shade the day I came away. Ailes looks better at last—still has to syringe her ear and gargle her throat—her hearing has been tested and is unimpaired—she might have been deaf as a result of all this. Mrs. Wood is in the country running a boarding house, so our original plans could not be carried out. Mr. Wood came to relieve me a little, but practically I was at the store most of the time—much cooler anyway than Paradise Alley. How is the sculpture coming on? I imagine Mrs. Brokaw will look nice in marble. And have you been able to arrange an exhibition in London? I do wish you might have the "Lady in a Garden" in marble.

Don't forget to go to the north coast of Ireland if you have time, and to visit Coaleraine, the town of my father's home. It is necessary to get away from work and the usual routine sometimes, for your soul's good. I like to be all alone, as I am here. Have an attic room, and get my food. Mostly live on berries and fish, like the Cape Cod Indians who formerly habited hereabout. Have not quite decided whether to go home Tuesday, when my week is up, or to stay a little longer.

The swimming here is fine—quiet salt water of a pleasant temperature—I have been in every day for a short swim, then bask in the sun—rather bad sunburn, but guess the next dip will relieve it. I was not made for city life, nor Ailes either, I fancy. Write soon, if you receive this before you start, and don't be in a hurry to get back to New York.

Your very loving mother

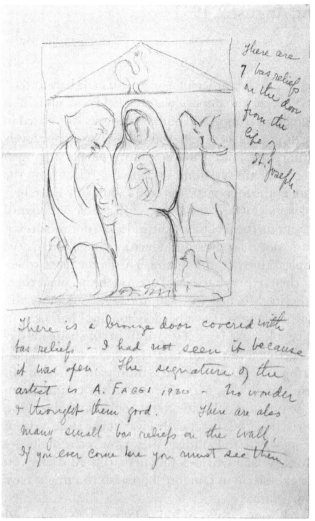

There are 7 bas reliefs on the door from the life of St. Joseph.

There is a bronze door covered with bas reliefs - I had not seen it because it was open. The signature of the artist is A. FAGGI 1930 - No wonder I thought them good. There are also many small bas reliefs on the wall. If you ever come here you must see them

Léonie's sketch of the middle left panel. *Isamu Noguchi Foundation.*

When Léonie returned to the Garden of Our Lady at St. Joseph's Rectory, she discovered that the tiny room at the foot of the tower did have doors, with bas reliefs as well, and that the artist whose work had so impressed her was none other than Alfeo Faggi, the Italian-American artist whose head of Yone Noguchi adorned the *Selected Poems of Yone Noguchi.* "No wonder I thought them good," she wrote, sketching one of the panels to send to Isamu.

Alfeo Faggi's *Life of St. Joseph,* **St. Joseph's Rectory.** *Edward Marx.*

Aside from the sunburn, Léonie made no reference to any health problems, so there was certainly no reason for Isamu to be concerned about Léonie's health. His first portrait in marble, of New York editor and playwright Clare Boothe Brokaw (later Clare Boothe Luce) had been completed and shipped.

From Isamu Noguchi, August 9, 1933

Dear Mother

Today finally, I am moving into a studio—the address Oak Cottage Studio Chiswick Mall London. Have taken it for 2 months so I will not get back to America until October.

Just received word from Paris that a marble head of mine has been shipped to you (really sent inadvertently as I had asked that it be not sent for yet a month).

So please explain to the customs people that it is the work of an American—should there be too much difficulty in getting it through I suggest that you let them hold it in a bonded warehouse until my return. In any case be careful about how they handle it as it is marble.

Chiswick Mall is very beautiful—by the river and outside of London, the home of Keats and William Morris. The river rises and floods the streets.

Now I am off to move in—
All my love mother
Isamu

From Isamu Noguchi, August 17, 1933

Dearest Mother,

I am so glad that you have been able to have some time out in the country—how I wish you could spend all the time in such a beautiful spot as you describe.

I have had a great deal of difficulty getting to work over here—but finally I am at it in this studio the adress of which I believe I gave you in my last letter "Oak Cottage Studio" Chiswick Mall London. Its [*sic*] a transformed barn good light but no heating or lighting—so I do not expect to remain here after the end of September.

Still I have made no money all Londoners being away in the Country—but I do hope to get something done within say a month.

Here it is usually cold, and I can imagine how frightful it must become when the fog settles in the winter time—you say it has been so hot in New York.

I am thankful that Ailes is better—it must have been terrible.

Surely now things will be getting better.

My plans are simply to bring something good home with me.

Your loving son
Isamu

Isamu began to worry when another two or three weeks had passed and there was no word from his mother in New York.

From Isamu Noguchi, September 3, [1933]

Dear Mother,

It's a very long time since I last heard from you—so please write quickly.

Just now (7 p.m.) I have just stopped working—it is Sunday, a beautiful day, and the Church bells are ringing—that is the only noise, otherwise utter quiet here by the river. I have never had such relaxation in a long long time.

All my thoughts and energies and attention are just now most taken up by this statue which I hope to have finished for delivery in New York next month.

I feel out of touch with actuality here—sometimes I get so very lonesome for you for Ailes and New York—indeed I begin to love N.Y. for what it is, what it contains. London is still a complete stranger to me.

Please write soon

Lots of love

Isamu

Enclose $10

On October 10, Catharine wrote thanking Léonie for a gift of Franciscan sandals. Florence had ridden down with a neighbor and was "studying hard on locations to which to remove herself and the four-footers." Their old classmate, Kitty Dame, who had suffered from tuberculosis for many years, had died suddenly while convalescing after a complicated operation. "Ah well, we all want to go suddenly," Catharine wrote, "and have our friends go so, but not yet. This year has taken heavy toll of mine."

Isamu, who had relocated to West Kensington, wrote in November from Oxford where he was staying with Sir Michael Sadler, Master of University College, a prominent educationist who had been one of Britain's early promoters of modernist art.

Evidently Isamu had heard from Léonie at this point, for he does not repeat his earlier concerns about her silence.

From Isamu Noguchi, November 4, 1933

Dear Mother,

Please forgive my protracted silence, which was due to my being distracted as to what I was to do—there was every sort of a difficulty—the necessity of moving into town—looking for a commision [*sic*] etc.—and I did not know what in the world to decide—how long to stay.

Finally there is a breathing space (having gotten over a terrific cold)—I have decided to take the Bremen on the 29th or the Europa sailing on the 8th December.

I will bring with me a statue and a stack of drawings—let's hope that they may find a market. I imagine things over there are getting very bad with the prices of things rising. I am almost tempted to think that should I be able to earn money over here it might be wiser to remain yet awhile—I wonder.

In any case I will be able to send you a check within a week—sold some drawings.

I do hope things are not too hard—

Now I have a studio temporarily until the 16th at 24 Ryder St. then I must find another place. In the meantime please adress [*sic*] all mail to c/o Am. Ex. Co. Haymarket.

All my love from
Your loving son Isamu

From Isamu Noguchi, November 13, [1933]

Dearest Mother,
Here is a draft for $102.40.

Myself will in all probability arrive on the Bremen sailing here the 29th.

The marble head of which I wrote you long ago was only sent about 4 weeks ago so you should now have notice of it. Suggest that you ask them to keep it in bond pending my arrival.

All my love to you and Ailes.
Isamu

From Isamu Noguchi, November 17, [1933]

The Master's Lodgings, University College · Oxford

Dear Mother,
My birthday evening, and I am visiting here Sir Michael Sadler for the night, a thing so appropriate. He has a remarkable collection and we spent the afternoon looking at his paintings and sculptures.

It seems now that the bronze founder can not possibly finish that which I have given him before the end of the month and I am afraid I will miss the boat for the 29th—so do not expect me on that but rather on the Europe sailing from here on the 8th December, should get me into N.Y. by the 14th and we will have a grand reunion.

I have again moved. This time to 10 Girdlers Rd W. 14. I occupy 2 rooms until Thursday when I will take over the studio until I leave.

Please see that the marble head is kept for me in bond—if they will not do that, of course, take it out. I will want it upon arrival.

Do keep on the lookout for a studio—altho I may find it convenient to move to some other city on account of my many creditors in N.Y.—or else it might be best that I went into bankruptcy—but we will talk about that later.

I like England away from London.
Love to Ailes
My much love
Isamu

Isamu wrote Léonie a note on November 28 to make sure she had received the check. He now thought he would leave on December 17 rather than the 8th but would "absolutely be there for Xmas"; he was "now working with wood and having a glorious time of it." The following day he changed his mind again; he would take the earlier ship:

From Isamu Noguchi, November 29, [1933]

Dear Mother,
I think I made a mistake in sending you that note yesterday—I think after all to leave on the 8th.

Why have I not heard from you for so long—of course I can not expect any reply to complaints before I leave so I will simply complain—and you will say the same of me.

One has so many things to adjust oneself to in this best of worlds!
Best love to Ailes
Your loving son
Isamu

At some point in late 1932 or 1933, Léonie began to read her old letters in an effort to start on "the book." Struck by Stoddard's September 12, 1906 letter predicting that her son was "to be like no other Baby Boy in all the world" and exhorting her to keep "one of those kid chronicles in which all the quaint and clever things he says or does are recorded," she determined to make a belated attempt at writing "The Kid Chronicle That Was Not Written." She began by typing Stoddard's letter, and then began her explanation:

The Kid Chronicle That Was Not Written

Unpublished typescript.

Charles Warren Stoddard had come to see me in New York a few years before, just once, brought by that young Japanese poet, Yone Noguchi to one of those little suppers which I and my friend Catherine Bunnell, sometimes gave in our tiny apartment on Washington Heights. One of us always played the role of cook, the other was hostess, turn and turn about. That day I was cook, and when, flustered and hot from wrestling in the kitchen (Catherine played that role better than I) I came at last to sit down at the table, Mr. Stoddard seemed to waft away all those kitchen fidgets while he kept us entertained with his suave wit, and vastly amused by the naive self-consciousness with which he enjoyed our appreciation, his fat rosy head hung on one side like a foolish baby's.

Evidently Mr. Stoddard made more of an impression on me than I on him, perhaps he just thought of me as "the cook" of a very simple home-made sort of supper he once took with some of Yone's friends in horrid New York. For in the first letter I ever had from him he wonders whether we met in New York.

No, Mr. Stoddard, I didn't write that kid chronicle recording the "quaint and clever" sayings and doings of my child. He was not given to that kind of thing, and I should not have encouraged him in it if he had been. And I never liked chronicles. The things worth keeping seem not to be in them. If one could capture the bright winged moment that like a humming bird flits over the garden and is gone, or net the shy anemones that bloom in the deeps of the heart and cannot be brought out into the sun! The real things are so far from speech.

Stoddard wasn't the only one to pester me for chronicles, however. I evaded them all. And now the Boy, grown to a man, and not unknown to fame, commands me to write of our early days in California and Japan, the days before he could remember.

Perhaps, my son, you think your mother has the kind of memory that is like a well-ordered storehouse from which one can fetch out things at a moment's notice, or at the very least like an attic, where one can rummage and pull out odds and ends helter skelter. No such thing. My memory is like a treacherous sea, where things are so covered with sand they are completely lost. Sometimes, it's true, the tide ebbs, and behold clearly revealed are the long lost days, bright and untarnished. I feel sure they are all there—somewhere—oh very safe. Not arranged chronologically. All quite equal in value and without any time sequence whatever. That is because for me time is something I do not understand. Forward and backward is all the same. The yesterdays play at hide and seek with today and all the tomorrows.

Now I am setting myself to a hard task. Sorting out old letters, and from their dates trying to put the yesterdays in their places. Alas, many of those letters are undated. Your father rarely dated his letters (I have to decipher the postmarks on the envelopes, what if the Japanese mark is the only one left?). You, my son, never do so. Anyway, it's a scheme, putting old letters together to make a pattern, not to mention saving a good deal of brain fag by simply using other people's phrases. And since Charles Warren Stoddard is a writer of fine quality, and was ready, in the goodness of his heart, to sponsor this record, as he was to stand godfather to my child, I'll start this with his first letter to me, written when the boy was a little over a year old.

Léonie ended by quoting Stoddard's letter of March 12, 1906 inquiring whether she had any thought of joining Yone in Japan. The two letters gave the piece a nice symmetry, and one wishes she had continued the contemplated account "of our early days in California and Japan." But the story stops after the letter, perhaps simply interrupted, perhaps bogged down by Léonie uncertainties. She had made a start. But she could go no farther.

In December, Léonie came down with a bad case of pneumonia, serious enough to send her to Bellevue Hospital. Located at the end of East 26th Street, overlooking the river, Bellevue, founded in 1736, was, and remains, the oldest public hospital in the United States. Its medical standards were adequate, the equivalent of other large city hospitals. But the open admission policy meant crowded wards, poor food, and a shortage of personnel. During busy periods, shortage of space might mean a sagging cot in a hallway or out on a balcony. And at Bellevue, the Great Depression was one long busy period. "Were ever the sick and suffering packed in more wretchedly anywhere, except in military hospitals after a great battle?" wondered one contemporary visitor. But the grim accommodations were at least egalitarian: the occasional wealthy patients, and the more numerous middle-class ones, received the same accommodations as the poor.

When Isamu returned to New York on December 17, Léonie had been hospitalized for nearly a week. She had been in poor health for some time, suffering from heart trouble, exacerbated by hardening of the arteries. As Christmas approached and passed, her condition remained poor. On New Year's Eve, she suffered a heart attack, and died at 6:30 in the evening. It was the last night of the worst year of the Great Depression. The grim fairy of poverty that had presided over her birth had followed her to the end.

Little is known about Léonie's funeral. No doubt it was no grand affair. Her mother, Albiana, had been buried in Aaron Smith's spacious plot in the sprawling Cypress Hills Cemetery in Brooklyn. Léonie was interred beside her. The grave "is no longer possible to find," Masayo Duus writes. "It may lie beneath one of the weathered headstones scattered on the family plot, whose inscriptions have been worn away." Instead of the "splendid tooniform" he had planned at the age of eight, "Isamu placed in the grave an unglazed ceramic piece that he made in Kyoto to keep her from being lonely."

Among Ailes Gilmour's papers was a letter dated January 17, 1934 from Léonie's often mentioned college classmate, Alice Hammond, expressing her sorrow at the loss. Léonie, she wrote, had been a big part of college memorias. In recent years, she wrote, it had been an annual treat to see Léonie in New Haven at the Book and Quill, exhibiting her prints and jewels.

Amid the deepening depression, New York artists had been offered a chance of relief that winter by the announcement of the Public Works of Art Project (PWAP), which promised to put 2,500 idle artists to work on murals and other forms of public art. As Isamu considered how he might respond to this unprecedented outpouring of governmental goodwill, thoughts of his mother and his childhood must have been on his mind. Though his ideas drew on deep sources, they were not at first very coherent. His first proposal was an abstract monument to Benjamin Franklin. Seeing a large Ben Franklin portrait hanging in the Bar Harbor library, Léonie had commented that "he must be the fashion now." She might have been thinking of the famously frugal and industrious Franklin as an appropriate model for an age of poverty. Yet Franklin was also the original American modernist. Isamu thought his monument might go nicely in front of the Franklin Institute in Philadelphia. The PWAP officials asked Isamu to clarify his proposal, by which time his idea had changed to an enormous pyramid of earth to be entitled *Monument to the American Plow*, in some sense inspired by Edward Rumely, whose family fortune came from tractors. The idea now floating around in this head was "sculpture made from earth." It did not go over well with PWAP administrators, who were mainly interested in representational art, and in the case of sculpture, works of "a pure sculptural character," but somehow he was put on the PWAP payroll. In February 1934, he wrote again explaining he had "plans for musical and illuminated weather vanes" to be placed on public buildings, but this went nowhere, and in the spring he was dropped from the payroll, inspiring him to write to the PWAP in disgust that "one might as well abandon the expectation of enthusiastic leadership from those imbued with timid hope." He was not quite ready to give up the chase, however, and produced a set of drawings for an earth sculpture for children entitled *Play Mountain*. With the help of Murdock Pemberton, an art critic at *The New Yorker* whose head he had sculpted, Isamu arranged a meeting with New York Parks Commissioner Robert Moses, who "just laughed his head off and threw us out more or less."

Over the following decades Isamu gradually managed to realize various aspects of his "earth sculpture" conception, but it was only toward the end of his life that Play Mountain was realized in a larger but somewhat simplified form, in Sapporo's Moerenuma Park. In this 400 acre converted landfill, Isamu finally was finally given a place to dig, though he was able to make only one visit to the site in 1988, the last year of his life. The park was completed in 2005 and has been a great success.

Descending Play Mountain, Moerenuma Park, August 2010. *Katsuko Marx.*

Matsui ends the Japanese version of her film with a scene of children playing in Moerenuma Park, and the voice of Isamu saying (as Isamu had once said in an interview): "I am the son of my mother's imagination."

Miscellaneous Writings

George Meredith—A Study

National Magazine, December 1905

"I fear yet this iron yoke of outward conformity hath left a slavish print upon our necks; the ghost of a linen decency yet haunts us." Milton: "Essay on Divorce."

"Whoso would be a man must be a nonconformist." Emerson.

The nineteenth century has been called the age of individualism. The numberless new sects that are springing up, the many "isms" of the day that are raising their rebellious standards against the existing order of things and penetrating with their revolutionary doctrines into all parts of the social structure, are but expressions of the spirit of nonconformity. Custom no longer means sanction. If the custom is not good, let us make a better one, say the revolutionists of today. Away with dead forms, away with hypocrisy and cant. "Reality" as opposed to "nominality" is the order of the day. And shall we be surprised that the first result of the search for reality has been, in literature, realism, with all that the word has come to imply of shameless inquisitiveness, irreverent familiarity, garish vulgarity placarded across a vast dead wall of materialism? "Peruse your realists"—writes George Meredith—"really your castigators for not having yet embraced philosophy," i. e., the study of the laws of Nature in her manifold aspects. Nature is the proper study of philosophy, the living plant with the sap coursing through it, not the botanical specimen. "As she grows in the flesh when discreetly tended, Nature is unimpeachable, flower-like, yet not too decoratively a flower; you must have her with the stem, the thorns, the roots and the fat bedding of roses."

Meredith is a nonconformist, and he stands out boldly as the opponent of conventionalism. There is something Carlyle-like in the independent ring of many of his phrases. He hates sham. He is continually crusading against the false sense of delicacy that dares not look upon Nature for fear of being shocked, that would rather suffer untold corruption than soil its hands in the attempt to get rid of corruption. "Imagine the celestial refreshment of having a real decency in the place of sham," he cries. Nature, great all-embracing Nature, "mother of mighty harmonies"—how often and how loudly he proclaims his delight in her. He would fashion his books out of such stuff as Nature uses, molding it in her own right queenly manner. And indeed, in the scope and breadth of his treatment as well as in the boldness and richness of his language there is felt not merely the original and brilliant writer, but the really broad, much-embracing mind. One is sure not to find life painted in a monotone by him, sure that he will try to catch many of the colors of this "dome of many-colored glass." He realizes the complexity of our human nature, containing as it does much of the earthly as well as the divine. A close and subtle analysis of psychological phenomena, tracking actions to their motives with unerring instinct, tracing the wayward involutions of thought with unwearied patience,—that is the method of his work. "The brain stuff of fiction is internal history," he writes. But in his case a taste for psychological analysis does not, as with so many writers, mean that the public are to have thrust upon them the spectacle of the dissection of the writer's personality—a species of exercise leading fatally around to morbidness on the part of the writer and weariness on that of the reader.

Perhaps it is Meredith's humor that saves him from that. Humor with its quick sense of the ridiculous laughs at the pompous strut of egoism. Humor, the broad, Shakespearian humor, the "laughter of the gods" as Meredith calls it, keeps things in their true proportion, gives us a perspective as it were by drawing us back out of the gigantic shadow of the little personality.

Humor, moreover, tempers satire, which too often arises from bitterness of spirit and is always personal in tone. In only one of Meredith's novels, "The Egoist," have I found that sort of relentless satire which pursues its prey to the death, tearing off its covering shred by shred and then tossing it contemptuously aside. The treatment is so cruel here that, in spite of its being no more than the hero's just deserts, we are inclined to pity him. True, egoism, the fault chastised, is one that our human nature is most subject to, and perhaps nothing but the most drastic measures can ever eradicate it.

But usually Meredith is kindly in tone. Though he laughs at sentimentality—"pinnacle-flame of sensualism" he calls it—and again, "Sentimentalists fiddle harmonics on the string of sensualism" he has a deep reverence for real feeling. Humor and pathos come closely together. The deep well-spring of feeling bubbles in laughter and overflows in tears. It is the power of emotion that distinguishes rich from poor natures. Even the tropical redundancy of the foliage of passion gives proof of the richness of the soil underneath. What monastic ascetic is that who would teach us to stamp out passion as a thing unholy? The love scenes of Meredith vibrate with passion. Emilia writes to her lover: "Come on a swift horse. The thought of you galloping to me goes through me like a flame that hums." O, the romantic tenderness of that boy and girl love in "Richard Feveril," of the fresh morning fruit of love with the dew still on it. "The young who avoid that region" (of Romance), says Meredith, "escape the title of fool at the cost of a celestial crown."

With his conception of Nature as living, throbbing and palpitating beneath the touch, with his diligence in the study of her and his perennial spring of humor, George Meredith has created for us in his novels a series of flesh and blood men and women rivalled by no other living writer. And it is no slight praise to say that his women are as good as his men, if not better.

For there are few among our great novelists who have given us any adequate conception whatever of women, or taken the least trouble to distinguish the particular from the type. George Eliot has indeed given us good, all-around women. Charlotte Bronte's women are quite wonderful, but—aren't they simply lyrical embodiments of her own passionate nature? Thackeray and even more especially Dickens are wofully lacking in good women characters. Meredith has the honor of being preeminent in his treatment of women: indeed he has been called the "ultra feminine Mr. Meredith." He has a power that is really marvelous of throwing himself into women's feelings and analyzing their motives of action. He makes his women think, too. "The motive life with women must be in the head equally with men." His women one feels all along are essentially feminine, not men masquerading as women. The subtle shades of feminine character are admirably brought out. He patiently sets to work to analyze the so-called caprices and moods of women, due, according to him, to women's more delicate nervous susceptibility to outside influences, to their quicker habit of thought, rather than to mere volatility of character, as men often erroneously suppose.

It would be interesting to make a special study of his women. One might find a list of heroines that would compare with Shakespeare's. Emilia, with her passionate intensity of feeling, her childlike simplicity and "straightforwardness of soul" (*droiture d'ame*) matches Juliet, Shakespeare's "loveliest girl figure." And Clara Middleton in "The Egoist" might be compared with Rosalind. There is an exquisite reserve in the treatment of Clara Middleton—of the elusive lights and half lights of her character. The lighter touches too are good. "She had the look of the nymph that has gazed too long on the faun and has unwittingly copied his lurking lip and long, sliding eye." Of Emilia he says: "Her face was like the sunset across a rose garden, with the wings of an eagle poised outspread in flight."

Diana Warwick is perhaps the greatest of his women creations, surely a favorite with him. She is certainly a glorious type of womanhood, with her superabundant vitality, her fresh, strong intellect, her delightful wit and humor and the general warmth of tone of her whole nature. Meredith has here attempted the difficult task of creating a witty and clever woman who really says witty and brilliant things—and he has succeeded. The dialogue is splendid. The racy Irish wit, the overflowing humor, steeped in emotion, the nervous concentration and vividness of language are sustained throughout. Among less admirable women but admirably treated may be mentioned the Countess in "Evan Harrington," a sort of second Becky Sharp, though not really wicked—simply a very clever intriguer. What a cleverly arranged thing that book ("Evan Harrington") is, by the way, from the mere point of view of technique. As a general thing, Meredith's technique is good. The stories are well arranged as to plot, there is sufficient incident to make them interesting from that point of view alone, and his management of plot and incident as a means of bringing out character is splendid. "Evan Harrington," as I have said, is particularly clever. The book is full of incidents. The plot centers in the attempts of the Countess to conceal her origin—she is a tailor's daughter who has married a Spanish nobleman and to act the grand lady. We laugh at her languid affectation of aristocratic manners, her assumed foreign accent, her choice vocabulary culled from the longest words in "Johnson's Dictionary." We are forced to admire her talent for intrigue, the indefatigable energy with which she pushes her plans, the way in which she rises to every occasion and manages to extricate herself from the most hopeless entanglement of circumstances. There is not so much philosophizing in this book as in most of the others, and very little description. The characters are brought out chiefly by incidents and in the conversation.

In the matter of style Meredith has often been criticised, with some degree of justice, as being too metaphorical, too extravagant, too far removed from the ordinary usage of language. It is claimed that in the attempt to be original he has often become unintelligible. There is no doubt that in his earlier works—take for example "Richard Feveril" he is much simpler than in his later works, of which "One of Our Conquerors" is a very good example. The question is whether he gains or loses by the departure from simplicity. Meredith defends himself by saying that fiction does not "demand a smooth surface, —" that "any mediaeval phantasy of clothing" suits it as well as classical robes. If simplicity is synonymous with the commonplace, with sameness, we should rejoice that one has come to lift us out of the dead level of monotony—even though it be on a winged steed whose swift flight into the dizzy regions of poetry inspires terror and a swooning of the senses in the clinging wretch. "The poet knows that he speaks adequately then only when he speaks somewhat wildly, or 'with the flower of the mind,'" says Emerson. So long as it is a real Pegasus, not a prodded hack. The new-coined word or metaphor must have the spontaneity of inspiration, and it must be true. Meredith's language is no doubt sometimes strained and affected. It must indeed be difficult to keep up that nervous tension of high imagination. But on the whole his language is spontaneous, is brilliant with that richness of imagination which, like a prism, breaks up the central thought into a rainbow of many colors. It adds vividness to have things so presented to us. Facts may be stated baldly. But the idea, the philosophy, the poetry of the fact, is more elusive. He circles round and round it in similes and metaphors, gradually closing in on it

The change from the comparatively diffuse style of the earlier works to the condensed, highly metaphorical style of the later work is accompanied by a corresponding change in the thought. Emotions and incidents give place largely to ideas. "One of Our Conquerors" is a sort of running commentary in images and symbols on the story, which is very simple. The style becomes top-heavy—I mean over-weighted with thought. Too little attention is paid to lucidity. I should say that "Diana of the Crossways" combines the advantages of the early and the later work. The language is adequate to the ideas.

Since Meredith always lays such stress upon ideas, it may be well briefly to touch upon some of his own ideas in concluding this study of him. As I have said above, he is a nonconformist in all things. In politics he is with that small but steadily increasing minority who are not satisfied with the present social order and who would take radical measures for its remodeling. If not a socialist, I should say that he approaches socialism very sympathetically.

He stands out, too, with Ibsen and Tolstoi and many other thinking men as an earnest student of the problems that beset us in this present day with regard to the relations between men and women. He has thrown down his gauntlet as the champion of modern woman. And that not in any sentimental way. He does not tell woman that she is the cause of most of the progress that has been made in the world, that she has a peculiarly exalted moral nature, that her entrance into public life will introduce a high standard in politics. He recognizes woman as weak, as degraded by being prevented the use of her functions, and he bids her arise and throw off her chains. She must fight her own battles, he tells her. Does she wish men to admit her equality with themselves? Let her prove it. A very healthy doctrine and much better for women than that of the sentimentalists. He helps women by showing his faith in them, his belief in their ability to fight their own battles and by showing them how to do it. He does not minimize the difficulties that surround them.

He is perhaps chiefly intent in solving the problems of women in connection with, marriage. Man's jealousy and tyranny are constantly the subject of his attack. "Men may have rounded Seraglio Point; they have not yet doubled Cape Turk." In his very earliest works we see traces of his interest in women's problems, which come to absorb him more and more. "Diana of the Crossways" is entirely the story of a brave woman struggling against the world—not that she has not to struggle against her own nature too, for that matter. "She is by no means of the order of those ninny young women who realize the popular conception of the purely innocent." "I thank Heaven I am at war with myself," exclaims Diana.

In "One of Our Conquerors" we have the story of a woman who has taken the "leap" out of society by leaving her husband to live with another man. The story is told with such sympathy, her life seems so to justify her course, that one does not condemn her. She, however, never seems to get away from the haunting sense of guilt. Her one grand impulse of daring spent, she retreats into the innate timidity that has ever marked her gentle and sensitive nature. How like a woman!

In one of Meredith's later books, "Lord Ormont and His Aminta," (a very dull book, by the way, quite lacking in Meredith's usual fire) the story is even simpler. Lord Ormont, a man of sixty, marries a girl of twenty. She finds him uncongenial—and certainly his treatment of her is wholly indefensible—though he is not a bad man—and meeting with a young man who had loved her before her marriage, she runs away with him. No regrets or doubts as to the justification of their course ever assail the young couple, who live happily ever after. It is to be supposed Mr. Meredith has said his final word on the subject. It is the same solution that many other modern writers have hit upon. Whether this simple method of cutting the knot, if universally accepted, would be of advantage to the community at large, is an open question. In any case it is to be remembered, as Meredith says elsewhere, that conventions protect the weak, and that women are at present the weaker half of humanity—aye, and in the scale of woman's weakness put the children, such soft and tender things! Yet not more helpless than even the strongest of women may be in the hours when she walks unabashed up to the grim Death to snatch from his hands a new life for this world: in that hour, let it be remembered, woman and child are both utterly dependent upon the caprice of man; and the Mighty Convention of Marriage.

The Ways of Mirabel and Dousabel

National Magazine, October 1906

There's no doubt Mirabel and Dousabel are the two darlingest chickabiddies that ever delighted the heart of a fond mamma. Such zest in life; such untiring activity; such fertile invention; such endless resources. A bit troublesome at times? Bound to be naughty? Behold Mirabel's anxious little face, her quivering underlip holding back a sob. Behold Dousabel's eyes of heavenly blue upturned in angelic innocence. Then start to scold if you can. Alas, your harsh words are met by such tenderly reproachful glances that your heart fails. Leastways, Mamma's scoldings generally turn straightway to kisses and hugs, and then the gayest sunbeams sparkle where a storm was threatening.

Mamma likes to take a nap once in a while. That's the time for Mirabel and Dousabel to pace stealthily about her, wondering in subdued whispers whether "Mummy is really asleep, or only makin' b'lieve." A gentle snore from Mamma settles the question in their minds. They venture to cast aside some of their restraint. They crawl over her to investigate the insides of her ears, her nostrils, even her eyes, gently prying them apart to see "how Mummy's eyes look when Mummy is asleep." They approach her mouth with some trepidation, for Mamma is liable to play the wolf in "Little Red Riding Hood," and opening and snapping her mouth, suddenly exclaim: "All the better to eat you with, my dears!" What exciting fun.

Mamma can always get a good nap on Sunday afternoon, because those two young ones are out walking with Papa. Papa offers other diversions. What delight to sit, one on each shoulder, and survey the country from their tottering eminence. But pretty soon, alas, Dousabel starts to making faces at Mirabel, or Mirabel takes more than her share of Papa's head in her clinging embrace, and presto—a sudden scuffle knocks Papa's hat off, and then why that treat is over, and two very meek little girls must trudge one on each side of Papa—no dodging back and front, if you please!

Mirabel has lovely golden curls which Mamma curls over her finger every morning, and is often called an "angel-child." Say the name Mirabel over slowly, with a sweet smile and upward glance at the end, and perhaps you'll realize Mirabel's winning powers. Dousabel wears her short, brown hair in a top-curl, like a boy; has a dainty, turned-up little nose and a generally "pugnacious" expression, to quote one of Papa's happy phrases.

Once they had their picture taken, hand in hand, Mirabel intent on keeping her curls in place, Dousabel in for the fun of the thing. A facetious young man labelled it "The Little Mother and the *Enfant Terrible*." Mirabel liked the name "little mother"—she was awfully fond of babies—and Dousabel quite enjoyed the idea of being a "terrible infant" —wrinkling up her little nose wickedly. It is pleasant that people like to act different parts in the comedy of life. How dreadful, if everyone should want to be a star or an angel-child.

One morning—here my story begins—Dousabel waking up suddenly, turned and found Mirabel still in a deep slumber. Dousabel propped herself on one elbow, brought her face close to Mirabel's, and gazed steadily and intently. Mirabel stirred uneasily under the scrutiny, and finally opened her eyes wide. Dousabel hopped up in glee, seized a pillow and hurled it at Mirabel. Mirabel batted it back with her two little fists. Dousabel pranced on the bed with provoking airishness, singing out: "Do-yer-want-ter-have-a-fight, Missouri, Missouri?" In the scuffle that ensued, Dousabel was thrown down, Mirabel on top of her, and a loud howl brought Mamma to the scene of battle.

Dousabel lay on her back like a beetle, uttering tuneful variations of her original howl. "What's the matter, Dousabel?" "Mirabel hurled me," Dousabel interrupted her melody long enough to say. "Naughty Mirabel. Where did ze hurt oo, oo pwecious lambkin?" inquired Mamma tenderly. Dousabel gave her to understand that it was her little "tum-tum wot was hurted." Mamma undid her night-drawers and proceeded to investigate. Dousabel, taking a sudden interest, in her own case, sat up and bent over. Whether a tear dropped from Dousabel's lashes at that moment, none ever knew, but what Mamma saw was—a drop of water apparently spilling from Dousabel's little tum-tum cup. Sakes alive!

"Does it hurt when I touch it?" said Mamma, pressing Dousabel's plump little belly with her forefinger.

"Ow! Wow!" Dousabel's vocal chords responded sympathetically.

"Stand up, dearie."

"Can't stand!" said Dousabel with sudden conviction.

"Oh, my darling child, I'm afraid I'll have to take you to the doctor. Mirabel, haven't I told you over and over again that you should *never* hit anyone in the stomach? Now you see what comes of not obeying. See how you've hurt poor little sister—" Mirabel was sobbing in chorus with Dousabel by this time. "Can't you stand up a little, dearie, while I dress you to take you to the doctor's?"

Dousabel was dressed, apparently in great agony all the while. The baby carriage was trundled out—"Oh, she couldn't walk,"—and Mamma and Dousabel set out for New York—Dousabel looking like the poor king "who never smiled again."

At home, Mirabel went through the agonies of a murderer awaiting trial. She thought of committing suicide, to anticipate the noose that awaits murderers. Then she got down on her knees and tried to pray, "O, God, don't let my little sister be kilt!" But she dared not hope that God would ever listen to such a wicked little sinner.

In the doctor's office, Dousabel cheered up a bit. The doctor's funny way of looking down on her from over his spectacles was highly amusing. She put out her tongue and wiggled it at him. She let him feel her pulse, with a wink. And when he began feeling among her ribs, she chuckled with the delight of being tickled. He rolled up her little Rubens shirt. "Does it hurt?" said the doctor, pressing his finger against her little body first in one place and then in another. And to each such inquiry Dousabel answered with a charming shake of her head and squirm of her body, "N-o-o-o."

"Madame," said the doctor to Mrs. Waters, when he had heard all the details of the affair, "my prescription is that you make that young one wheel the baby-carriage all the way home herself, and if she *still feels sick* when she gets home, put her to bed and give her something *very hot and nasty* to drink."

Dousabel blinked hard at the doctor.

When they reached home, Mirabel, peeping from behind the gate, caught Mamma's skirt against her face, sobbing: "O, Mamma, is she dead, is she dead?"

"Why, you little goose," said Mamma, "don't you see her there before your eyes?"

But all Mirabel could do was to wring her hands and sob, "O, Mamma, is she dead?"

"Mirabel," said Dousabel, striding up to her, "you is one goose."

Of Pride and the Fall

National Magazine, December 1906

Such a bright, clean Sunday morning! The streets had been thoroughly washed and scoured by yesterday's rain. The little grass blades that stuck up between the paving stones were glossy as if they had each been polished with a clean dust-rag. The dandelions had had their faces scrubbed as with the best laundry soap, till they shone like the sun. Downy clover blooms fluttered and plumed themselves along the curb border. High up in the sparkling blue sky the clouds, like newly-washed lambs, roamed. The lambs do not skip on Sundays as on week-days,—they "roam." And these cloud-lambs, roaming through fields of azure, shook out their snowy fleece just as Mirabel shook out her freshly-laundered white skirts as she started to walk out with Papa.

Mirabel's white muslin dress was a sea of billowy ruffles. Her Leghorn hat flapped like a sail in the breeze. On the hat waved blue cornflowers. Her sash was blue. So were her shoes.

Mirabel glanced up at the sky and then down at her shoes. Then she was vividly conscious of her eyes. All such a lovely, lovely, blue!

She stepped daintily, holding her parasol at a discreet angle to keep off the sun. No shoulder ride today! Shoulder rides were for children. Mirabel was for the day a young lady.

She even refused Papa's proffered hand. Her hands were both occupied, one in holding her parasol, the other in lifting the edge of her skirt with aristocratic finger-tips.

In order to fully enter into the feelings of Mirabel you must understand that white muslin and leghorn hats were not everyday affairs with her, as they are with some children. On week-days she wore a checked gingham apron dress.

How often had she felt ready to cry when the other girls in her block stared at her gingham dress pityingly, and wondered "why she didn't tell her mamma to dress her in something more decent." Mirabel bravely imitated little Miss Brag on these occasions, eagerly explaining the advantages of a checked gingham apron dress, which was so comfortable to play in, so kind in hiding the dirt, so easily done up, don't you know. She had not read dear Eugene Field's poem about "Little Miss Brag," but she knew intuitively that it was one of the first principles of good breeding to keep up a brave front before the world, and if you were ashamed of your clothes, not to let anybody see it.

However, she was mighty glad to shed that gingham dress when Sunday came. Sunday was the most beautiful day in the week. On Sunday, those other little girls couldn't hold a candle to Mirabel.

With such self-conscious pride, Mirabel paced today by Papa's side. The day, clean as a new pin, was a fitting setting for her ladyship.

They passed a field of nodding, winking daisies. "Come and see! Come and touch! Come and kiss!" they called to Mirabel.

"Don't you want some daisies, Mirabel?" said Papa.

Ah, but daisy-babies' lips are covered with crumbly yellow flour, as if they were always eating cookies, and daisy-babies' fingers leave green stains where they touch your skirt! So Mirabel knew.

"No, I don't want any," she said, quietly, though looking longingly.

"I'll climb over and get you a bunch," said Papa.

From the daisy-field he cried: "Look here, Mirabel! See what I've found!" He held up a kicking hoppy-toad by one leg.

"Ugh!" said Mirabel. "I don't want him."

Papa came forward with the hoppy-toad.

"Don't come near me with that dirty toad!" said Mirabel, backing away.

"Nonsense, he's as clean as you are."

"I don't want to touch him." Mirabel still backed away.

"Mirabel, look out!" cried Papa, springing forward. Too late! Mirabel's last step plunged her backward into the turbulent stream that flooded the gutter. All of the week's dirt which the rain had so carefully washed away was in that stream, hurrying to carry it out of sight.

Papa fished Mirabel out by her sash. But her Leghorn hat with the blue flowers frantically struggling to keep above water, was drowned before her eyes. The billowy ruffles of her dress turned into muddy creeks, which oozed into her grimy shoes. She walked in puddles.

And as she slopped ignominiously home—at a respectful distance from Papa, so as not to soil his new pants—Mirabel wished, ah she wished! that she were a hoppy-toad, and had some small hole wherein she could creep away into the dark.

St.Bridget's Child.

It is a story of poverty and heroism, those grim fairies who presided at my birth, to whom I owe whatever fibre of strength is in my being.   So often have I heard my father and mother speak of these things that it seems as if I remembered them, as if I wept when my mother bent her slender neck in toil for my sake - I yet unborn - as if I still felt the cold kiss of the snow on my cheek, while my father paced under the stars watching my feeble breath of life.

They were such an amazingly foolhardy young couple to marry, my father earning - was it six dollars a week ? - my mother a spoiled darling, as innocent of the old time art of housekeeping as of the more modern art of earning money. And when my father fell"out of work" I can well imagine my mother's dismay in telling him of the wonderful dignity of motherhood that was come upon her, a dignity, alas! - too heavy for poor folks to bear. He walked the streets in a frenzied despair, demanding work, work, at any cost, while she made the best pitiful woman-struggle to help that ever it were possible for woman to make. What could she do, oh, what could she do ? As a child she had watched the printers setting type for the printing of her father's paper - the Brooklyn Daily Eagle, in the days when he and James Gordon Bennett had been partners in that enterprise ("I furnish the money , and you, Smith, the brains" had laughed Mr.Bennett) - and so she knew "upper case" and "lower case" and "font" and "stick" and other words of the printers vocabulary. She boldly went to a printing shop and

Acknowledgments & Sources

Acknowledgements

For permission to publish copyrighted materials used in this volume, the author wishes to thank: The Isamu Noguchi Foundation, Long Island City, New York, for extracts from Isamu Noguchi, *A Sculptor's World* (New York: Harper and Row, 1968), letters of Léonie Gilmour, Isamu Noguchi, Ailes Gilmour, Yone Noguchi, Catharine Tomlinson Bunnell and Matsuo Miyake, as well as archival photographs, and permission to reproduce photographs of artworks by Isamu Noguchi. Essen Communications, Ltd., Tokyo, for dialogue and images from the film *Leonie*. The Bancroft Library of the University of California at Berkeley, for letters of Charles Warren Stoddard, Ethel Armes, and Frank Putnam. The Lilly Library, Indiana University Bloomington, for letters of Léonie Gilmour and Isamu Noguchi. The British Library, St. Pancras, London, for letters to Marie Charlotte Stopes. The Ethical Culture Society, New York, for photograph of the Workingman's School's first graduating class. The Bryn Mawr School, Baltimore, for Léonie Gilmour's high school graduation picture. Bryn Mawr College Archives, Bryn Mawr, Pennsylvania, for Felix Adler's letter to Eleanor Andrews and photographs. Yale University Special Collections, Sterling Library, for Bunnell Family Papers. The Stratford Historical Society, Stratford, Connecticut, for the photograph of Catharine Tomlinson Bunnell.

The author also wishes to acknowledge the kind assistance of Ikuko Atsumi, Heidi Coleman, Elizabeth DiCataldo, Jenny Dixon, Yoshinobu Hakutani, Miyako Hada, Amy Hau, Robert Maeda, Katsuko Marx, Hisako Matsui, Marleigh Ryan, Hiromi Saitoh, Amy Sueyoshi, Lorett Treese, and Keiko Wada.

Léonie Gilmour's previously published works (chronological)

A Scrap of Paper, tr. of Victorien Sardou, *Pattes de mouche*, in *Dramatic Masterpieces by Greek, Spanish, French, German, and English Dramatists*, revised ed. (New York: Co-operative Publication Society, 1900), 443-512.

"George Meredith—A Study," *National Magazine* 23 (Dec. 1905): 272-77.

"Founding a Tent-Home in California," *National Magazine* 23 (Feb. 1906): 554-57.

"Nursery Menus for a Week," *Good Housekeeping* 42 (May 1906): 565.

"The Ways of Mirabel and Dousabel," *National Magazine* 25 (Oct 1906): 93-94.

"Of Pride and the Fall," *National Magazine* 25 (Dec 1906): 299-300.

"A Little California House: Living Close to God and Nature In Sunland," *The West-Coast Magazine* (Dec. 1906).

"Regarding Yone Noguchi," *Japan Advertiser*, 7 Oct. 1917, 4.

"Cherry Blossoms in Tokyo," *Christian Science Monitor*, 28 April 1921.

"Dorobo, or the Japanese Burglar," *New York Times*, 17 July 1921, 44.

"Home, Sweet Home, in Japan," *Japan* 11:9 (June 1922): 15-19, 44-45.

"Glory of the Morning in Japan," *Christian Science Monitor,* 24 July 1922.

"Rare Goyo in Exhibition at Library This Week," *Bar Harbor Times*, 20 Aug.1930.

"A Correction," *Nation*, 29 July 1931, 110.

"House and Garden in Beauty-Loving Japan," *Asia* 35 (June 1935): 358-62.

Previously unpublished articles

"A Mayor of Tokyo," undated typescript, collection of Edward Marx.

"Ai-Chan Goes to Frisco," undated typescript, collection of Edward Marx.

"Inside Looking On When East Weds West," undated typescript, collection of Edward Marx.

"St. Bridget's Child," undated typescript, collection of Edward Marx.

"The Kid Chronicle That Was Not Written," undated typescript, collection of Edward Marx.

Preface

Marleigh Ryan's comments are from an email to the author, June 5, 2009. Robert Maeda's are from his essay, "From Shape and Shadow: The Mother and Father of Isamu Noguchi," *Amerasia Journal* 20:2 (1996): 104-120.

Masayo Duus' biography of Isamu Noguchi was first published in Japanese as *Isamu Noguchi: shukumei no ekkyosha*, 2v. (Tokyo: Kodansha, 2000), and subsequently in English as *The Life of Isamu Noguchi: Journey without Borders*, tr. Peter Duus (Princeton, NJ: Princeton UP, 2004).

Hisako Matsui's comments on her interest in Léonie's story are from "The Strength to Lead One's Own Life—Film Portraying the Mother of Sculptor Isamu Noguchi," *Radio Japan Focus*, NHK World, 6 July 2010. Further comments on the making of Leonie are derived from chapter five of her book, *Sorisuto (dokusou suru hito) no shikoujutsu, dai 3-kan: Matsui Hisako no ikiru chikara* [A soloist's way of thinking 3: Hisako Matsui's way of living] (Tokyo: Rikuyosha, 2011) and from the author's personal conversations with the director.

Reviews of Matsui's film cited: Rex Reed, "Emily Mortimer Inspires in Triumphant Tale of Leonie Gilmour's Harrowing Journey," New York *Observer*, 19 March 2013; Rachel Saltz, "Emily Mortimer as the mother of Isamu Noguchi in 'Leonie'," *New York Times*, 21 March 2013; Alan Scherstuhl, "Emily Mortimer's Leonie Is Stifled by Mortifying 'Poetry'," *Village Voice*, 22 March 2013; Frank Scheck, "Leonie: Film Review," *Hollywood Reporter*, 22 March 2013; John Anderson, "Film Review: 'Leonie'," *Variety*, 24 March 2013.

Ikuko Atsumi described her discovery of the letters in "The Newly Discovered Letters of Yone Noguchi During His Stay in America," *KBS Bulletin On Japa-*

nese Culture 107 (April-May 1971): 1-12 and in her introduction to Yone Noguchi, *Collected English Letters*, ed. Ikuko Atsumi (Tokyo: Yone Noguchi Society, 1975).

Laurence Housman's description of Yone's English comes from Housman's letter to George Galloway, 8 Sept.1903, Special Collections, University of Iowa Libraries.

Prologue

Stoddard's transcriptions of Ethel Armes' and Elizabeth Converse's letters are in the Charles Warren Stoddard Collection of Papers, 1867-1918, Bancroft Library.

Origins (1873-1896)

On Tompkins Square, see Albert Webster, Jr., "Evening in Tompkins Square," *Appleton's Journal* 10 (20 Sept. 1873): 366.

On the origins of the *Brooklyn Daily Times* see Eugene L. Armbruster, *Brooklyn's Eastern District* (Williamsburg, N.Y, 1942), 10. On Whitman's self-promoting review, see Kenneth M. Price, *Walt Whitman: The Contemporary Reviews* (Cambridge: Cambridge UP, 1996): xi.

The Workingman's School

For a biography of Adler, see Howard B. Radest, *Felix Adler, An Ethical Culture* (New York: Peter Lang, 1998). On the origins of the Ethical Culture movement, see *Twenty Years of the Ethical Movement in New York and Other Cities, 1876-1896* (Philadelphia: Weston, 1896). For Adler's early views on Ethical Culture, including his views on gender relations, see *Creed and Deed: A Series of Discourses* (New York: G. P. Putnam's Sons, 1877), especially 111-14. For his educational ideals see "The Democratic Ideal in Education," *Century* 38:6 (Oct. 1889): 929 and *The Moral Instruction of Children* (New York: Appleton, 1912). Florence Scholle's recollections of the kindergarten are from Jacob Rader Marcus, ed., *The American Jewish Woman: A Documentary History* (New York: Ktav, 1981), 338-40. On Gabriel Bamberger, see Joseph H. Leiser, "The Influence of the Jews on Manual Training," in *The Craftsman* 3:6 (March 1903): 380-389. Quotations from Fanny Schwedler [Barnes] are from her "Child Culture Studies" column, *Kindergarten Magazine* 4:8 (Apr 1892): 477 and 10:3 (Nov. 1897): 218. The later activities of Léonie's fellow graduates are mainly derived from the *Ethical Culture School Record* (New York, Ethical Culture School, 1916).

The Bryn Mawr School, 1887-1891

The letter from Felix Adler to Eleanor Andrews is in the Bryn Mawr School archives. On the Bryn Mawr School, see Andrea Hamilton, *A Vision for Girls: Gender, Education, and the Bryn Mawr School* (Baltimore: Johns Hopkins UP, 2004).

Bryn Mawr College, 1891-1896

See Helen Lefkowitz Horowitz, *The Power and Passion of M. Carey Thomas* (Urbana: University of Illinois Press, 1999). Early volumes of the *Bryn Mawr College*

Program and its successor, the *Bryn Mawr College Calendar*, may be found in The Internet Archive. Helen Thomas Flexner's comments about the college are from her book, *Bryn Mawr—A Characterisation* (Bryn Mawr, 1905).

Letters between Catharine Tomlinson Bunnell and members of her family are in the Yale University Special Collections department at Sterling Library. Letters between Catharine and Léonie are in the Isamu Noguchi Foundation collection.

On Lindley Keasbey see Walter F. Pilcher's biography in the *Handbook of Texas Online* <http://www.tshaonline.org/handbook/online/articles/fke46>, Texas State Historical Association and Keasbey's *The Nicaragua Canal and the Monroe Doctrine* (New York: Putnams, 1896).

On Umeko Tsuda, see Yoshiko Furuki, *The White Plum: A Biography of Ume Tsuda* (New York: Weatherhill, 1991). A Japanese biography of Michi Matsuda may be found in the Doshisha Women's College magazine *Vine* (Autumn 2005) <http://www.dwc.doshisha.ac.jp/vine/39/index.html>. For a brief account of Masa (Dogura) Uchida and her husband, see William Elliot Griffis, "The Japanese Ambassador," *Outlook* 94 (26 Feb. 1910): 473-5.

On Gertrude Stein and the Hodder-Gwinn-Thomas saga, see Stein, *Fernhurst, QED, and other early writings* (New York: Liveright, 1971); Brenda Wineapple, *Sister Brother: Gertrude and Leo Stein* (New York: GP Putnam's Sons, 1996), 145-6, 409-14; and Linda Wagner-Martin, *"Favored Strangers": Gertrude Stein and Her Family* (New Brunswick, NJ: Rutgers UP, 1995), 52-55.

New York and New Jersey, 1896-1904

The letters from Yone Noguchi to Léonie Gilmour in this volume are in the collection of the Isamu Noguchi Foundation except for the letters of [April / May 1901], 28 Jan. 1906, 2 Apr. 1906, [Mar. 1906], and 22 Apr. 1906, which are in the collection of Edward Marx, and that of 5 May 1906, in the collection of Seiji Itoh. Nearly all the letters may be found, with some errors of transcription, in Ikuko Atsumi's edition of Noguchi's *Collected English Letters*. In the present work, Noguchi's errors of English usage are presented as written, without the customary [*sic*].

The American Diary of a Japanese Girl was excerpted in *Frank Leslie's Popular Monthly* in November and December 1901, and published in book form by Frederick Stokes in October of 1902. For further information on the book and its sequels, see *The American Diary of a Japanese Girl: An Annotated Edition*, ed. Edward Marx and Laura Franey (Philadelphia: Temple University Press, 2007).

Amy Sueyoshi discusses Yone's relationships with both Stoddard and Armes in *Queer Compulsions: Race, Nation, and Sexuality in the Affairs of Yone Noguchi* (Honolulu: University of Hawaii Press, 2012). On Charles Warren Stoddard, see Roger Austen's *Genteel Pagan: The Double Life of Charles Warren Stoddard*, ed. John W. Crowley (Amherst: University of Massachusetts Press, 1991). Stoddard's Washington bungalow is described by Ethel Armes in "Aloha, Wela, Wela!," *National Magazine* 20 (Dec. 1904): 308-18. On Noguchi's relationship with Charles Warren Stoddard, see "Epilogue: Charles Warren Stoddard" in *The Story of Yone Noguchi*. Noguchi's letters to Stoddard are in the Huntington Library; Stoddard's surviving letters to Noguchi, now at Keio, are included in Noguchi's *Collected English Letters*. The Bancroft Library holds letters from Stoddard to Frank Putnam (*Charles Warren Stoddard papers, 1903-1906*), and letters to Stoddard from Putnam, Ethel Armes, and Léonie Gilmour (*Collection of Charles Warren Stoddard Papers, 1867-1918*).

Ethel Armes wrote two unsigned articles about Noguchi: "Dream Child Noguchi," *Washington Post*, 27 Jan. 1901, 24 and "Noguchi the Dreamer," *Washington Post*, 5 Jan. 1902, 29. Noguchi's comments on Ethel Armes are from his *Kicho no ki* [Homecoming chronicle] (Tokyo: Shunyodo, 1904). James R. Bennett gives an overview of Armes' career in his preface to a new edition of her *Story of Coal and Iron* (Tuscaloosa: U of Alabama Press, 2011), xv-xxvi.

On common law marriage laws in New York, see Göran Lind, *Common Law Marriage: A Legal Institution for Cohabitation* (Oxford UP US, 2008), 139 and "Common Law Marriage in New York," *New York Times*, 12 Apr. 1901, 8.

Los Angeles, 1904-1907

On California's miscegenation laws, see Megumi D. Osumi, "Asians and California's Anti-Miscegenation Laws," in *Asian and Pacific American Experiences: Women's Perspectives*, ed. Nobuya Tsuchida (Minneapolis: Asian/Pacific American Learning Resource Center and General College, U of Minnesota, 1982): 13; *Reports of the Immigration Commission: Immigrants in Industries*, Part 25, vol. 1 (Washington, DC: Government Printing Office, 1911), 162, note b.

"Yone Noguchi's Babe Pride of Hospital" appeared in the *Los Angeles Herald*, 27 Nov. 1904, 8.

Yone's November 1905 Japanese discourse on love, "Ai-ren!" [Love-passion!] was published in *Shirayuri* 3:1 (1 Nov. 1905): 12-14.

The Bancroft library holds letters from Putnam to Stoddard in the *Collection of Charles Warren Stoddard Papers, 1867-1918*, while those from Stoddard to Putnam are in the *Charles Warren Stoddard Papers, 1903-1906*.

Relatively little is known about Matsuo Miyake beyond the information contained in his letters. According to a 14 Jan. [1909] letter in which he writes, "I am just 23 years and two months old now, and still young," his month of birth can be given as November 1885. He worked for the *Osaka Mainichi Shinbun* and authored a volume of translations from Guy de Maupassant in 1914. His date of death has not been discovered.

On Theo Lowe and *The Raven*, see: "Raven Publisher Acquitted," *San Francisco Call*, 24 Sept. 1903, 10; "Want Return of Graphophone," *San Francisco Call*, 24 Apr. 1904, 28; "Stenographer Porter Insults The Raven," *San Francisco Call*, 15 June 1904, 16; "Woman Charges Editor With Swindling Her," *San Francisco Call*, 8 July 1904, 11; "Publisher Lowe Seeks Bondsman," *Los Angeles Herald*, 24 May 1906, 5; "Publisher Of Raven Charged With Felony," *San Francisco Call*, 7 Aug. 1908, 4.

On the California anti-Japanese movement see Herbert B. Johnson, *Discrimination against the Japanese in California: A Review of the Real Situation* (Berkeley: Courier Pub., 1907). Los Angeles schools commissioner E.C. Moore is quoted on page 34. On the Expatriation Act (or Perkins Law), see Susan Koshy, *Sexual Naturalization: Asian Americans and Miscegenation* (Stanford, CA: Stanford UP, 2004), 7, and "Expatriation Bill Reported," *New York Tribune*, 19 Jan. 1907, 3.

Tokyo, 1907-1911

"Isamu's Arrival" is derived from "Isamu and Others," *Sunset* 25 (Nov. 1910): 534-39; "Isamu's Arrival in Japan," *Nation* (London) 8:20 (11 Feb. 1911): 798-800, which was reprinted in *The Story of Yone Noguchi*, (London: Chatto and Windus, 1914), 185-99; and "Isamu Comes Home," *Southwestern Farmer*, 15 March 1911, 14-15. Though the story is essentially the same, there are a number of differences, beginning with the titles. The version given here mainly follows the *Sunset* version but includes several passages from the *Nation* version probably deleted by the *Sunset* editors because of space considerations. The photograph of a five-year-old Isamu included in the *Sunset* version appears later in the chapter; the other illustrations by Arnold Genthe of unrelated Japanese children are omitted.

Frank Putnam's nostalgic comments on Noguchi appeared in "The Poet of East and West," *The Stylus* (Houston) 1:13 (6 April 1912) 3-4, 15.

The three Japanese newspaper accounts of Léonie and Isamu's arrival were discovered by Prof. Keiko Wada of Osaka Gakuin University, and are discussed in her essay, *"Noguchi Yonejiro no Rondon (16) Shijin no skyandaru"* (Yone Noguchi's London 16: scandals of a poet), *Osaka Gakuin Daigaku gaikokugo ronshu* 49 (March 2004): 41-59.

Isamu discussed his "Blue Wave" sculpture in an interview with Paul Cummings, 7 Nov. 1973, Smithsonian Archives.

Umeko Tsuda's school is discussed in Yoshiko Furuki, *The White Plum: A Biography of Ume Tsuda* (New York: Weatherhill, 1991), 101-27. On the Joshi Gakuin, see "The Joshi Gakuin, and other Schools of Tokyo," *Woman's Work for Woman* 18 (Sept. 1903): 201-07, and Rumi Yasutake, *Transnational Women's Activism: The United States, Japan, and Japanese Immigrant Communities in California, 1859–1920* (New York: NYU Press, 2004), 21-26.

Usaburo Toyama's chronology in Usaburo Toyama, ed., *Shijin Yone Noguchi Kenkyu* [Essays on Yone Noguchi], v. 1 (Tokyo: Zokei bijutsu kyokai shuppankyoku, 1963), 326, gives Hifumi's birthdate as January 1, 1908, but births were customarily recorded at the new year. Duus, p. 53, gives December 1907 as Hifumi's birthdate, but expresses some uncertainty and does not name a source. The recollections of Hironobu Noguchi, the Noguchis' houseboy, may be found in *Shijin Yone Noguchi Kenkyu*, v. 1, 309-21.

On the Hearn / Koizumi family, see Yone Noguchi, *Lafcadio Hearn in Japan* (London: Elkin Mathews, 1910), which collects most of his earlier articles on Hearn. Léonie's October 1908 letter to Kazuo Koizumi giving directions to

Myogadani is quoted in Duus, 55.

Marie Stopes diary entries are taken from *A Journal from Japan: A Daily Record of Life as Seen by a Scientist* (London: Blackie, 1910). Stopes' veiled account of her relationship with Kenjiro Fujii was published under the pseudonym G.N. Mortlake as *Love Letters of a Japanese* (London: Stanley Paul, 1911). The letters to Stopes are from the Marie Stopes Papers, Add. 58681 f. 86, British Library. In her *Journal* Stopes refers to Elizabeth Bisland's *Life and Letters of Lafcadio Hearn*, 2 vols. (Boston: Houghton Mifflin, 1906) and George M. Gould's "atrocious book," *Concerning Lafcadio Hearn* (Philadelphia: George W. Jacobs & Company, 1908), which was strongly criticized by Noguchi in "A Japanese Defense of Lafcadio Hearn," *Lafcadio Hearn in Japan*, 19-30. Hearn's former student from Matsue who lived in a part of the house was Hachisaburo Fujisaki.

Zona Gale became friendly with Noguchi in New York in 1903 and had known of his engagement to Ethel Armes. Noguchi's letters to her are among the Zona Gale Papers at the State Historical Society of Wisconsin.

Kanagawa, 1911-1920

Dr. Moody mentioned in Léonie's May 3, 1911 letter to Catharine was probably Mary Moody's brother, Dr. Robert Orton Moody, an anatomist at the University of California, San Francisco. The African postcard may have been a souvenir from Catharine's mother's recent trip to Algeria. Denjiro Kotoku, mentioned in the same letter, was one of the eleven anarchists whose execution on January 24, 1911 for alleged involvement in a plot to assassinate the emperor was the subject of many sympathetic articles in the United States.

Charles Kingsley's *The Heroes; or, Greek Fairy Tales for My Children* (Cambridge: Macmillan, 1859) was the book Catharine presented to Isamu as a Christmas or birthday present in late 1912. Léonie had been reading Isamu Josephine Peabody's *The Piper*, a dramatic retelling of the Pied Piper story. Peabody had been a friend of Yone's since 1903.

Pegotty and Barkis, mentioned in Léonie's November 29, 1913 letter to Catharine, are characters in Charles Dickens' novel *David Copperfield*. The "phlegmatic" carrier Mr. Barkis' proposes to David's affectionate nurse, Clara Peggotty, by asking David to mention in his letter that "Barkis is willin'." Léonie means to suggest that Isamu's "Please visit!" is similarly understated. "Impatient Griselda," as Léonie describes herself in the same letter, alludes to "patient Griselda" in the medieval folktale who uncomplainingly endures a series of torments designed by her husband to test her virtue.

Paul Cummings, Oral history interview with Isamu Noguchi, 1973 Nov. 7-1973 Dec. 26, Archives of American Art, Smithsonian Institution <http://www.aaa.si.edu/collections/oralhistories/transcripts/noguch73.htm>.

"Dinna doff your clout till May goes out" cited by Léonie in her May 6, 1914 letter to Catharine is a Scottish proverb ("cast not a clout . . . " is the Anglicized form) advocating keeping one's winter clothing until the end of May. In Japan, *koromogae* (seasonal change of clothes) took place in the fourth month.

Catharine's Christmas gift books of 1916, alluded to in Léonie's February 20, 1917 seem to have included Juliana Horatia Ewing's 1884 story "Daddy Darwin's Dovecot" (a rather conventional English tale originally published by the Society for Promoting Christian Knowledge) for Isamu and a poetry collection for Léonie that included "The Passing of the Prince" by the unpopular and critically disparaged English clergyman, Rev. F. William Orde Ward (pseud. F. Harald Williams, 1843-1922), a book by Scottish poet William Sharp (Fiona MacLeod), and a poem about Lilith (the supposed first wife of Adam, who had been the subject of poems by D.G. Rossetti, among others). According to some theologians, Lilith had no soul; Anatole France, in his 1889 story, "The Daughter of Lilith," wrote that Lilith "voluntarily separated" from Adam when he "was still living in innocence" and therefore had no part in the original sin. "Because of this she also escaped from the curse pronounced against Eve and her descendants. She is exempt from sorrow and death; having no soul to be saved, she is incapable of virtue or vice. Whatever she does, she accomplishes neither good nor evil" (Anatole France, *Works, in an English Translation*, v. 17 [London: John Lane, 1909], 77).

The Interlaken article that attracted Léonie was "The Daniel Boone Idea in Education," *Scientific American* 109 (3 Nov. 1916): 361-62.

Noguchi's article *Beikokujin no kaibo* [Analysis of the Americans], *Chuo Koron* 32:10 (Sept. 1917): 108-15 was translated as "American Men Mere Rustics—Women Sentimental, Says Poet," *Japan Advertiser*, 21 Sept. 1917, p. 6, 10. After Léonie's response appeared on October 2, the *Advertiser* published another letter critical of Noguchi, "A Poet's Gratitude," *Japan Advertiser*, 9 Oct. 1917, p. 4. Noguchi complained about the *Advertiser*'s "un-American and even ungentlemanly" conduct in "Analysis of the Americans," *Japan Times*, 21 Oct. 1917.

Return to America, 1920-1933

On Onorio Ruotolo, see Amy Wolf, *On Becoming an Artist: Isamu Noguchi and His Contemporaries, 1922-1960* (New York: Noguchi Museum, 2010), 15-16.

Isamu's portrait sculptures are described in detail in Nancy Grove, *Isamu Noguchi: Portrait Sculpture* (Washington, D.C.: Smithsonian Institution Press, 1989).

On Isamu Noguchi and Martha Graham, see Martha Graham, *Blood Memory* (New York: Doubleday, 1991), 218; Agnes De Mille, *Martha: The Life and Work of Martha Graham* (New York: Random House, 1991), 210, and Alice Helpern, *Martha Graham* (New York: Routledge, 1999), 45. Ailes Gilmour's recollections of working with Graham, recorded at a 1988 colloquium at the Asia Society in New York, are included in Marian Horosko, *Martha Graham: The Evolution of Her Dance Theory and Training, 1926-1991*, revised ed. (Gainesville, Fla.: UP of Florida, 2002): 8-10.

"Mr. Kasai in San Francisco" in Léonie's July 28, 1927 letter was probably San Francisco stockbroker Kenji Kasai, whose wife Aya gave birth to a son, George Shoichi Kasai, on April 28, 1927.

Ruth Furness Porter and Pauline Goldmark, mentioned in Léonie's October 9, 1927 letter to Isamu, were both members of Léonie's Bryn Mawr class (the Class of 1896). Ruth, a classics major, had married James Porter, whose parents' plot of farmland in once-rural Chicago had become the Chicago loop, the most valuable real estate in the city. Their son Fairfield, then an art student at Harvard, went on to study painting at the Art Students League in New York and gained fame as both art critic and painter, his abstraction-influenced representational painting style appealing to the literary art critics of the New York School. The Porters owned a summer house on Spruce Head Island, an adjacent private island.

Léonie's Galleon exhibition was noted in "New York Items," *New York Times*, Apr 22, 1928, 123.

On Isamu and Buckminster Fuller, see Shoji Sadao, *Buckminster Fuller and Isamu Noguchi: Best of Friends* (New York: 5 Continents Editions, 2011).

Isamu's 1930 meeting with his father is discussed in Yoshinobu Hakutani, "Father and Son: A Conversation With Isamu Noguchi," *Journal of Modern Litera-*

ture 17:1 (Summer 1990): 13-33.

Dorothy Bird's recollections of Ailes are in her *Bird's Eye View: Dancing with Martha Graham and on Broadway* (Pittsburgh: University of Pittsburgh Press, 1977), 82, 93. Ailes is identified as the model for Walt Kuhn's "Miss A" in *Philip Rhys Adams, Walt Kuhn, Painter: His Life and Work* (Columbus: Ohio State Univ. Press, 1978), 257. The painting is now in the collection of the Colby College Museum of Art.

Inajiro Tajiri's soybean promotion effort was the subject of an article in *The New East* 2 (1918), 481. Richard Whittington, a medieval merchant-politician, was appointed Lord Mayor by King Richard II in 1397, and thrice reelected. According to an apocryphal story made into a popular pantomime, he rose from dire poverty with the aid of his rat-hunting cat. John Burns, working class labor leader was appointed to the new London County Council shortly after emerging as a labor leader in the London Dock Strike of 1889.

Isamu's *Lady for a Garden*, a plaster sculpture Léonie wished to see in marble, had been displayed in Isamu's February-March exhibition at Philadelphia's Mellon Galleries.

On Bellevue Hospital, see Sandra Opdycke, *No One Was Turned Away: The Role of Public Hospitals in New York City Since 1900* (New York: Oxford UP, 2000).

INSIDE LOOKING ON

WHEN EAST WEDS WEST

When the Editor of ~~Liberty~~ asked me to write on article, based
on my own observations and experience, on the subject of marriage
between Europeans and Japanese, I promptly ~~responded that I would~~
~~make~~ a few little sketches from life among my friends in Japan. Alas,
my trifling sketches seemed to him too flippant, too cursory, not to
attack the problem in the serious spirit due to a very serious subject.
"And where," said he, "are your conclusions ?"   Conclusions ?   Where,
indeed ?   He talked in such an earnest way that I felt sure I ought
to go to the bottom of something.   So I put out a few feelers to find
out what he would consider the more serious aspects of the question.

He assumed, to start with, that there were certain fundamental
differences between Japanese and Europeans, differences in their
philosophy of life, differences in religion, differences in customs,
and that these differences might easily become a source of that
"incompatability" which is the frequent excuse for a broken marriage.
(Incompatability is sometimes pieced out to make quite a decent cloak)
He assumed that there was a Japanese "type," with variations to be sure,
just as there is an American type , or types, pretty clearly recognized
in literature - sometimes we recognize traits of the type here and
there among our friends, tho a complete type is pretty hard to find.
(The literary "type" is largely a vogue, the persistence of a type
depending largely on the brilliancy, or popularity, of his originator.
The American type having been studied at first hand, at least, the
features are fairly xxxxxxx clear. The Japanese type has hardly
emerged in literature, because few have taken the trouble to study the
Japanese through the medium of their own language and literature, or
through personal contact.   Lafcadio Hearn is a notable exception. He

About the author

A native of Los Angeles, Edward Marx began following the Noguchi family after finding a copy of *The Spirit of Japanese Poetry* in a second-hand bookshop in Berkeley. He subsequently completed a doctorate in English at the City University of New York, and has taught at CCNY, the University of Minnesota, Kyoto University, Nara Women's University, Ehime University, and the University of Kochi. He is the author of *The Idea of a Colony: Cross-Culturalism in Modern Poetry* and co-editor, with Laura Franey, of Yone Noguchi's *The American Diary of a Japanese Girl: An Annotated Edition*. His articles on Yone Noguchi have appeared in *Re-Collecting Early Asian America, Modernity and East-West Literary Criticism, Transactions of the Asiatic Society of Japan, Genre,* and *Yeats Annual*. The present work is a companion to a forthcoming biography of Yone Noguchi.

Made in United States
Orlando, FL
10 August 2024